Democracy
in America

A Public Choice Approach

Democracy

A
Public
Choice
Approach

R. L. MEEK *Colorado State University*

L. L. WADE *University of California, Davis*

Duxbury Press *North Scituate, Massachusetts*

Duxbury Press

A DIVISION OF WADSWORTH PUBLISHING COMPANY, INC.

Democracy in America: A Public Choice Approach was edited and prepared for composition by Julia Stair. The interior design was provided by Dorothy Booth. The cover was designed by Oliver Kline.

L.C. Cat. Card No.: 75-41975
ISBN: 0 - 87872 - 107 - x
PRINTED IN THE UNITED STATES OF AMERICA
1 2 3 4 5 6 7 8 9 — 80 79 78 77 76

Contents

---

8 Congress: Rules of Collective Choice

9 The Presidency: Leadership and Policy Exhortation

10 The Bureaucracy: Generating Goods and Services

Preface

This book presents a somewhat personal interpretation of democracy in America. The theory, data, and arguments it contains were selected from a vast body of knowledge that could have been organized in many different ways. We selected those aspects of American politics which seem to us the most important for the understanding of American politics. The orientations and commitments brought to this work have to be made explicit in order that the reader may be alert to the many points at which an unarticulated bias has been inserted into the analysis. Even though our choices were dictated in part by our own goals and values, we believe they were required as well by the academic argument sketched in Chapters 1 and 2.

Serious academics nearly always believe that it is better to know than not to know, that it is better to understand the things which shape one's life than to be moved about by obscure or mysterious social forces. We share this view. The individual lives in a political world. Everyone consequently must make political choices and, if wise in doing so, will look for the implications of alternatives, options, and opportunities that are available in any choice-making situation. Assessing the implications of different decisions calls for predicting the probable reactions of other people and understanding the nature of the political process. Politics is often a dangerous business, and the more knowledge individuals have, the less likely their choices will be to harm themselves, those who are most important to them and, if their ethical value systems are sufficiently developed, other members of the society or the world community.

The central purpose of this book, in short, is to help readers make political choices that are realistic and consistent with their personal interests and ethical values. Such rational conduct is possible only if one understands the crucial elements of the political process and their interrelationships. Our purpose is not to dictate choices — there is no shortage of moral teachers prepared to assume that chore — but to broaden awareness of the *real* political options available. Thus the book aims to increase sensible political behavior.

This purpose is related to our conception of the individual and his or her proper role in the American polity. We presume that all adults are the best judge of their own interest and that individuals should be allowed to make their own political choices as long as they do not conflict with widely accepted and freely chosen political rules and institutions. The book rests on the traditional liberal democratic assumption that no elite, whether based on self-proclaimed rectitude, alleged wisdom, wealth, race, sex, force, or status, should dominate public decisions. Our perspective is equalitarian in the procedural sense that one should be free to take responsibility for one's own fate, to extend one's individual political resources, and to improve one's own political, social, and economic positions. Gross substantive inequities arising from the exercise of such freedoms must be remedied through an open, competitive, and reasonable democratic political system.

This individualistic perspective does not require the naive corollary that society is, should be, or could be unimportant in shaping a person's political choices. Indeed, the *interdependence* of individuals provides the basis for both social conflict and cooperation and the focus for the public choice approach to political analysis (explained in Chapters 1 and 2). Ideally, government should serve as a positive instrument to achieve goals established through a political process which, however robust, contentious, or turbulent, is consistent with democratic principles — that is, with some acceptable variation on majoritarianism and with certain protection for minorities. The fact that individuals have different and frequently contradictory interests, needs, and wants, which are held with varying degrees of intensity, makes us prefer also that the political process be marked by negotiation, bargaining, and compromise. The politics of compromise makes possible adjustments in the lines of greatest social stress, an outcome we prefer to results often associated with the politics of intransigence and dominance. The politics of unyielding principles is unattractive also because it suggests rule by some faction, a rule altogether inconsistent with democratic norms.

It follows that the primary technique for effecting political change or for maintaining existing privileges should be persuasion. People who have discovered what is good for society have an obligation to convince others of the truth of their discovery. Failing to do so, they should not attempt or be allowed to coerce other members of the community into accepting their personal visions of the good society.

The value perspective from which we proceed — and the weight we give to responsible freedom and procedural equality — is derived from the tenets of traditional liberal democratic theory. Hence we oppose those now familiar forms of contemporary radicalism which are based on arrogant certitude and elitist principles. In asserting an attachment to traditional liberal values, we are placed, ironically enough, in what popular usage might now define as the conservative mold. It is a mold that emphasizes knowledge and rationality, human equality and freedom, and the politics of compromise.

For readers who are just now coming to the serious study of American politics, we should explain briefly how this book differs from other interpretations of the American political process. For the past quarter-century or so, American politics was conventionally explained in terms of a pluralistic or group conception of things (a conception explained thoroughly in Chapter 6). The two central facts of political life — the existence of stability, cooperation, and agreement on the one hand and instability, conflict, and disagreement on the other — were analyzed in terms of the interaction of groups and predominantly in terms of formally organized groups. There was conflict because groups had different interests and sought to improve their respective positions in society by making claims upon others through the political process. Conflict was limited and social life was made possible, however, by the willingness of all to accept certain "rules of the game," or rules of fairness, of due process, of self-restraint. Beginning perhaps in the mid-1960s, this appealing description of American politics became less and less realistic. While millions of

Americans continued (and continue) to behave with the old restraints required by group theory, many others adopted other political outlooks, including what to us is the obnoxious notion that unless the political process translates one's *own* values into public policy that process is necessarily corrupt, unresponsive, or undemocratic. The growth of intransigence, an increased propensity for the unrestrained use of power, the decline in civility, and an enhanced tendency to base political demands upon a stance of moral certitude have dramatically laid bare the weaknesses inherent in the group approach and have substantially diminished its utility as an efficient means of understanding American politics.

It is our view that an individualistic theory of politics, in which cooperation and self-restraint are problematical and not presumed, is the logical parsimonious academic alternative to the older group approach. This is a melancholy conclusion in some ways. By suggesting that the virtues of restraint are increasingly rare, we seem to be calling in question the future of self-government, which requires such virtues. Still, a focus on individualism has certain attractive aspects (both analytical and normative) which will become clear. We do not mean to say that groups are any less important in the political process than they were; indeed, our analysis has a good bit to say about groups and their importance to an understanding of American politics. However, the focus is on the role of the individual in collective decision-making and the impact of the political process upon the achievement of individual values even though much of collective choice goes forward in a group context.

The now problematical nature of self-restraint and shared understandings has similar implications for the elite theories advanced by some critics of the group approach. In an age of egotism and the delegitimation of authority, the disarray and growing impotence of political institutions in the management of political affairs is a more obvious feature of the polity than the presumed capacity of elites to mobilize resources on behalf of their covert objectives. That poor scholarship — assertion rather than demonstration — has marked most contemporary American elite theories is another reason for their less than compelling force. The elite approach tends to explain the obvious political reality of the unequal distribution of political power in terms of presumed covert and conspiratorial activities and to evade tracing the complex social linkages that guide, restrain, and modify the exercise of power.

Finally, many modern treatments of American politics are based on the so-called behavioral approach, an approach that focuses on what people actually do with respect to political things and not on formalistic and unrealistic descriptions of the Constitution, the law, political institutions, and so forth. We are generally sympathetic to behavioralism, properly understood, but it is now time to restore a focus on the formal rules (constitutional law, statutory law, legislative rules of procedure, administrative regulations) that limit and direct individuals in the making of political judgments. Accordingly, we pay more attention than is now conventional to the formal decision-rules of the American polity. Such rules are related conceptually to the other essential elements of the political system in Chapters 1 and 2.

A word about the organization of this book is in order. The theoretical and methodological stance of the book is laid out in Chapters 1 and 2, followed by the substantive chapters (Chapters 3 to 11) on rules, actors, processes, and institutions. The last chapter seeks to place the study of American politics and government in a broad intellectual context. Political analysis is an ancient undertaking and turns today on many of the same questions that preoccupied the Greek philosophers of the fifth century B.C. The academic study of political science in America has its history as well. The continuing issues in political thought and the nature of American political science are taken up in Chapter 12. A reading of this chapter may improve one's understanding of what has gone before and what awaits students who continue, as we hope that many do, to have a serious interest in political science. For reasons which seem pedagogically sound to us, we have placed these topics at the end of the book, but the curious may choose to turn there immediately.

R. L. M.
L. L. W.

1

Some Assumptions About (American) Politics

The study of politics is both intrinsically difficult and inherently incomplete. Politics is a very strange business, involving sensational contrasts and striking incongruities; in fact, it is at least as strange as sex.[1] Nevertheless, many people believe that the understanding of politics is a simple matter and that the answer to most political problems is self-evident. Those who decline to recognize the vicissitudes of politics and the tentativeness of political knowledge are perhaps themselves worthy of political study. If so, it is already apparent why politics is full of hazards for the authors and readers of this book, who seek to explain it. We must study ourselves. There are two related intractable questions before us: Why do some people refuse to face up to the obvious truth that politics is not to be comprehended even partially without effort and endurance? And why do they refuse to accept the fact that no fully satisfactory theory of politics has ever been developed? Since political life is composed of wild eccentricities and extravagant events of all kinds (as well as boredom), we should not be surprised to learn that such people exist. Who are they?

They present themselves in the pages of ancient manuscripts, in contemporary monographs and learned periodicals, in journals of opinion and the mass media, in the councils of government, on the campaign trail, in classroom lectures and conference halls, from the soapbox and the picket line, in jeering mobs, in seminaries and publishing houses, on local planning commissions, in corporation boardrooms, in interest groups and political parties. In short, they are the people who claim that political "truth" is either self-evident to any right-thinking person or discoverable by some process of inquiry, either occult or "scientific," which they, and perhaps some other party-liners, have mastered. Fanatics, mad philosophers, dogmatic ideologues, certified lunatics, and assorted mystics are not the only ones guilty of distorting the reality of politics. Sober-minded businessmen, accomplished scholars, responsible politicians, concerned citizens, and involved students sometimes maintain opinions and beliefs that are fundamentally at odds with the facts of political life and the actual state of political knowledge. That so many people can be so confused about politics suggests another of its dimensions, its *excitement*. What could be more exciting than the coming together of masses of people with very different views of the "truth" who must, sometimes reluctantly and too often without success, decide how (if at all) they are to live together? This is perhaps the most basic political problem. How Americans solve it is explored at length in this book.

Much of the discordance in politics arises from the profound differences in the material, social, and personal positions of individuals in society. Social groups and classes are based on unequal access to material advantage, social status, and political influence and on unequal talents and intelligence. The great American political engineer James Madison was quite correct when he wrote in *The Federalist,* No. 10, "The most common and durable source of factions has been the various and unequal distribution of property." (According to one cynic, Americans are people who came originally from all over the world having only one thing in common — a desire to get rich. This is a gross oversimplification, but it does point up the keen interest in the distribution of material goods.) Like other people, Americans divide over how the enduring tension between those who command property and those who do not is to be resolved.

But Madison also believed that humans are naturally so quarrelsome that they will find *any* excuse to start wrangling. He put it nicely, again in *The Federalist*, No. 10: "So strong is this propensity of mankind to fall into mutual animosities that where no substantial occasion presents it-

*"Now let's be absolutely certain I have this all straight.
Your taxes, regardless of circumstances, are not—
I repeat not— to be used for waging war, manufacturing munitions, financing espionage, or for any
other activity designed to subvert the legitimate democratic aspirations of peoples at home or abroad.
Rather, these moneys will be spent to reduce poverty,
advance education, fight pollution, and, in short,
to do whatever is necessary to improve the human
lot and make this planet a viable habitat for mankind
once again."*
Drawing by Mulligan; © 1973 The New Yorker
Magazine, Inc.

self the most frivolous and fanciful distinctions have been sufficient to
kindle their unfriendly passion and excite their most violent conflicts."

The belligerent positions adopted on political, economic, and social
questions may be viewed as deriving, then, from two sources: objective or
perceived *external* differences in the distribution of advantage and
natural or *internal* impulses which lead to contests over all manner of issues, real or illusory, important or trivial, material or immaterial.[2] We
shall have more to say about the sources of social and political conflict
later but do not have to choose here between social and personality
theories of conflict in seeking to explain human contentiousness. As
Madisonians, the authors believe both to be important. This book, however, unlike most others in modern political analysis, is less concerned
with the *origins* of human conflict than with the implications of its *existence*. It strives to explain how what people are and what they want leads

them to engage (or decline to engage) in the political process. What individuals want politically, together with the resources they command, shapes what they do, and what they do shapes public policy.

There is no doubt that individuals want and believe very different things. For example:

> "We want *pig*meat." (Demonstrators at the 1968 Democratic Party Convention in Chicago.)

> "I thoroughly enjoy attending debutante parties and the like. These parties are, to me, a visual representation of the wealth and power of this country. This leads me to be even more interested in preserving this country to the utmost of my ability." (A college student, quoted by Robert E. Lane, *Political Thinking and Consciousness*, p. 256.)

THE PUBLIC CHOICE APPROACH TO POLITICS

In this book, a number of assumptions are made about human beings and their political behavior, not because they are the only assumptions that one might make in order to better describe, explain, and predict behavior but because, in our view, they are particularly *efficient* in doing so. Moreover, in addition to assisting in the understanding of (American) politics, the assumptions discussed in this chapter lead potentially to the making of certain recommendations concerning how public policy "ought" to be made and how it benefits and costs might be "better" distributed. Initially, the assumptions stated below may appear either difficult to grasp or so unrealistic as to lead to false or preposterous conclusions about political behavior. To these objections, a couple of answers might be made: (1) No reasonably intelligent person should have trouble comprehending the following concepts, although a close reading of their meaning is necessary and failure to keep them in mind during subsequent discussions may lead to serious misunderstanding of the analysis developed. (2) The "realism" or accuracy of the assumptions is, of course, open to challenge. Frankly, the authors themselves are not entirely sure how well the assumptions *actually* describe the behavior of people in politics. However, the assumptions are, to some extent at least, accurate summations of human tendencies and (even more importantly), whether "true" or not, enable us to make some interesting statements and even some predictions about political things.

A Model of American Politics

What we present is a way of looking (a "model" or a "map") at American politics which deliberately omits and radically simplifies what is "actually" true of the subject. We know of no way of writing a book on American politics which does not omit and simplify. For the reader unaccustomed to an academic analysis which *purposely* sets out to do what one might think impressionistically that serious people should *not* do, a word of explanation is in order. Everyone knows that the United States is an awesomely complex society and that its political system alone is of such complexity that comprehensive knowledge of it is rare even among scholars who do nothing else but study it. Experts in constitutional law are often quite ignorant of the precise operations of Congress; experts in political parties and interest groups are frequently unfamiliar with the intricacies of intergovernmental relations; and specialists on the presidency may know relatively little about comparative state politics. In short, most of even the most thoughtful full-time observers possess only limited knowledge of the American polity. Therefore, any book that attempts to introduce students to the structures and processes that constitute the American polity must select from the fund of political knowledge only those elements that are considered fundamental for understanding the subject.

What political scientists, political sociologists, and political historians seek is not detailed familiarity with *all* the "facts" of politics but an abstract set of statements that makes sense of the features of politics most interesting and important to them. These invariably simplified and to some extent distorted abstract statements about political reality constitute the various "theories" of politics. The theories dictate which facts are to be considered significant and suggest the relationships between significant facts. If the statements relate fewer facts of politics and entail more expectations (= **hypotheses**) concerning what one *thinks* may be true, they are characterized as "models" of politics. Thus theories are less abstract than models and attempt to interrelate a greater range of political knowledge. This distinction is introduced to differentiate between abstract statements of political relationships which are *apparently* true and statements which *may* be true.

A simple example should make clear why, in this book, a model (and partial theory) of American politics is presented and no comprehensive description is attempted. Not only is the latter impossible — although some old-fashioned and even some current texts attempt it — but it would be virtually useless to anyone. A Standard Oil Company road map (model) of California is not a representation of all things Californian (only the real California is that) but merely a concise and helpful guide to getting around the state by automobile and even then only on the main highways. Its shape and content, understandably, are determined by its expected use. A topographical or climatic map of the state would have a different look about it. The same is true of political analysis. The political phenomena sorted out for representation will lead to the omission of much of political reality, will distort relationships, and will be grossly oversimplified, all in the same way that a road map omits, distorts, and oversimplifies. Accordingly, this book does not attempt to describe all of politics but only the features of American politics that are particularly salient to an initial comprehension of — and now we state the *use* of *this* map — the making of the main outlines of public policy. It is necessary to stress the phrase *main outlines*, since a detailed examination of any particular aspect of public policy will reveal dimensions, activities, interactions not fully accounted for in the model constructed here. This book, then, provides a picture of American politics from a lofty perspective; its "scale" is very coarse indeed. Yet familiarity with such an overview is helpful to subsequent more detailed investigation and enables one to link up aspects of politics which are of greater personal interest with other, and often interrelated, features of political life. In this and the next chapter two things are done. First, the assumptions that will guide the construction of our model of American politics are stated and explained. Second, the main elements of the model are presented in rudimentary form. Once the assumptions and the elements of the model are in mind, understanding of the substantive analysis developed in later chapters should be greatly facilitated.

A brief cautionary remark is in order. Everyone has a model or theory about how the world works. Yet all of the many models held about the world are probably false in some degree, a conclusion which is easily confirmed by pointing to the logical inconsistencies or empirical gaps they contain. A theory is deficient to the extent that it contains logical incompatibilities, fails to explain important aspects of the world it seeks to explain, or produces highly inaccurate predictions about what is likely to occur in the future. In such circumstances the task of scholarship is not to select the "correct" from among the "incorrect" models or theories — for no correct one exists — but to select and accept for the time being, albeit critically, whatever statement explains best (i.e., most fully and consistently) the world events that interest us. Of course, our interest here is not with phenomena generally but only with some small but important part of the whole of reality, namely, politics and government in the American nation-state. Even so, as Robert Dahl has pointed out, the field of American political theory is one in which both large and important questions are still open, not having been dealt with adequately by any theory.[3]

The Trouble with Answers

To say that we have no fully adequate theory of politics is not to say that we have no answers. Indeed, there is an inexhaustible supply of answers, and almost everyone claims to have some of them; some people claim to have all of them. The trouble is that the answers are often inconsistent with the facts. In addition, the people who supply such answers ordinarily fail to tell us how, if their answers are wrong, we might be able to find that out. The fact is, if we have no way of finding out whether an answer is wrong or not, we call such an answer (theory) untestable, which is not to claim that it is false but that, in a scientific sense, it is uninteresting. Answers to political questions from politicians, bureaucrats, media representatives, aroused citizens and the proverbial "man in the street" often have this puzzling untestable quality. Statements which seem to be about reality are not that at all but are figments of the fancy or of a disordered mind. Moreover, statements which are "supposed" to inform us about the world are in fact often designed to give a deceptive or illusory appearance to things. Political activists and politicians are particularly fond of such propaganda statements; the theories they actually are operating on may be very different from the theories they express publicly. Thus, the public advancement of various theories of politics by various (and in their own minds benevolent) enthusiasts is frequently intended less to inform others of the real relationships of things than to serve the *strategic* function of rationalizing a preference or a course of action. The propensity to attribute one's action to creditable motives without adequate (at least public) analysis of one's true motives is almost universal. The task of the student of politics is therefore most difficult, if only because on any specific occasion it is hard to know whether a public statement of reality conforms to even minimal standards of evidence. In politics, such uncertainties must be lived with.

ASSUMPTIONS

Scarcity Is the Most Important Problem in Politics

Virtually everything that people want is in short supply: income, housing, fame, health, pure air, peace, time, jobs, beauty, intelligence, parks,
dental floss. If such things were *not* in short supply, politics might or
might not exist (as we have said, some theorists claim that people like to
fight for natural [biological] reasons over the most spurious issues and
that politics is therefore an irrepressible human activity which cannot be
brought to a conclusion this side of heaven). Whichever, it surely would
not have its present cast if all desirable things were obtainable simply for
the asking. In any event, it is mere wish-dreaming to attempt to say what
society might be like if all wants were capable of satisfaction or, conversely, if all valuable things were suddenly made available without
costs. In this book, wish-dream theory is avoided; our purpose is to
analyze the behavioral consequences of what will be taken as an immut-
able fact of life: the pervasive, insoluble problem of scarcity, the limited
availability of all valued things.

The fundamental behavioral manifestation of scarcity is that people
are forced to *choose*, to weigh alternatives, to decide on one course of action rather than another. Each of us controls only a small share of all the
nice or desirable things in the world and even total control might be insufficient for some individuals, as it was for Alexander, who was falsely
accused of weeping when he ran out of worlds to conquer. Not all choices
are political in character, however, though ostensibly nonpolitical choices
can have profound political consequences. It is therefore necessary to distinguish between choices that will and will not be analyzed in this
volume.

Since this is a book about politics and government, the focus is
primarily upon **public choice.** It is not a book about decision-making in
general or about decisions involving the selection of a mate, the purchase
of a toothbrush, or the planting of a tree. Yet each of these matters could
become a problem of public choice if, in order to resolve it, what was originally the subject of voluntary and private concern became bound up with
coercion and the interests of other people. Public choices, therefore, are
choices involving the authoritative (= ultimately coercive) resolution of
matters affecting all or significant portions of a population. In politics,
individuals with different wants must often make a single choice which is
binding upon all.

The fundamental process of choosing or weighing alternatives is important in both political and nonpolitical situations. *Bruce Anspach/from Editorial Photocolor Archives*

Everyone chooses in one way or another, but that statement tells us nothing about who chooses what. As later exposition will demonstrate, only a small proportion of the population participates very actively in the making of public choices. Participation in public decisions varies with issues, circumstances, and incentives. From the standpoint of **descriptive theory** it is important to understand how public choices are made in fact. From the standpoint of **normative theory** it is important to consider how public choices might be organized so as to produce both efficient and equitable social outcomes. The normative problem is undoubtedly more difficult than the descriptive. Individuals in America number in the millions and maintain a bewildering variety of beliefs, attitudes, and opinions. How, if at all, can their individual tastes and preferences be put together, or taken into account, or authentically aggregated in the making of a *single* choice which is consistent with those preferences? How, indeed, can their preferences be discovered in the first place?

Moreover, just what is meant by "efficient and equitable"? Could one identify an (in)efficient or (in)equitable public choice if it were observed? If so, what criteria would one have in mind in making such a determination? These are some of the questions we hope the reader will keep in mind. No fully satisfactory answer can be given to any of them — perhaps because of deficiencies in all existing approaches, methodologies, and theories but mainly because of the nature of the questions themselves: When approached seriously they become extremely complex and contain innumerable variables. Nevertheless, they are unavoidable and important questions.

Individual Wants Are Insatiable

Scarcity is a problem, of course, only because human beings, as constituted at present, are not satisfied to live under conditions of scarcity. If everyone would accept, as St. Francis did, the dictum of Jesus that we lead lives of self-denial, scarcity would be no problem. The world is able to maintain even larger populations than now exist if bare subsistence standards were satisfactory. But demands for population control are often justified on the grounds that poverty is not a wholesome state, that the satisfaction of basic and nonbasic wants is necessary among nonascetic people. St. Francis was, in a statistical sense, an aberrant personality whose fame stems from that very fact. There are few saints, and, while some people might wish for more saints, and more people might be encouraged to become saintly, most people keep wanting more things. For this reason, the assumption is made here that individual wants are **insatiable.**

This is not to say that *specific* wants are necessarily insatiable. Most (not all) people can get their fill of just about anything, whether of Scotch whiskey or applause from the masses. What is presumed is that, when any particular want is satisfied for the time being, an individual will begin to *shift* remaining resources (energy, money, good looks, "connections") to secure other wanted opportunities and commodities. For most people, specific wants are rarely fully satisfied, either because they lack the necessary resources or because they recognize that satisfying want A entirely would mean foregoing want B entirely. The problem, then, is to allocate scarce resources to multiple uses so as to improve one's own position as much as possible: to maximize. There are, of course, so-called obsessive-compulsive people who are, or appear to be, single-mindedly devoted to securing just one thing (or a few things) and who, no matter how much of it they obtain, remain unsatisfied. Politicians are occasionally of this character, as are some bureaucrats, people who speak for various political movements and crusades, and assorted crackpots who displace their concentrated affections on political objects and processes. Regardless of any success they may have in changing public policy or political institutions, they are unsated in their search for notoriety, injury, or impact. No amount of success will bring them into equilibrium with their surroundings; they will continue to make claims on others.

From a normative point of view, evaluation of the ends (wants) of people is extremely important, but we should keep in mind that one person's dangerous psychotic is another's "culture hero," or one who brings new, if initially private, insights into the possibilities of a culture. By so doing, such an individual may expand social welfare by opening up new vistas for others, perhaps by creating or redefining political ideologies so as to make possible effective social action with respect to political crises. On the other hand, the unsated political ideologue may pose a positive danger to others, both within and without a given society; think of Hitler or Stalin. Paradoxically, what is personally harmful or destructive may turn out to be socially beneficial and what is personally rewarding may be socially catastrophic.

Most if not All People Are More Concerned with Their Own Welfare than with the Welfare of Others

At first glance, this might seem to be a cynical assumption which denies the likelihood, if not the possibility, that people will act in beneficent ways toward other members of the collectivity. While the authors confess to occasional skepticism vis-à-vis the motives and behavior of others, we would be disappointed if readers were to accuse us of cynicism. So, in spite of the fact that cynical people may believe firmly in this particular assumption, we obviously do not feel that one is necessarily to be judged a faultfinding, captious critic of others *simply* because one may subscribe to the view that, for the most part, individuals are preoccupied with the question "What will become of *me*?" or "What am *I* to do in order to be saved?"

From one point of view the question is an **empirical** one (= depending on experience or observation alone), and the evidence, we submit, confirms (or at least does not *dis*confirm) the assumption. Individuals seem to be more worried about their *own* health, their *own* incomes, their *own* offspring, their *own* "happiness" than about others' possession of these values.[4] The assumption of individual self-interest (like the other assumptions presented here) is not, however, introduced as a prescriptive norm. That is, we are not advising people that they *should* be primarily self-interested. On the contrary, we agree that genuine efforts in behalf of the welfare of others are, consistent with the doctrines of Gandhi, Jesus, Kant, and Pope John XXIII, to be applauded when undertaken with proper humility. Political history, of course, is replete with actions taken *in the name of the general welfare* which, upon examination, were actually seen to stem from the self-interest of some political leader or elite or, even when "sincere" from a public interest point of view, led to devastating results. The road to hell, they say, is paved with good intentions.

Individuals Are Rational

Suppose a person knows that to do a will lead to X and that to do b will lead to Y. If the individual must (or wishes to) choose between a and b, and chooses the alternative that is expected to yield a more preferred outcome, the decision is said to have been rational. This is the simplest possible example of what is meant in this book by rational behavior. The reader will observe that nothing contained in the example has anything to do with whether X and Y are morally good or sinful, healthy or unhealthy, provident or wasteful, laudatory or scandalous, pleasant or unpleasant, nonaddictive or habit-forming. Rational behavior, in our usage, has to do only with *means* and not with ends.

For a decision to be rational, three formal criteria must be satisfied. They are quite obvious when one thinks about them and should not be considered complex or difficult to understand. The three criteria are (1) **consistency,** (2) **instrumentality,** and (3) **transitivity.**[5] *Consistency* means that, to be rational, individuals cannot prefer X to Y and Y to X at the same time. *Instrumentality* means that, if X is preferred to Y, the individual must, as in our example, choose a rather than b if it is a which will lead to X. *Transitivity* means that if X is preferred to Y, and if Y is preferred to Z, then X must be preferred to Z.

There are two possible uses to which this concept of rationality can be put. One use is *prescriptive* and is familiar to all who listen, or have listened, to the admonitions and counsel of parents, teachers, clergymen, probation officers, judges, politicians on the stump, or concerned friends. Such people frequently make statements like (1) "If you don't want to return to prison, you should find a job" or (2) "If you want to avoid pregnancy, you should practice abstention." This sort of advice can be wrong, misguided, or inapt, but its purpose is clear: to encourage others to think consistently, instrumentally, and transitively — in short, rationally with respect to the ends they wish to achieve. The other use of the concept is *descriptive,* that is, as a way of making sense of what people do in fact, not what they should do. **Descriptive rationality** is a tool of science; **prescriptive rationality** is a tool of ethics. Descriptive rationality makes statements like (1) "President Nixon imposed wage and price controls in an effort to halt inflation (or, if you prefer, to maintain political support)" or (2) "Prime Minister Heath took Britain into the Common Market in an effort to improve living standards in his country (or, if you prefer, to maintain political support)."

Our concern is with *both* uses of the concept. We shall rely upon the context to make clear the sense in which the term is being used at any particular point.

Everyone Who Participates in Politics Seeks to Impose His Preferences on Everyone Else

Stated as baldly as this assumption is, the conclusion might be drawn that the authors view every person as a potential dictator, and, to be quite frank, we know of no way around the problem. When individuals with different wants must make a *single* choice binding on everyone, *they are placed in the position of choosing not only for themselves but for everyone else as well.* Someone who chooses for everyone else is a dictator. That autocratic or high-handed methods may be avoided in imposing one's preferences on others does not alter this aspect of collective decision-making. One does not vote to impose taxes on oneself; the taxes are imposed on everybody. One does not vote for a park for himself or herself; a park is chosen for everybody. And a vote against the school budget is not a vote to deny just one's own children a "better education" but a vote to deny all children within the same jurisdiction that kind of education.

This troublesome (yet intriguing) feature of "democratic" politics raises profound questions concerning the possibility of achieving efficiency and freedom through the political process. Hence it is important to

Political participants impose their preferences on others, just as the above authority figure does, though in a more subtle manner. *G. D. Hackett*

know, when individuals must choose for others as well as for themselves,
whether they consider (1) their personal welfare and/or (2) the welfare of
others in doing so. And if one *does* consider the welfare of others, how is it
possible to know what their welfare is? Are not they themselves the best
judges of that? How can anyone presume to speak for them?

Public Decisions Are Neither Rational
Nor Irrational

As we shall use the term, rationality is something that *individuals* alone
possess. On the other hand, public decisions which arise from putting together the preferences of several or many individuals, as in elections,

may very well violate the standards of rationality discussed above: consistency, instrumentality, and transitivity. For example, an election based on simple majority rule may produce an *in*transitive collective decision: where X is preferred by the majority to Y, Y is preferred to Z, and Z is preferred to X. Under such conditions the voters as *a group* are unable to give a consistent ranking to their several preferences. We cannot know, therefore, what the group "really" wants. Some writers have concluded that group or public decision-making in a "democracy" is, with some unknown degree of frequency, irrational.[6] From our point of view, however, it is misleading to describe group (democratic) decision-making as either rational or irrational. Groups do not have minds. They are not organisms. They do not have preferences. To talk of their rationality or lack of it, then, is silly. What we may say is that the consequences of individual decisions, once aggregated into a collective choice or public policy, may be good or bad for everybody, good or bad for some people, or neither good nor bad for anybody. But whether they are beneficial or deplorable, this book makes no statements about the rationality of public choices. Intransitive public choices may present a problem to democratic theory but not to an interpretation of political life which views individuals as rational. Individual rationality is presumed to exist even in the face of intransitive public choices.

One purpose in making this assumption is to avoid the inference, through slipshod analytics, that "society," the "public," or "government" as such has wishes, intentions, tastes, or purposes. Society is not an organism and cannot be said to be directed toward an end or shaped by a purpose in the sense in which individual human beings are organisms and have designs on things and ends in view. The **organic fallacy** (a subfallacy of the reification fallacy) involves converting an abstraction or mental construction into a supposed real thing; it is, unfortunately, a fallacy accepted by all too many people who comment on politics. When phrases such as "social needs," "the public interest," "the government has decided," "this is a government of laws, not of men," and "as history tells us" are used in political discourse, we must decide whether the speaker is attributing organic characteristics to the terms or is merely using a shorthand expression for the sake of convenience while recognizing that *individuals* alone are acting, telling, and deciding. This book focuses upon individuals for both positive reasons (individuals are the choosing agents in politics) and normative reasons (only individuals are valuable and important). Its basic methodology, therefore, is *individualistic*. Such an approach in no way rules out the use of collective nouns and pronouns in political analysis, if only because they are necessary for reasonably concise communications, but the foregoing discussion should be kept in mind when considering the collective terms used in this book.

No One Can Predict the Future
with Certainty

To say that human beings (aside from a few perspicacious practitioners of the occult) are not quite sure what will happen tomorrow or the next day is not the mere truism that one might suppose. Hackneyed or not, the observation contains important implications and may on occasion clarify political events that appear analytically impenetrable or crazy. Ignorance of the future is a function of *uncertainty;* uncertainty, in turn, is a function of poor or inadequate information, the absence of a theory that would make available data meaningful, and (some claim) a measure of randomness in the world. Although the authors are not strong believers in randomness, a concession must be made as to its possibility. If random conditions obtain, it means that no theory or data base could ever yield absolutely accurate predictions about the future. In any event, the fact of uncertainty in human affairs is the important thing here. Even the hardest and most rigorous of the sciences confronts the problem of uncertainty in some degree, and political science may have greater problems with uncertainty than other social sciences do. The reason is not necessarily that political scientists are less able or more indolent than other scholars but because *in politics, more than in other aspects of life, individuals often have reason to hide their wants and intentions from their fellows.* Political life is uncertain partly because we do not know enough about the intentions of anyone but ourselves.

It is often rational for individuals to keep silent or to issue misleading statements about what they will do under particular circumstances. The practice of "concealing preferences" is sometimes — indeed, frequently — rational because it is a powerful tool in **strategic bargaining,** or bargaining engaged in for the purpose of improving one's position with respect to whatever achievement or possession is wanted.

An example drawn from a marketplace confrontation with a used-car salesclerk makes the point. The seller not only "conceals preferences" in refusing upon initial approach to state flatly the lowest value placed on a particular vehicle but may have every inducement to conceal the facts about the product: Setting back a car's odometer is not unknown; fanciful exaggerations, such as claiming that the prior owner was a little old lady from Pasadena, are rather common. By the same token, the potential purchaser of a Cadillac El Dorado acts strategically when hiding both the excitement of contemplating its ownership and the price he or she is actually prepared to pay to secure it. Both the seller and the potential purchaser conceal their preferences because their interests are in perfect conflict: One wants a high price, the other a low one. However, both must at some point reveal their preferences if a mutually beneficial exchange is to be conducted. Politics, it turns out, provides even more interesting examples of the concealment of preferences, examples with an additional dimension.

The reason politics provides more interesting examples of concealing preferences is this: In the marketplace, individuals are *sooner or later required* to reveal their preferences if they want to exchange the resources which they control for those which they value more highly; *in politics, no such requirements exist* in many circumstances. On the contrary, the individual has every reason *not* to indicate how strongly he or she wants something in the hope that others who want the same thing will take the time and go to the expense of securing it; once secured, it will be enjoyed by the individual along with everyone else. A brief example will clarify the point.

Suppose a certain farmer would like the government to provide him with a subsidy. If he calculates that *other* farmers will organize, go to Washington, pressure government, and secure the subsidy (in which each of course will share), then the individual farmer has no incentive to share the costs necessary to get the subsidy policy enacted into law. The farmer wants to secure the subsidy but does not want to incur any costs in doing so. The fact is that one may be successful by pursuing this "strategy of inaction" *in getting what one wants at no cost.* Such an outcome is impossible in the marketplace, where people must eventually pay (and in doing so reveal their preferences) for anything they want. Those who successfully conceal their preferences and get beneficial returns from government at no cost may be referred to as "**free riders**" (or, as someone put it more pejoratively, "freeloaders").

Consider the problem of a political decision-maker who, full of goodwill and intent upon satisfying the real wants of his constituents, is frustrated because the latter persistently conceal their preferences. How can the decision-maker possibly legislate in a manner that will satisfy them, or, in the vocabulary of the day, how can she or he be "responsive" to them? This is a profound dilemma which theorists of democracy must consider. In any event, the problem of the free rider, which arises out of the inducements to silence and nonparticipation, means that political analysts, political participants, and political decision-makers are often in the dark as to what the future holds. Not knowing the preferences of others, they do not know what they are likely to do under various circumstances. Moreover, the *normative* problem confronting the intendedly responsive democratic politician, who must make judgments as to which scarce resources should be distributed to which people, is vexing to the point of insolubility. If one does not know what one's constituents want, or how much of it they want, or how they are prepared to pay for it, one can scarcely be expected to read their minds to find out. Politicians sometimes fail to respond to the "needs" of constituents simply because no one will tell them what those needs are. There are additional reasons why elected officials in the United States are often insecure in their positions but this is an important one.

Uncertainty has one other important effect on political choices. The extent of uncertainty associated with the various preferences of an individual will help shape the final choice. A second-ranked preference which can be secured with near certainty may be sought over a more doubtfully attainable first-ranked preference. Thus, an individual's choices are determined not only by (1) the ranking assigned to various wants, (2) the apparent costs of the wants, and (3) the resources controlled by the individual but, as well, by (4) the probability (= extent of certainty) that any particular preference can or cannot be achieved. In many economic exchanges, uncertainty is minimized by the one-to-one relationship of buyer and seller, the short time span between decision and transaction, the sanctity and explicitness of contract, and so forth. In politics, however, uncertainty is both greater and more ubiquitous. Collective choices (as in elections) involve processes which produce different outcomes depending upon ingredients that are usually, or often, beyond the control of the individual (e.g., **the decision-rules** in effect, the number of participants, *their* preferences). The time between choice and action, if defined at all, may be lengthy, giving rise to confusion and ambiguity, as do the often inexplicit and vaguely formulated agreements made among political actors. No wonder that, for many people, "making up one's mind" politically is most difficult; uncertainty makes it so.

SUMMARY OF ASSUMPTIONS

The controlling assumptions of this book can now be stated in one sentence: *Rational, potentially dictatorial individuals, who seek to maximize benefits and to minimize their costs in doing so, interact with others under conditions of scarcity and uncertainty to make binding public choices which are understood to be neither rational nor irrational.*

SOME QUALIFICATIONS

Having stated these assumptions, we must now enter some important qualifications as a gesture toward greater realism and concreteness. Individuals are not interchangeable as are parts in a mass-produced product. Therefore, while individuals calculate their actions in the manner described above (and, more explicitly, below), their calculations are affected by their *individual propensities* as well as by the objective costs and benefits associated with any particular situation. Thus, two individuals in the same situation may make very different decisions if, for example, they subscribe to very different types of morality. As Professor Edward C. Banfield sees it, morality is essentially an attitude toward rules, both legal and moral.[7] A person with a "preconventional" moral attitude believes that any action is proper as long as it is personally rewarding and can be carried off with impunity. Countervailing raw power alone can check the claim such a person will make upon others. The altogether ruthless politician and the sociopathic outlaw are examples.

"Conventional" morality, on the other hand, emphasizes obligations to everyday laws and commands developed by those in authority, whether in government or in, say, church, school, and home. When no great disproportion exists between potential benefits and expected costs, adherents to this morality may eschew potential benefits if, to secure them, some abridgment of conventional morality is required. The outcome is increasingly problematical, however, as benefits increase relative to costs (or, what is the same thing, as costs decrease relative to benefits). Most Americans, — indeed, most people everywhere — are doubtless of this moral type. For the most part, they are "honest" as conventionally defined but may yield to temptation when a large return becomes available at slight cost or risk. Legitimate authority alone may check some high proportion of the claims people of conventional morality make upon others. It cannot be emphasized too strongly, therefore, that adherents of a conventional morality make possible a tolerant and ordered society; this is not the case for the preconventional moral type or, for different reasons, for the "postconventional" moral type, discussed next.

Postconventional morality is characteristic of those who seek moral guidance not from social conventions or legal codes but from some surpassing ethical value system. Laws which are personally considered stupid or unjust are regarded with amusement or contempt, and "true" virtue consists in "having the courage of one's convictions" and breaking or otherwise undermining the law. Legitimate authority will therefore not limit the demands such moral types will make upon others in the society. Paradoxically, only power and coercion can limit the claims of both those who are preconventional and those who are postconventional in their moral stances. Ordered social life would be impossible among individuals all acting as their own lawgivers.

From one point of view, there is no difference between the preconventional morality of the street mugger and the postconventional morality of the advanced intellectual who steals state secrets in the name of justice and humanity: Both are their own behavioral legislators, and both can be constrained not by legitimate authority but by coercion or the threat of coercion alone. Their behavior is also likely to be less predictable than that of the conventionally moral person. Insofar as conventional points of reference do not condition their behavior, they are "free spirits" moved either by impulse or by shifting interpretations of moral obligations in light of a transcendent source of guidance.

In sum, a moral system orients one to the choices to be made. A person is predisposed to choose and act in one direction rather than another. Nonetheless, the importance of the situation itself, morality notwithstanding, should not be lost sight of, although the relative influence of morality and opportunity in any concrete situation is a matter to be discovered and not asserted.

INTRODUCTION TO MAJOR TERMS

The assumptions discussed above provide the foundation upon which we can now construct the model of American politics to be developed and utilized in the remainder of this book. In a sense the controlling features of the model have already been introduced, although incompletely, in the description of certain qualities of individuals—self-interestedness, rationality, insatiability, limited resources, etc. The next chapter provides some "life" or dynamism by considering the ways in which the individual characteristics and behaviors of members of the society are structured into a system of collective choice that defines the operation of the polity. We begin this process by focusing attention upon (1) the individuals or *actors* who play certain definable political *roles* and, by doing so, perform certain *functions* for the political system as a whole; (2) the *rules* that structure and control the political behavior of the actors as they engage in their roles and functions in the system; (3) the *distribution of resources* among the actors

a ? of or ? ? ?in? ?o? ? the polity; and (5)

8

ing on to the next this book is to be s *equilibrium* and will be explained choice model can

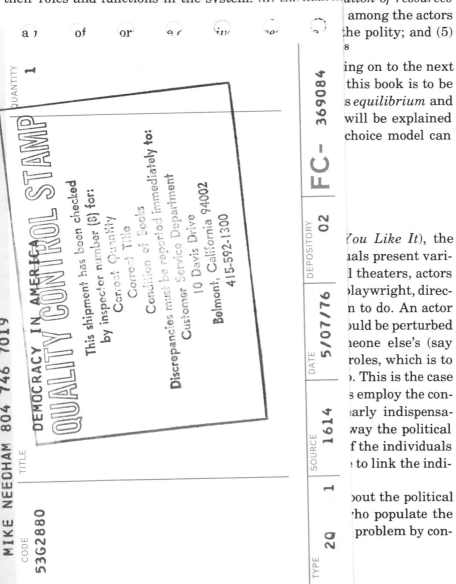

You Like It), the uals present vari- l theaters, actors playwright, direc- n to do. An actor uld be perturbed eone else's (say roles, which is to . This is the case s employ the con- arly indispensa- way the political f the individuals to link the indi-

out the political ho populate the problem by constructing a limited and intellectually manageable number of roles into which, if need be, specific individuals or certain of their traits can be grouped. A role is understood to summarize a pattern of behavior. Thus, the role "constitutes a *strategy* for coping with a recurrent type of situation."[9] We will illustrate directly the types of strategies associated with various American political role-players. A role is also defined as a socially identifiable entity; hence the concept can be used for identiying, placing, and analyzing individuals in the political system. The behavioral patterns which are grouped into a particular role are referred to as *actors*. Actors are the dynamic part of the role. The roles actors play are parts of a larger culture and, for that reason, contain standards of behavior to guide the actor in making choices. These standards of behavior, called here **decision-rules,** or simply rules, may be both formal (legal) and informal (customary). Thus, in an important sense, the concepts of role, actor and rules are inseparable.

Function

In social and political analysis, the notion of function is defined variously. For our purposes it is sufficient to define the term narrowly and simply to refer to the contribution that a role makes to the way the political system as a whole operates (e.g., "one function of the role of 'voter' is to elect the government"). Since the social impact of every role is manifold, it is necessary in the present book to restrict attention to the most important or influential contribution of various roles to the working of the polity. Our treatment of function will be limited to the analysis of the most significant impacts of political choices upon the operation of the American polity.

Equilibrium

By the term **equilibrium** we mean two things. (1) The parts that make up a model of a political (or any social) system must, in their interrelationships, form a closed or **determinant system** if one is to assess (and evaluate) the weight or influence of each element relative to the whole. In the absence of such a determinant system, one cannot know how much importance to assign, say, to elections in the political order, if elections are an element of that order. (2) In the particular equilibrium (="equal weight") model developed here each element is balanced in terms of power with all other elements in the model. Once that balance is presumed, the source and consequence of imbalance may be considered. Almost any useful model of the American polity involves acceptance, if only implicitly, of equilibrium in the first sense. The second sense (balance of power) is congenial to the discipline of political science in which power remains the central organizing concept but need not be accepted universally.

Marginality and Individual Decision-Making

The model of the American polity stated below is (at least temporarily) an equilibrium one. The actors in the model must themselves come into equilibrium with other actors and with the environment generally. (To say that actors reach an equilibrium state is emphatically not to say that they are satisfied but only that they are doing as well as they can under the circumstances. Also, one must avoid presuming that a social system in equilibrium is necessarily normatively attractive.)

In this model, individuals are presumed to reach equilibrium by following the marginal rule in making decisions. Two aspects of the rule are relevant here. The first concerns the notion of **diminishing marginal utility.** This rule states that as more of some valued good is consumed, satisfaction increases. However, each additional increment of the good yields somewhat less satisfaction than the previous increment. Total satisfaction increases but at a decreasing rate. The rule applies both to private goods purchased in the marketplace and to public goods (social security, education, national security, and many other things) purchased from government through taxation.

The second aspect of the marginal principle of importance here is the notion of **equal marginal utilities per unit of resource.** Each good or service, either public or private, will be sought by the individual up to the point where the marginal utility per resource unit (say, money or time) spent to secure it will yield the same marginal utility as the same resource spent on some other good or service. If any one good or service yielded more marginal utility per resource unit, the individual would allocate less scarce resources to other goods or services and more to that good or service. This allocation would be continued until the operation of the first principle described above, that of diminishing marginal utility, brought its marginal utility down to equality. When equal marginal utilities have been achieved, the individual is in equilibrium with the situation; the decisional problem is solved for the time being. Each actor in the model described below is presumed to act on the basis of these principles.

Public or Collective Goods

Individual wants and needs may be satisfied through the acquisition of either private or public goods. Private goods are those that are allocated through the free operation of voluntary activities, individual choices, and market mechanisms. Choices made in the process of allocating private goods often have only limited external effects upon other members of the community. Individual choices involving, for example, the purchase of toothpaste rather than beer or playing golf rather than attending church are at most of only trivial significance to most members of the collectivity. The individual controls the enjoyment attached to the private good acquired and generally assumes whatever costs are associated with its acquisition.

The choice of a public good (given the nontechnical usage presented here) significantly affects other members of the community. Such choices involve the wants and needs of large numbers of persons and binding allocations. They normally cannot be controlled completely by the individual but are the subject of collective decision-making. The choice to build a highway rather than a school or to allocate more available resources to military hardware—typical problems in the selection of **public goods**—has a strong impact upon sizable portions of the community. These choices not only dictate what benefits will be allocated by public policy but involve a judgment, explicit or implicit, about how the costs will be allocated among the members of the community. Frequently people receiving the greatest benefits from public goods are not those who have to pay the costs. The processes that determine the amount and kinds of public goods that will be provided, and the distribution of the costs and benefits associated with them, are the central concern of political science.

SUMMARY

Politics is a complex, exciting, and strange activity that occurs in all societies. It grows out of conflicts over contradictory goals pursued by the individual members of the community. It involves conflicts over whose interests will be served by the collectivity and how benefits and costs should be distributed among the members of the community. Collective decision-making is required in order to obtain many goals that are beyond the reach of the individual acting alone and to provide a means through which large numbers of competing individuals can live together in relative peace.

To make sense of phenomena as complex as politics requires simplification. Our treatment of American politics rests upon a set of abstract statements which guide the selection and ordering of the facts presented. These statements comprise a theory or model of the American polity. Every treatment of American politics rests upon a theory, whether clearly articulated or not. We believe that the model developed in this book provides an efficient tool for the initial understanding of public policy formation in America. Like all models of the political process, it leaves out much that is known about politics and provides something less than a comprehensive explication of the American political process.

The model is based upon certain assumptions that are useful in the understanding of the political process. It places the individual in the center of analysis. The individual is seen as having insatiable wants and as being faced with relative scarcity. Since not all wants can be satisfied, each person must allocate resources among available opportunities so as to maximize total satisfaction. Choices are seen as rational in that the individual selects those alternatives that are expected to yield the greatest total satisfaction. Choices must be made under conditions of uncertainty, which greatly influence the nature of the choice process. Everyone is guided by personal interest in making choices about the allocation of public goods and seeks to impose his or her own image of the good society on all other members of the polity. Collective decisions represent an aggregation of the preferences of certain members of the society and cannot usefully be characterized as either rational or irrational. Individual decision-making based upon the marginal principle proceeds until the individual can be said to be in equilibrium with the environment. The dynamic relationships between these concepts and processes are examined in the next chapter.

NOTES

1. Harold Lasswell, *Psychopathology and Politics* (New York: Viking, 1960).
2. One of the finest expositions of this view is developed by Alexander Hamilton, James Madison, and John Jay in the *Federalist Papers*.

3. Robert A. Dahl, "The City in the Future of Democracy," *American Political Science Review,* 61 (December 1967), 953–969.
4. Hadley Cantril, *The Pattern of Human Concerns* (New Brunswick, N.J.: Rutgers University Press, 1966). As far as *public* issues are concerned, questions of war and peace — or issues that are also likely to bear directly on the well-being of all individuals—are most salient to most people (pp. 34–44).
5. For a good discussion of these criteria see Anatol Rapoport, *Strategy and Conscience* (New York: Harper & Row, 1964), pp. 7–11.
6. Expressions of this view will be found in ibid., p.10, and are discussed at length in Kenneth Arrow, *Social Choice and Individual Values,* 2nd ed. (New York: Wiley, 1963).
7. The caveat entered here is developed by Edward C. Banfield, *The Unheavenly City* (Boston: Little, Brown, 1968), pp. 160–163.
8. A more technical statement of a similar model may be found in R. L. Curry, Jr., and L. L. Wade, *A Theory of Political Exchange* (Englewood Cliffs, N.J.: Prentice-Hall, 1968), Chapter 2.
9. Ralph H. Turner, "Role," in *International Encyclopedia of the Social Sciences,* Vol. 13 (New York: Macmillan, 1968), p. 552.

2 Actors in the American Political System

In Chapter 1 the several assumptions which will guide the remainder of the book were specified. When reference is made to particular participants in American politics — the president, members of Congress, judges, and so forth — the reader must remember that all the qualities described there are being attributed to such people. In addition, the previous chapter introduced a number of concepts which are useful in understanding social and political systems generally and which are applied below in elaborating this book's view of the American polity: model, role, actor, decision-rule, function, equilibrium, collective goods, and marginal utility. If the meanings of the assumptions and concepts are clear, both this and following chapters should be easily appreciated.

Attention is now directed toward the principal actors in the American polity, their central functions in terms of the present model, and the decision-rules that direct their behavior. These matters are first discussed in a cursory manner and pursued at greater length later on. The actors are, specifically, voters, members of interest groups, leaders of interest groups, and formal officeholders (i.e., elected officials, bureaucrats, and judges).

VOTERS

No analysis of the major actors in American politics could exclude from concern the electorate, the voting public. While it is not correct to contend that all decision-making power in the United States rests ultimately upon the consent of the governed manifesting their desires through competitively elected "representatives," it would be singularly unwise to conclude that voters are unimportant in the determination of major aspects of public policy.[1] The connection between the preferences of voters and the content of public policy or the allocation of public goods is difficult to trace. There are logical (as distinguished from empirical) reasons why any consistent (and hence, for a democrat, praiseworthy) connection between the hopes and wants of voters and policy decisions *must* in many circumstances be either weak or nonexistent.[2] These reasons are very important indeed as a corrective to any utopian conception of political democracy.

Nonetheless, voting by democratic means often *does* produce policies which are in fact favored by consistent majorities and which are in fact implemented by political authorities. Moreover, whether the impact of voting on policy or leadership is consistent or not, it is an empirical determinant of the outcome; that is, voters (or a majority of them) may not get what they "want," but, even so, the final shape of a policy would have been something else if no voting had taken place at all.

Thousands of electorates exist in America, ranging in size from a mere handful of participants (as, say, in a small water or school district election) to the over sixty million individuals who vote in presidential elections. By presumption, all these voters have certain things in common: Each has limited resources and many unsatisfied wants, and each hopes to improve his or her own position with respect to those wants. Also by presumption, voters (or potential voters) are rational; they will make decisions concerning voting which, intendedly, maximize the differences between what they want to secure and what they must give up in order to get it.[3] (The potential voter who is in the happy position of being a free rider of course pays no costs.)

For the student who has recently come to political science, the characteristics imputed to the voter here may seem either obvious and unsurprising or dead wrong. Indeed, experts disagree as to whether politics, including voting behavior, can better be understood through a rational-choice model of the sort advanced here or by some alternative model which does not ascribe a high measure of rationality to political actors.[4]

In order partly to bridge any disagreement that may arise over the alleged rationality or nonrationality of political actors, we emphasize again that one of the major, if often scarce, resources in politics is information. Rational decisions made under uncertainty may resemble in all descriptive particulars decisions made under conditions of irrationality or nonrationality defined, say, psychoanalytically. Rational decisions are sometimes regretted; remorse and disillusionment, to say nothing of havoc and loss of life, may flow from decisions that are quite consistent with a rational view of politics. Nonetheless, improved information may reduce the unforeseen consequences of decisions made under uncertain conditions. Accurate or improved decision-making is enhanced by conducting a thorough search for feasible alternatives, collecting and ana-

Drawing by Weber; © 1973 The New Yorker Magazine, Inc.

lyzing data defining the costs and benefits of those alternatives, and choosing the obviously best course of action from among them. Improvement in decision-making through scientific analysis has its limits, however: Even if all relevant data concerning a particular alternative were available, the *reactions* of other people to the alternative chosen can never be known entirely. *Asking* them how they feel about it might be helpful, but one cannot be certain how much strategic bargaining is involved in their answer.

The Voter's Resource

The political resource held by the electorate is, of course, the vote. It is fixed in supply ("one adult, one vote") and can be managed in a number of ways in the American polity.

A rational political voter in, say, a presidential election, must decide whether to (1) vote at all; (2) vote for the Republican party's nominee; (3) vote for the Democratic party's nominee; (4) vote for a minor party candidate, if one is on the ballot; (5) vote for a write-in candidate, if allowed. How any particular voter will respond to these choices depends upon the individual's *preferences, resources,* and *alternatives.*[5]

The individual who decides to play the role of elector and vote participates positively in the selection of a government. (Obviously the nonvoter participates negatively in the selection process; in a two-candidate election, for example, the individual's effective or "real" choice is to give each candidate 50 percent of his vote, as opposed to giving one candidate 100 percent.) By presumption, each voter has calculated that the effort involved in voting is worthwhile, and each nonvoter has come to the opposite conclusion. By deduction, each voter has made a calculation also that one candidate will probably improve the voter's position more, or damage it less, than another candidate. In analyzing each candidate's stands on the public issues of the day, the voter makes a voting decision not on the basis of a candidate's stand on one issue (unless, untypically, all other matters pale into insignificance compared to one issue of overwhelming importance) but across the whole range of issues present in the election. The potential voter decides whether, on balance and across all issues, his or her position will be more improved (or less damaged) by candidate A than candidate B.

In deciding whether or not to vote, citizens (1) consider to what extent their position will probably be improved if their preferred party wins (minus the costs of voting); (2) multiply that probable improvement by the extent to which their vote is likely to change the outcome of the election (by judging both the estimated size of the turnout and the closeness of the election); and (3) consider the value to them of maintaining a democratic political system.

Thus the more important an election is to individuals, the more important they judge their vote may be in determining its outcome, and the more firmly they are committed to democratic procedures, the more likely they are to vote. This might seem to be a fairly straightforward conclusion; in fact it is a controversial one. Some scholars have argued[6] that, in a large society, any single vote has only a trivial impact on the result of the election. If this point is granted, it would seem to follow that no rational, self-interested person would absorb any of the so-called costs of voting. A self-interested citizen would not choose to accept costs when no offsetting benefits were in prospect. Therefore, it is said, the mere existence of voting proves that a rational-choice view of politics is wrong.

Is there a way of salvaging the theory? One authority has claimed that, in our terms, voting is part of the democratic citizen's role; the individual votes because that is what democratic citizens do, and the gratifications (benefits) in playing one's civic role correctly more than offset the costs of voting.[7] Is this a sleight-of-hand trick? Are *unnecessary* reaffirmations of attachment to the political order, which have no impact and produce no return, consistent with a model of rational voters? Perhaps, if nothing else were involved, no. But there are other ways of explaining voting within a rational-choice context. In the nature of things there is always *some* difference, however slight, between and among candidates in terms of their positive and negative effects upon a potential voter, and there is always some possibility, however remote, that the potential voter's vote will be important to the outcome of the election. If the costs of voting are less than the perhaps extremely low probability of affecting the outcome, voting will still be rational. The costs of voting should not be exaggerated; they are, for most people in America, negligible. Many efforts are made to reduce the costs of voting if not to eliminate them entirely in any practical sense. In most jurisdictions registration requirements have been greatly simplified in recent years. Most voting precincts are open at other than working hours and are conveniently located; sample ballots with statements of contending views (free information) are frequently circulated to registered voters; and the mass media provide free information on the candidates and issues. To become a well-informed voter is costly, true enough, but the act of voting itself is usually not. In this context the importance of one vote to the electoral outcome need not be large in order to justify voting in light of the low costs of participation.

In addition, an election (such as a presidential election) may involve more than the issues posed in selecting a particular candidate. Ostensibly irrational voting may be shown to be rational if the citizen votes not so much because of a cost/benefit calculation made in terms of the issues of some specific election but, instead, in order to maintain the democratic system itself. If the preservation of democracy *depends* upon voting, as in large part it does, and if democracy confers overwhelmingly important benefits compared to any alternative political order, then voting is a rational act, particularly in view of its insignificant costs. Anthony Downs refers to *this* calculation as one involving the "short-run" cost of voting in return for a "long-run" benefit (the maintenance of democracy).[8]

Actually, the "maintenance-of-democracy benefit" need not be viewed as a long-run one. If rational calculation based on other premises leads to nonvoting on the part of everyone, democracy will have been forsaken at the same time (in the short run). Still, why should the individual citizen not let *others* incur the cost of voting and, by "saving" democracy, produce a benefit in which the nonvoter will share? On the other hand, if only a few citizens decide to vote in order to save democracy, while everyone else is induced not to vote (following the reasoning just described), will those few votes suffice to maintain a system of free elections? Probably not. A large turnout is required, with the result that abstaining increases the risk of undermining the democratic system.

One point often insufficiently stressed in discussing voting is that the potential voter, in assessing the value of democracy, specific electoral issues, probable turnout and competitiveness, and the costs of voting, is not in the same situation as all other potential voters. Citizens are *not* identical in their concerns; the problem is *not* why some people vote and others do not, as if they were all similarly situated in all politically relevant ways. People differ radically in information and other resources. For some, specific issues in an election are so important, the costs of voting are so small, and information about turnout and the likely importance of one's vote is so uncertain that voting is clearly a rational act *for those people*. For others, for whom likely benefits are small, voting is difficult, democracy has proved to be *personally* disadvantageous, and the outcome is rather obvious beforehand, nonvoting may well be rational *for those people*. For yet others, if they are aware that the impact of their vote on the specific outcome will probably be insignificant and if the costs of voting, while slight, exceed the likelihood of having an appreciable effect on the outcome, voting will still be rational if they have a strong attachment to democracy and if they are in some measure ignorant, as they must be, of how others in the electorate are going to behave. Thus citizens who would, in their own interests, save democracy by voting must evaluate not only the formal *logic* of whether nonvoting is rational (let others vote and hence save democracy; or, since others will not vote, my vote alone will not be enough to save democracy, and therefore I should not vote) but the likely calculations of people dissimilarly situated. Nonvoting for the supporter of democracy who has nothing else at stake is rational if he has reason to believe that the facts in the election will induce a large or "satisfactory" turnout. On the other hand, voting is rational to supporters of democracy if they believe that the facts in an election will produce a low or "unsatisfactory" turnout. By voting in such an election the supporter of democracy may assist in keeping democracy alive. The important point is that, in this view, even the strongest supporters of democracy and the electoral system are not required to vote in *every* election. We should never lose sight of the fact that *specific conditions* determine whether voting or nonvoting or any political act is rational or not.

Role and Function of the Voter

The voter's *role,* we may conclude, is to analyze the opportunities presented by local, state, and national elections in terms of the marginal principle discussed in Chapter 1. Given his scarce resources, the citizen will allocate resources to electoral politics — by studying issues, candidates, turnout rates, competitiveness, the viability of the democratic order — until the expected marginal benefits from doing so equal the marginal costs of doing so. When that point is reached, involvement in the electoral system ceases for the time being except for individuals for whom, out of rational calculation, it never began. It is not to be inferred that equilibrium has been achieved with the entire political system; as shown below, calculations with respect to other possible forms of political participation are still required.

The principal political *function* of the voter is to participate in the selection of a government.

MEMBERS OF INTEREST GROUPS

Most people recognize that the electoral process is not the only, or even the most influential, method of political participation. We turn now, therefore, to an explanation of why individuals might be presumed to participate (or not participate) in other political processes.

Many, perhaps most, American political scientists, in estimating the relative impact of various forms of political activity on the formation of public policy, have concluded that special interest or "pressure" groups are particularly powerful in American politics.[9] Certainly an understanding of voting and elections and the institutions and personalities that operate them (e.g., political parties, politicians, voters) will, at best, provide a partial theory of American political life. But by the same token, a theory of political interest groups will, by itself, be partial as well. All individuals have limited resources; their problem is to allocate their resources to alternative uses so as to maximize their overall well-being. For a good many people, therefore, few if any political actions — all of which are in some measure costly — will be pursued. Resources of money, time, and energy are better allocated among, say, love affairs, career improvement, and rock music. In terms of the purposes of these people, engagement in any political activity would simply be *inefficient*. There are others, however, for whom modest political involvement — voting, for example — is rational. By presumption, they have assessed the uses to which their scarce resources might best be put in terms of probable benefits and decided that some minimal political action is consistent with an efficient distribution of resources.

For still others — rather few, as it turns out — an efficient allocation of personal resources leads to higher levels of political involvement, one form of which is membership in political **interest groups.** By joining one or more interest groups, they seek to maximize their personal position with respect to the things they want and to minimize their costs in doing so.

Bases of Interest Groups

Why might a rational person join a political interest group such as the Chamber of Commerce, the United Farm Workers, the American Medical Association, the Farm Bureau, the American Civil Liberties Union, the NAACP, the Teamsters, the American Federation of Teachers the American Legion, or any of the myriad groups that compete and advocate in the political arena? Initially, one might think that the *political goals* of a particular group appeal to the self-interest of particular members of the public, who, realizing as much, join it in order to facilitate its success. If the American Medical Association (AMA) is perceived by medical doctors as pursuing political goals that are personally advantageous to them, it would seem to make sense for doctors to join and support the AMA. This logic is in some measure flawed. Membership in all groups which pursue personally advantageous ends would be rational were it not for several constraints. For one thing, membership is rarely free. For another, public policy decisions made because of pressure group activity usually confer benefits not only on the formal, "card-carrying" members of the **pressure group** but upon classes or interests more broadly defined. If the AMA is instrumental in defeating a policy proposal that might limit the opportunities of doctors, all or most doctors benefit, not merely those who happen to have joined the AMA. Therefore, an individual doctor might well avoid the costs of joining the AMA on the grounds that its political successes will redound to his or her benefit anyway. That is to say, one might act as a free rider. But if each person pursues the logic of the free rider, why should people join political interest groups at all?

According to some authorities, the answer is that, normally, *individuals do not join "political" interest groups for political or public policy reasons in the first place.*[10] Rather, they join groups, if at all, in order to secure certain immediate, usually material, benefits that are not otherwise available or are available elsewhere only at higher cost. Think of a geographically isolated farmer who lacks access to a satisfying social life, to a credit union, to group life insurance programs, to cooperative purchasing arrangements, or to marketing information. If the Farmers Union, the Farm Bureau, the Grange, or the National Farmers Organization can provide services such as these, the farmer may well be prepared to join and to accept the cost of membership in return. One conclusion is that, in many cases, the political activities of organizations are of secondary importance to individual members; indeed, individuals may actually *disapprove* of the policy positions of an organization but retain membership because of its offsetting concrete advantages.

Historically, as government has supplied more and more goods, services, and consumer protection, the specific benefits available for singular dispensation by private associations have declined. For example, the big-city political machine, which once provided social services to poor and untutored citizens in return for their votes, was a casualty of the success those millions of aggregated votes had in compelling politicians to erect the main outlines of the welfare state. The machine collapsed, its services being provided now by the government. Another conclusion, therefore, is that unless an organization can require (coerce) people to join and maintain their membership (as in closed or union shop arrangements) it may

Dairy farmers like those pictured above at a Wisconsin World Dairy Exposition may join political interest groups such as the National Dairymen's Association with the intention of securing certain benefits otherwise unavailable. *Daniel S. Brody/Editorial Photocolor Archives*

alienate members to the extent that it is successful in getting government to meet the desires of the members.[11] The raison d'être of an organization may be obviated by its success.

Still another conclusion is that, while members may join for the immediate, tangible goods and services offered by the organization, the political activity of its leadership is a spillover or by-product of resources attracted to the organization for nonpolitical reasons. Nonetheless, there are surely many occasions on which the primary interests of individuals get attached to the political system and are pursued through membership in political groups.

In certain groups, for instance, the members are motivated by some shared vision of the public interest: groups concerned to abolish (or restore) capital punishment, improve (or justify) foreign policy, or eliminate (or preserve) pornography. Such groups are concerned less with maintaining or redistributing material values than with imposing a particular ethical value system on society. Even if they are successful in altering public policy, no important alteration in material dispensations normally takes place. Moreover, since the selective material incentives the groups make available to their members are usually meager or nonexistent, memberships tend predictably to be small. As a haven for like-minded ideologues, such a group offers values of sociability that are often strong enough to maintain some members. It should be remembered, too, that virtually all formal organizations in America — publicly involved or not and no matter how small — have leadership positions to allocate which are of great interest to some people. Established organizations have a president, a chairman, an executive secretary, a publicity director, a treasurer, a board of directors, and so on. In some politically radical groups where there is hostility to "bourgeois" or "parliamentary" systems of internal rule other niches will be allocated: membership in the cabal which calls meetings, sets the agenda, and defines the political line; positions as outraged orators who attack the cabal from the floor; roles for both deviationists and revisionists as well as ideological purists. Playing or seeking various roles can be an intense experience and for some personalities constitute the attraction that leads them to form and reform political associations of all kinds.

Benefits and Costs of Membership

But the larger thesis still holds: The contribution that individuals are normally prepared to make to an organizational objective varies with the value of the personal and selective benefits they are able to gain through group membership. They will make *just enough* of a contribution (and no more) to procure those selective benefits. This is an important point, for it means that interest groups usually have far less in the way of resources than they would have if they were able to eliminate the free-rider problem and to pursue through political action benefits which would accrue only to their own members.[12] But as we have said, interest groups that achieve some policy objective almost always produce favorable consequences for others as well. For nongroup members, those consequences are *external benefits,* or benefits accruing to individuals who did not participate in the costly decision-making process that made them available. Think of benefits you may enjoy (e.g., agricultural subsidies, veterans' allowances, good roads) even though you did not take part in the complex political process through which they became available. Knowing that one stands a good chance of receiving an external benefit is often a strong reason for deciding not to assume the cost of going out and working for it. It is one explanation of political inactivity or "apathy."

Do *any* interest group members join even though all selective benefits (even attractive roles) may be lacking and even if, assuming they are successful politically, they are aware that others who did nothing to secure a benefit will share in it anyway? The answer is yes; there are undoubtedly people who are intensely interested in some political objective for whom the cost of participation is subjectively much less than it might seem to most others.[13] The argument, however, is that such people are relatively few and that the decision not to belong to groups — or, if one belongs, to participate and contribute at a low level — is often quite rational.[14]

To summarize: Individuals bear the costs of joining a group as long as the expected rewards from doing so exceed those costs. The expected rewards need not be familiarly "political" in nature. For example, benefits may be derived from the specific material advantages which group bargaining power in the marketplace can provide in the way of attractive life, health, or auto insurance. Or benefits may be derived from directly confronting another specific group, as in labor-management bargaining. Government allocations made only to members of certain private groups serve to induce individuals to join or stay in that group (as, formerly, the Defense Department provided sporting ammunition to members of the National Rifle Association at reduced rates). The main point, again, is that in large, impersonal, and noncoercive groups, contributions from members to the achievement of political goals, which, if achieved, will benefit nonmembers as well, will be less than optimal. This is one consequence of the free-rider problem discussed earlier.

Many costs limit group membership: dues, time, forgone opportunities, adverse publicity. Given scarce resources, the individual is presumed to allocate resources to group memberships (if at all) until the marginal benefits from doing so equal the marginal costs from doing so. When that point is reached, the individual has done as well as possible for the time being with respect to interest group activity and is in equilibrium with the pressure group system.

The major political *function* of the members of interest groups is to establish, however cumbersomely, demands upon others in society which the leaders of those groups seek to advance in the political arena.

LEADERS OF INTEREST GROUPS

Except for certain groups that are exclusively political, such as Americans for Constitutional Action or the National Committee for an Effective Congress (which tend to be quite small), most members of most groups are interested more in the social or immediately tangible benefits provided by membership than in the political activity of the organization. Indeed, many members are poorly informed if not altogether *unaware* of the involvement of the group's leaders in political affairs. Some 50 percent of labor union members, for example, appear not to recognize that their leaders devote considerable energy and group resources to the political process.[15] Many members of groups have not found it worthwhile, then, to inform themselves fully about the purposes to which their dues and purported sympathies are put. Once the calculations described in the last section have been made, it would be irrational for them to investigate such matters in view of the costs in time and other resources their inquiries would require. There is a measure of "trust" that the leadership will not use the group's resources to the disadvantage of the membership, based either on the past performance of the leadership or on the realization that the member's contributions are too small for serious damage to be done to the individual's interest in any event.

For rational reasons, then, uncertainty (ignorance) about the political activity of the leadership is widespread and stems partly from the position of good faith that the leadership may maintain toward much of the membership. Betrayal of that trust and an ensuing loss of confidence in the integrity of the leadership is to be avoided at all costs by self-interested leaders. In voluntary associations particularly, the leadership must fear not so much a revolt from below as a simple withdrawal of members from the organization. Leadership is less vulnerable in more coercive groups (e.g., some labor and professional organizations), but counterelites can form even there. The recent internal struggle against the established bosses of the United Mine Workers is a case in point.

The leaders' doubt about the rank and file's interests also gives rise to the relationship of trust just described. Leaders can never be sure that the demands they advance in the name of the membership are accurate representations since members are notoriously inarticulate on such matters. The uncertainty of organizational life provides leaders with both opportunities and restraints. Ignorance of the members' precise interests compels an anxious leadership to innovate on behalf of their anticipated or presumed interests. Union leaders who seek "more and better" for their members through political action are entirely reasonable in believing that success in their efforts will be applauded (if recognized) even though the precise public policies (e.g., fiscal, monetary, and trade policies) that produce success are best understood by a handful of politicians, academics, bureaucrats, and technicians. Here the leadership is free to combine its resources in unique, creative, and efficient ways. The leaders' ignorance of the members' preferences also constrains their behavior, however. Most union leaders equivocate on issues of culture and style (forced busing for purposes of school integration, capital punishment, abortion, for example) precisely because they fear a backlash from some of the membership if "advanced" positions should be taken. This fear may be based on accurate perceptions or, our concern here, on *uncertain* ones.

Function and Role of Leaders

However roughly and vaguely the members of organizations present their political demands to their leaders, the major political *function* of leaders of interest groups is to translate, aggregate, mobilize, and advance those real and imputed demands in compelling ways to the holders of political power. The political authorities are thus alerted to the diverse priorities of the multitude of interest groups in society.

Leaders undertake to perform this function out of a regard for their own interests. The *role* of the interest group leader is to distribute the scarce resources of the group (money, prestige, size) so as to maximize the presumed welfare of the membership; the leader's own welfare is of course maximized as well. Thus, the leader distributes group resources to competing uses (for example, to social functions, recruitment drives, informational activities, immediate benefit programs, *and* to political matters) until the resources allocated to each activity produce equal expected benefits at the margin. In making these decisions efficiently, group leaders are able to command a commensurate return for themselves from group resources. Their skills at organizing, managing, and propaganda enable them to retain some portion of the resources as their own reward. Inefficient leaders who dissipate group resources fail to maximize their own position.

Whether or not a group's resources, or some portion of them, will be devoted to the political fray depends, therefore, on the strategic calculation of the leadership. Politics is entered into when it is efficient to do so, and abstinence may be chosen under different conditions. But when political action is indicated, and when the leadership has distributed the group's resources so as to maximize its (and its membership's) interests, the leadership is in equilibrium with the political system. No other decision is called for for the time being.

Costs to Leaders

The costs which the group leader must bear in entering the political thicket include the time and effort of promoting, negotiating, propagandizing, threatening, and dissimulating — in short, of *talking*. The leader must also endure the disapprobation of people of alternative views and, of course, must forgo all the other things that could be done with the time, energy, and group resources available. The leader's benefits are or may be several: the salary derived from the application of expertise, public recognition, a measure of power, opportunities for self-expression.

We have concentrated so far on three classes of political actors: voters and members and leaders of interest groups. We presumed in the preceding discussion that their participation in politics (or lack thereof) was a matter of rational choice. Whatever individuals might choose to do or not do politically, their behavior was efficient in the sense that, given their information, resources, and wants, they would act on the marginal principle and select whatever course of action led to the highest expected payoff. In the following section, the same analysis is extended to include the holders of public office.

FORMAL OFFICEHOLDERS

For reasons which will become clear, it is convenient to regard formal officeholders as consisting of three types: politicians, bureaucrats, and judges. Politicians make the most fundamental and binding policy decisions regarding the allocation of rewards and deprivations in society. Their power is conditioned, however, by the strategic position and expertise of the bureaucrats and by the application and interpretation of policy decisions by judges in specific cases. Attention is directed first to the politician.

Politicians

The normal overriding aim of the politician is to win or retain public office. The politician's *role* is to make the choices and engage in the behavior most likely to attain that end. His or her *function* is to make authoritative choices for all or significant portions of society. In order to play this role successfully, the politician must, when forced to compete with other politicians for votes and for the support of interest groups, take into account the perceived preferences of both potential voters and members and leaders of interest groups. Only if politicians are *forced* to compete with others in the pursuit of public office will they have an inducement to respond positively to the wants expressed by the electorate and by pressure groups. Even though it is notoriously difficult empirically to discover what voters want, or even though, if known, their wants might be sufficiently consistent (or alike) to enable a politician to satisfy them, a competitive situation compels politicians to try to determine society's wants and to assume that some consistency of wants is present and can, however problematically, be discovered. It is this discipline that controls and restrains the politician.

The relationship of competition to responsiveness is obvious if we presume, on reasonable grounds, that politicians, like everyone else, have tastes and preferences of their own. If possible, they will choose to indulge their personal preferences regardless of the preferences of the public at large. One who values democracy, therefore, will try to ensure that politicians conform in some reasonable manner to the community by making it in their interest to do so. Competition alone will produce the rough discipline forcing such an outcome. Democracy without competition is impossible.

According to the present view, politicians are not, however much they claim otherwise, primarily concerned with the "public interest" (whatever that term may mean). They see public office as a means to personal power, social status, immortality, income, or whatever else an empirical investigation reveals their concerns to be. (Of course, occasional politicians are interested in furthering the common good to the exclusion of their personal preferences. This position could become known if they decided in favor of some "public interest" project significantly out of keeping with their personal interests when they were under no compulsion to do so. You may want to think of examples, if you can, when this seems to have been the case.) Out of simple prudence democrats will want to *force* politicians to respond to the community and will be reluctant to rely solely on their benevolent intentions. The competitive mechanisms for keeping politicians in line are mainly (1) elections and (2) the potential support (or withdrawal of support) of interest groups and assorted opinion-making elites.

Politicians: Vote Maximizers.   It is a matter of dispute whether, in this effort, rational politicians will try to maximize the number of votes received or will seek only the number of votes absolutely necessary to win. The latter argument is based upon the view that the winner of an election gets *all* the power and prerogatives a public office has to offer and not merely some part based upon the proportion of votes he has received. Since winning politicians get all the power of the office, they can offer larger payoffs to their supporters the smaller their numbers are.[16] Obviously, the presumption is that the resources controlled by the winning politician are fixed or limited (in the short run) and that large coalitions contain people with diverse and contradictory tastes and preferences. The more numerous and more heterogeneous a politician's supporters are, the more likely it is that the individual politician will find it impossible to please some of them.

Consider, for example, Lyndon Johnson's overwhelming victory over Senator Barry Goldwater in 1964. Johnson won with slightly over 61 percent of the total votes cast, a winning coalition consisting of interests, factions, and personalities united in opposition to Goldwater but otherwise as diverse, perhaps, as any large political coalition ever assembled in presidential politics. It was soon in disarray, of course, as first one and then another group of one-time supporters announced its disaffection. In attempting to maintain his support, Johnson had pursued inconsistent

It is difficult to ascertain whether politicians campaign for the maximum number of votes or only enough to win. Here John Lindsay greets the public in a campaign motorcade in New York City. *Katrina Thomas for Pictorial Parade*

policies — guns in Vietnam and butter at home — that could not be realized and that ultimately forced him from office. An interesting question is: Would President Johnson personally have been "better off" if in 1964 he had adopted a policy stance designed barely to win election, thereby obviating the embarrassment caused him by the dropping away of erstwhile supporters? Any answer must presuppose that politicians *know* (1) precisely the measure of support they can attract by adopting various policy positions and (2) the response that competing politicians will make in return. In truth, politicians are *uncertain* of both things. Attempting to be all things to all people may be unwise strategically for the politician — if voters become aware of the impossibility of being so — but acting as if one knew how much of what has to be done for whom in order to win may be unwise also. Given the problems of uncertainty, victory is most likely to be achieved by pursuing all the votes possible. Victory is more important to politicians than the possible collapse of their coalition in the longer run.

Further, in a two-party system, in which politicians of different political parties *share* power in many ways, as a consequence of federalism and the separation of powers, they *cannot* know how an opponent will respond to any particular policy stance taken in the quest for votes.[17] The opposition party is not only fighting, say, a presidential election but seeking to control other offices — governorships or congressional seats. To adopt a viable strategy for the presidency alone would be shortsighted if that strategy put at risk the party's control over other offices.

The matter is further complicated when the question of *time* is introduced into the rational politician's calculations. Does one seek to maximize votes — or to secure a minimum winning coalition — in *this* election only? The answer depends upon age and health, office(s) sought, constitutional limitations upon terms of office, commitment to party ideology, and so forth. We end up with seemingly contradictory possibilities: *Depending upon the politician's own estimate of the situation, either* vote maximization will be pursued in the short run in order to assemble a long-term minimum winning coalition, *or* a minimum winning coalition will be sought in the short run in order to maximize votes in the long run. No complete resolution of this problem can be given until we know the preferences of the politician in question and *his* or *her* (and not some political "expert's") judgment of the consequences of adopting one strategy rather than another. Clearly, some politicians, fully aware of the consequences, have "squandered" their constituency support in pursuit of policy objectives which they have regarded as of crucial social importance.[18]

In seeking office, politicians stake out policy positions on a wide range of issues designed to gain the support of whatever proportion of the electorate is necessary in terms of the politicians' short- or long-term objectives. The composition of party platforms depends very much upon (1) the policy positions of the opposition; (2) the perceived demands of the voting public; and (3) (in America) the two-party system.

Policy Positions of Politicians. Another determinant of policy positions is the need to placate or mobilize significant interest groups and, to some extent, powerful individuals — media personalities or financial "fat cats." How much of this kind of support must be secured is a matter to be decided in specific cases.[19] But concessions have to be made to get such support. Money, it has been said, is the "mother's milk of politics," and defeat at the polls, while not guaranteed by an impecunious campaign or poor public relations, may be facilitated thereby. Although the impact of a campaign upon voter intentions appears to be slight, and its relation to turnout on election day remote, the uncertainty of these outcomes is a strong reason why the party seeks a positive media image and an active, well-financed campaign.[20] By providing fluid resources to politicians and by assisting them in the building of positive public images, interest group leaders try to reduce the uncertainty and hope to receive, in return, some political benefit. Attempting to maximize their personal welfare, politicians act on the marginal principle already described: They offer programs, benefits, and opportunities to the electorate and to interest groups until the marginal costs of the offers (in losing the support of taxpayers, interest group leaders, militant minorities, etc.) equal the marginal gains. At that point, they are in equilibrium with the political system; no other pattern of decisions will improve their position.

The connection between groups and parties is to be discovered empirically, although one writer suggests that newly created parties must rely more upon group support than established ones.[21] The relationship is "of critical importance to the process of transforming power. . . . Interlocking leadership and membership, a common policy orientation expressed in party platforms, and the groups' action programs may lead to a frank participation of the groups in the electoral process through subsidies and the nomination of candidates."[22]

Ehrmann presents two interesting ideas: (1) Group influence over parties has increased in those democracies in which ideological politics is said to have declined; and (2) groups in modern pluralistic politics have tended in recent years to shift their activities from party concerns to the bureaucracy, where "the expansion of governmental activities and the dispensations of governmental powers in the modern state, the delegation of rule-making to the civil service, and the technical difficulties of rational rule application all invite intimate collaboration between groups and administrations."[23]

Examples of consultation between interest groups and public administrators abound. Logging operators in the West and South seek access to the decision-makers in the Forest Service; corporation financial officers to those in the Internal Revenue Service; women's groups to the officials in the Department of Health, Education, and Welfare who develop guidelines on "affirmative action" employment opportunities; cattlemen to the Bureau of Land Management officials who administer grazing rights on public lands; banking interests to the Federal Reserve System officials who establish discount rates and reserve requirements for member banks; consumer groups to the Federal Trade Commission and the Food and Drug Administration, which have some control over industrial organization and the marketing of various products. These interactions are part of the daily stuff of politics and do not serve merely the interests of the pressure groups themselves.

Public administrators also have an interest in collaborating with groups in this manner. Consultation acts as an "early warning system," alerting administrators to probable public reaction to policy decisions; provides an opportunity to induce group leaders to prepare their members ("keep them in line") for impending policy shifts; gives occasion to persons of often similar policy views and technical backgrounds to share information; and facilitates the building of consensual public policy. And just as bureaucrats often find it personally congenial to respond to the concerns of interest group leaders, so too do politicians and party leaders.

Bureaucrats

The bureaucrat is a nonelected career official whose position has been achieved by merit and seniority and by anticipating and meeting the needs of superiors in the organization. If the bureaucratic position is not important in the determination of policy, the bureaucrat's role is to make the choices most pleasing to those in the agency who allocate salary, promotion, and assignment.[24] By so doing, bureaucrats maximize their personal welfare as they receive the rewards due loyal service. Of greater interest, however, is the policy-making bureaucrat, who provides crucial influential information and advice to the formal makers of public policy, the politicians.

The *role* of policy-making bureaucrats is to make choices that will maximize their agency's budget. As "budget maximizers" they seek to extend the size, power, and dominion of their agency and hence their own rewards and opportunities.[25] The central political *function* of budget-maximizing bureaucrats is to expand the scope of government relative to other social institutions. In combination with other forces, bureaucracies work to consume and to allocate an ever greater portion of the social product and to employ a larger proportion of the labor force. (Under some regimes bureaucrats maximize their own welfare by seeking to *minimize* the size of their agency's budget. The budget-minimizing bureaucrat is a rather rare specimen, however.)

The Army Corps of Engineers, which develops many public projects throughout the nation's 435 congressional districts, has been among the more astute federal agencies in expanding its activities by undertaking projects which could not meet normal economic tests but which met the political needs of members of Congress. The Children's Bureau has discovered that the needs of children are unlimited, while the National Science Foundation has made the same discovery concerning the community of scientists, the Civil Aeronautics Board concerning the needs of aviation, the Defense Department concerning national security, the Veterans Administration concerning the needs of veterans, the Environmental Protection Agency concerning the environment. Since the matter of "needs" as understood by these and many other bureaucratic interests cannot in principle be met in a world of limited resources, the concept is used to try to improve the position of each agency relative to all others in the continuing struggle for bureaucratic expansion.

Bureaucrats and Public Goods.   If one accepts the argument of Professor William A. Niskanen, this tendency can have exceedingly unhappy outcomes.[26] To begin with, the committees of Congress that review agency budgets are comprised of members who generally *share* the expansionary bias of the agency bureaucrats. Members of Congress gravitate to committees on which they can advance certain interests. (Proportionately larger majorities on committees support the recommendations of the committees than is the case in the legislative body as a whole.) It is in the interest of members of Congress to be biased in this manner so that they can attract the support they need from the voters and groups who will most greatly benefit by new or expanded programs. They seek committee assignments that will maximize their political backing by allowing them "to do something for the folks back home." If the new or expanded programs in view are of the sort in which everyone may participate — if they are public goods and services such as roads, parks, police protection — they will be demanded most intensely by those who will pay least for them. A most important point may now be made. For some 80 percent of the population, the government takes about the same proportion (28 percent) of income taxes regardless of the amount of income being taxed. (The poorest 10 percent pay less and the richest 10 percent normally pay somewhat more than 28 percent.) Who, then, among the great bulk (80 percent) of the population will pay least for public goods and services (and, other things being equal, demand them more intensely)? For the large majority of the people who, regardless of income, find themselves in the 28 percent tax bracket, the answer is clear: Those with higher incomes will demand more public goods and services and those with lower incomes will demand less. The principle of diminishing marginal utility of income is in effect.

The taxes paid by the affluent are relatively less important to them than the taxes paid by poorer people. Further, more affluent people vote and participate generally in political life more frequently than less affluent people. No wonder politicians tend to respond to the demands of the politically active majority, a majority which is not representative economically. The expansion of the government in the social service sector, therefore, does not always or even usually accrue to the benefit of the poorer strata of the population. Public expenditures for bicycle paths, recreational programs, better schools, zoos, libraries, the arts, cleaner water, national and domestic security, and other public goods and services will be demanded more vigorously by higher-income groups than by lower-income groups under a system of proportional taxation and majority rule. Although public goods and services are freely available to all income groups, the costs of providing them fall more heavily on the less privileged than on the more privileged. Moreover, the propensity to consume many social and cultural amenities is greater among the middle classes than among the lower-middle and working classes. Tastes and preferences vary significantly by social class, and art museums, nature trails, and universities are used more frequently by the affluent than by the poor.

While, as previously stated, the political function of the budget-maximizing bureaucrat is to expand the scope of government, other actors and institutions are implicated in that function. The staffing patterns of legislative committees, the existence of a system of proportional taxation, the majority rule principle in legislative bodies, the higher rates of political participation among higher-income groups — all work to enlarge the polity and, on many occasions, to do so at the expense of its least privileged members. It is one of the many ironies of political life that this result often comes about with the active encouragement of those who, by self-appointment, speak for the poor; their good intentions exceed their understanding of how interests, the characteristics of public goods, fiscal (tax) systems, and decision-rules interact to indulge and/or deprive particular social groups.

The only constraints on the efforts of bureaucrats to expand their agency's budget are (1) their calculations concerning how other decision-makers will respond to their efforts and (2) their determination that the costs of supplying whatever goods and services are expected by the agency's clientele be less than the budget being sought.[27] The skillful bureaucrat seeks to win the confidence and high regard of other decision-makers by, for example, "playing it straight," behaving with integrity, making friends, and being willing to accommodate and compromise.[28] The bureaucrat who has made the above calculations and allocated personal and agency resources efficiently in light of a budget-maximizing objective is in equilibrium with the political system. For the time being, no other decisions are necessary. The skillful bureaucrat is not a decision-maker but a decision-avoider.

Judges

The primary political *role* of the judge is to understand (or to come to an understanding of) the formal rules of society — its constitutions, statutes, bench-made and administrative laws — and to apply the rules in specific disputes which are brought to the court for resolution. An important and innovative aspect of the judge's role is to invent *new* rules or to reinterpret old ones to meet the exigencies of the moment or otherwise to conform to his or her ideology or sense of legal probity. The extent to which judges are guided in their deliberations by legal doctrine and reasoning as opposed to their personal social philosophy is a matter to be settled empirically (and is discussed further in Chapter 5). Here we only point out that social policy has been designed to reduce if not eliminate the incentives that would otherwise lead judges to decide cases on the basis of personal interests.

Under the terms of the Constitution, all federal judges, for example, are appointed for life (contingent upon their "good behavior") and may not have their salaries reduced during their time in office. By reducing the extent to which judges are beholden to others, the framers of the Constitution clearly hoped to induce judges to issue decisions uninfluenced by particularistic political forces. Codes of ethics adopted by bar associations to which judges belong and codes of ethics explicitly applicable to federal judges (excepting members of the Supreme Court) also direct the behavior of judges and minimize the lure of some forms of personal aggrandizement. By conforming to the strict rules of judicial conduct, the judge does of course receive social indulgences of a substantial sort: deference, income, and, particularly if he or she is a high-ranking magistrate such as a federal judge, very high social status.

The primary political *function* of the Supreme Court judge is to make binding interpretations in cases involving basic or important disputes over the rules. The social scope of this function can be broad in the extreme, as in conflicts over rules involving whole classes of people, or people "similarly situated": blacks, women, voters, businessmen, taxpayers, trade unionists, and so forth. Judges maximize their personal welfare by agreeing to hear those cases, and by deciding to reward particular parties by rendering them a favorable decision, so as to most efficiently and most probably achieve their ends. A judge who has made an appropriate selection of cases to adjudicate, and has rendered a decision in those cases, is in equilibrium with the political system.

A CONCLUDING NOTE

For each class of actors described above — voters, members and leaders of interest groups, politicians, bureaucrats, judges — we have stated the conditions under which each individual actor might be said to have reached a personal accommodation with the political system. This accommodation — or equilibrium — is a state in which each individual has done as well as possible in view of limited personal resources, the power, purposes, and choices of other individuals, existing social and political organizations, and the controlling rules of the society. When each individual has reached this accommodation, the political system is in general equilibrium. The model posited above, therefore, is a *general equilibrium model of the polity*. Both individual and general equilibrium states are rarely, if ever, experienced, of course. Both are hypothetical constructs. They are expressions of tendencies which, because of constantly changing conditions, are never fully realized. Nonetheless, the model has some descriptive validity. Social and political systems have elements of stability that can be observed and described in their essential aspects. The "real world" of American politics can be studied and discussed against the equilibrium model. Any analysis must begin with certain presuppositions, and deductive model-building of the sort illustrated above is, in our opinion, likely to lead to a more succinct and accurate understanding of politics than will many alternative approaches. The reader who understands the present model is thinking *theoretically*. The ability to think theoretically is essential for the serious student of any academic subject and not least important in political analysis.

The model rests in part upon several heretofore unstated assumptions. For example, if the model is to operate, the *rules* of the society must provide for the individual's *freedom* to undertake the choices and actions described in the model. There must be freedom to vote, join (and quit) groups, run for public office, bargain with others, and approach decision-makers. Actually, such freedoms do exist, but only imperfectly. All are qualified, sometimes with reason. For some, group memberships cannot always be forgone (as in union or closed shops); voting requires that rules governing age, residency, and registration be met; certain bargains (in restraint of trade, racially restrictive covenants) may not be made; "standing" — or being a real party to a real dispute — is demanded before access to the courts is granted. And so forth.

Moreover, certain social, political, and economic *conditions,* involving what is normally referred to as *pluralism,* have to be met for the model to operate even conceptually. Resources, technology, information, values, and organization must be widely distributed and held, controlled, and manipulated in a decentralized manner. The model does not provide for dictatorial or oligarchical domination on all issues. Realistically, of course, decentralization in the control of resources is limited, and some resources are markedly skewed in distribution and control. Nonetheless, among all existing political systems, pluralism is relatively most advanced and developed in the United States. This book is clearly in the pluralistic tradition even while we recognize the limitations of that term in describing the actual operation of many social and political sectors.

In Chapter 3 we begin to identify more precisely—and more realistically—the basic formal rules governing American public life. They are clearly selective and illustrative, however, given the vast scope and complexity of the law in America.

NOTES

1. See, for example, William R. Keech, *The Impact of Negro Voting* (Chicago: Rand McNally, 1968).
2. L.L. Wade, *The Elements of Public Policy* (Columbus, Ohio: Merrill, 1972), pp. 171–179.
3. See Anthony Downs's brilliant book, *An Economic Theory of Democracy* (New York: Harper, 1957).
4. The relative merits of rational-choice versus so-called sociological approaches to politics are discussed by Brian M. Barry, *Sociologists, Economists and Democracy* (London: Collier-Macmillan, 1970), who concludes that these approaches can be reconciled even if they have not yet been.
5. Downs, *An Economic Theory of Democracy.* Preferences, resources, and alternatives will presumably shape the individual's response, and Chapter 8 will show how Americans "break down" along these dimensions.
6. E.g., Barry, *Sociologists, Economists and Democracy,* pp. 19–23.
7. William Riker and Peter C. Ordeshook, "A Theory of the Calculus of Voting," *American Political Science Review,* 62 (March 1968), 28.
8. Downs, *An Economic Theory of Democracy,* pp. 266–271.
9. The definitive post-World War II statement is by David Truman, *The Governmental Process,* 2nd ed. (New York: Knopf, 1971). The relative functions and weights of electoral versus group processes on collective choice in America are perceptively addressed in Robert Dahl, *Preface to Democratic Theory* (Chicago: University of Chicago Press, 1956).
10. The best statement of this view is found in Mancur Olson, *The Logic of Collective Action: Public Goods and the Theory of Groups* (Cambridge, Mass.: Harvard University Press, 1965).
11. An organization that attracts and holds members through a combination of coercive means, immediate material advantage, sociability, and political goals is described in S.M. Lipset, *Union Democracy* (New York: Free Press, 1958).
12. Contrary to much popular thinking, most interest groups, even economic ones, do not possess particularly lavish resources and often are "underfinanced" in the extreme. See Raymond Bauer et al., *American Business and Public Policy* (New York: Atherton, 1963).
13. Few nonsmokers will understand the old advertising slogan "I'd walk a mile for a Camel," the cost seeming to be entirely disproportionate to the reward. For an analysis of the impact of intensity on the willingness to assume costs in return for benefits, see L.L. Wade and R.L. Curry, "An Economic Model of Socio-political Bargaining," *American Journal of Economics and Sociology,* 30 (October 1971), 383–394.

14. Contrast this view with that expounded perhaps most influentially by Robert Michels, *Political Parties* (New York: Free Press, 1962), who argues that nonparticipation in voluntary organizations is a function of the so-called iron law of oligarchy, which works to concentrate all effective participation in the hands of a small elite. That many members, on rational grounds, may not want to participate very actively is not considered.

15. Harmon Zeigler, "Interest Groups in the States," in H. Jacob and K. Vines (eds.), *Politics in the American States* (Boston: Little, Brown, 1965), p. 105.

16. The view that rational politicians will seek to secure the smallest possible *winning* number of votes is set forth in William Riker, *The Theory of Political Coalitions* (New Haven, Conn.: Yale University Press, 1965).

17. The logic of this indeterminacy is developed in Curry and Wade, *A Theory of Political Exchange,* pp. 90–92. Where power-sharing does not obtain (as in the British parliamentary system), the relationship is in principle determinate. This point has been misunderstood even by sophisticated writers, who would like to find more structural determinacy in American politics than in fact exists.

18. John F. Kennedy wrote of some past members of the U.S. Senate who he thought had made such decisions in his *Profiles in Courage* (New York: Harper, 1956).

19. E.E. Schattschneider's *The Semi-Sovereign People* (New York: Holt, Rinehart & Winston, 1960) undertakes to show the meager impact that interest groups can have upon a political party's future at the polls. The contrary case, often stated with fine indignation, contends that political party "responsibility" is frequently if not routinely undermined by the insidious influence of "the interests" upon politicians and political parties.

20. In any event, marginal influences are often critical, though this point is understressed in P.A. Lazarsfeld et al., *The People's Choice,* 3rd ed. (New York: Columbia University Press, 1968). See John R. Owens, *Trends in Campaign Spending in California, 1958–70* (Princeton, N.J.: Citizens' Research Foundation, 1973), for a sophisticated discussion of the determinants of campaign spending.

21. Henry W. Ehrmann, "Interest Groups," *International Encyclopedia of the Social Sciences* (New York: Macmillan, 1968), Vol. 7, p. 487.

22. Ibid.

23. Ibid., p. 488.

24. This thesis is developed at length in Gordon Tullock, *The Politics of Bureaucracy* (Washington: Public Affairs Press, 1965). A more complex rational-choice analysis of bureaucratic behavior

is Anthony Downs, *Inside Bureaucracy* (Boston: Little, Brown, 1967).

25. The implications of this view are treated in William A. Niskanen, Jr., *Bureaucracy and Representative Government* (Chicago: Aldine-Atherton, 1971).
26. Ibid.
27. Ibid.
28. See Aaron Wildavsky, *The Politics of the Budgetary Process* (Boston: Little, Brown, 1964), Chapter 3, for an interesting empirical statement of the budget-maximizing strategies of bureaucrats.

The Constitution: Fundamental Rules of the National Polity

The **polity** is that social organization through which are made public choices that are binding upon all members of society. The political processes of society, following certain defined rules, determine which values (and in what degree) will be subject to allocation through public choices and which ones will be left to the private discretion of individuals. These processes define the content of public policy for the society. The rules that control their operation are, therefore, among the most significant determinants of governmental performance.

Every polity imposes someone's preferences and values upon the entire society. The basic structure of rules provides a means of determining the legitimacy of such choices. A democratic polity is one which, following certain rules, aggregates the preferences of *individual citizens* into binding public choices. The range of persons whose preferences are taken into account and the relative weight given to the preferences of different sets of citizens supply criteria for evaluating the degree to which democracy is operative in the society.

A set of decision-rules (statements defining what must be done to effectuate some outcome) exists in every political system. These rules guide and shape the activities of individuals as they seek to advance their welfare. The content of the rules (and the ability of individuals to use them to their advantage) plays an important role in determining the winners and losers in the political struggles of society. The fundamental rules that legitimately structure and control the operation of the polity are the society's political constitution.[1] In short, the constitution includes those rules that specify the procedural requirements for the making of *legitimate public choices*.

The constitution defines, sometimes vaguely, sometimes precisely, the range of public choices that may be made by government, provides

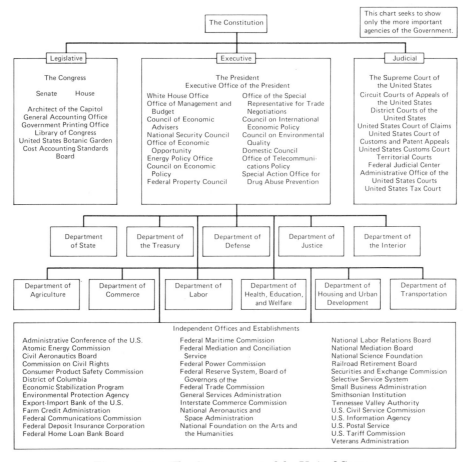

Figure 3-1. The Government of the United States.

criteria for determining the line between private and public sectors, and specifies *how* decisions in the public (and sometimes private) sector must be made. It also thus defines, at least in general terms, the *legitimate scope of government* and identifies areas of private choice that are shielded from governmental intrusion. Succinctly, the functions of a democratic constitution are to define the public process and limit the powers of government. In addition, the basic rules identify the public officials and institutions that may or must participate in public decisions. The rules therefore define and allocate the power to make binding social decisions.

The nature and content of constitutional rules are most significant in determining the degree of "fit" between the preferences of individual citizens and the public policy created by government and, consequently, how "democratic" or "undemocratic" a society is. Constitution-building — the choosing of rules that are to govern the operation of the polity — is thus a major problem confronting any political system. The content of public policy, the allocation of values in society, and the legitimacy of the political system in the eyes of the citizenry are strongly influenced by the nature of the prevailing constitution. Moreover, the processes followed in selecting the rules to be included in the constitution are fundamentally important to any political system: Consider, for example, the vast literature on the development of the U.S. Constitution. For all these reasons, an understanding of the rules of a political system is a necessary (but not sufficient) condition for estimating the public choices that may be made by government and for evaluating the performance of the government.

The basic rules involving the allocation and limitation of governmental power take various forms in different political systems and are, of course, derived from different sources. They may be primarily derived from a specific and deliberate rule-making effort and be included in a particular document, as in the United States, or they may be contained in more diverse, less formal, and less identifiable documents and usages, as in Great Britain. But whether written or unwritten, whether located in one or many sources, whether created by purposeful decisions or through customary practices, all constitutional governments are marked by the existence of rules that organize and guide the political system.[2] For two reasons, the oft-made distinction between written and unwritten constitutions is not always a very useful one. (1) Political systems with "unwritten" constitutions usually in fact have documentary sources which contain the major dimensions of the fundamental rules of the polity. (2) In systems where a particular document is identified as the "constitution," the words and phrases of the basic document are colored by traditions, practices, usages, and interpretations that become indispensable components of the governing rules. A critical problem in the analysis of any political system is to identify the basic decision-rules of the system as well as the processes and procedures — both formal and informal — involved in maintaining and changing them, and to assess the impact of the rules upon the distribution of values in the society.

THE NATURE OF THE AMERICAN CONSTITUTION

The formal decision-rules in America are to be found in a document written in Philadelphia in the summer of 1787, in the first ten amendments to that document, which were proposed by the first session of the Congress of the United States, in the sixteen amendments added still later, and in decisions of the Supreme Court that interpret the Constitution as amended. The first ten amendments are best considered part of the original constitution-building enterprise.[3] Although the nature of the rules found in the original document have changed substantially through usage, tradition, interpretation, and formal amendment, the Constitution is the touchstone of political legitimacy in America and of the organization of governmental activity. Virtually all important disputes over the allocation of governmental power to particular institutions turn on some provision of the original document or on some element of the first ten amendments to it. The words of the constitutional manuscript and the "intentions" of the framers are frequently introduced as unimpeachable guides to the determination of the proper limits of governmental power. Complex and critical political issues, such as war, governmental scandals, crime, abortion, capital punishment, and the desegregation of American institutions, are debated in the language of the Constitution, and antagonistic positions on these issues are justified and rationalized in appeals to the intentions of the Founding Fathers. *Every* major political issue becomes intertwined with constitutional arguments and eighteenth-century (and older) legal terminology. This is testimony to the broad acceptance in America of the rules of the Constitution and to the openness of those rules to competing interpretations and applications. The vagueness of certain constitutional phrases allows conflicting interests to find support in the opaque parameters of the Constitution. The ability to find such support is an important political talent and is often crucial to one's political success.

A striking public example of the process of attempting to resolve a contemporary political problem through a search for the precise meaning of the words of the Constitution and the intentions of the framers was seen in the debates of the House Judiciary Committee as it considered the impeachment of Richard Nixon. Much of these dramatic televised debates was given over to discussion involving the true meaning of the proviso that a president could be impeached for "high crimes and misdemeanors." The members of the committee frequently introduced arguments developed by Madison and other framers of the Constitution to justify their interpretation and to legitimize their decision on the matter. Anyone who followed the debates in the summer of 1974 was made aware of the importance and power that present-day leaders attribute to identifying their choices on controversial issues of the day with the wisdom, integrity, and intentions of the framers of the Constitution.

Support for, and veneration of, the Constitution has become a major component of the American political culture. Reverence for the document as a statement of social justice has sometimes meant that any decision which an individual believes inappropriate, unjust, unethical, or immoral must also be unconstitutional. Any act that can be so characterized has reduced acceptability and legitimacy.[4] Legitimacy, of course, involves the capacity of the polity to inculcate the belief that the existing institutions and ways of doing things are right, proper, and just. To many people an act that they personally perceive to be unjust, unwise, offensive, or otherwise unwarranted can scarcely be thought compatible with the tenets of the Constitution, which, after all, is the very fountainhead of Justice! Americans tend to accept the position that all the requirements of justice are necessarily dictated by some provision of the Constitution. Inasmuch as the Constitution has become a primary instrument of legitimacy, wedding any public policy to constitutional doctrine is an effective means of legitimating and building support for the policy.[5]

The desegregation of American institutions provides an excellent example. The determination in the mid-1950s that racial segregation was contrary to the Constitution served to legitimize and justify the protest activities associated with the civil rights movement of the 1960s. It was crucial to the protesters to be able to argue that the object of their demands was simply the achievement of rights clearly guaranteed by the Constitution. The linkage of civil rights group goals with constitutional doctrine was an important mechanism for gaining public support for the demands of the movement. The broadening public support led to intense pressure for the enactment of civil rights laws designed to extend constitutional rights to black Americans. Congressional support gave public recognition to the constitutional requirements and strengthened the thrust toward societal changes. This process has dramatically changed attitudes toward, for instance, school desegregation over the past two decades.

The Constitution functions most effectively as a political symbol and, like the Bible,[6] is more frequently cited and believed than read and understood. Since much of the political process is marked by heated debates over the meaning and implication of specific constitutional provisions in concrete situations, the Constitution does more to organize conflicts and to shape the language of political discourse than to resolve social conflicts. There is frequent dispute over the "proper" interpretation of the Constitution; on occasion "official" interpretations may lack the level of support necessary to be found acceptable.[7] The flexibility of the document in interpretation reduces demands for its overhaul. The celebrational mythology that has grown up around the Founding Fathers minimizes any faith that contemporary politicians could be trusted to improve upon the existing document in any important way. While calls for a "new" constitution are restricted to the eccentric (mostly academic) few, constant demands arise that the government and its policies be brought back to the "true" requirements of the Constitution. In short, the broad consensus upon the legitimacy of the Constitution is countered by substantial disagreement over the precise requirements of the document and the extent to which specific governmental actions are compatible with its provisions.

In the Constitution, major decision-rules are established and the bases, limits, and powers of the institutions of government are identified. As every schoolchild knows, the Constitution fragments power and disperses responsibility in complex ways among several interacting and competing political structures: the Congress, the presidency, the Supreme Court, the federal and state governments. Although the powers of government are laid out in a relatively ambiguous manner, even the provisions that appear altogether clear and self-explanatory have been handled *as if* they contain substantial ambiguity. For example, the word *no* in the First Amendment phrase "Congress shall make *no* law abridging the freedom of speech" has been the subject of continuing interpretation, even though many people have presumed that the word *no* means "no." It turns out that *no* is not an absolute negative but means such things as "under some circumstances," "when threats to society are not present," and "not too much."[8]

Constitutions in constitutional democracies provide only general outlines for the operation of the government and do not prescribe in any great detail the actual allocations of values among individuals. A constitution offers a framework for the formal management of the conflicts that arise in society. Fundamental rules supply the context within which public choices must be made but do not specify the substantive choices that will be made. An amazing and almost infinite array of particular public policies can be developed without coming into necessary conflict with the fundamental rules that comprise our Constitution. The American constitutional system has been found consistent (and inconsistent) with social arrangements ranging from slavery to the welfare state and from the sanctity of private property to the unlimited regulation of business.

FORMATION OF THE CONSTITUTION

The codification of the rules that are to govern the political process is among the most significant political acts that occur in a polity. The personal goals and values of the individuals who draft the constitution become implanted in the political system as rules and institutions and influence the polity for (usually) long periods of time. While Americans would hardly turn to the remedies of an eighteenth-century doctor to treat their physical ills, they freely consult eighteenth-century politicians for palliatives to the social woes of our time.[9] For this reason, a brief description of the process of constitutional formation is necessary to understand the development of the American political system.[10]

It has often been argued that political rules are never neutral, that they tend to favor some interests, values, or skills over others, and that they play a leading role in the determination of the winners and losers in any political struggle. (Although the rules, as they actually operate, are never neutral, it is not always easy in fact to say whom they favor.)

But this is not an invariable result.[11] Some rules may work to nearly everyone's benefit: rules maintaining domestic tranquillity, a common monetary system, equality of the franchise, freedom of speech and religion, due process in legal proceedings, for example. The individual is often secure in the enjoyment of such goods, freedoms, powers, and protections only so long as everyone else is similarly secure. By extending the benefits of such rules to others, one secures their agreement to extend them to oneself. There are other rules, of course, which do bestow disproportionate rewards and levy disproportionate burdens.

To some extent, the distribution of power among contending rule-makers (such as the men assembled at Philadelphia in 1787) is reflected in the rules they finally place in the constitution. Moreover — and this is a point often forgotten — the decisions taken by the makers of a constitution must themselves be arrived at according to some rule(s)! The distribution of power is reflected in these "pre-constitutional" rules. The process of rule construction and the rules under which the construction takes place, therefore, shed light upon the interests which are and will be favored in the institutions and rules provided for in the constitution. An understanding of the historical and social context in which constitutions are developed is obviously necessary to an understanding of the rules the constitution contains.

The American Constitution was created against the backdrop of two highly significant historical circumstances. On the one hand, the period of English dominion was still fresh in memory, and there was a widely accepted desire to protect American citizens against the tyranny that was thought or was asserted to have flowed from that centralized monarchical regime. Individual freedom and republicanism were much valued in the early post-Revolutionary period, as they are today. On the other hand, the strength and survival of the new independent nation were threatened by the fragmentation, lack of central economic control, inefficiencies in trade and finance, and perceived popular excesses in the states which obtained under the Articles of Confederation. Stability, order, and economic security needed to be secured and protected.[12] The Constitutional Convention was called to propose amendments to the Articles that would strengthen the Union by adding necessary powers to the central government to achieve those goals. But there was little support in the convention or in the nation for the development of a central government that would displace the states as the primary loci of political authority. The states were to be preserved as the main governmental influence upon the day-to-day life of the citizen.[13]

The prevailing ideological sentiment in the convention was that government in general and central government in particular were necessary evils and that governmental power must be strictly limited. Government should have only the powers absolutely necessary to society and must not

The formation and ratification of the Constitution by the Founding Fathers
were of great significance in developing America's political system.
Library of Congress

be allowed to follow the historically normal course of becoming an instrument of oppression. The threat of oppression was thought to exist regardless of whether power was held by a majority or a minority. Tyranny
by a majority was just as distasteful as tyranny by an elite. The convention undertook the difficult task of creating a complex set of public institutions and decision-rules that would provide for the stability *and*
dynamism essential to society without placing potentially tyrannical
power in the central government. In short, the framers' problem was to
create a political system in which the power of government would be limited and citizens could pursue their individual goals, when judged necessary, through collective political action.

The determination to completely overhaul the government went well
beyond the formal authority of the Constitutional Convention. The am-
bitiousness, not to say illegality, of this decision required broad general
support for the document by members of the convention in order for the
new Constitution to have a reasonable chance of ratification in the states.

The fact that the document had to be ratified dictated that each state delegation would have a single vote in the convention. The rules governing constitutional decisions were formally based on simple majority rule at two levels but were actually more inclusive. A *simple majority* of the delegates present from each state determined the vote of that state. While individual items were decided formally by *simple majority* rule, there was a massive attempt to gain consensus among the delegates and to project to those outside the convention an image of *unanimity* of support among the delegates. The final resolution by which the document was adopted was apparently supported unanimously though a number of the delegates refused to sign the document and Rhode Island had chosen not to be represented at the convention at all.[14]

The need for virtual unanimity greatly tempered the provisions of the Constitution. (Actually the delegates had decided that only nine of the thirteen states need ratify, although all eventually did, contravening a provision of the Articles of Confederation for unanimity in amending the Articles.) Fears that existing interests would be endangered by the new Constitution were minimized by this consensus-building process. These factors, wedded to a conviction that a stronger central government was necessary, established an atmosphere favorable to broad acceptance on principles and compromise on specifics. The result was a very general document marked by a series of fundamental compromises, containing a great deal of ambiguity, and many different rules to control future contingencies. Vagueness in the document has made it possible to mold its provisions to drastically changed circumstances. This is an instance of political serendipity, attributable less to the genius of the framers or to the triumph of a specific political philosophy than to the fact that common agreement could be achieved only in the most general terms. Agreement was often impossible on more specific provisions. The outcome was not unlike a good deal of modern legislation, which is necessarily written in general language by heterogeneous popular assemblies and particularized in its administration. The reason is simple: More detailed provisions would destroy the broad coalition required to enact legislation.[15] Likewise, the content of the Constitution reflects the art of the possible as practiced in the late eighteenth century.

There was no single coalition in the convention which was able to dictate its desires to the other delegates or to the emerging nation. In fact, differences requiring compromise were involved in most of the major issues that came before the convention. Some members wanted a very strong national government while others sought to maintain the basic arrangements of the Articles of Confederation. Support for broadening popular control of the government was counterbalanced by substantial fear of creating a tyranny of the majority which might flow from mobilizing the passions of the masses. Some delegates wanted strong executive leadership; others were committed to legislative supremacy. There were conflicting ideas as to the most appropriate ways to ensure that only a limited government would be created. And, in addition to the many views of what should be done, the historical circumstances surrounding the convention, the existing government under the Articles, the rules covering representation and voting procedures in the convention, and the requirement that the product be ratified by an extraordinary majority of the states focused much of the conflict on state interests and regional concerns.

The framers approached the task of developing a constitution in an environment of *uncertainty* and considerable *risk*, conditions not unusual to great political undertakings. The nature of the coalition that would come to control the new government was in doubt. The framers could not predict that the interests dominating the convention would be able to control the new political institutions. A strong government might be used to restrict the liberties of those interests and impose other costs as well. Uncertainty about their future prospects induced the authors of the Constitution to propose a system containing several separate and balanced powers that would prevent any single faction from gaining complete control of the government and destroying other legitimate social interests. In an effort to minimize the risks involved, they emphasized establishing a power structure capable of dealing with the most pressing problems of the society but severely limited in its ability to act against any major interest in the society. Their concern, in short, was to *maximize* benefits and to *minimize* risks. This "minimaxing" strategy entailed certain concrete choices: Most importantly, power was divided and fragmented in many ways, so that several institutions had to reach consensus before any major *affirmative* action could be taken. The preservation of the rights and liberties of most elements in the society was given precedence over the ability of the government either to act on its own initiative or to respond to demands for action.

The framers thought it important to guarantee liberty, as they understood it, even if, by doing so, they made it very difficult and time-consuming to form the large coalitions and broad agreements necessary to compose public policy. A premium was placed on minimizing certain potential costs (the danger that one's liberty might be subverted by the decisions of others) even though other heavy costs (those involved in getting wide agreements) had to be borne. James Madison and other constitutional logicians have considered it their task to devise the basic rules for minimizing the costs individuals must bear as members of society. That, in a nutshell, is what a democratic constitution should do.[16]

Much of the specific content of the Constitution was left to be resolved through the ongoing political process. Generally, the document represents a series of political compromises among the political interests of the day which together require continuing negotiation, bargaining, and compromise among factions and institutions. The political talents often attributed to the Founding Fathers were real enough and were applied pragmatically in achieving agreement in an atmosphere charged with distrust of government, intense political conflict, and uncertainty about the future. Political reality and a particular philosophical logic combined to produce the Constitution. The provisions for its ratification illustrate their general perspective. Ratification was to be carried out by the states, and the new government would be activated in the ratifying states when nine of the thirteen states had approved the document. The difficulty of gaining unanimous consent was recognized, as was the probability of failure unless the new government had broad support. The precedent was thus clearly established that a viable federation could exist only if fundamental decisions had the backing of an extraordinary majority. Unanimous consent — which would be ideal — could not be looked for, but basic decisions could still be made only when action was widely endorsed.

Unanimity of agreement on the Constitution was never expected by its authors. There was considerable opposition, and the outcome in a number of states was in doubt.[17] Many citizens of the day did not immediately recognize that a "perfect" document had been drafted which would usher in the New Jerusalem. The most significant reason for the opposition was fear that the central government was not sufficiently limited in its power. From influential quarters came demands for additional restrictions in order to protect the rights and freedoms of individuals. The controversy over ratification forced the proponents of the Constitution to assure their fearful countrymen that a detailed Bill of Rights would be added to protect those rights. And although the Constitution was ratified in the requisite number of states, a great deal of uneasiness remained that needed to be allayed by the new government if it was to survive. The myth that the Constitution embodies all that is good, true, and beautiful in political rules emerged in a much later day.

The creation and ratification of the Constitution were important events in the development of the American political system. The primary bias of the Constitution is one which favors limited government and rewards interests that can achieve widespread support throughout society. Designed to guarantee stability, the Constitution places a heavy burden of proof upon those who seek to alter the institutions and decision-rules of American government.

The document is a *political* one. Because of its ambiguity, the structures and decision-rules of the government are made precise only through the ongoing political process. Competing interests can mold the Constitution to the felt needs of any historical period and make it fit practically any ideological position. However, such manipulation of the Constitution is unlikely to be successful unless there is general support for the changes being sought; yet with broad consensus on the need to act, American political institutions have often acted quickly and effectively. Issues that divide society frequently result in slow, incremental, and sometimes ineffective governmental response. Of course, the aim of most of the framers was not to solve all problems of all citizens but to protect their liberties. In this very important sense, the preferences and philosophies of the authors of the Constitution are embedded in the fundamental rules of the polity and still guide behavior. Nevertheless, the Constitution itself is a mere scrap of paper, having no more effect than that given it by the internalization of its goals and values in the operating code of American citizens.

CONSTITUTIONAL CHANGE

Any rules designed to guide a polity will develop perceived defects as their practical impact becomes evident in operation and as social conditions change. In America, two peaceful means are available to secure changes in the fundamental rules. Orderly amendment may take place through formal legal channels, reducing the likelihood that appeals will be made to extralegal techniques. Or substantial change may be brought about informally, simply by interpreting and reinterpreting the terms that define the nature, content, and implications of the rules. Extensive use has been made of both these practices. The general and ambiguous nature of many rules has made possible a great deal of change without formal amendment. The veneration of the Constitution and the deep trust in the wisdom of the framers as compared with contemporary politicians have placed a high priority on reinterpretation of the document and the maintenance of at least symbolic continuity with its original words and phrases. The formal amendment process tends to be limited to occasions in which some unusual obstacle develops in the normal ways of resolving conflicts and to situations in which those in temporary control of political power believe that future decision-makers cannot be trusted to support values considered to be of surpassing and permanent importance.

Amending the Constitution

The original Constitution provides rules to be followed in changing the basic document, all of which require action at both the national and state levels before changes can occur. Actually, four separate combinations of procedures were established for amending the Constitution, but only two have ever been used. The methods that have been followed involve a process in which an amendment is proposed by a two-thirds majority of the members of each house of the Congress and must then be ratified by three-fourths of the states.[18] All the amendments that have been added to the Constitution with a single exception have been ratified by state legislatures. The exception, the Twenty-first Amendment, concerned with the politically charged issue of the repeal of prohibition, was ratified by special conventions in the states. No great discernment is necessary to understand that the rules are designed to protect against easy and frequent changes in the basic Constitution.

The procedures for the amendment of the Constitution that have not been used involve the calling of a new constitutional convention upon the "application" of two-thirds of the states. The states do submit such applications with great frequency as a means of communicating their interests, desires, and dissatisfactions to the Congress, but the rule functions more as a way of articulating a policy view than as an operative technique of constitutional change.

The Constitution has been formally amended only twenty-six times, and twelve of the changes occurred in the first fifteen years following the adoption of the Constitution. These early changes are best regarded as part of the constitutional formation phase of our history. In response to the concerns expressed in the ratification process, the First Congress proposed twelve amendments that rather precisely limited the powers of the national government. Ten of the proposals were ratified and are known now as the Bill of Rights. The First Amendment was designed to protect the freedom of speech, press, assembly, petition, and religion from intrusion by the national government. The Second and Third amendments were intended to prevent restrictions on the right to bear arms and to protect against the quartering of troops in private homes; they were clearly related to unacceptable practices of the British in the later stages of colonial rule. The Fourth through the Eighth amendments are basically guarantees to persons accused of crimes by the national government and were attempts to secure rights considered to be historically those of Englishmen. The Ninth and Tenth amendments were general statements establishing more definitely the principle of individual rights and limited government. Thus, the Bill of Rights limits the scope of the national government and protects the liberty of the individual. The thrust of these amendments was to prevent any recurrence of the excesses and deprivations that were thought to have developed in the colonial period.[19]

The initial period of constitutional amendment was closed with the ratification of the Eleventh and Twelfth amendments, which involve relatively minor defects in the original document. The Eleventh Amendment was made necessary by a controversial judicial judgment allowing citizens of one state to sue the government of another state in the federal courts.[20] This preference for out-of-state interests was rejected by state governments. The intensity of the rejection of the judgment is indicated by a resolution proposed in the Georgia House of Representatives which suggested that any federal official who attempted to enforce the Supreme Court's decree in the state should be summarily hanged.[21] The Eleventh Amendment was adopted to place the citizens of a state and foreign citizens on the same footing vis-à-vis the government of the state; that is, neither is allowed to sue a state without its permission.

In the election of 1800, the rules prescribed in the Constitution governing the selection of the president produced a tie vote in the electoral college between the majority political party's presidential and vice-presidential candidates. The Twelfth Amendment was passed to prevent a recurrence. Thus, the first twelve amendments that were added to the Constitution between 1789 and 1804 completed the basic process by which the new political order was established.

The institution of slavery had been one of the more difficult issues to deal with in the Constitutional Convention. Conflict between northern and southern and large and small state perspectives threatened to disrupt the proceedings. Agreement on the famous three-fifths compromise, by which slaves would be counted as three-fifths a person for purposes of taxation and representation, however odious in retrospect, was an essential element in holding the convention together and generating support for the new government. The salience of slavery to the South resulted also in one of the two specific limitations upon changing the Constitution. The original document clearly recognized the legitimacy of slavery, and its protection was a necessary precondition for gaining southern participation in the government under the Constitution. Conflict over slavery, however, could not be stilled by legal sleight-of-hand and endured until it erupted violently as one of the significant causes and justifications for the Civil War. A major outcome of that struggle was a series of amendments making the institution of slavery unconstitutional. The Thirteenth Amendment abolished slavery and most other forms of involuntary servitude.[22] The Fourteenth Amendment sought to guarantee the full rights of state and national citizenship to the newly freed slaves,[23] and the Fifteenth Amendment extended the suffrage to them. These so-called civil rights amendments were the first significant changes in the constitutional rules of the game since the adoption of the Bill of Rights some two generations earlier. Later court interpretations of the Fourteenth Amendment have altered political relationships in America in important ways.

The Fifteenth Amendment extended suffrage to newly freed slaves. In the above drawing blacks take advantage of their right by registering to vote. *The Bettmann Archive*

The next group of amendments came in a period of less than a decade some forty years after the adoption of the civil rights amendments. They were an outgrowth of the reforms agitated for in the so-called Progressive Era in American politics.[24] Reformers of the period demanded more popular participation in government, curbs on the power of the corporation and other "moneyed" interests, and additional reforms aimed at reducing the power of the political "bosses" and uplifting the moral tone of the community. The demands resulted in constitutional amendments that authorized the collection of an income tax,[25] provided for the direct election of members of the United States Senate, extended the vote to women, and outlawed the manufacture and sale of intoxicating beverages. The "noble experiment" to reshape American attitudes toward alcohol foundered on an unreconstructed population and was terminated with the adoption of the Twenty-first Amendment in 1933.

Only two amendments were added to the Constitution (except for the repeal of prohibition) between 1920 and the turbulent period of the 1960s. Both were anti-corruption amendments. The Twentieth Amendment changed the dates for the beginning of congressional sessions so that persons who had failed to be reelected would generally not serve after such a defeat in a regular session of the Congress. The idea was to reduce the temptation for corruption on the part of "lame duck" members. The Twenty-second Amendment formalized the traditional practice that presidents serve no more than two terms. This tradition had been successfully breached when Franklin D. Roosevelt was elected for a third and fourth term.

The 1960s was another time of nervous commotion in which intense interest was expressed in broadening participation in the political process. Flurries of constitutional amendments were proposed, and several were adopted. The suffrage was extended in presidential elections to residents of the District of Columbia, the poll tax was outlawed as a test of the right to vote, the vote was extended to all persons eighteen years old and older, and the equal rights for women amendment was proposed by the Congress. The political turmoil of the period was also reflected in the significant changes that were made in the rules covering the succession to the presidency in case of the death, resignation, or disability of the president.

Thus, the major formal changes in the Constitution have been concentrated in only four periods since the inception of the Republic. Moreover, the changes made in each of these periods stand together and rather clearly involve the prevailing issues of the time: limited government, rights, morality, participation. The first period was primarily concerned with making changes that were necessary to gain popular support for the new order by limiting government and by correcting minor technical defects in the basic document. The second period involved the destruction of slavery and the provision of certain guarantees of civil rights to the freed slaves. The third period was one of reform and social experimentation in which changes were made in order to extend popular democracy, broaden political participation in the political system, and reform society. The fourth period extended these goals after other issues had controlled the agenda of government for over forty years.

But putting the Bill of Rights aside, the process of *formal* amendment to the Constitution has made virtually no changes in the substance of the power allocated in the governmental system nor has it restructured the basic operations of the national government. No dramatic redistribution of power among governmental institutions has taken place through the

1789	1890
1st, 2nd, 3rd, 4th, 5th, 6th, 7th, 8th, 9th, 10th (1791)	
11th (1795)	
1800	1900
12th (1804)	
1810	1910
	16th, 17th (1913)
1820	1920
	18th (1919)
	19th (1920)
1830	1930
	20th, 21st (1933)
1840	1940
1850	1950
	22nd (1951)
1860	1960
13th (1865)	23rd (1961)
14th (1868)	24th (1964)
	25th (1967)
1870	1970
15th (1875)	26th (1971)
1880	1980

Figure 3-2. Formal Amendments to the United States Constitution by Decade.

amendment process — with the possible exception of the Fourteenth Amendment, discussed in the next chapter. The major thrust of the amendments has been to broaden suffrage and to extend the control of the citizenry over the institutions of the national government. The "people" have been defined in ever wider terms, and the techniques for popular control have been extended. Ten of the sixteen amendments ratified since the adoption of the Bill of Rights have extended political democracy. This movement toward much greater popular participation in public affairs would have been thought altogether undesirable by most of the framers in 1787.

Constitutional Development

It is incorrect to believe that the only changes in our fundamental constitutional rules have been produced by the formal amendment process. That process is more often a last resort, used only when other means of constitutional adjustment are perceived as inadequate. For example, at least four amendments were added to the Constitution after the Supreme Court had ruled that Congress did not have the power to make certain changes in the governing rules. The usual practice, however, is for the rules to be shaped by official (usually judicial) interpretations of relevant provisions of the Constitution in a manner that allows the government to respond to different circumstances without formally amending the Constitution. Judicial interpretations, legislation, executive actions, congressional rules, and conventional usage alter the meaning and significance of constitutional rules. These applications normally involve only incremental shifts in the content of the rules, but relatively dramatic changes may also be made. In all of these cases, the legal fiction is of course maintained that no change has actually occurred. Several examples follow of the ways in which such modifications have been made and illustrate how the process works and its importance in defining the basic rules of American society.

Judicial Review

The power of the Supreme Court to declare congressional actions unconstitutional and thereby null and void is not specifically provided for in the Constitution itself. However, the Court's interpretation of a number of constitutional provisions allowed it to assert that power.[26] The power of judicial review of legislation has become, through congressional acquiescence and popular acceptance, a fundamental rule in the American system. Characterized as the most original political innovation developed in America, this rule rests, then, on no formal grant of power. Yet judicial review has become so deeply internalized and accepted that a formal amendment to the Constitution would probably be necessary to abolish it.

In arrogating to itself the power of judicial review, the Supreme Court acted to reform the Constitution, but its act was by no means unique. Any policy-making act requires, at least implicitly, that some attention be given to the constitutional rules that are relevant to the subject matter under consideration. The shifting interpretation of the Constitution's "commerce clause" provides a classic example of how changes are made through the normal process of developing public policy. The traditional interpretation of the commerce clause by the Supreme Court was that matters such as manufacturing, mining, working conditions, retail trade, and agricultural production were aspects of local commerce and hence beyond the reach of the regulatory power of the national government.[27] However, the growth of powerful regional and national business corporations in the late nineteenth century resulted in demands for their regulation by the national government. The Congress, with presidential leadership and/or support, enacted a number of measures that regulated aspects of these businesses and broadened thereby the effective definition of interstate commerce. The Supreme Court resisted the redefinition for some time, holding that Congress had exceeded its power. Finally the Court accepted the redefinition of the commerce clause forced by the other branches of government and began to uphold legislation in this area.[28] At present the Congress is free to define the commerce clause as it sees fit. We will have occasion to refer to the commerce clause again in the next chapter in connection with federal relationships. All branches of government have now accepted congressional supremacy in this area. Obviously, there is no effective constitutional limitation when all three branches of the government concur in a particular interpretation of a constitutional provision, whatever the plain words of the Constitution may say.

The position of the president in the area of foreign affairs offers another example of the importance of interpretation and definition of the Constitution as it applies to concrete circumstances. The president has become more active in foreign affairs throughout this century as the United States has played an ever more significant role in world politics. The Supreme Court has interpreted the Constitution in such a way that the president's powers in foreign policy are virtually unlimited. It has concluded that the president is the "sole organ of the United States in international affairs" and has powers equal to those of the heads of state of other nations.[29] But the point here is that power in foreign affairs is *inherent* in the position of the president and is not defined or significantly constrained by the provisions of the Constitution. The Supreme Court has never found a president's actions concerning foreign affairs to be limited by the Constitution and refuses even to take jurisdiction in most cases involving this issue.[30] An unusual interpretation of the nature of the federal union and the constitutional system was required to develop a legal justification for this broad grant of power to the president. It resulted in a very significant rule which cannot be traced to any specific phrase in the Constitution.

In the last twenty years federal-state relationships have also been changed through judicial interpretations of the always ambiguous "due process" and "equal protection" clauses of the Fourteenth Amendment. Expanded meanings given the due process clause have applied virtually all the provisions of the Bill of Rights to the states, and the inclusion of corporations within the term *persons* in the amendment has greatly increased the power of the national government to intervene in areas traditionally reserved to the states.[31] Such interpretations have placed the federal courts in a position to supervise and oversee many of the activities of the state courts and other branches of the state governments. Consequently, the adoption of the Fourteenth Amendment and its recent interpretations have gone far in redefining the nature of the federal union.[32] Many currently held interpretations, incidentally, were rejected for extended periods of time.[33] The "nationalization" or "centralization" or "integration" (take your pick) of the American system has been accomplished or justified in this way.

Change Through Usage

The thrusts of constitutional rules may shift as a result of mere usage. Originally, for example, the electoral college was supposed to be made up of the "most qualified" members of the community who would use their best judgment to select a president and a vice-president. This notion fell into disuse long ago. Nowadays all the electoral votes of a state go to the candidates who receive the greater number of popular votes in the state. Little discretion is actually exercised by the delegates. It is not at all clear that state laws requiring this practice are compatible with the Constitution, but a pattern so widely accepted must be considered one of the operating rules of the polity.

These examples make a single but important point. The routine, everyday activities of government include an element involving the interpretation and reinterpretation of basic constitutional rules. The political process is shaped and limited by the rules in the Constitution, but the political process also shapes, defines, develops, and changes the content of those rules. The major rule changes have come about in the normal processes of policy-making, through usage, and through judicial interpretation. The formal amendment process has been a secondary means of changing the basic rules. This situation has allowed for the development of a relatively flexible regime, more flexible than if a rigid, formalistic adherence to the rules in the original Constitution were required. Such social benefits do, however, entail costs; for instance, the need to utilize legal fictions sometimes becomes the source of significant misunderstandings and even cynicism on the part of individuals whose confidence in law as a science is shaken by the same maneuvers that make flexibility possible. The obverse is also true: Legal fictions allow for a measure of symbolic continuity of public policy, which can be an important source of legitimacy and stability in the polity.

FRAGMENTATION OF POLITICAL POWER UNDER THE CONSTITUTION

The aim of the framers to establish a government of limited powers led to constitutional rules that distributed the powers of government among a number of independent institutions.

As observed in general terms above, the system of government they created was intended to hinder rapid, vigorous, and efficient responses by the national government to demands for action. Veto points were created which allow strategically placed interests to block affirmative decisions and which make it difficult for a transitory majority to have its way. Rules were developed to slow public choices and force multiple considerations before any policy can become the law of the land. Popular passions and temporary concerns are blunted, and priority is placed instead upon issues of broad and continuing social interest. At least three major interacting concepts are used to characterize the rules that divide power under the American Constitution: separation of powers, checks and balances, and federalism.

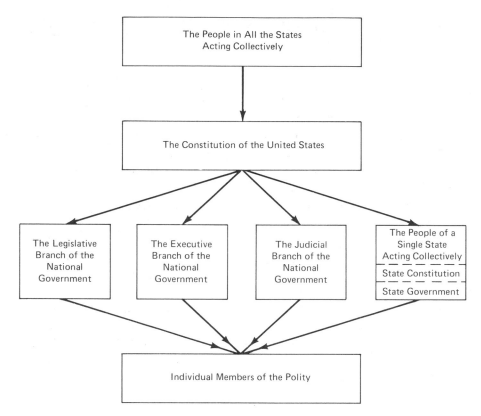

Figure 3-3.   The Structure of Legal Authority in the American Polity.

THE SEPARATION OF POWERS

The familiar doctrine of **separation of powers** among the branches of the national government is a primary principle under the Constitution. National powers are to be shared by three coordinate and separate and semi-independent branches of government. The system is provided for by the simple technique of using a separate constitutional article to define and limit the powers of each branch. All legislative power belongs to a bicameral Congress composed of a House of Representatives and a Senate. All executive power is concentrated in an indirectly elected president. Judicial power is granted to a Supreme Court and such inferior courts as may be provided by the Congress.

Each branch of government, then, receives its powers directly from the Constitution. This division of power establishes an exceedingly complex public policy process and involves the possibility of stalemate and inaction. Vigorous government, it was thought, might make possible public choices destructive of liberty.

Only the Congress has power to make laws, and any delegation of power to the national government for substantive action is largely the responsibility of the Congress. The focus of the substantive powers is upon matters that the Articles of Confederation were thought to have neglected, including the very significant powers to regulate foreign and interstate commerce, collect taxes, borrow and spend money, and independently raise a military force. These and other specifically identified powers were supplemented by the general grant of authority to Congress to make laws that are "necessary and proper" to carry out the enumerated powers. This provision is the constitutional base for the "implied powers" doctrine, which has supplied the legal justification for a substantial growth in the power of the national government over the decades.[34] The law-making power of Congress is restricted to the areas delegated by Article I of the Constitution or to laws that can be defended as necessary and proper in carrying out these delegated powers. There is no general undefined power of Congress to legislate for the common good or the national interest.

The powers granted to Congress can be effective only when the two houses agree precisely on a measure. Thus activities related to the making of law must be duplicated in both houses. This system was designed to harmonize political bodies representing very different interests in the society. The House of Representatives was to represent directly the people at large. The House was expected to be the only directly "popular" institution of the national government and, for that reason, the most "radical" as well. Transitory popular opinion was to be registered through the short two-year terms of members of the House. The Senate, on the other hand, was to represent the interests of the states qua states, and senators were originally selected by the state legislatures. Each state was given equal representation in the Senate, a principle so fundamental that, under the terms of the Constitution, it cannot be changed through the normal amendment process. The long six-year terms of members of the Senate were provided in order to isolate members from popular pressure, so that they might take a more sober and disinterested view of public issues than the House. The Senate, most people thought, would be a more conservative and perhaps wiser institution of the new government than the House.

With the Congress organized in this way, the vital interests of the larger states could be protected in the House of Representatives and those of the smaller states in the Senate. The major interests of the day, as they were perceived by the framers, were thus given both specific representation in the government and a veto point to protect them. While the conflict between large and small states is less intense today — if measurable at all on specific issues — the two houses continue to maintain their respective vetos and act as representatives for antagonistic social interests.

A public policy can be made effective only when applied and executed. Applying the law provides another opportunity for its reinterpretation and a means for limiting or enlarging its effect upon members of society. The president is given this power to execute the law by the Constitution. He is further authorized to appoint officials in the executive and judicial branches of government. His executive appointees are responsible to him and act as his instruments in executing the law. He is commander in chief of the armed forces and has the power and responsibility to use the forces that are provided by the Congress to protect the nation from external threats and internal disorder. The original powers lodged in the presidency to make treaties and to appoint ambassadors have been greatly expanded by judicial interpretations which have held that the president's powers in foreign affairs transcended the Constitution and were inherent in his office.

The president is elected for a four-year term and is limited to two terms in office. The president is the only elected member of the executive department, and all other members of that department are responsible to him. He is also the only public official (except the vice-president) in American government who is elected by a nationwide constituency and is accountable to all of the people. This relationship between the president and the nation places him in a unique power position in the governmental system. Similarly, the relationship establishes means of access and patterns of interest group activity quite unlike those in other public institutions.

The judicial power under the Constitution is vested in a Supreme Court and such inferior courts as Congress may provide. The judicial branch adjudicates disputes having to do with the content and application of the law. Issues must be brought to the federal courts in the framework of a case or controversy involving some aspect of the laws of the United States or involving altercations between citizens of different states. The Supreme Court was granted only limited original jurisdiction directly by the Constitution. It extends to cases in which ambassadors, public ministers, and consuls may be a party as well as those in which a state is a litigant. In all other cases the Supreme Court was given appellate jurisdiction which was to operate under rules provided by the Congress. The most fundamental power of the judicial branch is not specifically mentioned in the Constitution: the power of judicial review of actions of the other branches of the government. It is based upon the argument that the Constitution itself is a legal document, and that in all cases brought to the courts, constitutional requirements must be considered by it. Thus an interpretation of the Constitution is called for, and if there is conflict with other laws the court has no choice except to give precedence to the more fundamental law, the Constitution.[35] Perhaps the most significant effect of the power of the independent judiciary is that no person can legitimately have life, liberty, or property taken by the government without judicial approval of such action.

In a strictly formal way, the judicial branch is relatively independent of the "normal" political forces in the society. Judges are expected to be responsive to the law, not to a constituency. Federal judges are appointed by the president with the advice and consent of the Senate and serve for life unless removed from office by the impeachment process. Judges are supposedly immune to the more rough-and-tumble political forces that play upon the other branches of government. Their self-interests are thus aligned with the broader interests of others to have basic rules interpreted on universalistic principles.

The system of the separation of powers is a not unreasonable minimax approach to the problem of government. It grew out of a belief that governments have a marked propensity for tyranny and it was constructed to diminish the risks entailed in entering the new federal arrangement. The principle underlying the separation of institutions was to ensure that government and its agents could act against an individual only when there was very broad agreement that such action was warranted. Individual rights could be circumscribed only when (1) Congress had passed a law in precisely the same form through two independent houses, which were representative of different social interests; (2) the executive had applied the law to a given individual under a given set of facts; and (3) the courts had determined that the particular application of the law was appropriate under the law — constitutionally as well as otherwise. The division of power among the three independent, coordinate, and coequal branches was etched even more durably by requiring different means of selection to office and tenure in office. Risks that any single interest or transitory majority could gain control of all of these levers of government at the same time were minimized. Access was given to a variety of interests, with many having the capacity to thwart the desires of others.

THE SYSTEM OF CHECKS AND BALANCES

The foregoing description oversimplifies the allocation of powers under the Constitution. The separation of powers among the branches of government is complicated by a system of intermixed powers. This system of **checks and balances** was designed to integrate and coordinate governmental activity while at the same time providing another mechanism for limiting government. The rules that comprise the checks and balances give each branch at least some negative control over the action of the other branches.

Congressional Checks

The Congress can restrict the activities of the president in a large number of ways. It has the final affirmative power over both the purse and the sword, although it has on some occasions been reluctant to exercise power over the latter. All money expended by the executive branch must first be appropriated by the legislative branch, and the president has available only the personnel authorized by the Congress. Executive activities are almost always dependent upon congressional authorizations. Presidential appointments to many executive and to all judicial positions are effective only with the "advice and consent" of the Senate. Treaties made by the president must be ratified by the Senate, a limitation avoided to some extent (and with the quiet acquiescence of Congress) by "executive agreements" reached with foreign powers, which are much like treaties but do not require ratification. Most such agreements can be voided by a refusal by Congress to appropriate funds to make them effective or by a withholding of cooperation on other matters. The Congress can override a presidential veto by a two-thirds vote in each house and through this process make law in spite of the disapproval of the president. The Congress has the ultimate power through the impeachment process to remove a president from office and disqualify that person for any other office of public trust in the United States, a power initiated on only two occasions in our history: first against President Andrew Johnson following the

Civil War and then against President Richard Nixon in 1974 following the Watergate affair. There are, then, several means by which a Congress wishing to control the actions of a president may do so. Of course, it is misleading to speak of the Congress, as such, contesting with the president for power. Members of Congress are united only by their institutional associations, not their policy views. More correctly, we might speak of a struggle between the president and some coalition temporarily united in the Congress in opposition to the president. No one speaks for the Congress.

That caveat in mind, the Congress is also provided with means of restricting the activities of the judiciary. Appointments to judgeships must be supported by a majority of the Senate before the judges can take office, a power it has exercised extensively. The Congress can define through normal legislation the number of seats on the Supreme Court and has altered the size of the Court on a number of occasions. The entire appellate jurisdiction of the Supreme Court is controlled by the Congress, and any part of it can be removed through legislation.[36] This is a significant area of responsibility since almost all cases come to the Supreme Court under its appellate jurisdiction. All inferior courts in the federal system are created by the Congress and can be abolished by the Congress. Finally, through use of the impeachment process, the Congress may remove federal judges from office.

The general power to remove public officials through the impeachment process places the Congress at least formally in a position to control the other two branches of government. A broad use of this power could lead to a legislative supremacy in which all other public officials were subordinate to the will of the Congress. However, the impeachment power has been used sparingly; it is hardly a credible threat to other public officials who choose to act contrary to congressional will — if such a will were descernible on most issues. The requirement of a two-thirds majority in the Senate and the general public support for separation of powers dramatically restrict the ability of the Congress to use the impeachment power as an instrument of legislative supremacy.

Presidential Checks

The rules of the original Constitution and political practice give the president a number of checks over a congressional action. The executive power of the president can be exercised to defeat the aims of legislation.

The president can veto legislation, although the veto is conditional in that it can be overridden by a two-thirds vote of each house of Congress. In the last ten days of a legislative session the president can refuse to sign bills, which will not then become law. This, the pocket veto, is the only absolute veto held by the president. The power of the president to refuse to spend money that has been appropriated by the Congress is well established, though the "impoundment of public funds" has been a matter of substantial controversy in recent years. The courts have ruled against the president in this area on occasion, and Congress has lately provided rules designed to restrict the use of such power even though fiscal chaos would seem to be an inevitable consequence of denying it to a central authority. It is quite doubtful that the newly created congressional budget committee will be able to perform this vital coordination role. The president also is responsible for making recommendations to the Congress on legislative matters. This power has been so broadly expanded, often at the insistence of members of Congress, that the basic agenda for every legislative session is provided by the president, including the critical presentation of the executive budget. Thus presidential involvement in the legislative area is much greater than that anticipated by the framers when they devised the Constitution. In a profound sense, the roles of the president and Congress have been reversed as the former proposes measures that may be accepted or rejected by the latter. However, it must be emphasized that the Congress is under no constitutional requirement to accept any of the president's recommendations. The enactment of the War Powers Act in 1973 and the establishment of new budgetary procedures in the Congress in 1974 are attempts to redress what is widely perceived to be an imbalance of power in the presidency and to provide a more independent role for the Congress. It is too early to judge the success of these efforts, but in view of the requirement for centralized authority, coordination, and rapid response to crisis they will probably not strikingly reduce the power or responsibilities of the president in the long term.

The president's power over the courts is primarily related to presidential control of the selection process for all federal judges, although this power is greatly weakened by the life tenure carried by federal judicial appointments. The president can pardon and grant reprieves to persons charged with, convicted of, or sentenced for a criminal offense. The completeness of this power was dramatically demonstrated by President Ford's pardon of Richard Nixon even before he had been formally charged with any crime. Thus the ability of the courts to impose penalties upon individual members of the society is clearly limited. The president may

indirectly influence the behavior of the courts by making recommendations to the Congress to change the size of the Supreme Court, to shift the
appellate jurisdiction of that court, and to create or abolish inferior
courts. In fact, most congressional actions in these areas were initiated by
recommendations of the White House.

Judicial Checks

The judiciary has some important checks upon the other two branches of
the government. The Constitution requires that no one can be punished
without a trial in the judicial branch. The enforcement powers of the government can be effectively curtailed if the courts refuse punishment in
support of the demands of the other branches. The judicial dismissal of
the charges against the Chicago Seven and Daniel Ellsberg is an example
of the courts' rejecting intense administrative demands for the punishment of individual citizens. The development of the power of judicial review allows the courts to check the activities of the legislative and executive divisions. As the last branch of government to deal with an issue (for
the time being) the courts are strategically placed to limit the exercise of
power by the other branches.

The system of checks and balances provided in the Constitution, and
as it has evolved in the operation of the governmental process, contains
safeguards against tyrannical behavior on the part of any arm of government. Total control over a policy area by a single branch of the national government is precluded, and coordinated action among the several
branches is required for valid affirmative steps to be taken. This set of
rules generally operates as a negative force upon the performance of governmental agents and can be exceedingly frustrating to the impatient
and the certain. The Supreme Court, for example, can frustrate the actions of the other branches through the exercise of judicial review but
cannot require affirmative actions on the part of the president or the
Congress. The single exception so far is the court's order to President
Nixon to produce specified tape recordings.[37] The president's normal ability to reject such orders was undermined by the ongoing impeachment
process and heated public attitudes. Mr. Nixon submitted to the order.
Ironically, disclosures on the tapes further eroded presidential support
and led to his resignation. Although this example is likely to remain a
single deviant case, the institutionalization of the power of the courts to

require affirmative actions by the other two branches of government would dramatically change the distribution of power within the national government. A high priority is given under the rules of the Constitution to the use of persuasion, compromise, and bargaining in the making and execution of public policies. The manifest conservative bias of the Constitution is reflected in rules that favor those who prefer the status quo to the uncertainties of change inaugurated by either elite decisions or popular passions.

Again, the framers and Americans subsequently have accepted the high personal and social costs required to gain broad agreement before public policy can be initiated in return for the benefits associated with individual liberty and social stability. The same essential calculus has been used to explain other important features of the American system — federalism, civil liberties, and civil rights — which are dealt with in the next chapter.

SUMMARY

Every polity has a set of fundamental rules that guide its policy-making processes and give legal status to the subsequent public choices. These rules comprise the political constitution of the society. In America, the Constitution allocates and defines the powers of government and places limits on them. The subjects that are manageable through public choices and those that are reserved for individual decision-making are identified, and procedures by which authoritative and legitimate public choices may be made are established.

The Constitution was created in 1787 in response to the political conditions of the time. The values and material interests of the framers are stamped upon the document, and the product of their labors can be analyzed as either a philosophical statement, a complex effort to shore up existing privilege, or both. Its terms are general and elastic in nature primarily because of the divisions of opinion at the Constitutional Convention; ambiguity of expression permitted a consensus to build whereas precision would have caused the enterprise to collapse in disagreement. The motive of most of the delegates was to reach agreement on a stronger government which could deal effectively with commercial, military, and foreign relations problems. The document they created embodied a series of compromises among the major interests represented in the convention, necessary in gaining its adoption and ratification by the states.

Since the Constitution poses difficult tests for formal amendments, relatively little change has been made through the formal process. What are possibly the most important amendments — the Bill of Rights — were proposed and adopted almost immediately after the establishment of the new government. The major thrust of the other amendments has been to extend the suffrage and generally to expand popular control of the government. Perhaps the main changes in the Constitution, however, have resulted not from formal amendments but from the interpretation and application of its provisions in the ongoing political process.

The writers of the Constitution were fearful of tyrannical government. In order to protect against this threat, they divided the power of government among a number of political institutions. The doctrine of separation of powers was designed to require very broad consensus throughout the polity before any significant affirmative action could be taken by the national government. This requirement is reinforced by the system of checks and balances among the institutions of government. The framers were more willing to accept the potentially high costs of inaction than what were to them the still higher costs that might result from granting unlimited power to any one political faction or institution in society.

NOTES

1. The nature of constitutions and constitutional government has long been of major interest to political scientists. For classic considerations of these issues, see John W. Burgess, *Political Science and Comparative Constitutional Law* (Boston: Ginn, 1890); Charles H. McIllwain, *Constitutionalism, Ancient and Modern*, rev. ed. (Ithaca, N.Y.: Cornell University Press, 1947); Herbert Spiro, *Government by Constitution* (New York: Random House, 1959); and F. D. Wormuth, *The Origins of Modern Constitutionalism* (New York: Harper, 1949).

2. See A.V. Dicey, *Introduction to the Study of the Law on the Constitution,* 10th ed. (London: Macmillan, 1961), and Walter Bagehot, *The English Constitution.*

3. For a treatment of the adoption of the Bill of Rights, see Charles S. Hyneman and George W. Carey, *A Second Federalist* (New York: Appleton-Century-Crofts, 1967), and E. Dumbauld, *The Bill of Rights and What It Means Today* (Norman: University of Oklahoma Press, 1957).

4. The importance of this development is summarized in the following: "The Reformation superceded an infallible Pope with an infallible Bible; the American Revolution replaced the sway of a king with that of

a document." Edward S. Corwin, *The "Higher Law" Background of American Constitutional Law* (Ithaca, N.Y.: Great Seal Books, 1955).

5. See Charles L. Black, Jr., *The People and the Court* (New York: Macmillan, 1960).

6. The Constitution is a significant component of the credenda, or the basic things to be believed in the society. See Charles E. Merriam, *Political Power* (New York: McGraw-Hill, 1934). See also Thurman Arnold, *Symbols of Government* (New Haven, Conn.: Yale University Press, 1935), and Murray Edelman, *The Symbolic Uses of Politics* (New Haven, Conn.: Yale University Press, 1964).

7. See Henry J. Abraham, *The Judicial Process,* 2nd ed. (New York: Oxford University Press, 1968).

8. For examples see *Dennis* v. *United States*, 341 U.S. 494 (1951); *Ginzberg* v. *United States,* 383 U.S. 463 (1966); and *Schenck* v. *United States,* 249 U.S. 47 (1919).

9. Hardly any major debate in American politics goes forward without some appeal to the framers of the Constitution. The *Federalist Papers* (many editions) are also still frequently cited sources of arguments.

10. Max Farrand, *The Framing of the Constitution of the United States* (New Haven, Conn.: Yale University Press, 1913), has one of the better accounts of the framing process. Farrand collected most of the available records of the Convention in a four-volume work entitled *The Records of the Federal Convention of 1787* (New Haven, Conn.: Yale University Press, 1911), which is now available in paperback edition.

11. The argument that rules are never neutral is pressed with the greatest vigor in David Truman, *The Governmental Process,* 2nd ed. (New York: Knopf, 1971). A different and notable treatment of the impact of rules and the ways people may be brought willingly to accept a common set of rules that benefit everyone is developed in James M. Buchanan and Gordon Tullock, *The Calculus of Consent* (Ann Arbor: University of Michigan Press, 1962). Many of the arguments in this chapter rest implicitly upon their analysis. Technically, rules may be neutral when decisions must be taken unanimously by affected individuals or by their true delegates.

12. See Charles A. Beard, *An Economic Interpretation of the Constitution of the United States* (New York: Macmillan, 1962) (paperback), first published in 1913, for a vigorous statement of this point of view. Cf. Robert E. Brown, *Charles Beard and the Constitution of the United States* (Princeton, N.J.: Princeton University Press, 1956). See also Clinton Rossiter, *Seedtime of the Republic* (New York: Harcourt, Brace & World, 1953).

13. Farrand, *The Framing of the Constitution of the United States.*

14. Alfred H. Kelly and Winfred A. Harbison, *The American Constitution: Its Origins and Development* (New York: Norton, 1948), discuss this issue.

15. Edward Levi, *An Introduction to Legal Reasoning* (Chicago: University of Chicago Press, 1953), has a useful treatment of the nature and significance of purposeful ambiguity in legal documents.
16. The importance of limiting the power of factions was forcefully stated by James Madison in *The Federalist*, No. 10. The problem of reconciling expected external costs and expected decision-making costs so as to minimize overall costs (or costs of interdependence) is considered in Buchanan and Tullock, *The Calculus of Consent*.
17. See Kelly and Harbison, *The American Constitution*.
18. See *Coleman* v. *Miller*, 307 U.S. 433, for a discussion of these procedures.
19. See Hyneman and Carey, *A Second Federalist*.
20. *Chisholm* v. *Georgia*, 2 Dall. 419 (1793).
21. See Charles G. Haines, *The Role of the Supreme Court in American Government and Politics, 1789–1835* (Berkeley: University of California Press, 1944).
22. The amendment restricts peonage in the society as well as slavery. See *Bailey* v. *Alabama*, 219 U.S. 219 (1911); *Pollock* v. *Williams*, 322 U.S. 625 (1944); and *Robertson* v. *Baldwin*, 165 U.S. 275 (1897).
23. It was necessitated by the interpretations of the Supreme Court in the famous case of *Dred Scott* v. *Sanford*, 19 How. 393 (1857).
24. See Richard Hofstader, *The Age of Reform* (New York: Random House, 1955).
25. The ruling of the Supreme Court in the case of *Pollock* v. *Farmers' Loan and Trust Company*, 158 U.S. 601 (1895), was effectively overruled by this amendment.
26. *Marbury* v. *Madison*, 1 Cr. 137 (1803).
27. See, for example, *Hammer* v. *Dagenhart*, 247 U.S. 251 (1918); *Carter* v. *Carter Coal Company*, 298 U.S. 238 (1936); *United States* v. *E.C. Knight Company*, 156 U.S. 1 (1895); and *United States* v. *Butler*, 297 U.S. 1 (1936).
28. See *National Labor Relations Board* v. *Jones and Laughlin Steel Corporation*, 301 U.S. 1 (1937), and *United States* v. *Darby*, 312 U.S. 100 (1941).
29. See *United States* v. *Curtiss-Wright Export Corporation*, 299 U.S. 304 (1936).
30. The Court places most such cases under the "political questions" doctrine, which asserts that the Constitution gives final power in an area to some branch of the government other than the courts. See *United States* v. *Pink*, 315 U.S. 203 (1942), for an example.
31. See *Santa Clara County* v. *Southern Pacific Railroad*, 118 U.S. 394 (1886).
32. See Justice Miller's interpretation in the *Slaughterhouse Cases*, 16 Wall. 36 (1873).
33. See *Adamson* v. *California*, 332 U.S. 46 (1948); *Hurtado* v. *California*, 110 U.S. 516 (1884); and *Palko* v. *Connecticut*, 302 U.S. 319

(1937). Cf. *Gideon* v. *Wainwright,* 372 U.S. 335 (1963); *Malloy* v. *Hogan,* 378 U.S. 1 (1964); and *Miranda* v. *Arizona,* 384 U.S. 436 (1966).
34. See *McCulloch* v. *Maryland,* 4 Wheat. 316 (1819).
35. See arguments presented in *Marbury* v. *Madison.*
36. See *Ex parte McCardle,* 7 Wall. 509 (1869).
37. *United States* v. *Nixon,* 94 S. Ct. 3090 (1974).

The Constitution: Limitations on Public Power

The systems of separate powers and checks and balances operating at the national level, as described in Chapter 3, are reinforced by the federal system which distributes power between the central authority and the states. A premium is placed once again upon maintaining liberty by fragmenting power, even though to do so may at times increase the costs of developing coherent social policy. Much of American politics involves arguments rationalized through different understandings of the rules governing national and state relationships. Alexander Hamilton and John Marshall favored having the national government dominate the states in case of conflict; Thomas Jefferson and John C. Calhoun favored precisely the opposite: having national power strictly limited vis-à-vis the states. Another view has supported the notion of dual federalism, by which national and state powers are held to be roughly equal and sovereign in their respective domains. Still another view, that of so-called cooperative federalism, emphasizes not matters of dominance, competition, or sovereignty but teamwork and power-sharing among national and state governments in accomplishing common ends.[1] And another writer regards the federal relationship as a contract agreed to for reasons of mutual advantage by interests with little in common except a concern to maximize their own social positions.[2]

These need not be mutually exclusive propositions. An individualistic approach reminds us that the many citizens, party politicians, bureaucrats, judges, interest group leaders, and scholars who have dealt with questions of federalism have, at the same and different periods in history, advanced different answers in those matters. There is no "correct" opinion on the federal relationship beyond existing practice and judicial interpretation of the constitutional issues involved. The "intent" of the framers is also unclear. They faced the reality of an ongoing union of the colonies *of some sort* that went back to the early seventeenth century, one officially recognized in the Articles of Association (1774), made "perpetual" by the Articles of Confederation, and embedded in the Constitution. But political history does not exhaust the perspectives that might be taken: As political engineers seeking to act rationally with respect to their preferences, having certain shared agreements about the proclivity of government to degenerate into tyranny, and applying their resources efficiently to the task at hand, the framers adopted federal rules designed to minimize government's threat to liberty and to maximize their own value positions thereby. Political values and aspirations have their impact, just as do the political exigencies of the moment.

Further, a sophisticated political science literature seeks to show the logical basis for choosing a federal system at the time of constitutional choice, even though the nature and boundaries of the American states may bear little relationship to what that logic requires. Suffice it to say, there are arguments that individual benefits will be maximized (and costs minimized) when a political subunit is organized on a geographical basis to provide services efficiently, with respect to both producing them and making collective decisions about them.[3] According to this logic, public goods, such as national defense and the monetary system, should be provided by the national government (states could protect "national" security inefficiently if at all). By the same token, the benefits accruing to a Californian from a public beach in Florida are, if not nonexistent, certainly attenuated. The suggestion is, therefore, for subnational jurisdictions to handle matters which have limited effects. Needless to say, no precise line can be drawn around these effects. Opinions will differ as to where they fall and when costs may be *minimized* by a federal arrangement rather than compounded by establishing diverse centers of authority. While the American federal system did not grow out of such theorizing, it is not entirely alien to it.

THE SHARING OF POWERS

The United States Constitution establishes a federal republic in which the power to govern is shared between the national government and the member states of the federation. What constitutes "proper" sharing of the powers of government, as just observed, has been a persistent and disputed issue in American political history. Our form of government requires that determinations be made not only as to *what* activities may be undertaken by government but as to *which level(s) of government* will or may act in a given area. Theories and debates concerning states' rights and national power are colored by consideration of which level of government is most likely to support policies and programs compatible with the goals of the disputants. A more philosophical dimension of the debates involves how much homogeneity is needed or is appropriate in a political community in order for justice, freedom, order, and individual preferences to prevail.

The states and their governments predated the writing of the Constitution. Under the then prevailing political system sovereign power was lodged in the states. The Articles of Confederation supplied a cooperative, noncoercive arrangement in which the central government had almost no enforcement power against the states. It depended upon the willing support of the states for the enforcement of nationwide rules and for the effective implementation of national public policy. State officials could normally ignore policies of the central government without fear of formal sanctions, and any basic change could be made only with the unanimous consent of the states. The Congress of the United States, the primary decision-making organ of the central government, was little more than a debating society of ambassadors from sovereign states. Its inability to make system-wide choices, especially as regards the regulation of commerce, provided the thrust for calling the Constitutional Convention. The challenge was clear to many delegates: The central government required expanded authority in several important areas of collective or national concern, but the primary powers and prerogatives of the states would have to be maintained in all other areas if the states were to ratify the contemplated changes.

Opinions differed as to the best balance between state and national power. The decision following the constitutional debates was again a compromise between those who wanted a very strong central government and those who wanted to maintain most governmental powers in the states. In the end, a limited set of specific powers — those considered essential for the development and maintenance of a viable political system but no others — was delegated to the national government. Rules were also provided to curtail the powers of the states to intervene in matters of central concern and to require necessary cooperation among the governments of the states. All other powers of government were reserved to the states. This scheme is reflected in a good number of constitutional provisions, and the agreed-upon relationships are summarized in the Tenth Amendment to the Constitution. That amendment really adds nothing new to the basic allocation of power but it does, in explicit form, summarize the relationships which were to obtain between and among national and state governments.

The national government was to be supreme in the areas in which it was authorized to act by its delegated powers. The Constitution, laws made in conformity with its provisions, and all treaties made under the authority of the United States were to be aspects of the "supreme law of the land" and as such were to be binding upon the states. The powers of the central government were mainly those of interstate and foreign commerce, foreign affairs, military affairs, and monetary issues. This manner of allocation has forced the national government on all subsequent occasions to relate *all* its actions to some specific provision of the Constitution which can be said to authorize central governmental activity. The "implied powers" doctrine described in the preceding chapter does have some impact, but even here the "necessary and proper" clause must be joined with a specifically delegated power to legitimate its use. Thus, the central government was to hold only that share of the total power of governance directly granted to it by the Constitution, although practical and historical necessity have produced such expansive interpretations as to make the concept unrecognizable to eighteenth-century understandings.

All powers not granted to the national government and not specifically denied to the governments of the states are reserved to the states by the Constitution. The actual powers to be exercised by the states within the confines of these rules are to be determined by the constitutional processes in the states. Independent processes in each state determine which powers reserved to it will become matters for public choice and which will remain matters for individual decision-making. Formally, the states exercise the full right of sovereignty in the areas reserved to them under the Constitution. These residual powers are more difficult to describe than are those of the national government inasmuch as they are undefined in the Constitution itself. The states, for example, have a generalized police power that allows them to take whatever actions are considered necessary to protect the "health, welfare, safety and morals" of their citizens. This kind of open-ended power is unavailable to the national government, except possibly in the area of foreign affairs. The vast majority of rules and laws that apply to individuals in the American polity, the bulk of all criminal law, contract law, tort law, property law, and commercial regulations flow from the decisions of state governments.

A central problem in any federal system is to devise an authoritative means for determining which level of government, if any, has legitimate power in concrete conflicts between the national government and the states. The process of interpreting the relative powers of the two segments is one of the most significant of all political processes in any federal republic.

The philosophical conception underlying the American constitutional system is that all power derives from the people. Governmental authority stems from the people's decision as to which matters are appropriate for collective management and which rules must be followed in legislating on those matters. All power, and all rules governing that power, may be delegated to the national government or to the states or may be retained by the people.[4] The legitimate scope of government can be expanded or contracted by the people, and the powers of government can be reallocated between the two levels of government. The Constitution describes the allocations of power made by the people, but its rules are not precise, well-defined statements designating which level of government has the right to act in any particular circumstance. Inasmuch as it was written to solve practical problems, one should not be surprised at its frequent ambiguity and its philosophical contradictions. It was not written as an academic treatise.

Conflicts frequently arise as to whether any public policy, state or national, is compatible with the power allocations made by the Constitution. It is generally conceded that some entity has to be in a position to resolve such conflicts authoritatively. If this entity is part of, or is ideologically aligned with, the national power, it will tend to centralize authority, while decentralization is more likely if the states can make final determinations.

Any legitimate public choice rests, at least implicitly, upon a determination that it falls within the prerogative of the level of government which made it. Legislative and executive officials must interpret the Constitution as they carry out their responsibilities. However, the final interpretation is often made by the judicial officers who have to make decisions in cases involving the constitutionality of governmental actions. Thus the Supreme Court is in the strategic position of being the final arbiter in state-national conflicts — of being "the balance wheel of the republic."[5] The basic responsibility of the Court flows from the requirement that it discover the "supreme law of the land" in all cases brought before it. The constitutional interpretations of the Court on these issues may expand or contract the power of either level of government. The nature of actual interpretations has varied substantially through time.

THE REGULATION OF COMMERCE

The expanding-contracting-expanding interpretations of the commerce clause serve as an important illustration of the changing patterns of judicial interpretations of federal relationships.

The Constitution allows the national government to regulate commerce among the several states; by implication, the regulation of intrastate commerce (commerce wholly within a single state) is reserved to the states. The interpretation and definition of these terms is crucial in drawing the line of authority to regulate commercial activities between the two levels of government. This is not the place to attempt to explain in detail the strange and convoluted history of the commerce clause, but a few examples of the shifting interpretations given to it will illustrate the dynamic character of federal relationships as they undergo continuing redefinition.

The national government has full power to regulate commerce between the states, and any state regulation that is inconsistent with that power cannot stand.[6] However, the national government may allow the states to regulate portions of interstate commerce that do not require national uniformity.[7] The Congress and the courts must determine what matters do not require such uniformity. For a substantial period of time the courts defined commerce in such a way that many primary economic activities (mining, agriculture, etc.) could not be controlled by the national government.[8] The problems of wages, hours, prices, and working conditions in these businesses were held to be external to the power to control commerce by the national government. Such interpretations narrowed the capacity of the national government to deal with some profound social concerns. The revolution in judicial doctrine which occurred in 1937–1938 dramatically changed these interpretations.[9] Cases decided at that time broadened the power of the national government and destroyed traditional constitutional reference points. The Congress was now free to regulate business and the economy when economic (and some other) activities could be construed as being of national concern or as markedly affecting interstate commerce. The concept of interstate commerce became so wide that much federal regulation in fields as seemingly unrelated as that of civil rights is now based upon the commerce power. The courts have not found any significant federal legislation to be in violation of the commerce clause in over three decades. This pattern leaves the Congress quite free to define for itself the confines of the national power over commerce.

The states are free to regulate commercial activities within their borders if such regulation does not interfere with the free movement of commerce among the states. The main limitation is that they cannot discriminate in favor of local businesses or against those from other states.[10] State regulations cannot place undue "burdens" upon interstate commerce.[11] The understandings as to the activities that burden interstate commerce have also changed. In 1900, for example, the Constitution was interpreted in such a way that states could allow or require racial segregation on common carriers passing through them but could not *prohibit* such segregation without unconstitutionally burdening interstate commerce.[12] The reader may marvel at this instance of judicial reasoning. More recently, of course, the interpretation has been completely reversed. The states may now prohibit segregation but cannot require it on common carriers without placing an unconstitutional burden on interstate commerce.

The complex history of the commerce clause illustrates a more general proposition, namely, that while there have been few formal constitutional amendments concerning the allocation of powers between the national government and the states, the actual operating rules have shifted this allocation, molding it to the preferences of changing interests and combinations of power. The Supreme Court has played a vital part in legitimizing these major changes in power alignments and in finding ways to link the changes to fundamental constitutional concepts. The operating relationship between national and state governments continues to adjust to ever changing political interests and policy coalitions. The dialogue continues over which level of government is the appropriate locus for decision-making on the issues of the day. Normally, virtually every social and political issue has a states' rights–national power dimension. Not uncommonly, a partisan's stance on current issues determines his or her position on which level of government will best address the issues.

COOPERATIVE FEDERALISM

The above discussion emphasizes the potential for conflict between the states and the national government. However, any treatment of federalism would be incomplete without mention of the very significant modern state-national relationship known as cooperative federalism, in which the national government and the states cooperate in formal and extensive ways in many policy undertakings. The vast grant-in-aid programs developed in the last several decades comprise the core of this system. Briefly, they involve financial aid by the federal government to the states to support services authorized, administered, and, to some degree, financed also by the state governments. These federal inducements are often so financially attractive that the states have little serious option except to participate. To do otherwise would be to forgo the benefits that federal aid makes possible without reducing the federal taxes levied on the citizens of the state. Numerous public goods and services such as highway construction, welfare, pollution abatement, education, and urban development are provided through this kind of cooperative (in fact, sometimes mildly coercive) activity. "**Revenue sharing**" is one much-discussed variation, allowing the states far greater discretion than they had before in determining how federal contributions will be expended. Revenue sharing moves the primary power to determine which services will be provided to whom and in what degree to a lower level of government. Different patterns of policy decisions, produced by different political interests, will arise from the enhanced powers of subnational governments. The various models of national-state cooperation are designed to meet effective political demands that cannot be met by either level of government acting alone. The point is that, although there are areas of conflict between national government and the states, and controversy rages over the relative merits of lodging policy-making power at each level, many contemporary relationships between the states and the national government are characterized as much by cooperation as by conflict.

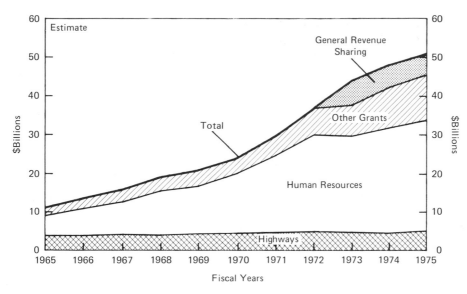

Figure 4-1. Federal Grants to State and Local Governments. *Source: Special Analysis, Budget of the United States Government, Fiscal Year 1975*, p. 203.

RULES RESTRAINING STATE POWER

The political aim of the framers to create a system of limited government has been emphasized throughout our discussion of the checks upon power which are built into the Constitution. However, a number of issues were considered so critical for the maintenance of a free society that *specific denials* of governmental power were inserted at the insistence of some political influentials. The result was the addition of ten amendments to the Constitution almost immediately after its ratification. These, the Bill of Rights, have long been considered primary bulwarks against tyranny of either the minority or the majority and basic guarantees of a free society. A brief analysis of these rules and what they have come to mean is essential to an understanding of the American system.

The limitations placed in the original Constitution were meant to protect both the states, as corporate units, and individual citizens. The main import of the rules designed to protect the states was that there could be no discrimination against any one state or a combination of states. The national government was not allowed to place a tax on state exports, all direct taxes had to be appropriated among the states on the basis of population, and all indirect taxes were required to be uniform throughout the United States. The Congress was given the power to admit new states into the Union, but all states were to be admitted on an equal footing with all other states. The equal suffrage of the states in the Senate could not be destroyed even through the process of constitutional amendment. The right of the states to maintain the slave trade was guaranteed until 1808, and a strict limit was placed on the taxes that could be imposed on the slave trade. Although the meaning of the provision is somewhat in doubt, the national government was required to guarantee every state a republican form of government. The force of the limitations upon the national government in this area was to prevent the development of preferences either for or against any state.

Several guarantees in the original document were designed to protect against governmental tyranny over the individual. The right of the national government to suspend the writ of **habeus corpus** (the right of a person to be charged with a crime and brought to trial) was severely restricted. Thus, a person had the right to demand a judicial hearing on whether he or she was being justly held in custody by federal officials. The national government was not allowed to enact bills of attainder or ex post facto laws. **Bills of attainder** are legislative acts that directly punish an individual or an identifiable set of individuals without trial or judicial process.[13] An ex post facto law is any law that provides punishment or increases punishment for an act committed before the law was passed. This is an extremely important guarantee that assures citizens they will not be held punishable for an act that was consistent with the law when carried out. The Constitution defined the crime of treason narrowly and required stringent tests for conviction of the crime. Similarly, the punishment for treason was limited to the individual and could not extend to other family members. The trial of anyone charged with a crime was required to be by a jury in the state in which the crime had been committed. There could be no religious test for holding any public office under the Constitution. These restraints were primarily designed to protect individuals from the felt excesses that had developed in the later years of colonial rule and to guarantee subsequent security from arbitrary acts of the national government.

The limitations that were placed upon the governments of the states by the Constitution fall into three categories. (1) The states were restricted in those functions delegated to the national government and considered to be essentially national in character. They were not allowed to make treaties or other agreements with foreign nations or to coin money or issue bills of credit. They were not allowed to maintain a standing military force in peacetime. They were not allowed to impose taxes on imports and exports, in either interstate or foreign commerce. They were not allowed to enter into compacts with other states without the specific authorization of the Congress. These limitations were directed toward resolving problems present under the Articles of Confederation and molding the states into a single Union. They were also ways by which eighteenth-century American elites attempted to achieve two of their prime goals: national power and commercial stability.

(2) Requirements for cooperation among the states were developed to reinforce these general objectives. For example, all the states were required to give "full faith and credit" to the public documents and records of all the other states — an extremely important consideration if commercial activity was to be conducted on a nationwide basis. The states had to grant to the citizens of all states the privileges and immunities attached to citizenship. The states were not allowed to discriminate against the residents of other states and in favor of their own citizens. Finally, the states were required to return any fugitives from another state. This has proved to be an unenforceable provision of the Constitution, but it does indicate the interest of the framers in promoting cooperation among the states which would be conducive to national unity.

(3) Few limitations were placed upon the states in relations with their own citizens, this being a matter to be worked out in the political processes of the states. However, the states were not to enact bills of attainder or ex post facto laws. They were also constrained in their power to impair the obligation of contracts, a matter again related to the need for commercial stability and financial predictability that was so important to the authors of the Constitution.

THE GOVERNMENT AND
THE INDIVIDUAL

There was a widespread sentiment at the time of the original Constitution's promulgation that it did not limit the national government sufficiently vis-à-vis individuals. Demands for further safeguards resulted in the Bill of Rights. These restraints were designed to protect individual liberty from threats by the national government and were not imposed upon the states. Primary protections from the activities of state governments were to be sought in the constitutions of the states and not in the national Constitution. However, the guarantee included in the Fourteenth Amendment that states could not deny persons life, liberty, or property without due process of law has been interpreted in recent years to impose limitations on the states much like those imposed by the Bill of Rights on the national government. The Supreme Court has never held that the Bill of Rights is "incorporated" in the due process clause of the Fourteenth Amendment, although it has held that limitations like those included in the Bill of Rights are operative upon the states if they are necessary for "fundamental fairness" or "ordered liberty" to prevail.[14] This process of selective inclusion has reached such a point that virtually all of the protections against the national government found in the Bill of Rights are also protections against state actions as well.

The way these rules apply to the national and state governments at present is an exceedingly complex topic. Here they are described only in general terms; no attempt is made to consider the more subtle interpretations that have developed. However, the nature and implications of the basic legal rights of Americans will be identified and their significance evaluated.

Personal Freedoms

A major protection found in the First Amendment relates to the freedom of social intercourse. This amendment guarantees freedom of speech, press, and assembly and the right of citizens to petition the government. A primary justification for it is to guarantee the right of political dissent and the free discussion of political issues even though the government or public officials may be criticized. This type of freedom is generally considered necessary to the continuing practice of democracy in any society. The First Amendment has been characterized as the "first article of our faith" and the cornerstone of political democracy in America. Controversy over it has turned mainly on attempts to "protect" the society from subversive speech aimed at "overthrowing" the government. The right of political speech is not unlimited under current interpretations of the Constitution. Speech is limited which advocates some illegal action, such as the overthrow of the government by force and violence, and which includes a call for action in the immediate future that has some probability of invoking illegal action of the part of others. When these conditions are met, the maker of the speech may be punished.[15] Quite importantly, American practice is to permit punishment subsequently for speech which is not protected by the First Amendment, but censorship or "prior restraint" of such speech is generally not permissible.[16] Except for extreme versions of speech, as described above, there is broad protection for speech in the political arena. Indeed, public officials generally cannot collect damages in libel suits for unfair criticism or defamatory statements made about them.[17] Only in the most extraordinary case can there be punishment or civil recovery against individuals who criticize the government or public officials.

The protection of speech outside of the directly political arena is somewhat less complete. A major issue involves pornography and obscenity, which have been defined as being beyond the protection of the First Amendment. They fall into a general category including libel and fighting words — "mere utterances" — which are not treated as speech at all. The major problem is one of definition. What is obscenity? What constitutes libel? What are fighting words? The courts are frequently called upon to consider these problems in cases brought before them. Once the court finds that a given utterance falls into one of these categories it loses

The acquittal of Peter Zenger, printer of the New York Weekly Journal who was accused of libel, established the precedent of freedom of the press in the United States. *The Bettmann Archives*

its protection under the First Amendment.[18] The current interpretations of the Supreme Court hold that the freedom of speech provisions of the First Amendment are fully applicable to the states. The definitions and interpretations used to determine whether government has restricted speech illegitimately apply to the national and state governments equally.

A second major protection found in the First Amendment involves the socially sensitive issue of religion. The Constitution decrees that the Congress "shall make no law respecting the establishment of religion." The "establishment" clause was designed to prevent the national government from establishing a national church or from intervening in state practices with regard to religion. The current judicial doctrines hold that the Fourteenth Amendment imposes a similar limitation upon the states. But the chief area in which the meaning of the establishment clause has been contested is education. The primary focus of the issue has perhaps been the use of tax funds to support religious exercises in public schools. Another controversy has concerned federal aid to church-operated schools. The courts have ruled that neither the states nor the national government can aid religious activities of church-operated schools, although aid can be given to students and nonreligious education functions of these schools.[19] The most emotional controversy in recent years has involved Bible reading and prayers in the public schools. The courts have decided that such activities are sectarian in nature and in violation of the establishment clause of the First Amendment.[20] The thrust of these and other rulings is that the power of the state, including its financial resources, cannot be used to support or promote religious activities under the Constitution.

By the same token, the government is not free to weaken religious activity. The First Amendment also attempts to protect the free exercise of religion — a fairly difficult problem inasmuch as the government is not allowed to determine the truth or falsity of a religion. People have claimed altogether eccentric and antisocial practices to be an exercise of religion and therefore protected under the Constitution. Judicial rulings in response to this problem have held that any nondiscriminatory exercise of the police power designed to protect substantial community values is not limited by the "free exercise" clause.[21] Merely unusual religious practices may not, of course, be restricted, and the courts have held that a number of rules developed in local communities have discriminated against particular religious groups and were unconstitutional.[22] The fact that the United States has extensive religious freedom is as much the result of its religious diversity and the consequent inability of any single religious group to control the institutions of government as the result of applications of the free exercise of religion provision in the First Amendment. Perhaps the major significance of this provision is its guarantees against purposeful discrimination by governmental agents against unpopular religious groups.

The First Amendment is, then, the constitutional basis for two important values in American society, freedom of speech and freedom of religion. However, these liberties have not been interpreted to be absolute and can be limited when they threaten other more deeply held values such as the survival of the nation. The courts engage in a difficult balancing process in determining how much these liberties may be restricted in order to obtain a "greater good" for the community.

Personal Security and Privacy

The guarantees of the Second and Third amendments have had little formal impact on American history. The right to bear arms, protected by the Second Amendment, has been interpreted narrowly and in practice applies to activities of the state militia.[23] However, this provision is widely cited in discussions of gun registration and control. Interestingly, even though under current judicial interpretations the amendment is not relevant to the issue of gun control, it has added substantially to the forces opposed to gun control legislation. If popular convention accepts a matter as unconstitutional, it may become so. The Third Amendment has only historical interest, as no notable cases or incidents have arisen in the area it attempts to control. Even so, we cannot say that the quartering of troops in private homes would or would not have developed in its absence. Basically, these two amendments were designed to eliminate practices engaged in during the colonial period which have not yet emerged in the Republic.

The Fourth Amendment guards against unreasonable searches and seizures by governmental agents and protects the individual's right of privacy in person, papers, and effects. The two conditions that make searches and seizures "reasonable" and allowable are a valid arrest or the presence of a valid search warrant. A search may be conducted of any person (and of the place the person is found) who is the subject of an arrest warrant or who the arresting officer has probable cause to believe has committed a felony. Search warrants are valid only if the area to be

Drawing by Niculae Ascinu; © 1974 *The New Yorker Magazine, Inc.*

searched and the items that are the subject of the search are clearly
identified. A warrant can be issued only if the judge has probable cause to
believe a crime has been committed and relevant items are present in the
place to be searched.[24] Recently the most controversial aspects of the
Fourth Amendment have been related to the use of wiretapping and elec-
tronic eavesdropping as means of gaining evidence of criminal activity. The
current doctrines hold that such means are unreasonable unless they are
carried out under the direction of a search warrant issued by a judge.[25] The
major means of controlling law enforcement officials is to make illegally
gathered evidence inadmissible in a court of law as well as any evidence
based on illegally obtained material. This requirement is now applicable to
both national and state judicial systems.[26]

Protection of the Accused

The Fifth Amendment protects any person charged with a criminal offense and includes more general protections of individual freedom in the
society. The national government is not allowed to try anyone for a major
crime without indictment by a **grand jury** — a group of impaneled citizens
who hear the state's evidence against the person and determine whether
there is sufficient evidence to warrant a trial but do not make any determination of guilt or innocence. The grand jury system screens cases so

that individuals will not be required to defend themselves in a trial in which evidence of guilt is lacking. The grand jury is *not* required in state jurisdictions under the provisions of the national Constitution as currently interpreted. The Fifth Amendment also protects the individual from double jeopardy, or being tried twice for the same crime. However, a single action may violate both a state and a national criminal statute, and the person may be tried in both jurisdictions because two criminal acts have been committed. A person who has been found guilty of a crime and whose conviction is overturned in an appeals court can be retried without being placed in double jeopardy. The protection against double jeopardy is operative in both the national and state jurisdictions.[27]

One of the most significant and controversial guarantees of the Fifth Amendment protects against compulsory self-incrimination. People may not be required to give testimony against themselves in a criminal trial or any formal hearing conducted by the government. If a citizen invokes this right, the prosecutor is not allowed to indicate to the jury that such an invocation may indicate guilt. The protection extends to any attempts, physical or psychological, to coerce anyone into confessing to a crime. If a confession is found to be coerced, it is not admissible as evidence. The courts have held that any confession made before an individual is clearly apprised of her or his rights and has an opportunity to consult with a lawyer is inadmissible as evidence against the individual.[28] The right against self-incrimination is, however, a personal right not to testify to information that can be used in a criminal trial. One *cannot* claim this right in order to protect another person or to avoid personal embarrassment. An individual may be given immunity from prosecution for any testimony that is given, and if such grant of immunity precludes any trial for any crime resulting from the testimony, the right to remain silent without punishment is removed. The protection extends to state courts as well as to those of the national government.[29] This protection has often been criticized — usually perhaps by those who have not (yet) had occasion to invoke the rights provided by the Fifth Amendment themselves — as being a means by which the guilty may avoid their just punishment.

The most general protection included in the Fifth Amendment declares that no person shall be deprived of life, liberty, or property without due process of law. Property is thus placed among the fundamental rights to be protected in the polity and replaces the more ambiguous ideal of "pursuit of happiness" which had been included in the Declaration of Independence. The concept "due process of law" is vague, and the courts have refused to give any full or final definition of it. In general, it has come to mean that all deprivations must be rooted in the law of the land and that the processes through which deprivations are made must meet tests of justice and fundamental fairness. Before an individual may be punished under the law, there must first have been a law defining the duties and responsibilities that have been transgressed. The individual must have clear notice of the charges being brought and must have an opportunity to develop and present a defense in a fair hearing. The context of the hearing and the procedures used to conduct it must be compatible with standards of justice and fairness. The due process provision gives the courts a chance to prevent a prosecution or deprivation when they believe that justice is not being served and even though all of the specific guarantees of the Constitution have been followed. The major goal is to prevent punishment that rests upon arbitrary and/or capricious action by agents of the government. The due process clause is repeated in exactly the same form in the Fourteenth Amendment, and its protection operates to limit the actions of the governments of the states.

The final provision of the Fifth Amendment stipulates that private property cannot be taken for public purposes unless "just compensation" is given to its owner. The two critical issues involve the meaning of "public purpose" and "just compensation." The courts have granted the other branches of government considerable latitude in defining the nature of public purposes. As long as there is not a clear intent to take property from a person (or group of persons) and redistribute it to another private person or group, legislative interpretations have been upheld. The nature of just compensation must be determined in individual cases. The real guarantee of this provision is that the individual has the right to a judicial hearing to determine the just price for any property taken by the government. The Fifth Amendment recognizes the government's power of **eminent domain** (taking private property against the wishes of its owner), but it does provide limits and means by which a person can demand to be compensated for such losses.

The Sixth Amendment guarantees an impartial, speedy, and public trial of anyone charged with a criminal offense. The fact that the trial must be conducted as soon as is practicable after the offense is committed limits the period an individual can be held in custody without conviction and restricts the government's opportunity to prepare its case. The trial must be held in the state and district in which the crime was committed, and a jury from that district must be used. The accused has the right to legal assistance of counsel and the right to confront all witnesses who testify for the prosecution. A trial cannot proceed until the individual has been apprised of the precise charges that are being brought. The basic thrust of these provisions is to guarantee a fair trial on clear-cut charges following an opportunity to develop a fair defense. The trial must be held near at hand and the expectation is that the defendant will have the assistance of friends and relatives in preparing a defense and their support during the course of the trial. The major provisions of the Sixth Amendment were a reaction to the colonial practice of sending people to England for trial, far from friends and relatives, without the aid of counsel and in secret "star chamber" proceedings. The most important change in the original rules is the requirement that the government furnish legal counsel if individuals are financially unable to secure their own. This is now required by current interpretations of the Constitution in both the federal and state courts.[30] The guarantee of a fair trial for all persons accused of a criminal offense was a crucial element in the development of constitutional limitations and is an indispensable aspect of a free society. These protections have frequently come under attack, regarded as mere technicalities which allow the guilty to "go free." The authors of the Sixth Amendment believed that the danger of freeing the guilty was less than that of punishing the innocent for acts they did not commit in a process that was unfair. The formal balance is purposely weighted against the government and in favor of the criminal defendant. Even granting that bias, the criminal defendant probably has no actual advantage over the government in most criminal trials. Nonetheless, these rules do attempt to protect the individual from the superior power of government as far as possible.

Jury Trial and Punishment Provisions

The Seventh Amendment guarantees trial by jury in most civil cases that arise under the law of the United States. These are cases involving non-criminal disputes among individuals or institutions. Disputes over property, contracts, and personal injuries fall into this category. The amendment further guarantees that the determinations made by the jury in such cases will be binding upon all courts in the national system.

The Eighth Amendment protects against excessive bail and fines and forbids cruel and unusual punishment. The question of what amounts to an excessive bail or fine has never really been settled in American law. Generally, decisions must be made on a case-by-case basis. However, this provision has figured in a number of recent political controversies concerning justice for the poor. The movement toward developing a system of releasing on their own recognizance persons unable themselves to establish bail is a significant step toward achieving the goals seemingly implicit in the Eighth Amendment. The provision against cruel and unusual punishment has also begun to have greater formal impact. Punishment for alcoholic and drug addiction has been brought under this protection and substantially limited.[31] The recent, albeit confused, determination that the death penalty as it was applied in most jurisdictions amounted to cruel and unusual punishment is the latest important application of this rule.[32]

The Bill of Rights as a Whole

The first eight amendments contain the major specific limitations upon the national government. Many of these provisions have also been made applicable to the states through interpretations of the Fourteenth Amendment. The main elements of the Bill of Rights have the purpose of protecting freedom of political discussion and preventing the national government from imposing religious beliefs upon the population. The chief function of the remaining provisions is to keep individuals safe from attempts of the government to take their life, liberty, or property arbitrarily. To this end the procedures and processes required before any such deprivation would be legitimate are spelled out in some detail. Procedural guarantees are at the heart of a free society and at the core of the Bill of Rights.

The Ninth Amendment has served as little more than a disclaimer. Its primary purpose was to indicate that citizens might be able to claim rights not specifically listed in the other provisions of the Bill of Rights. Throughout most of our history the amendment has had very little impact. An individual claiming a right that was being illegitimately restricted by government has been required to point to some specific constitutional provision defining that right or to one limiting the action being taken by government. There does seem to be an emergence of a new right under the Constitution which rests at least in part upon this amendment. It is a generalized right to privacy and is based on the contention that some activities of individuals are beyond the legitimate interest and control of the government. The two specific areas in which the Ninth Amendment has been used as a justification for limiting governmental power have involved the free distribution of birth control information by a doctor to his patients and the right of women to arrange for an abortion.[33] The argument places the privacy of an individual's relation with a member of the medical profession beyond the control of governmental officials as long as it has no clear destructive effects on the interests of others. This beginning could, in the long run, lead to the pouring of substantial content into the Ninth Amendment.

The Tenth Amendment is largely a reaffirmation of the federal nature of the government under the Constitution. It specifies that the powers not "delegated" to the United States or prohibited to the states are reserved to the states or to the people. The proponents of states' rights have pressed for interpretations of the Tenth which would amount to adding the word *specifically* before the word *delegated*. The purpose is to force a narrow interpretation of national governmental power and to limit the so-called implied powers under the Constitution.[34] This position has never been fully adopted, and the primary achievement of the Tenth Amendment is its clear and concise statement concerning the nature of the government created by the original Constitution. It has had more importance in ideological discourse than as an operative rule restricting the powers of government.

The Fourteenth Amendment

Undoubtedly, the most significant constitutional limitations on government that have been added since the adoption of the Bill of Rights are found in the Fourteenth Amendment. Unlike the Bill of Rights, the Fourteenth Amendment limits the power of the states rather than that of the national government. Its provisions constituted (as they continue to do) a fundamental shift in the nature of the federal system. They break with the tradition that the citizens of each state determine the boundaries of state powers and allow those boundaries to be imposed by national political processes. They thus restrict certain powers of the states even though the people in that state might prefer that their state government exercise them. This shift has placed the federal courts in a position to supervise and oversee many activities of the states. Obviously, a new balance of power has been created in the federal Union and has generated much controversy. The Fourteenth Amendment forbids the state to deny to any person (1) due process of law, (2) the equal protection of the law, and (3) the privileges and immunities of citizenship.

The important "due process" clause places limitations on the states much like those imposed on the federal government by the Bill of Rights.

Consequently, many fundamental rights discussed in our treatment of the Bill of Rights have come to apply to the states. At present the main area of concern is that of criminal rights, but the due process provision was used for a time to restrict the power of the states to regulate hours and wages of workers in the states.[35]

The "privileges and immunities" clause has had little significance in American law. The first major interpretation of this provision construed it narrowly and it has not yet been given much substance.[36] The clause does ensure the right of individuals to move freely across state lines and to do business in the different states,[37] although that right could probably be protected just as well by the commerce and the equal protection clauses of the Constitution.

The last, and perhaps most critical, rule of the Fourteenth Amendment is the "equal protection" clause. It has been used as a basis for requiring state legislatures to be reapportioned on the "one person, one vote" principle. It has been used to demand a whole range of protections for the poor in the criminal process — protections involving the right to counsel, free trial transcripts to be used in appeals, and changes in bail requirements. It has been used to guarantee welfare rights to persons who are not legal residents of states and to restrict discrimination against businesses from out of state. However, its most important — and most controversial — application is to the problem of racial equality.

The initial impulse for the equal protection clause was to make sure that the states, particularly the southern states, did not discriminate against the slaves freed by the Thirteenth Amendment. The first reaction to the rule was to give it a very narrow interpretation in that a person alleging discrimination had to show that the action was carried out by state officials. This "state action" doctrine was used frequently to limit the efficacy of the equal protection clause. Another landmark in the evolution of the clause was the judicial interpretation that racial segregation required by state law did *not* necessarily violate this provision of the Constitution. The courts ruled that as long as "separate but equal" accommodations were provided for different racial groups, segregation did not violate the Fourteenth Amendment.[38] For more than a generation, the states were by and large left to determine for themselves when such requirements were met.

The most significant shift in the interpretation of this provision occurred in 1954, although the separate but equal doctrine had been eroded previously in a number of lesser cases. The Supreme Court ruled in that year that segregation of the races in public schools was in itself a violation of the equal protection clause.[39] Since then the courts have been called upon many times to decide cases involving state-enforced or -required segregation of the races. The Supreme Court has held consistently that this is contrary to the Fourteenth Amendment. The current interpretation is that the states cannot, either directly or indirectly, make race a category for legal action without violating the Fourteenth Amendment. The interpretation rests on the ground that the Constitution requires state policies and programs to be "color blind." There remain many social barriers to racial equality in America, but current constitutional interpretations destroy any legal bases for discrimination when supported or reinforced by the actions of the states or their agents.

SUMMARY

Among the several ways in which the power of government is limited in the United States is division of that power between the national government and preexisting state governments. By the terms of the Constitution, the national government acts in areas delegated to it while all other powers of government are reserved to the states. In this complicated system of dual sovereignty each level of government is presumably supreme in its own sphere of action. There is in fact considerable conflict involved in determining when either level is operating in an appropriate area. When conflicts arise, the Supreme Court plays the most important role in deciding constitutional allocations of power between national and state authorities.

The need to gain ratification of the Constitution led to the inclusion of specific limitations upon the power of the national government. The first ten amendments to the Constitution, the Bill of Rights, are the legal basis for freedom of speech and religion in the United States and contain a large number of protections for persons accused of violating the criminal law. The original interpretation of these amendments restricted their protections to the national government. However, more recent interpretations of the due process clause of the Fourteenth Amendment have resulted in similar limitations upon the governments of the states.

The major restraints on government that have been added to the Constitution since the adoption of the Bill of Rights are contained in the Fourteenth Amendment. By limiting the power of the states, this amendment has substantially changed the nature of the federal Union. Current interpretations impose a broad range of restraints and obligations upon the criminal processes of the states and eliminate the power of the states to discriminate on the basis of race. The interpretations of the Supreme Court play an extremely important role in defining the impact of constitutional limitations upon the states.

Federalism and the protections of individual liberty and rights contained in the Constitution often make it more costly to conduct government as vigorously and "efficiently" as might be possible under some alternative set of rules. But Americans have accepted these high "decision-making" costs — just as they have accepted the costs associated with the separation of powers and the system of checks and balances — in return for a vastly more important benefit. That benefit is limited government and, thus far, the absence of tyranny.

NOTES

1. For an excellent discussion of different widely held theories of national-state relationships, see Richard H. Leach, *American Federalism* (New York: Norton, 1969), pp. 1–23.
2. William H. Riker, *Federalism: Origin, Operation, Significance* (Boston: Little, Brown, 1964).
3. See James M. Buchanan and Gordon Tullock, *The Calculus of Consent* (Ann Arbor: University of Michigan Press, 1962), Chapter 8.
4. See, for example, the arguments presented in *Kansas* v. *Colorado,* 206 U.S. 46 (1907).
5. See John R. Schmidhauser, *The Supreme Court as Final Arbiter of Federal-State Relations* (Chapel Hill: University of North Carolina Press, 1958).
6. See *Gibbons* v. *Ogden,* 9 Wheat. 1 (1824).
7. See *Cooley* v. *Board of Wardens,* 12 How. 299 (1851).
8. See note 27, Chapter 3.
9. Ibid.
10. See *Bibb* v. *Navajo Freight Lines,* 359 U.S. 520 (1959); *Dean Milk Co.* v. *Madison,* 340 U.S. 349 (1951); and *Southern Pacific Company* v. *Arizona,* 325 U.S. 761 (1945).
11. See *Robbins* v. *Shelby County Taxing District,* 120 U.S. 489 (1887).
12. See *Hall* v. *DeCuir,* 95 U.S. 485 (1878), and *Plessy* v. *Ferguson,* 163 U.S. 537 (1896). Cf. *Morgan* v. *Virginia,* 328 U.S. 373 (1946), and *Bob-Lo Excursion Company* v. *Michigan,* 333 U.S. 28 (1948).
13. See *United States* v. *Lovett,* 328 U.S. 303 (1946).
14. The most important source of this argument is found in Justice Cardozo's opinion in *Palko* v. *Connecticut,* 302 U.S. 319 (1937).
15. In particular, see *Yates* v. *United States,* 355 U.S. 66 (1957).
16. See *New York Times Company* v. *Sullivan,* 376 U.S. 254 (1964).

17. See *Near* v. *Minnesota,* 283 U.S. 697 (1931).
18. See *Roth* v. *United States,* 354 U.S. 476 (1957), and *Chaplinsky* v. *New Hampshire,* 315 U.S. 568 (1942). The major problem in this area is the very difficult one of determining an adequate definition.
19. See *Everson* v. *Board of Education,* 330 U.S. 1 (1947). Cf. *McCollum* v. *Board of Education,* 333 U.S. 203 (1948).
20. See *Engel* v. *Vitale,* 370 U.S. 421 (1952), and *Abington Township* v. *Schempp,* 374 U.S. 203 (1963).
21. See *Jacobson* v. *Massachusetts,* 197 U.S. 11 (1905), and *Two Guys from Harrison-Allentown* v. *McGinley,* 366 U.S. 582 (1961). Cf. *Sherbert* v. *Verner,* 374 U.S. 398 (1963).
22. See *Murdock* v. *Pennsylvania,* 319 U.S. 105 (1943), and *Kunz* v. *New York,* 340 U.S. 290 (1951).
23. See *United States* v. *Miller,* 307 U.S. 174 (1939).
24. See *Trupiano* v. *United States,* 344 U.S. 699 (1948).
25. See *Katz* v. *United States,* 389 U.S. 347 (1968).
26. See *Mapp* v. *Ohio,* 367 U.S. 643 (1961).
27. *Benton* v. *Maryland,* 395 U.S. 784 (1969).
28. See *Miranda* v. *Arizona,* 384 U.S. 436 (1966).
29. See *Ullmann* v. *United States,* 350 U.S. 422 (1956).
30. See *Gideon* v. *Wainwright,* 372 U.S. 335 (1963).
31. See *Robinson* v. *California,* 370 U.S. 660 (1962).
32. *Furman* v. *Georgia,* 92 S. Ct. 2726 (1972).
33. See *Roe* v. *Wade,* 93 S. Ct. 705 (1973); *Doe* v. *Bolton,* 93 S. Ct. 739 (1973); and *Griswold* v. *Connecticut,* 381 U.S. 479 (1965).
34. Perhaps the most significant example is found in *Hammer* v. *Dagenhart,* 247 U.S. 251 (1918).
35. See *Lochner* v. *New York,* 198 U.S. 45 (1905).
36. See *Slaughterhouse Cases,* 16 Wall. 36 (1873).
37. See *Edwards* v. *California,* 314 U.S. 160 (1941), and *Colgate* v. *Harvey,* 296 U.S. 404 (1935).
38. See *Plessy* v. *Ferguson,* 163 U.S. 537 (1896).
39. See *Brown* v. *Board of Education,* 347 U.S. 483 (1954).

Interpreting the Rules: Judges and the Judicial System

$\mathbf{T}$he effective operation of any democratic society requires a set of known or knowable rules to guide and control the behavior of both policy-makers and citizens along reasonably predictable channels. The Constitution is only one of the more significant sources of the rules provided by the polity and applied and enforced through the coercive processes of the government. Rules are found in constitutional documents, legislative enactments, executive and administrative orders and judicial decisions, and, at the state level, in the common law. The creation of the rules that guide the operation of the polity is the single most significant activity of government. We generally refer to the complete body of these rules as *the law*. The formal rules of the American polity, together with the institutions and processes through which they are established, interpreted, applied, and enforced, constitute the American legal system. The primary goal of any legal system is the achievement of predictability, certainty, and stability in human relationships. Laws are designed to control and pattern the relationships among individuals in a manner that reduces the uncertainty and risk inherent in such interactions. The confidence that governmental agents will enforce private agreements embedded in contracts, for example, when these contracts have been made in accordance with the law, is indispensable for the operation of a developed private enterprise economic system. The body of law in a democratic society is a major public good and it functions to benefit, ideally, all members of the society. Law may also be used, of course, in the pursuit of purely private and divisible advantage.[1] The formation of public policy places collective choices into the body of the law, and the execution of public policy involves the application of aspects of the law to specific individuals and situations in the society. The law and the legal system thus serve as a mechanism for making binding allocations of values among the population.

WHAT IS THE LAW "REALLY"?

This simple description of the nature of law and the legal system evades a number of the historic controversies that have sometimes clouded, confused, and agitated discussions of the concept of law. The public choice approach helps to cut through some of the confusions. On the one hand, there have been frequent arguments that rules not accepted generally or enforced completely or obeyed (such as some laws concerning sex) are not "really" law, even though they are embedded in seemingly legal documents. On the other hand, claims have often been made that rules prescribed by governmental agents are not "really" law because they are in conflict with a "higher" moral law or someone's personal conception of justice or some other virtue. These positions assume a different and more complicated conception of the law from that presented here.

Much confusion results from an inadequate distinction between the law as an actual body of rules, and preferences as to what the rules "should" be. Our view is that any rule from a recognizable governmental source is law as long as it does not conflict with another rule emanating from the same or a superior structure *of the polity*. This formulation represents a modern variant on the Austinian or "**positive**" **law** doctrine that was developed in the nineteenth century.[2] Such a doctrine directs attention to fundamental issues of law and public policy rather than into obscure and discursive channels. The self-interested individual will approach the law with questions like the following:

1. What rules exist in the society at any point in history?

2. What political forces established this particular set of rules?

3. How do these rules affect *my* welfare and interests and values?

4. How could the rules be changed to better achieve values that *I* want to see maximized?

Under this view, rules decreed by governmental agents may be contrary to some conceptions of justice, but they are law nonetheless. Opinions on justice are as varied as the values of individuals in the society.[3] Ideas of justice may stem from religious beliefs, political faiths, socialization processes, or toilet training practices but, in any event, are likely to change with one's understanding of one's own concrete interests. The law, at any given time, represents a visible index of the dominant interests in society. The extent to which the law is considered "just" or "unjust" by politically relevant members of the society determines to a substantial degree the support present for the political system and the vigor with which demands for change in the law will be made.[4] For example, the segregation laws in the South until the early 1960s became the focus of intense discontent and demands for change. These governmentally developed rules for behavior came to be widely seen as unjust and were eventually "found" to be contrary to a superior law of the polity. Much of the law of a society will be considered unjust by people who disagree with those in control of the government and successful in getting their values crystallized into law. The only escape from such dissonance is in a society so homogeneous in values that everyone agrees completely as to what justice requires in all cases. This outcome is not possible outside the confines of the narrow tribal society or the fully developed totalitarian state.[5] Legitimate authority in a democratic society is therefore always somewhat problematical. There are always people negatively affected by some laws — angry, distressed, injured people — who are prepared to pronounce them unjust and, hence, the authority of the government illegitimate.

The political process is, then, from a legal perspective, an ongoing struggle over whose conception of justice will be fixed in the society's formal rules. Public choice refers in good part to the certification of the winners in the struggle. Debates over the requirements of the "higher law" are often simply political tactics.

The status of a law that is generally disobeyed or is seldom or never enforced presents a very different problem but one which is still more related to matters of doctrinal purity than to the actual operation of political systems. All laws are to some extent disobeyed and lack complete and uniform enforcement. The significant social resources allocated to law enforcement agencies and to the courts attest to the fact that laws are not always obeyed. Similarly, the number of uncleared criminal complaints, the undetected and unpunished white-collar crimes, and the continued operation of organized crime indicate that something less than complete enforcement of the law is achieved in contemporary America. Moreover, the law may be administered in a selective, arbitrary, and capricious manner which makes a mockery of the *ideal* of equal justice. For example, many persons have served jail sentences for possession of marijuana when they had believed that the laws were so ignored that they were really not law at all. Such a belief provides little comfort during long months in a prison cell. The greater the deviation from full enforcement of a rule, the greater the degree of potential arbitrary action that is available to law enforcement officials. Arbitrary application of a rule may depart from the achievement of justice but it does not necessarily lead to a violation of the law. The purist argument that a nonenforced law is not law can have one of two absurd conclusions: (1) Either there is no law at all, as no law is completely enforced; or (2) there is some point at which the degree of noncompliance and nonenforcement of legal rules is such that the rules suddenly become non-law.

The major question is not the nitpicking and basically nonpolitical determination of how much disobedience can be present before a law ceases to be law, but finding out which laws are obeyed, by whom, and with what degree of consistency. The causes and consequences of obedience and disobedience, of enforcement and nonenforcement, can be assessed in terms of their implications for the welfare of individuals.

The determination of formal rules is a critical component of the political process. The question of justice may be a central element in the struggle over the appropriate content of the law and may provide, for some, criteria for judging the acceptability of any existent or proposed set of rules or their enforcement. Patterns of disobedience or lax enforcement may indicate the degree to which certain segments of the society find laws to be unjust, avoidable, or unimportant. It must be remembered that enforcing the law is also a political act and is an integral part of public choice.

TYPES OF LAW IN AMERICA

Law: Constitutional, Statutory, Common, Administrative

The legal rules in the United States flow from diverse sources. This diversity has led to the development of a number of ways of categorizing the law that tend to be confusing inasmuch as the terms frequently overlap or are used differently in the same discussion. Some understanding of the categories by which rules are conventionally grouped is needed for the analysis of the operation of the American legal system. The most frequently used classification schemes are based upon the sources of the law and/or the substantive content of the rules. The major categories are: constitutional law, statutory law, common law, and administrative law.

Constitutional law involves the rules that are found in the Constitution and the basic judicial interpretations of this document. In the American system of government, it is the most fundamental type of law, and all other forms of law are subordinate to it. The law of the Constitution, the "supreme law of the land," includes the rules that are specifically stated in the Constitution and the rules that have been found to be implied by it through interpretations of the Supreme Court.[6] Any other rule that is found to be in conflict with a constitutionally based rule is null and void.

Statutory law includes all rules that originate in legislative enactments. In America, these rules result from the lawmaking powers granted to legislative bodies by constitutions. Rules created by the legislature are a part of the supreme law of the land if they are made in "pursuance" to the Constitution. Thus, statutory law must be made in accordance with constitutional rules and must be compatible with the Constitution. The national law has its basis in legislative enactments.

Common law is a body of law that develops directly from judicial decisions.[7] In its purest form, it is simply judge-made law, having no constitutional or statutory base. A very large body of common law flows from state courts in the United States, but technically there is at present no general national common law. The national courts do use common-law techniques, as will be described later, but the substance of the law announced by the courts at the national level has either a statutory or a constitutional base. The common law may be changed through legislation and it must be compatible with the Constitution.

Administrative law is found in orders and rulings that flow from agents within the executive branch of government. These rules result from the decisions of executive and administrative officials as they go about the business of executing and administering the laws that have been provided by the legislature. They are primarily related to the filling-in of the details within broad grants of power made to the executive branch by the Congress. They must be compatible with the legislation upon which they are based as well as the Constitution.

With minor exceptions, each type of law operates in the national government and the states. This dual legal system adds to the scope and complexity of the rules which guide decision-making and behavior in America.

These categories of law provide a rough hierarchy of legal forms in the United States. Constitutional law is the superior law; statutory law assumes a similar position in the legal system if it is compatible with the Constitution. Administrative law and common law are both technically subordinate to constitutional and statutory law.[8] However, the system is complicated by the fact that when courts interpret the provisions of any of these types of law they rely heavily upon the concepts found in the **common-law tradition** in seeking to determine the intention of the legislators or constitution writers. Therefore, even though the common law is subordinate to the other forms of law, its doctrines are used by the courts to guide their interpretation of all forms of law with which they must deal.

Law: Civil and Criminal

The criminal law includes rules whose violation is considered a crime against society punishable by the state through the imposition of penalties. Cases involving the criminal law are always so titled as to indicate this relationship: *The People* v. (versus) *Jones, The State* v. *Jones, Idaho* v. *Jones,* or *The United States* v. *Jones.* The bulk of the criminal law in the United States is found in statutes enacted by the legislative branches of government at the national, state, or local level, but in some jurisdictions there are still common-law crimes that may be punished for violation of judge-made rules. Generally, the criminal law is divided into three categories: felonies, misdemeanors, and petty crimes. They reflect the seriousness of the crime and to some degree the amount of punishment that is possible when a person has been found guilty. Criminal laws provided by the national government are few compared to those of state and local governments.

The civil law is concerned with the violation of a rule of government or any private agreement that the government has obligated itself to support. The wronged party in civil cases is not the society at large but some identifiable person or group within the society. The enforcement mechanisms are designed to vindicate the rights of the injured party. The form of these cases usually symbolizes this private aspect: *Smith* v. *Jones* or *Finance Company* v. *Jones*. The rules of the civil law are meant to reduce conflict and increase predictability in private relationships. The government and its agents also rely upon the civil law for protection against the illegal activities of private parties. A suit by the government against a private person for damages for noncompliance with the terms of a governmental contract, and the refusal to transmit private property to the government to be used for a public purpose when just compensation has been offered are typical examples of cases in which the government might be a party to a civil suit.[9]

Civil law is divided into the elements of law and equity. **Equity** is a form of civil law which grew out of certain historical conditions in England but which maintains great importance in contemporary society. It developed because so many actual or threatened wrongs were incapable of being prevented under the common law. Equity represents an attempt to achieve justice in individual cases. Originally it was very fluid and followed few formal rules. Now it is highly formal, complex, and binding upon judges when deciding cases under their equity jurisdiction. In the United States, all courts have jurisdiction in cases at law and in equity.

Law: Written and Unwritten

One sometimes hears discussions of "written" and "unwritten" law in the United States. All of the types of law that have been described can be characterized as written law, discoverable in documents such as constitutions, statutes, administrative rules, and judicial decrees. Appeals to unwritten laws are typically based on some conception of higher law, on vague interpretations of written rules, or on custom. Perhaps the clearest example of the use of unwritten law in the Anglo-American legal tradition occurred when, in the formative period of English common law, courts frequently looked to custom to guide their decisions. This practice has little significance in the United States today. Custom becomes law only when it has become so recognized by an authoritative governmental agent.

THE COURTS AND THE LEGAL SYSTEM

Although all branches of government participate in making, interpreting, and executing the law, the courts play a particularly critical role in the legal system. The courts, in the final analysis, interpret and apply the law to individuals when a dispute arises. The remainder of this chapter will focus upon their role and function in the American system of government. The primary emphasis is upon describing why courts behave as they do and evaluating the impact of judicial behavior upon the larger governmental and social system.

The main function of courts is to adjudicate disputes over rights, obligations, duties, and requirements of law in particular incidents.[10] This activity is basically one of conflict resolution, in which quarrels and their potentially disruptive consequences are settled or moderated.[11] It is no less a process in which some individuals improve their welfare positions while the welfare of others deteriorates. The courts give binding interpretations of the law which in criminal cases result in the awarding or withholding of punishment and in civil cases answer the important question of "who gets the money." The stylized and formal set of rules governing the American courts gives them a certain mystique. Since these rules reduce the flexibility of the courts and restrict their behavior, decisions can be made only after the rules have been molded into standardized formats.

A critical attribute of American courts is that they generally operate as passive agencies of government.[12] They are restricted to deciding issues brought to them by persons external to the court system — either private persons or other nonjudicial governmental actors. They do not and cannot go out in search of law violators (except in contempt of court cases), civil wrongs, or unconstitutional laws. They can only decide issues that come before them in the context of a properly formulated dispute involving the question of how a particular law should be applied to a specific case. Illegal behavior, destruction of fundamental rights, and un-constitutional enforcement of the law may go forward unabated while the courts remain powerless to act until someone brings these matters to them in the context of a dispute between two or more persons with a real interest in the outcome of a case. The parties must present competing arguments of the requirements of the law as it applies to them. This state of affairs is an outgrowth of the doctrine of separation of powers, constitutional allocations of powers, and a commitment to the adversary proceeding — wherein there is always a prosecution and a defense — which is a central component of Anglo-American law.[13]

The adversary proceeding leaves its imprint upon American law in other ways as well. It developed from the ancient practices that marked the trials by ordeal and combat in the formative period of Anglo-Saxon law. The basic presumption was that the "truth" would emerge from the conflict between a person and the elements or between two persons. These rituals had a strong religious component in that God would supposedly decide the truth of the matter by protecting the innocent individual or by strengthening the person's right arm if need be. In modern court battles the truth is expected to emerge if each party puts forward those arguments that present the individual's side in the best possible light. Then the judicial actors, the judge and jury, decide which side has won the struggle and make sure that the rules of the combat are followed by both parties.

The nature of adversary proceedings underlies much of the misunderstanding concerning the attorney's role in American courts. The lawyer is expected only to put forward the client's case in the best manner possible and is not responsible for finding the truth. If that is anyone's function, it is the court's. A truth-seeking lawyer is actually usurping the judicial role.[14] The skeptic might argue that the truth is more likely to be on the side of the party who has the more competent lawyer. This state of affairs is a major stimulus for guaranteeing the right of (competent) counsel to poor persons as a means of equalizing the chances that truth, virtue, and the law will at least sometimes be on the side of the economically disadvantaged.

The courtroom wraps the stylized ritual of the trial in the trappings of dignity and evokes the aura of a religious ceremony. The judge is seated on a high bench, clothed in black robes, and by manner and authority demands the attention and deference of all those present. How different from the conduct of business in other public places! Exalted authority projected by the courts plays a critical role in one of their more dramatic functions, which is to *particularize* the law. The court decides whether X shall go to jail, or whether Y shall lose his property, or (more ambiguously as this is written) whether Z's life shall be taken away.[15] If these judgments were viewed as handed down by mere mortals or, even worse, by political hacks, they might be intolerable to defendants or plaintiffs, their supporters, and the society. A tough-minded recognition of the political role of the courts has much to commend it as a means of understanding the law, but the judgments of the court become more acceptable in the context of ritual, judicial dignity, and the internalization of the myth that nonpolitical judges simply render the judgment required by the law.[16] There is a very great difference between the abstract legislative judgment that any person who takes the life of another with malice may be put to death and the concrete judicial decision that John T. Jones shall be hanged by the neck until he is dead on September 12, 1978.

For such reasons, the myth that judges are "above politics" and make their decisions not on the basis of personal interest or preference but en-

"I feel I give them their thirty-two thousand five hundred dollars' worth of justice every year."
Drawing by D. Fradon; © 1975 The New Yorker Magazine, Inc.

tirely as required by law is one of the mechanisms through which the decisions of the court are made legitimate and acceptable. Similarly, it is a major foundation for the maintenance of an independent judiciary. This myth demands the attendant fiction — present in most official explanations of the role of judges and the courts — often summarized in "This is a government of laws and not of men."[17] The official theory is that judges do not make but merely discover the law that is applicable to the case at hand.[18] The basic argument is that, if only it can be found, some preexistent rule can properly resolve the dispute before the court. The judge who decides the case never creates the rule he applies.[19] The frequent searches by judges for the "intentions" of the framers of a constitution or a statute are examples of this view. The argument, although not always descriptive of the actual behavior of judges, is useful in making the judgments of courts acceptable, legitimate, and enforceable.

JUDICIAL REVIEW

Judges are not limited to determining how a given law should be applied to a particular case; they must often decide which of two laws that are in conflict should be followed. The doctrine of **judicial review** allows judges to hold that a law is null and void if it is found to be in conflict with the Constitution. A judge must decide between rules when opposing rules are applicable to a case presented for decision. On the one hand, there may be a statute that governs the case and, on the other hand, a constitutional rule demanding a contrary outcome. In such event, the judge must support one of the mutually exclusive rules. Since the Constitution is the "supreme law of the land" and takes precedence over inferior rules, the judge has no viable choice but must support the Constitution, which every judge has sworn to obey and defend. The statute *must* be found null and void and thereby unenforceable. This is, in brief, the basic argument for the necessity of judicial review developed in 1803 by Chief Justice Marshall in the famous case of *Marbury* v. *Madison*.[20] It is widely accepted as the justification for the power of judicial review in the United States.

Judicial review is among the most unusual and important political rules developed in the United States. The Constitution does not specifically grant this power to the Supreme Court or to any other court. However, in the *Marbury* case the Supreme Court successfully claimed it, and, at least by usage, it has become deeply embedded in the American way of governing. The logic followed by Marshall was much like that described above and was based upon his interpretation of the nature of a written Constitution. He did not indicate that both the statute and the Constitution were subject to judicial interpretation *before* a conflict between the two became obvious. The power of judicial review has been extended through time to include the power of *all courts* in the United States to hold any legislative or executive action null and void if it is in conflict with what the judges believe the Constitution requires.[21]

The courts, then, are extraordinarily important institutions. They have to give final interpretations to the laws, whether they originate in legislative, executive, judicial, or constitutional sources. They decide how the dictates of a law fit into a specific situation and they determine exactly the obligations of the parties in a dispute involving the application of a legal rule. The power to interpret the law becomes most significant when there is conflict between two sets of rules. The exercise of this power places the judges in a position to block the actions of the other branches of government when they are found to be in conflict with a constitutional precept. Conversely, a finding by the Supreme Court that a

Table 5-1. Congressional Actions Declared Unconstitutional by U.S. Supreme Court (by decades).

Period	Number[*]	Chief Justice(s)
1789–1799	0	Jay, Rutledge, Ellsworth
1800–1809	1	Marshall
1810–1819	0	Marshall
1820–1829	0	Marshall
1830–1839	0	Marshall, Taney
1840–1849	0	Taney
1850–1859	1	Taney
1860–1869	4	Taney, Chase
1870–1879	10	Chase, Waite
1880–1889	4	Waite, Fuller
1890–1899	5	Fuller
1900–1909	8	Fuller
1910–1919	7	White
1920–1929	16	White, Taft
1930–1939	17	Hughes
1940–1949	2	Hughes, Stone, Vinson
1950–1959	4	Vinson, Warren
1960–1969	13	Warren
1970–1974	2	Burger

[*]Compiled from information presented in *Guide to the Congress of the United States* (Washington: Congressional Quarterly Service, 1971), pp. 311a–316a.

controversial statute is compatible with the Constitution broadens the social acceptance and enforceability of a statute.[22] The powers of the Court place judges in a strategic position in the public policy process in the United States, a position not shared by courts in any other country in the world. The only nations that have developed the power of judicial review have used the United States as a model, and nowhere is the power of judicial review so broad as it is here.

THE ORGANIZATION OF COURTS IN AMERICA

Like other governmental institutions, the courts reflect the federal structure of the polity. Each state has an independent system of courts, and there is a set of national courts. The courts in these fifty-one separate jurisdictions are loosely organized into the American judicial system. Although our primary concern is with the national courts, even a minimal understanding of the American legal system requires a brief description of the structure of the state courts and their relationship to the national court system.

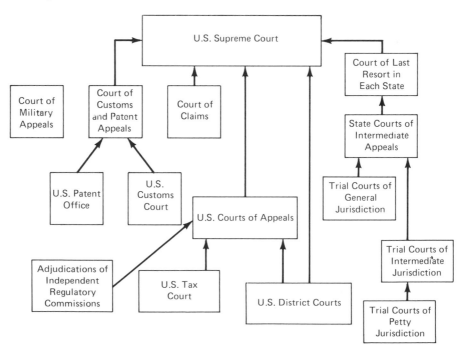

Figure 5-1. Organization of the American Judicial System.

State Courts

The organization of state courts has a large number of variations. Consequently, the present discussion refers only to some common features of these systems and does not attempt to depict any single state structure completely.[23] The base of a state system is its trial courts. Trials are started in these courts, and, as courts of original jurisdiction, they frequently make use of the jury. All state cases originate in a trial court. A typical state has at least three sets of trial courts.[24]

There are also courts of petty jurisdiction in all states. Relatively minor cases (traffic violations, small claims, disturbing the peace) are processed through these courts, which ordinarily operate with rather informal rules and practices. Examples of courts of petty jurisdiction are the municipal court, the police court, the justice of the peace courts, the corporation courts, and small claims court. The criminal cases tried here involve minor offenses in which fines and/or short jail terms can be levied. The civil cases involve small sums of money. The main feature of these courts is that they resolve a large number of conflicts quickly, simply, and inexpensively. They are generally not courts of record; that is, no formal record of their proceedings is established, and if an appeal is taken to another court the case must begin anew.

Many states have a set of courts of intermediate jurisdiction. They hear cases in which the controversy is more serious than in those tried in the courts of petty jurisdiction. There are also upper limits provided by law as to the penalties that can be awarded and the value of civil suits that can be heard at this level. Jurisdiction in criminal cases here tends to follow the definition of misdemeanors in that jurisdiction. Frequently, the largest penalty that can be given is a year in jail. The county court is the most frequently used title of these courts. Cases are processed with much greater formality than in the courts of petty jurisdiction. Indeed, these courts function very much like the courts of general jurisdiction (see below), and they are usually courts of record.

All states have at least one set of trial courts that are courts of general jurisdiction. They hear major felony cases and any civil cases that involve substantial amounts of property or money. They operate with great formality, a jury is frequently impaneled, and major cases having to do with questions of state law are tried in these courts in the first instance. They are often designated as district courts or superior courts.

The state trial courts are an extremely important component of the judicial system. Most legal disputes are first heard in these courts, and most of the decisions reached are final, as the losing party chooses not to appeal to a higher court. The bulk of the law that impinges upon the average individual on a day-to-day basis is state law as interpreted and applied by trial courts. The probabilities are high that if one ever appears in court on a major issue it will be in a state trial court.

All states provide at least one level of appeals courts, primarily designed to determine whether the trial courts have correctly interpreted the law and whether the trial was conducted under the proper procedures. These courts will only review cases that are brought to them by the party who lost in the original trial and they generally limit their consideration to issues raised by the two parties. They do not reconsider the facts of the case but restrict their review to legal issues raised in the original trial. All cases can be appealed to at least one court of appeals.[25] Some states have intermediate appeals courts to remove some of the burden from the court of last resort in the state. They may consist of panels of judges who hear cases drawn from throughout the state, or they may be divided among geographic regions of the state. While trial courts are normally presided over by a single judge, courts of appeal are almost always multimember courts.

All states provide some court of last resort for cases arising under state law. The Supreme Court is the most common title given to the judicial body that has final power to review interpretations of state law. This court provides a means of developing uniform interpretations of the state laws to guide the activities of the lower courts of the state. It performs the same general functions for the government of the state as are carried out by the Supreme Court of the United States in the national government.

Federal Courts

The structure of the national court system flows from a simple grant of power in Article III of the Constitution: "The judicial power of the United States, shall be vested in one Supreme Court, and in such inferior courts as the Congress may from time to time ordain and establish." Thus, the Supreme Court is the only national court specifically provided for in the Constitution. The remainder of the national court system has developed out of congressional legislation and could be abolished in a similar manner.

The present national court system has three levels of regular courts of general jurisdiction and a number of special courts of limited or specialized jurisdiction. At its base are the district courts — the trial courts of the national system — of which there are ninety-three distributed over the United States and its territories. About 300 judges serve in these courts. The district court is presided over by a single judge and is the only national court that makes use of the jury. It hears most cases in which the federal courts have jurisdiction in the first instance.

The district courts hear both criminal and civil cases. They have jurisdiction in cases involving the application of federal law and in cases in which the court has jurisdiction because of diversity of citizenship between the parties. Diversity of citizenship means that the parties are citizens of different states. Currently, Congress has limited this part of district court jurisdiction to cases in which $10,000 or more is involved in the controversy, and the court must apply the law of the state in which the incident occurred as interpreted by the highest state court. There is at least one district court in each state, and the districts do not cross state lines. Most cases that arise in the national court system originate in the district courts and relatively few of them are appealed to any other court.

In 1895 Congress established a set of intermediate courts of appeal. There are eleven courts of appeals, having jurisdiction over specific regions of the United States and the District of Columbia. Some ninety-five judges serve on these courts at the present time. Cases are normally heard by panels of three judges, but in certain very important cases all of the judges assigned to the court may hear a case *en banc* so that as many as nine judges may be sitting on a case.

Courts of appeal were designed to guarantee that all persons whose cases were decided by the lower federal courts could have at least one appeal and were expected to reduce the burden being placed upon the Supreme Court. The courts of appeal also play a vital role in supervising the adjudication activities of the independent regulatory commissions that have been given quasi-judicial functions. When disputes are adjudicated by the National Labor Relations Board or the Federal Trade Commission, for instance, there may be direct appeal from the decision to the courts of appeals. Decisions of these courts may be appealed to the Supreme Court of the United States.

The Supreme Court stands at the apex of the judicial system. It is currently made up of a chief justice and eight associate justices. The number of justices is determined by Congress. Its size has been changed a number of times, but there have been nine members of the Supreme Court since 1868. Although cases may come to the Court on either original or appellate jurisdiction, virtually all of its work at present is appellate. The Constitution provides that the Supreme Court shall have original jurisdiction in "all cases affecting ambassadors, other public ministers and consuls, and those in which a State shall be party." However, Congress has given the district courts concurrent jurisdiction over most of these cases, and the original jurisdiction of the Supreme Court is seldom activated.

The Supreme Court gives final interpretation to the requirements of the Constitution and to statutes enacted by the Congress. Its interpretation of constitutional provisions cannot be changed except by the Court itself. The Constitution must be amended to bring about a different rule. But Congress does, of course, have the power to modify interpretations that the Court has given to statutes.

Cases come to the Supreme Court from the district courts, the courts of appeals, state supreme courts, and certain special national courts. There are two primary means of activating the processes of the Supreme Court: the **writ of appeal** and the **writ of certiorari.** Cases come to the Supreme Court on writ of appeal when the power of judicial review has been used in the lower court. The Supreme Court is technically required to hear all such cases but it frequently dismisses these appeals because they "lack a substantial federal question." All other cases come to the Court on a writ of certiorari, and it has total discretion in choosing which ones it will hear.[26] The justices do not have to give any reason for refusing to grant certiorari in a case, and no legal inferences can be drawn from such a denial. The general rule is that certiorari will be granted if a case involves a question of great national significance or if there is conflict between the interpretations given to a single law in the different courts of appeals. The justices are the sole judges of when these conditions have been met. Under current rules, a case is called up for formal consideration if four justices believe that it should be heard. By determining which cases appealed to them they will hear, the justices control the flow of cases to the Court. The role of the Supreme Court is not to do justice in all cases but, as we have said, to clarify formal rules for the society. Attaining uniformity in the interpretation of constitutional provisions and statutes throughout the judicial system serves that end.

Congress has developed a number of courts of limited jurisdiction that should be mentioned in passing. The Court of Customs and Patent Appeals is a specialized appellate court that hears appeals from the U.S. Customs Court and the U.S. Patent Office. The Court of Claims hears cases involving claims for damages against the government of the United States. The adjudications of these courts are subject to review by the Supreme Court.

There is one specialized segment of the judicial system that is technically quite independent of the regular court system. This is the structure of military trials. It is under a civilian Court of Military Appeals and, while the law does not allow any appeals beyond this court, legal practice is such as to provide appeals in certain cases.

In summary, the judicial system of the United States consists of a variety of structures. The Supreme Court stands at the apex with the power to provide at least some coordination of their activities. Its power can be used to bring about uniformity in the interpretation and application of national laws. The Supreme Court provides the only linkage between the state and national court systems and this linkage can be used only after the highest state court that has authority to act in a case has given its decision — and only then if the decision was based upon the interpretation of a national statute or constitutional provision.[27] The state courts are supreme in the interpretation and application of state laws, and the national courts cannot intervene unless an issue of national law is involved in the case.

THE SELECTION OF
JUDICIAL ACTORS

Courts make significant choices that determine the allocation of rewards and deprivations in the society. The judicial system operates in the context of a complex set of highly developed rules, but in the final analysis individuals, not rules, make decisions and choices. Although the official explanation of the operation of courts would indicate the contrary, it does make a great deal of difference *who* performs the act of judicial judgment. The values, preferences, and identifications of judicial actors influence the patterns of allocations that flow from the judicial structures. The means used to select the people who will serve in these vital roles influence to some extent what kinds of people will serve and hence what kinds of decisions are likely to be reached.

The two primary sets of decision-makers within the judicial system are judges and jurors.

Jury Selection

The right to trial by a jury of one's peers is a fundamental right in Anglo-American law.[28] It is operative in both criminal and civil cases. It may be waived but cannot be denied. A critical problem is deciding who one's "peers" are. This question has created a good deal of controversy in recent years. A number of contentions have been made that would redefine the traditional concept of the requirements of a representative jury. Many young people assert that no jury of middle-aged Americans can legitimately be defined as the "peers" of a person under twenty-five, particularly one who is charged with the violation of a law (say, involving drugs) that is rejected by a youthful bohemian subculture. Similarly, there have been claims that blacks can properly be tried only by other blacks, that Chicanos can fairly be tried only by other Chicanos, and women only by other women.

The courts have not accepted these particularistic criteria and maintain that a jury of one's peers is simply a jury composed of persons drawn by some randomized process from the entire community. The general rule is that some quite inclusive list of the residents of the jurisdiction must be created and that the jury list must be drawn randomly from it. Most lists are now drawn from voter registration rolls, and they are often supplemented by names drawn from city directories and other available lists of the adult members of the community.

The guarantee of a representative jury comes to this: that no identifiable group will be purposely excluded from the jury list. The finding of bias has been most frequently related to race, ethnic origin, sex, and economic position. There is no guarantee that a jury will be made up of persons who share some relevant characteristic with the defendant, although such persons cannot purposely be excluded from the jury list. The one exception to this rule is that juveniles may be excluded from juries even when a young person is on trial.

Selection of Judges

Many processes for the selection of judges are used in the states.[29] Some follow the national pattern and allow the chief executive of the state to appoint judges with legislative ratification. In others, judges are elected. A growing form of selection is a combination of appointment and election in which a nonpartisan commission submits nominees to the governor, who actually appoints the judge. After a time the judge's name is placed on the ballot and the voters decide whether the incumbent should be retained. This, the "Missouri Plan," represents another example of the often pursued goal of "removing judges from politics." Under all plans the bar association plays a critical role, and interest groups that want to influence judicial decisions are active in the actual selection process.[30] The general goal of removing judges from politics is not likely to be achieved as long as judges make decisions that have a substantial impact upon the allocation of values in society.

The formal process of selecting judges for the regular national courts is quite simple. They are appointed by the president with the advice and consent of the Senate. Their term of office is "during good behavior." That is, their appointment is for life unless they are removed from office by the impeachment process. No Supreme Court judges have actually been removed by this process, and only a handful of lower court justices have been impeached and convicted. Lifelong tenure has led to fairly long periods of service for many federal judges; it is not unusual for a Supreme Court justice to serve twenty or thirty years on the Court. Thus, when choosing a person for this position, the president may shape the orientation of the court for many years into the future. The Court has been criticized frequently for being burdened with superannuated judges. All attempts to establish a mandatory retirement age have failed, however, and the development of rules to allow retirement with substantial benefits has not led to early retirement by many Supreme Court justices.[31]

District court judges are appointed by the president upon the recommendation of the senior senator of the president's party from the state in which a vacancy develops. *Michael Meadows/from Editorial Photocolor Archives*

While there are no constitutional qualifications for judges, certain practices seriously lessen the options available to an appointing president. In the selection of district court judges, it is the senior senator of the president's party from the state in which a vacancy develops who actually chooses the person who will be nominated by the president. This custom has developed through usage and is supported by the rule of senatorial courtesy.[32] If there is no senator of the president's political party from the state, the local party organization normally makes nominations to the president to fill a vacancy. Thus federal judgeships are most frequently awarded to persons who have been loyal to the party and active in it. However, it cannot be inferred that the appointees are typically not qualified to hold the position. The quality of federal judges is ordinarily high by any standards.

Appointments to positions on the courts of appeals are more directly controlled by the president. The pattern followed is very much like the process for the naming of a person to the Supreme Court, except the range of interests that come into play tends to be somewhat narrower. Therefore, the following discussion of the selection of Supreme Court justices is in general applicable to the filling of courts of appeals judgeships.

Selection of Supreme Court Justices

How a vacancy on the Supreme Court is filled varies somewhat from time to time and with the proclivities of the incumbent president. However, a number of stable patterns and recurring issues do exist.[33] When a vacancy occurs or is expected, names of potential nominees are submitted to the president from senators, party leaders, interest group leaders, and other concerned parties. The names are screened by the Justice Department. Republican presidents have become accustomed to submitting names to the American Bar Association for review of the judicial qualifications of potential nominees, although this practice may soon fall into disuse. The president finally chooses a name to submit to the Senate for confirmation. Until President Nixon's difficulties in getting two nominees (Haynesworth and Carswell) accepted, the Senate tended in recent years to accept presidential nominations. Historically, however, nearly one-fourth of all persons proposed to the Senate have been rejected.

This description of the major steps in the appointment process does not reveal the political struggle that goes forward both openly and behind the scenes.[34] The struggle is particularly intense when political alignments have formed in the country concerning the public choices made by the current Court. The fight over Supreme Court appointments at the end of the Johnson administration and at the beginning of the Nixon administration is a good example. Conservatives were able to block the nomination of Justice Fortas to become chief justice, and their questioning of his probity finally drove him from the bench. Similarly, President Nixon undertook to change the orientation of the Court when there was a substantial group of liberal senators committed to blocking such efforts. Two of his nominees to the Court were rejected. However, President Nixon was able in the end to secure the ratification of persons who, on the basis of their early decisions, generally (but with important exceptions) accepted his view of the proper direction in which the Court should move. This final success emphasizes one of the most significant points that can be made about the Supreme Court: Its decisions tend to follow the election returns. When the mood of the country changes, new appointments to the Court are likely to reflect the new mood, although the justices' long tenure may produce a considerable lag between changes in public opinion and changes in judicial decisions.

A number of political factors come into play in the process of judicial selections and they impinge upon both the president and the Senate.[35] The critical variables are party, ideology, geography, and constituency. Some combination of these factors is always important in the appointment process. Although competence is the most frequently discussed variable, it is often a euphemism for the *correct* combination of factors.

Presidents quite consistently choose members of their own political party for judicial appointments, not only to have members who share the president's ideology but to reward people who have been helpful in the president's political career. When presidents deviate from this normal pattern, it is frequently either to broaden their personal following or to extend the constituency of the party of the president.

Table 5-2. Political Party Membership of Judges Appointed by Recent Presidents.

	Democrats	Republicans
Roosevelt	188	6
Truman	116	9
Eisenhower	9	165
Kennedy	111	11
Nixon (1969–1970)	3	86

Source: Guide to the Congress of the United States (Washington: Congressional Quarterly Service, 1971), p. 237.

The political and legal philosophy of the nominee is a major factor in the selection process. Presidents tend to name persons to the Court who share their orientations toward the proper direction of public policy and judicial decision-making. This action is particularly likely when the Court has become a center of public controversy. The appointments of President Roosevelt in the late 1930s and of President Nixon are cases in point. Sectionalism is a source of demands for the appointment of certain persons, and there is generally a vague attempt to maintain a geographic balance on the Court. Acquiescence in such demands may allow the president to develop a broadened political following, as, for instance, in President Nixon's attempt to get a southerner named to the Court. The geographic factor is frequently subordinated, however, to other factors, such as ideology, but remains an aspect of the selection process.

In this century, characteristics such as race, religion, ethnic background, and sex have become increasingly relevant to judicial selection. Minority groups demand "representation" on the Supreme Court. There was long a "Jewish seat" on the Court, although President Nixon may have rejected this tradition, perhaps because of the relatively low level of support the Republican party receives from the Jewish community. Similarly, the Court usually has at least one Catholic jurist. President Truman ignored this tradition when Justice Murphy left the Court, but it was seemingly reestablished by President Eisenhower with the appointment of Justice Brennan. With the appointment of Justice Marshall, President Johnson may well have instituted a more or less permanent allocation of a seat to a black American. A current issue is whether a "woman's seat" should be established. Senator George McGovern as a presidential candidate in 1972 promised that, if elected, he would fill the first vacancy on the Court with a woman. All of the seats for minority members exist only by tradition and any president may reject it. However, the repudiation of so established a tradition may be looked upon by the group involved as an affront and may result in the loss of political support for the president.

The consideration of nominees to the Supreme Court by the Senate revolves around the same kinds of issues as those taken into account by the president. The most important basis for the rejection of a nominee is the expected voting behavior of the potential justice. The debates in the Judiciary Committee and on the floor of the Senate often reflect an intense interest in the ideological commitments of the nominee and an implicit concern with how the person will vote on critical issues if he takes a seat on the high bench. Senators do usually give at least lip service to the concept of a nonpolitical court by referring in their criticism to such ambiguous terms as judicial temperament and competence. In general, when lack of judicial temperament, experience, or competence is alleged, the real issue is that senators do not believe the nominee's political and legal philosophy will lead to votes on the Court that are personally acceptable to them.

The point is that judges are influenced to some extent by their backgrounds and attitudes and that these factors are taken into account by people who participate in the selection of judges. Knowledge of this fact is shared by presidents, senators, other politicians, journalists, and interest group leaders. The following description of the decision-making activities of judges will attempt to clarify the nature and the extent of the influence of these factors on judicial decision-making.

THE JUDICIAL PROCESS
IN AMERICA

The courts in the United States are passive bodies that operate under a highly structured set of formal rules. According to these rules, issues brought before the courts must be focused narrowly before the processes of the courts can be activated. Since the nature of the adversary process severely limits a court's fact-finding ability, courts become captives of the factual and legal arguments brought forward by the two parties to a case. Certain techniques have been developed to guarantee that the issues presented have been identified and narrowed before trials can begin. The simplest is found in criminal cases, in which quite specific charges are made in an indictment or an information. These must be answered in a plea by the defendant. Then the issues are joined, and the precise dispute to be resolved becomes clear. The defendant may admit to the facts as presented but argue that the law does not define such actions as a crime; or the defendant may deny the facts as they are presented, accepting that, if they are true, then a crime has been committed; or both the factual and legal allegations may be denied. The jury decides disputes concerning the factual allegations, and the judge decides disputes concerning the law. If the trial goes forward without a jury, the judge performs both roles. Civil cases involve a similar but even more complicated sharpening of the issues before the trial can begin.[36]

Access to the Judicial Process

A large number of general rules have been developed to control access to the courts and to assure that only properly formulated cases will enter the judicial process. The most important of these "entrance norms" require that the case be taken to a court having jurisdiction over the issue in question; that the person bringing the action show that an injury either has taken place or is threatened; that a real conflict of interest exist between the parties; and that a remedy available to the court be requested.

The complex rules controlling access to the courts and the processing of cases make it virtually impossible for the average citizen to use the judicial system effectively without professional assistance. Lawyers, whose profession it is to know and manipulate the rules, are important in getting access by citizens to the courts. Consequently, under present doctrines every person charged with a crime which may be punished by even a short jail sentence is guaranteed the right to legal counsel.[37] If the individual lacks sufficient financial resources to retain a lawyer, the government is required to provide one. There is no similar guarantee in civil cases, but some attempt has been made to provide lawyers to economically disadvantaged persons involved in civil cases.

Rules Governing Access to the Supreme Court

1. One must have "standing" — that is, be seriously impinged on by some state action.

2. If one has taken advantage of a law, he or she may not then challenge its constitutionality.

3. One must have exhausted all lower federal and state court remedies.

4. A federal question must be involved; it must be substantial, not trivial, and it must be part of the plaintiff's case.

5. For the most part, a question of law, not fact, must be posed.

6. "Political questions," or those the Court decides are properly matters for other branches of government, will not be heard. (The apportionment of state legislatures, for example, was long considered a "political" matter.)

Rules Governing the Court's Disposition of Cases

1. Precedent can be overturned — but never lightly.

2. Presumption of constitutionality is always in favor of the statute involved.

3. If a case can be decided on statutory grounds and without reference to the Constitution, it will be.

4. If a law is found to be unconstitutional, the Court will limit its judgment to that portion of the statute involved, and will not consider the statute as a whole.

5. The Court will not formally dispose of a questioned statute or executive action on the basis of its wisdom, impartiality, or degree of democratization. There is no constitutional requirement that a law be wise or popular.

Interest Groups and the Judicial Process

The importance of legal representation in the judicial process has long been recognized by interest groups, which have used the courts as a primary means of achieving their goals. A historically important example of such activities was the development of an effective legal staff by the National Association for the Advancement of Colored People as it pursued its interests in the courts during and prior to the great civil rights campaigns of the 1950s and 1960s.[38] Several techniques exist for maximizing group benefits through litigation. Having made the tactical decision to enter the judicial arena, the group leaders find, through legal counsel, persons considered to be injured by the operation of a law the group believes to be unconstitutional and develop a case to test the validity of that law. Often such a case is presented as a **class action**; that is, the plaintiffs request vindication of the rights not only of themselves as the primary litigants but also of all persons who are "similarly situated." The interest group may furnish legal counsel to carry the case through the trial court and all necessary appeals. It may file **amicus curiae** briefs (as a "friend of the court") arguing the case for overturning the law from a perspective other than that presented by the primary litigants.

By presumption, the decision to enter the judicial system in pursuit of a group's interest is made to use its scarce resources efficiently in maximizing gains and minimizing costs. Civil rights groups, and the NAACP most importantly, concluded by the early 1950s that to win gains in the civil rights field from the Congress and the president was either not possible or possible only marginally and at great costs. In the Supreme Court's great 1954 school desegregation decision in *Brown* v. *Board of Education*[39] the NAACP's tactics were seen to be well chosen.

It must be said here that government is not merely a referee or an idle bystander in group struggle through the judiciary. Government at all levels maintains skilled lawyers to activate the judicial process in the name of the government and to protect governmental interests that may be involved in cases prepared by private parties and interest groups.

There are two types of outcomes in any case decided by a court. (1) The dispute between the actual parties to the suit is resolved, and (2) a rule is formulated to justify the decision, which rule may be used by the courts in a future case involving the same issues. The second outcome is normally of greater interest to the political scientist, whose concern is more with the bindingness of rules generally and less with the effect of a rule upon two or a limited number of individuals. Under the rule of **stare decisis** (rule by precedent), every decision reached by a court establishes a precedent which should be used in the decision of all similar cases. This is one means of guaranteeing that people in similar situations will be treated the same way by the courts and that equality before the law will be preserved. Thus, the decision of a court has an impact on the legal system far beyond the settling of the case. When interest groups engage in litigation, they are frequently much more concerned with the development of a particular rule than with winning the actual case. For example, the NAACP was far more interested in the rule developed in the case of *Brown* v. *Board of Education,* which held that segregation in the public schools was a violation of the equal protection clause of the Fourteenth Amendment, than in whether the Brown children would be admitted to the white schools of Topeka, Kansas. These two types of outcomes have quite different impacts upon the political system and the society.

Influences in Supreme Court Decision-Making

The most far-reaching of judicial decisions are those reached by the Supreme Court of the United States. The influence of its decisions radiates throughout the judicial system and beyond to the entire society. A critical problem in analyzing the judicial process concerns the determinants of the decisions. The following discussion of factors that shape judicial decision-making focuses on the Supreme Court. However, it is applicable in large extent to the decision-making behavior of other American judges as well.

The official explanation of decision-making in the Supreme Court holds that the Court simply mirrors the dictates of the law. The justices are considered "above politics" and responsive to the law and to no other consideration in the disposition of cases. While this explanation does maximize the legitimacy of the Court's decisions — by emphasizing its objectivity, disinterestedness, universalism — it is not very accurate. We have noted that, in the selection of judges, their personal characteristics are important. When a new Supreme Court justice is appointed, the media commentators are lavish in their predictions of how the new judge will behave on the Court. However, the predictions are frequently wrong. Judges are often capable of learning and, in many instances, have succeeded in concealing their true views from others until a particular question or convenient situation makes it opportune to reveal their preferences. Presidents have been wrong in their expectations of persons they have appointed. Such errors are generally based upon an altogether too simple conception of the factors which influence judicial choice. Preferences, beliefs, identifications, and evaluations of the justice must be taken into account in any explanation of his or her decision-making. The four most significant dimensions are (1) personal interests, (2) political and social philosophy, (3) conception of the proper role of the judiciary in the American system of government, and (4) commitment to the legal rules that have developed in Anglo-American law. Judges vary along all of these dimensions, and their individual voting behavior is determined by a combination of these factors as they interact with the facts of the cases that come before them.

The ideology or social and political philosophy of justices is the most frequently discussed factor in judicial decision-making. It has long been a favorite practice of scholars and journalists to label incumbent or potential justices as either "liberals," or "conservatives."[40] The argument is that voting behavior is determined by the social values the judge holds. One popular technique for determining the "proper" label is to analyze the statements made by the justice — speeches made, books and articles written, opinions written as a judge — to identify his or her political philosophy.[41] Judicial biographers often approach their subjects this way. A second method is to analyze the "social background" (e.g., class, race, religion, ethnicity, and work history) and to project the justice's voting behavior from the kind of values a person with this background can be expected to have internalized. Such a connection is tenuous at best. Finally, analysts have used a justice's voting record on the Court as a means of placing the judge along a liberal-conservative continuum. It is then presumably demonstrated that a consistent pattern of voting for a liberal or conservative outcome, as defined by the analyst, is simply an extension of the justice's ideology.[42]

Ignoring here the logical and methodological differences among these various formulations, we see that the several arguments have much in common: The voting behavior of the justice is thought to be determined by a personal political philosophy. Definitions of **liberalism** and **conservatism** in the literature have much the same general thrust and can be characterized in a general way. According to these definitions a "**liberal**" justice votes against the interests of business and industry; for the demands of organized labor and the worker; for the interests of disadvantaged minorities, particularly in civil rights cases; in favor of a broad interpretation of the right to freedom of speech; for a rigid separation of church and state; and for a broad construction of the protection of the criminal defendant. The "**conservative**" justice votes in a contrary pattern. Deviations from these polar opposites are caused by varying degrees of commitment to liberal or conservative values. Thus the justices of the Supreme Court can be arrayed along a continuum from most liberal to most conservative.

Now there can be little doubt that political philosophy, social values adhered to, interests of groups identified with, and interpretation of goodness and badness affect — directly or indirectly — the way a justice reads the requirements of the law. However, this is quite different from the argument that there is a simple and mechanical connection between ideology and voting behavior. The gross generalizations derived from that argument must be tempered considerably if the choices of judges in the American polity are to be understood.

Among other things not always related to political values and philosophy, a justice's evaluation of the proper role of judges and the courts in the system of government has a significant impact upon his decision-making behavior. The most frequently used concepts to characterize this aspect of judicial conduct are "**activism**" and "**self-restraint**."[43] These terms refer to how active a role the Court takes in government and under what conditions a justice is willing to review and modify the decisions made by other agents of government. The activist believes that the Court has an obligation to do justice in individual cases. To achieve this goal, the activist is quite ready to overturn the decisions of the Congress, the president, independent regulatory agencies, or the agents of state government. The activist thinks it appropriate to use the power of judicial review to guarantee that the other officials of government perform their functions in a "proper" manner. An activist judge defines the powers and responsibilities of the judiciary broadly. For example, a general activist orientation tended to dominate the work of the Warren Court as it assumed an innovative role in the American polity. A more cautious approach characterized the early Burger Court.

The activist justice is more likely to impose personal political values upon the society through judicial decision-making than is the justice who believes that the primary role of the Court is to apply the law passed by the representative branches of government. Supporters of self-restraint argue that the elected representatives in a democratic society have the main responsibility for lawmaking and that the Court should restrict that activity only where the Constitution has been violated.[44] They prefer a limited role for the Court in a system of limited government and have charged their activist colleagues with engaging in "judicial legislation."

It is important to understand that if a justice takes a consistently restrained position, the resulting voting record may support *either* liberal or conservative outcomes inasmuch as the ideological component of a decision is not dependent upon the values of the justice but upon those that prevail in the elected branches of government. For this reason, the justice's decision-making behavior and assessment of the proper role of courts and judges are interrelated. The relative weight given to the support of social values and the conception of judicial role varies greatly among justices, but all are aware of the implications of both of these factors as they approach their work.

The discussion of the influences of social values and conception of judicial role makes the obvious point that courts are political bodies which make real public choices. This idea was long ignored by students of the Court. But courts are also legal bodies applying legal rules to factual situations that are brought before them for resolution. The extent to which particular judges feel bound by particular legal rules varies, but they cannot ignore the legal nature of their role and give free reign to their personal values and whims. The complex legal rules are largely accepted by all justices and cannot arbitrarily be neglected. Commitment to rules such as stare decisis, strict interpretation of criminal statutes, presumption of constitutionality, and definitions of jurisdiction shape the pattern of choice followed by the justice. While these rules may be rejected by a justice, they cannot normally be ignored. Judges have been trained in the law and taught to look at legal problems in terms of the historic development of the Anglo-American law. By training and by their identification with the legal profession they are predisposed to consider seriously the relevant legal rules bearing on a case. The impact of these rules is much stronger among lower court justices but is felt to some degree in all cases decided by all courts. The courts are political-legal agencies, and both legal and political influences shape judicial decision-making. Both factors must be taken into account in order to understand the nature of judicial activity.

To put the above discussion succinctly: The power of the courts is limited by the kinds of cases brought to them. Individuals other than judges have a large part in shaping the way issues are framed for the judges. The issues presented by the involved parties interact with relevant legal rules and the personal and philosophical attitudes of the justices to determine the basic output of the judicial system. Thus, the courts play a significant political as well as legal role in the polity. The importance of the Supreme Court in the development of public policy is clear. In the United States, virtually all major political issues are transformed at some point into legal questions to be decided finally by the Supreme Court.

The Impact of Judicial Decisions

In the past, political scientists did not always consider what happened after a final judgment made by a court of last resort in important cases. The assumption was that the court's decision would be complied with by all affected parties and fully enforced by executive officials. This assumption overlooked two conspicuous problems which involve (1) the effect of judicial decisions upon the allocation of values in society and (2) an understanding of factors that lead to noncompliance with the law. The actual impact of judicial decisions is obviously critical in any evaluation of the judiciary process.

As has been pointed out, every judicial decision has two segments. One affects the parties to the dispute directly; the other frames a rule which will presumably be binding in similar cases in the future. Such a rule, when developed by a high court, is expected to guide the decisions of all inferior courts as they are called upon to decide related issues. Moreover, the rule is expected to guide individual behavior by informing people how the court is likely to handle disputes in which they may become involved. Only when the courts have brought about general acceptance of the rules developed in their decisions do they provide the indispensable legal function of adding certainty and predictability to society.

An obvious question about the problem of compliance is: Do the parties to a dispute do what the court tells them to do? Further, if they do not, will executive officials support the decree of the court? If executive support — from the president, governor, sheriff, etc. — can be depended upon, the probability that the parties will willingly comply is increased. Under the doctrine of separation of powers, the courts have no independent enforcement powers and must rely upon executive officials to enforce their decisions. A court decree becomes a law to be executed by the agents of the executive department. Executive officials generally, but with significant exceptions, back specific court orders with whatever force is necessary to gain compliance. For example, President Eisenhower sent troops to Little Rock, Arkansas, to carry out a court-ordered desegregation plan even though he may not have favored the decree. Subsequent presidents have also found it necessary to use force to bring about compliance with individual desegregation orders. Although in many cases state officials refused to accept the legitimacy of the decrees, the federal executive furnished the power necessary to obtain compliance with the decrees. With few and minor exceptions, gaining compliance with *specific* court decrees has been little problem, although there has been frequent and sometimes violent resistance to them.[45]

The major problem of compliance is related to the generalized rules of the court. Rules stating that school segregation is unconstitutional, that prayers in the public schools violate the First Amendment, and that persons must have their constitutional rights explained to them at the time of arrest are examples of judicial decisions that have resulted in noncompliance. Each of these examples represents an area in which there has been considerable evasion, defiance, and subsequent litigation.[46]

Such rules cannot be enforced except on a case-by-case basis as new cases are brought to the courts. A decision indicating that prayers in the schools are unconstitutional means that the court by decree orders a specific school to stop a particular practice of holding prayers. If the decree is not followed, the specific person(s) responsible for the non-compliance can be cited and punished for contempt of court. However, no penalty can be levied against officials of other schools that engage in the same or similar practices until a case has been framed that specifically cites them. Therefore, unless school officials are in willing compliance with a judicial rule, the rule can gain uniform application only if an independent suit is filed in every school system that maintains prayers. This is a very inefficient way to change social behavior. Obviously, therefore, acceptance and willing compliance are critical determinants of the impact of judicial decisions. Consider the following example.

In 1954 the Supreme Court held that school segregation was in violation of the equal protection clause of the Fourteenth Amendment; in 1955

Rules stating that prayers in public schools violate the First Amendment can be enforced only by court decree on a case-by-case. *Camerique*

it held that school segregation must be ended "with all deliberate speed."[47] The correctness and legitimacy of the 1955 *Brown* decision (desegregation of schools) and rule were questioned by many southerners including most of the public officials of the South. Many related cases were brought in succeeding years. This case-by-case pattern led to very slow change in the racial integration of the public schools, except in those areas, such as the border states, where willing compliance prevailed. A full decade after the *Brown* decision there were a number of states in which not a single black student had been admitted to a previously all-white primary or secondary school.

Compare that record with the one resulting from the passage of the Civil Rights Act of 1964, which established a *legislative* sanction against segregated schools. Any school found to discriminate on the basis of race was to lose all federal funds. This was a general rule that could be enforced through the administrative activities of the executive departments. The shift in the progress of desegregation after 1964 was dramatic and in striking contrast to that derived from the relatively ineffective judicial rules. Legislative enactments provide greater powers of enforcement than do judicial rules and can better obtain basic changes in society. Nonetheless, the case of civil rights does indicate that the courts may play a vital role in the process of social change. Many individual students *were* in fact integrated into previously all-white schools as the result of court orders. The constitutional interpretations found in the *Brown* case *did* legitimate and strengthen political demands for civil rights legislation. The court decisions also increased public support for the principle of desegregation, which support was necessary to bring about the sweeping legislative changes that have occurred since 1954. One may conclude that the courts, by developing generalized rules, have some, but certainly not unlimited, power to alter social relations.

The varying impact of the courts is illustrated by a final example. In 1963 the Supreme Court ruled in *Schempp* v. *Abington School*[48] that Bible reading and certain prayer exercises in public schools violated the Constitution. The court order directed to the school involved in the case was followed. However, in some areas especially dissatisfied with the Court's ruling the number of school prayers actually *increased*. Again, the Court could act only if specific cases were brought to it. No general sanctions were applicable to the many public school officials who maintained the practice of school prayer. Emotions run deep on this issue and there are great social pressures against any effort to bring suit to restrict the use of prayers in schools. Therefore, relatively few cases have been forthcoming. Congress has not sought to aid the Court in this matter by passing legislation, and public opinion has been mostly unfavorable toward the school prayer decisions. In fact, the heaviest pressure applied by political groups and legislators is directed at finding means to block the effect of the rule. Changes in this area have been much less pervasive than in the case of school desegregation.

These cases indicate a number of factors related to the enforcement and acceptability of judicial decisions. The degree to which the decisions conform to attitudes and interests that are broadly supported or rejected in society at large is crucial. The greater the dissonance between the values contained in judicial decisions and those held generally in society, the greater the probability of noncompliance. But even when these value sets are at odds, compliance will be enhanced if the decisions of the Court are thought to be legitimate — that is, in conformity with legal processes and requirements.

The Constitution is a revered and broadly supported element of the American polity. If people believe, or act as if they believe, that the Supreme Court only applies the Constitution as written and that the personal values of the justices do not pervert this application, willing compliance is much more likely than if they believe that the judgment represents merely the political prejudices of nine unelected old men.[49] The myth that the Court is "above politics" and only applies the law as written and intended by the framers of the Constitution has, therefore, important consequences. Sad to say for supporters of the myth, perhaps the most significant defect of the Warren Court was its destruction, via its hyperactivism, of much of the credibility of the myth, resulting in a dramatic reduction of support for the Court and a major increase in attempts to evade judicial pronouncements. Intense demands developed for returning the Court to its traditional role of interpreting the Constitution rather than engaging in "judicial legislation." The effects of these demands are seen in the Burger Court. Once again the Court is following the election returns — if only belatedly.

SUMMARY

All societies provide rules to achieve order and predictability in human behavior and to allocate rewards and deprivations to individuals. The rules levied by the political system are the law. They are found in constitutions, statutes, administrative and executive orders, and judicial decisions. The law is a set of known or knowable rules that guides human behavior in directions provided by the formal actions of governmental agents.

The courts supply a regularized means of interpreting and applying the law in the context of individual disputes involving the rights and obligations of persons within a given factual situation. American courts perform this function within a highly developed, stylized, and formal set of rules and an adversary process. The courts thus have a passive role which must be activated by others.

The selection of judges is meant formally to maintain the independence and disinterestedness of the judiciary. The purpose is to guarantee that judges will remain above the everyday struggles and venal interests of political partisans. However, actually the personal and political views of a potential judge are crucial in the selection process. Judges are chosen in large measure because of their ideology, party identification, place of origin, and racial, religious, and ethnic characteristics. Judicial competence is taken into account but it tends to be of secondary importance.

The personal interests, ambitions, political philosophy, social values, and group identifications of justices have an impact upon their judicial decision-making — whether the justice is a liberal, a conservative, or a radical. Justices' views as to the proper role of the courts in the polity also effect their judicial choices. A third factor is their commitment to the legal forms and rules that have developed in the Anglo-American system of law. These elements, in interaction with the facts of the case before the court, determine the outcome of judicial decisions.

There are two main consequences of judicial decisions: (1) A decree resolves the dispute between the parties, and (2) a general rule is stated to be applied in similar cases. Normally, there is compliance with the direct decrees of the courts but frequent attempts have been made to evade the effect of a general rule developed in controversial cases. Willing compliance is indispensable if the general rule is significantly to change behavior in the society. Willing compliance is based upon the correspondence between the values contained in judicial decisions and the values held in the broader society, as well as the extent to which the legitimacy of the Court is accepted. In convincing people that its judicial decisions are dictated by the provisions of the Constitution, the Court may maintain and enhance its legitimacy in their minds.

NOTES

1. See Harold J. Berman, *The Nature and Function of the Law* (Mineola, N.Y.: Foundation Press, 1958); H.L.A. Hart, *The Concept of Law* (London: Oxford University Press, 1965); and James M. Buchanan and Gordon Tullock, *The Calculus of Consent: The Logical Foundations of Constitutional Democracy* (Ann Arbor: University of Michigan Press, 1962).
2. John Austin was the leading spokesman for what has come to be known as the analytical school of jurisprudence. His positive law doctrine was first presented in his *Lectures on Jurisprudence,* published in 1832.
3. See Jerome Frank, *Courts on Trial* (Princeton, N.J.: Princeton University Press, 1949), and Hans Kelson, *What Is Justice?* (Berkeley: University of California Press, 1957), for discussions of this problem.
4. See David Easton, *A Systems Analysis of Political Life* (New York: Wiley, 1965), pp. 153–170, for a discussion of the significance and effect of support by the politically relevant members of a society.
5. Consult Hannah Arendt, *The Origins of Totalitarianism* (New York: Harcourt, Brace & World, 1966) and *The Human Condition* (Chicago: University of Chicago Press, 1958), and Carl J. Friedrich, ed., *Totalitarianism* (Cambridge, Mass.: Harvard University Press, 1954).
6. Rocco J. Tresolini, *American Constitutional Law,* 3rd ed. (New York: Macmillan, 1970), p. 14.
7. See Karl N. Llewellyn, *The Common Law Tradition* (Boston: Little, Brown, 1960).
8. See James Hart, *An Introduction to Administrative Law* (New York: Appleton-Century-Crofts, 1950), pp. 13–15, for a discussion of the relationship between administrative and constitutional law.
9. These are only two of many examples of the operation of the agents of government as litigants in civil suits. Actually the bulk of litigation involving the government goes forward in civil rather than criminal cases.
10. C. Gordon Post, *An Introduction to the Law* (Englewood Cliffs, N.J.: Prentice-Hall, 1963), pp. 40–41.
11. Ibid., pp. 18–21.
12. See Alexander M. Bickel, *The Least Dangerous Branch* (Indianapolis: Bobbs-Merrill, 1962).
13. See Carl A. Auerbach, Lloyd K. Garrison, Willard Hurst, and Samuel Mermin, *The Legal Process* (San Francisco: Chandler, 1961), pp. 188–235.
14. Ibid., pp. 31–42.
15. See Herbert Jacob, *Justice in America* (Boston: Little, Brown, 1972), pp. 21–29.
16. See Thurman W. Arnold, *The Symbols of Government* (New Haven, Conn.: Yale University Press, 1935).

17. A classic statement of this position is found in Horace H. Lurton, "A Government of Laws or a Government of Men," *North America Review*, 193 (January 1911), 8–25.

18. See Zechariah Chafee, Jr., "Do Judges Make or Discover Law?" *American Philosophical Society: Proceedings* (December 1940), pp. 405–420.

19. See Edward H. Levi, *An Introduction to Legal Reasoning*, rev. ed. (Chicago: University of Chicago Press, 1962).

20. 1 Cr. 137 (1803).

21. Bickel, *The Least Dangerous Branch.*

22. See Charles L. Black, Jr., *The People and the Court* (New York: Macmillan, 1960).

23. Discussions of the organization of the state courts may be found in Herbert Jacob and Kenneth Vines, eds., *Politics in the American States* (Boston: Little, Brown, 1971), pp. 288–291, and Lewis Mayers, *The American Legal System* (New York: Harper & Row, 1964), pp. 367–378.

24. See Mayers, *The American Legal System.*

25. A major exception to this rule is that generally the prosecution is not allowed to appeal a verdict of not guilty.

26. See Alpheus T. Mason and William M. Beaney, *American Constitutional Law*, 4th ed. (Englewood Cliffs, N.J.: Prentice-Hall, 1968), pp. 5–8, for a concise discussion of Supreme Court procedures. This description does not include the process of certification, a seldom used technique whereby certain courts can request that the Supreme Court answer certain questions about a case pending before the lower court. This method is utilized by the courts of appeals and the special courts. See Tresolini, *American Constitutional Law*, pp. 32–34, for a discussion of this matter.

27. John R. Schmidhauser, *The Supreme Court as Final Arbiter of Federal-State Relations* (Chapel Hill: University of North Carolina Press, 1958), has a recommended discussion of the role of the Supreme Court in the federal system.

28. Mayers, *The American Legal System*, pp. 119–120, has a short discussion of the structure of the jury selection process. For more extended treatment, see H. Kalven, Jr. and H. Zeisel, *The American Jury* (Boston: Little, Brown, 1966), and A.T. Vanderbilt, *Judges and Jurors: Their Functions, Qualifications, and Selection* (Boston: Boston University Press, 1956).

29. Jacob and Vines, *Politics in the American States*, pp. 282–287, and Mayers, *The American Legal System*, pp. 38–401, discuss state selection processes.

30. See Joel B. Grossman, *Lawyers and Judges* (New York: Wiley, 1965).

31. See Charles Fairman, "The Retirement of Federal Judges," *Harvard Law Review*, 51 (January 1938), 397–443.

32. Joseph P. Harris, *The Advise and Consent of the Senate* (Berkeley: University of California Press, 1953).

33. John R. Schmidhauser, *The Supreme Court: Its Politics, Personalities, and Procedures* (New York: Holt, Rinehart, & Winston, 1961).

34. David J. Danielski, *A Supreme Court Justice Is Appointed* (New York: Random House, 1964), presents an interesting case study of the selection process that describes the complexity of the transactions involved in choosing a Supreme Court Justice.

35. See Schmidhauser, *The Supreme Court.*

36. See Charles G. Howard and Robert S. Summers, *Law: Its Nature, Functions, and Limits* (Englewood Cliffs, N.J.: Prentice-Hall, 1965), pp. 49–103, for a useful discussion of the way this process operates.

37. *Argersinger* v. *Hamlin,* 92 S. Ct. 2006 (1972).

38. See Clement E. Vose, *Caucasions Only* (Berkeley: University of California Press, 1959).

39. 347 U.S. 483 (1954).

40. Consult, on this point, Alpheus T. Mason, *The Supreme Court from Taft to Warren,* rev. ed. (Baton Rouge: Louisiana University Press, 1969), and C. Herman Pritchett, *The Roosevelt Court* (New York: Macmillan, 1948).

41. Alpheus T. Mason, *Harlan Fiske Stone: Pillar of the Law,* rev. ed. (New York: Viking, 1956), and Carl B. Swisher, *Roger B. Taney* (New York: Macmillan, 1935), provide excellent examples.

42. Glendon Schubert's *The Judicial Mind* (Evanston, Ill.: Northwestern University Press, 1965) is a highly developed example of this approach.

43. See Wallace Mendelson, *Justices Black and Frankfurter,* 2nd ed. (Chicago: University of Chicago Press, 1966), for an extended consideration of this problem.

44. See Learned Hand, *The Bill of Rights* (Cambridge, Mass.: Harvard University Press, 1958), for a particularly insightful treatment of this issue. Cf. Fred Rodell, *Nine Men* (New York: Random House, 1955).

45. See Stephen L. Wasby, *The Impact of the United States Supreme Court* (Homewood, Ill.: Dorsey, 1970).

46. Ibid.

47. 347 U.S. 483 (1954) and 349 U.S. 294 (1955).

48. 374 U.S. 203 (1963).

49. See Black, *The People and the Court.*

Factions and the Public Interest

$\mathbf{P}$olitics involves the collective behavior of individuals. How individuals are connected to the larger collectivity generally is the concern of sociology. How they are connected to the political system, and particularly to government, is the concern of political science. The relationship between a typical American and the polity and government may be more or less direct, as when an individual receives a tax bill or a draft call or votes for a public official or enters a case in court. Frequently, however, relationships are more attenuated and are mediated and shaped by intermediate social structures or groups.

In Chapter 2, the manner in which the individual is presumed to relate to groups which are actively involved in the political process was described. People normally join interest groups, if at all, in search of immediate material or social protection, advantage, or rewards, and the political activity of the group, if it occurs, is a *by-product* made possible by individual contributions to the group but not a subject of great or direct concern to the member. A rational basis for such behavior was suggested: The members seek to maximize their own welfare and, while willing to share in any gains from political action, are unwilling to bear exclusively or disproportionately the costs involved in securing, or seeking to secure, some benefit which noncontributors may enjoy as well. Large and noncoercive groups perform suboptimally in the political process, therefore, because of the indirect, not to say reluctant, relationship of group members to the policy-making process.

Further, communications from citizens to governments are ordered and shaped by group structures which combine individual preferences into such generalized statements that they cannot often be said to represent the position of any single individual.[1] Communications from governments to group members are often interpreted by these same intermediaries — group and opinion leaders — and processed in terms of the leaders' value premises before being transmitted to the rank and file.[2] Groups in America influence public policy to a significant degree. Because of their importance, an understanding of the nature and consequences of group activity is a necessary dimension of the analysis of the politics of any society.

FACTIONS: NATIONAL UNITY
VERSUS INDIVIDUAL FREEDOM

Political scientists give considerable attention to the description and evaluation of the many groups that mediate relationships between government and individual. In general, political theorists who view the state as a positive or benign force argue that groups which compete with the state for the loyalty and identifications of the individual are divisive and a threat to the unity essential to a decent, stable, and harmonious society. Government should, they say, guard against the formation of organized **factions** that divert, divide, and hence weaken the community. Social pluralism beyond some point becomes anarchy or decadence, and dangerous to social life itself.

Others believe that the state represents the most profound of all threats to personal freedom and rely upon private voluntary groups to share the power of the state and to reduce its influence over individuals. Although the normative conclusions of these positions are at odds, both assume that the formation of groups independent of the state does limit

Drawing by Lorenz; © 1969 The New Yorker Magazine, Inc.

the unity of the society as well as the power and control of the state. Freedom and order are often antagonistic values.

Plato, for example, believed that the good or ideal state requires the absence of any bases for competing group loyalties. The family should be abolished, and private property should be severely restricted in order to maintain a uniform, permanent, and primary commitment to the larger society. Any departure from this commitment was seen as a serious threat to the unity of the state and a source of social retrogression.[3] Rousseau argued that factions in society preclude the achievement of the "general will," which is required if the state is to serve the *true* interests of all. His fear rested partly upon the belief that loyalty to groups other than the state would lead to the control of the state by those groups, which would then use their power to achieve private gain and to impose their personal values upon all members of society.[4] The modern idealists such as Hegel, Fichte, and Bosenquet also rejected the appropriateness of factions that would compete with the state for the allegiance of citizens.[5]

The assumptions and interpretations that underlie the conceptions of such diverse philosophers include a belief that certain social goals can only or best be achieved through the operation of a unified state, and that they are superior to those of individuals or factions. Any competition among groups with different values may make impossible the achievement of these preferable social goals. Debate over the determination of the goals that should be pursued is not appropriate. The proponents of this position believe theirs is the only "true" version of the needs and interests of society and the individuals within it. Modern totalitarians, too, who would destroy any structures that mediate between the individual and the state, feel justified by the "need" to achieve an ideal form of society, understood by the political leadership if no one else. The leadership must not be hampered by those who propose other and clearly erroneous goals. The attainment of the ideal society is facilitated by developing social situations that leave the individual atomized, weak, and exposed vis-à-vis an all-powerful and all-embracing state.[6]

An alternative "**pluralist**" tradition sees the state as only one of many social groups created to meet human needs. Supporters of this view argue that individuals have different preferences and values and that their entrance into a multiplicity of groups confirms their diversity. Groups other than the state are essential to fulfill the wide range of interests and needs of individual members of society. The groups may (1) serve interests beyond the reach of the state, or (2) stand between the individual and the state by providing a means by which persons with similar interests can heighten their impact upon the policies of the state, or (3) protect the freedom of the individual from attack and destruction by other groups or the larger community itself. The development of groups that can compete successfully with the state for authority in guiding people's activities results in a division of loyalty and power in the society. The alternative channels of collective activity they provide can be used in pursuit of individual goals and values. The historic struggles between church and state represent a significant variation of this problem, one that stands at the foundation of a great deal of pluralist thought.[7]

Pluralists generally want a limited state with many social affairs conducted by private voluntary groups altogether independent of the state. To them limited social conflict is desirable for the highest development of both the individual and the society. Competition among diverse intermediate organizations is seen as a means of achieving more acceptable or "better" public policies. Maximum freedom requires that individuals have some choice in the institutions to which they grant their allegiance and that no single institution command the undivided loyalty of all members of the society.[8] Pluralists seek a division or even a fragmentation of political power. They tend to subscribe to Lord Acton's aphorism that "power tends to corrupt and absolute power tends to corrupt absolutely."[9] Their approach rests on a profound skepticism about the achievement of perfection and therefore supports the maintenance of openness and tentativeness in social organization.

THE PLURALIST PARADIGM

The American experience has been strongly influenced by pluralistic conceptions.[10] General support for the maintenance and integrity of groups that are independent of the state stems from the historically widespread suspicion of the powers of government. Competing versions of the truth and substantial toleration of deviant viewpoints have existed throughout most of our history. There has also been, of course, rejection by various means of groups that support values radically at odds with the mainstream of American thought and practice. Nonetheless, that mainstream has been quite broad by all historical or comparative standards allowing for the development of groups holding very different values and goals. This prevailing attitude reflects both the influence of pluralist thought and a recognition of the realities of diversity.

In America, then, factions have frequently been regarded as a positive good.[11] The traditional distrust of government and a fear of the tyranny of the majority, classically stated by James Madison in *The Federalist*, No. 10, are shown in purposeful attempts to promote voluntary groups. Given the size and diversity of American society, the uninhibited organization of groups around private interests will supposedly prevent any one faction from controlling the polity and imposing its will upon other members of the society. For this reason, the development of competing veto groups is often articulated as a worthy, even necessary, goal.

The legal system was designed to protect the formation of voluntary groups. The guarantees of the First Amendment to the Constitution in the areas of religion, speech, press, petition, and assembly are clear examples. The diverse constituencies of national officials and the Constitution's basic requirements of simple or extraordinary majority decision-rules ensure that major policy decisions represent compromises among competing interests. One assumption has been that these checks and balances protect against radical and destructive changes in the core values of the society.[12] Conflict, within acceptable limits, is to be cherished and nurtured as a means of evolving public policies consistent with the interests of the greatest possible number of people. The ideology, institutions, and formal decision-rules of American politics recognize and sanction conflict, competition, relativity, compromise, and individual welfare as positive values. It is not very surprising to learn that these same values dominate economic thought and practice in America.

Although the pluralistic paradigm is dominant in American politics, it is frequently attacked. There is discomfort among both intellectuals and anti-intellectuals with the relativism of the pluralist position on questions of values. Demands have been made, consequently, for the recognition of some form of overarching "public interest" that must be sought and maximized. Decisions, it is argued, should be guided by the public interest and not by the higgling and bargaining of the political marketplace. People who have found the path to social salvation are often impatient with the slow, incremental, piecemeal, and circuitous character of policy development in a pluralistic society and the neglect of what they perceive to be pressing social problems.[13] Among those who claim at least occasional knowledge of what the public interest requires in the way of public policy are the editors of the *New York Times* and the *Chicago Tribune,* the National Association of Manufacturers, Common Cause, authors of a spate of recent American government textbooks, and the John Birch Society. These persons and organizations tend to characterize politically active groups of which they disapprove as "special interests" whose major purpose is to undermine the public interest for private gain. They frequently demand that the influence of the so-called special interests be restricted and their own preferred world view imposed on those of alternative persuasion. This position is typical of many, even most, left- and right-wing reformers in American politics. Such people often are so convinced of their own principles and rectitude, and so intensely committed to substantive policy changes, that they do not understand, or do not consider important, the effect of their demands upon the values of civil liberties, civil rights, and due process. These values of process — so called because the consequences of their exercise cannot be predicted — do, of course, reflect America's pluralistic orientation. Yet however much radicals and reformers disdain process, preferring ultimate values, they generally insist that the pluralistic rules of the game protect them even while they are denouncing the rules. In short, they use the tactics of the special interests in their own attempts to shape the political universe. And no wonder, for they are special interests too!

In recent years there has been a good deal of impatience with the procedures of democracy, and demands have been made to restrict those procedures in the name of various conceptions of the public interest. The pluralist paradigm is rejected by many as an inappropriate guide to "proper" political decision-making, which should be evaluated in terms of substance and not process. Some politically exercised students, black revolutionists, racists, violence-prone "peace" demonstrators, radical feminists, and ecological extremists are quite willing to impose their peculiar notions of the truth upon their less-informed, timid, or intimidated fellow citizens. The compromises and tentativeness required by the pluralist paradigm are altogether intolerable to certain bearers of an incandescent Truth.

The influence of the pluralist philosophy in the American polity is seen in the emergence of a "group approach" to the study of politics. This is primarily of American derivation and has been paramount in American political science in the last several decades. It assumes that interest groups are the main forces shaping public policy. Extremely persuasive among scholars of politics, **group theory** also carries much weight with journalists and contemporary politicians as indicated by analyses of politics that appear in the popular press.[14] Because of the dominant status of group theory, it is necessary for all students of American politics to become familiar with its basic outlook. This book, of course, is based not on the group but on the individualistic approach. The two approaches are not always in conflict and, indeed, may be reconciled at many points. Both, for example, view politics as the interplay of diverse interests and not as a morality play or spiritual exercise.

THE GROUP THEORY OF POLITICS

Group theory proceeds from the assumption that all politically relevant activities occur in a group context. People naturally find themselves in social groupings and they create other social groupings to satisfy their wants and needs. Their interpretation of the world is in large part conditioned by the perspective of the group or groups to which they belong. Political attitudes and values are derived from the same sources. The group is held to be the primary means by which the activities of the polity can be influenced. The group, then, must be the central unit in all fruitful political analysis. Both the political behavior of the individual and the operation of the political system are shaped by the group process — even if one is personally unaware of the forces that determine individual reactions to political stimuli. While all group life — family, neighborhood, school, etc. — is important to the politics of a society, the explicitly *political interest group* is one of the greatest significance and provides the major focus for the group approach.[15]

A group is any number of persons who share some characteristic: a political attitude, an economic outlook, a skill, a hair color, interest in a sport. It is generally of little political relevance until the members begin to *interact* around the shared characteristic, at which point it becomes an interest group. Interest groups may pursue their interests in any number of ways, but an effort to achieve their goals by making demands on other groups through the government transforms them into political interest groups. Now they may have some effect on the operation of the polity. Once they begin making demands on government, they are frequently characterized as pressure groups. The group approach is one way of studying pressure tactics in the political system. However, the major proponents of the approach would reject such a narrow application of their theory.[16]

The group perspective defines politics in terms of group interactions. Public policy is determined by the resolution of group conflicts, or by the certification by government of the winners and losers. The dynamic of the political system is provided by groups that are pursuing their self-interest through demands on it. In its most extreme form group theory holds that the agents of government simply respond to these demands as more or less neutral referees who enforce the rules and confirm the winners on the basis of the relative power the groups are able to muster in support of their goals and values. A more general view would be that the government is itself a group or set of groups which competes with other groups for scarce values.[17] According to still another conception, the structures of government are mere extension of external groups. The Department of Labor is an agent of organized labor; Commerce, of business interests; Agriculture, of agri-business; etc. The groups behind more apparently "neutral" political institutions, such as federalism and the three coordinate branches of government, must be sought presumably in unobtrusive or tacit coalitions of groups. (The fact that these coalitions have turned out to be difficult to locate empirically suggests that either they do not exist or they are devilishly clever in concealing their existence.)

GROUP THEORY AND THE "PUBLIC INTEREST"

In the perspective of group theory, the "public interest" is undefinable or nearly so. Normatively, one can only observe that the political process works at any time to reward certain values and not others. The identification of any value beyond those held by the groups in the system is impossible, given the basic concepts of the theory. True, there is an implied norm that the group struggle should continue to operate in an open and competitive manner. Perhaps, then, the preservation of the process can itself be regarded as the public interest.

Beyond this norm is the assumption that an acceptable social balance will be achieved among competing groups and that no single group will be able to dominate all others. Action by one group to press its demands through the political system activates a counterreaction by groups whose interests are threatened. Decisions are then made through negotiation and compromise, intensities of preferences are reconciled, and the greatest good for the greatest number is achieved. Unfortunately, a number of empirical problems with group theory indicate that its normative basis, however attractive initially, is not altogether persuasive. Consequently, some additional propositions, which are not derived from group theory, are required to supplement the basic approach.

LIMITATIONS OF GROUP THEORY

Public choice theory of the sort developed in this volume would reject the dynamic notion — critical to group theory — that countergroups will form to limit the success of any particular group in realizing its claims upon others. On the contrary, the success of most special interests is not likely to result in counterorganization because the incentives to mobilize in opposition are not sufficiently attractive. For example, success by the farm lobby may mean an upward adjustment in tax rates which disadvantages taxpayers (who are themselves a special interest even though their numbers are legion). Will taxpayers form a group specifically to counter the farm lobby as group theory requires? No, and for reasons which should now be clear: The slight increase in taxes which might be forced by a new farm program is not enough to justify the costs of forming an opposition to counter the claims of agricultural special interests. A new farm program may increase a taxpayer's taxes $1.00, while the costs in time, money, organizing, and deciding necessary to oppose the program are much more. Moreover, the free-rider problem discussed earlier operates most obviously in connection with interests as large, diffuse, and impersonal as "taxpayers." Still further, taxpayers may not be opposed keenly to the success of certain organized farmers but may object, instead, to the success of all special interests in the aggregate. That is, the taxpayer *qua* taxpayer is more concerned with the *overall* size of his tax bill than with the particular items in it. But since there is no group to defend the overall level of taxes, there is no identifiable "spending lobby" against which to mobilize on the issue of the total tax bill. Group theory fails to point out that, when interests make claims on other interests through the political system, the put-upon interests may be diffuse, unorganized, and, given the distribution of costs and benefits involved (externalities), essentially *unorganizable*. The social balance which the interplay of groups is sometimes thought to achieve is more conceptual than real.

At another level, the theory does not deal adequately with the interests of individuals who are not members of organized groups.[18] This problem has been "solved" by some group theorists who put forward the idea of *potential groups*. Governmental agents, they contend, will be restrained in their actions by the recognition that certain decisions would probably encourage adversely affected individuals to form opposition groups. Thus, even those not organized into formal groups have influence because they are potentially active forces in the political process. This conception is necessary (1) to explain why unorganized interests (e.g., safe-elevator enthusiasts) are apparently important from time to time in the decision-making process and (2) to save the group explanation of politics (remember, everything must be explicable in terms of groups).

In addition, the problem of keeping conflict among groups within certain boundaries is not explained by the theory, unless it is willing to concede that the preservation of the group struggle through universally supported rules constitutes the public interest. This concession is not always forthcoming; indeed, it is undeniable that the values of stability, democratic practice, due process, and individual liberties (comprising, altogether, the "rules of the game"), which are essential to the preservation of the pluralist paradigm, are *not* universally shared. For one thing, rules are not always neutral; they work to the advantage of some groups and to the disadvantage of others. For another, universal support for the permanent maintenance of the rules suggests that in the view of political interest groups the rules are going to work to their particular advantage in the long run. Actually, there seems to be no compelling reason to suppose that groups are more interested in the long than in the short run. In the long run we are all dead, as John Maynard Keynes once pointed out. Such observations muddle the otherwise attractive notion that all groups can or do reach consensus upon support of the rules of the game. Perhaps the best evaluation is that many significant aspects of the political process are not explicable in terms of group theory alone. However, interest groups do play an important role in the American polity and the conceptions and findings of group theorists can give valuable insights into the political process.[19]

POWER AND POLITICAL
INTEREST GROUPS

The goal of all political interest group leaders is to induce the agents of government to support their policy preferences. Group leaders attempt to gain access to government, access being defined as the capacity not only to be heard but to gain favorable action. In Chapter 2 it was observed that leaders distribute their groups' resources among contending uses and that these uses may be primarily organizational and nonpolitical: Leaders may incur costs in order to enlarge membership, or increase organizational amenities, or defeat their intraorganizational opponents, and so forth. Only when political access is deemed more efficient in terms of securing their objectives will group leaders take on the costs of entering the political process. Such access can be gained only if the group leaders are able to generate effective **power.**

The idea of power is central to political analysis. A successful group is a powerful group. A powerful group is a successful group. Therefore, a group's leaders must give attention to the power resources that are available to them and to their competitors. The concept of power is best understood as a *relationship* (and not always an abstract one) between the winners and losers in any particular competition.[20] The margin of victory — defined as how much the winners won, minus their costs, relative to how much the losers lost, plus what they won, if anything — is the same as the power margin. Group leaders will seek to enter transactions that will enable them to win by the greatest possible margin or, when winning is impossible, to lose by the smallest possible margin. Interest groups cannot survive persistent losing; either the leadership will be replaced or the membership will vanish.

Certain characteristics of group members can be related to the power available to them as a group. These characteristics represent their **potential power.** The extent to which potential power is used and to what effect is an empirical matter. However, a group's power resources limit the force it can apply at any given point. The most important aspects of group power are membership size and cohesion, financial resources, organizational and leadership capabilities, and the social status of the group and its members.[21] The greater these resources, alone and in combination, the greater the power and influence of the group. Resources are not always cumulative, and an increase in one may result in a decrease in another. For example, an increase in membership frequently results in a decline in the group's cohesion.

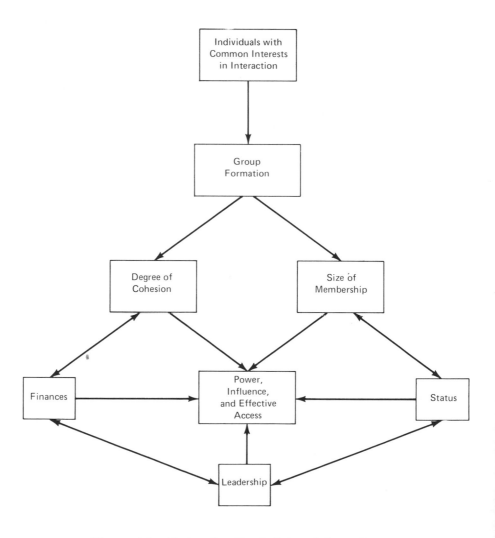

Figure 6-1.   Factors Leading to Interest Group Power.

Group Size

An obvious measure of the strength of a political interest group is its *size*. The more persons who share the values that define the group — or can be asserted by the group leadership to share them — the more likely group leaders will be able to influence political decision-making. Generally, when a group leader speaks about the size of a group in this context, all persons who share (or who can be claimed to share) the values, orientations, and policy demands of the group are counted, including those who are not formal members and formal members who are not sympathetic with the demands being expressed. This practice can be extremely irritating. Think of a student "leader" who insists that he or she speaks for all students; or a labor "spokesman" who informs the press what "labor" wants even though laboring people never have been consulted on the issue in question; or a politician who claims to express the will of the "people" even though many people are known to oppose the position being articulated. Much group size can be discounted when it is known what proportion is based upon assertion and what on actual support.

Certainly the power resource of size can normally be said to include the formal members of the association *and* those who can be considered or asserted to be "fellow travelers." This resource is of greatest significance when important decisions are to be made by majority rule. Clearly a group that is large enough to constitute the required majority can control such situations. Similarly, where individuals possess equality of voting rights, the size of the block of votes under the influence of the group may be decisive. In many circumstances, a single group does not, at least initially, control a majority; thus effective use of persuasion and coalition-building is necessary to control the outcome of the decisional process. If all other resources that are available to groups are equal, the larger group has a better chance of winning than the smaller group.[22]

Group Cohesion

Cohesion of a group and the related dimension of its **intensity** are of critical importance for the power of a political interest group. Regardless of the size of a group, it will probably be unsuccessful unless its members are capable of acting in concert to achieve their goals. The greater the intensity of their commitment to a common objective, the more likely the members are to submerge their idiosyncrasies and act in a unified way to promote the interest they hold in common. The influence of group members is maximized when, once a policy line has been chosen, unanimous action is taken in pursuing that line.[23] If, for example, a group decided to support a certain political candidate, it would be most successful if all members gave their time, energy, and money as well as their votes to that end. We have emphasized throughout that under very few conditions will such a uniform pattern of action by all members occur. The incentives to give minimal support or none at all to group activity are often substantial. However, some groups are more effective at achieving unity than others.

Unified groups are able to generate more power than those which lack a unified and intense commitment by the membership. The power resource of cohesion tends to be somewhat in conflict with the need for increased membership. Expansion frequently brings in many members with less concern for the original core values of the group, thus reducing its cohesion and presenting a problem for the leadership in getting unified action. A possible result is the dilution of the force of the leadership's original policies as new policies are developed to maximize the involvement of marginal supporters. American labor leaders face this problem. Growth in the size of organized labor has brought in many workers with a weak commitment to the formal policies of the group. Therefore, the leaders cannot concert its total potential resources. The members of organized labor cannot even be counted on to vote, much less to vote unanimously, at election time. Unity of action would obviously increase the power and influence of organized labor, but unanimity is impossible.

Conversely, conspiratorial groups often rely almost entirely on the power resource of cohesion. Their recruitment procedures require total commitment to articulated group goals before membership is permitted. Thus their plans can go forward in a unified manner. Purges of membership lists are a means of retaining only those members whose support for group policies remains pure and intense. Cohesion, therefore, is a significant resource achieved perhaps through the sacrifice of other factors which might also increase the political power of the group.

A critical strategic problem for any group is to strike a "proper" balance between size and cohesiveness. By presumption, leaders will attempt to reach whatever balance maximizes their own welfare. The balance which is achieved largely determines the likelihood of success of the group in the political process and dictates the tactics and strategies that are available to the leadership. The purposes of both leaders and members are, of course, multiple, and the optimal balance between size and cohesion for political purposes may not be the optimal balance in terms of other interests within the group. A suboptimal balance between size and cohesion may develop, therefore, if there are nonpolitical interests in the group.

Money

Many of the alternative tactics for influencing the course of public policy by an interest group depend upon adequate *financial resources*. Whether group leaders wish to influence the agents of government directly, through means usually characterized as **lobbying,** or indirectly, through means such as swaying public opinion, money is required to conduct their activities effectively. The more diverse the political interests of the group, and the greater its concern to affect policy at the national rather than the local level, the more important money becomes. Money may be acquired from many sources, ranging from voluntary contributions of members and sympathizers to dues collected from all members of the group. The extent to which the group can substitute other activities of members for money reduces the reliance on financial support, but these activities are the functional equivalent of financial resources. The more funds that are available to a group on a continuing basis, the greater the range of strategies that are available to its leaders and the greater its relative power. Money contributions by individuals are made normally to secure immediate and tangible benefits and not, in dependable and large amounts, to support political action. If the leadership is able to arrange a surplus of contributions over the costs of supplying immediate benefits to the membership, it may use that surplus to conduct political activity. The free-rider problem is involved once again as well but should not require further elucidation.

Leadership

The leadership and organizational skills available to a group are extremely important indices of its capacity to develop power. The ability of the leadership has a substantial impact upon the group's effective intervention in the political process. The leadership must usually be able to articulate the values of the group in such a manner that it can gain and maintain optimal membership. As we have observed, it is in the leadership's own interest to come up with internal and external processes, programs, and policy alternatives which maximize individual contributions to the group. The talents that are required to do these things vary with different groups.

Small conspiratorial groups and some mass movements tend to rely on charismatic leaders (leaders who have attributed to them a quality of extraordinary, sometimes spiritual, power). In more stable, diverse, and heterogeneous groups, leaders serve as brokers of the complex interests represented in the group. Not only does the required leadership style vary from group to group but it varies within each group throughout its history. The nature of leadership is an absolutely critical aspect of power development. Efficiency in the group struggle requires a good match among the interests of the rank and file, the interests of the leaders, and the kinds of tactics and demands that are pursued. The interests of the members are related to but independent of those of the leaders, but, as shown in Chapter 2, the interests of all are likely to be maximized when they are considered in the development of organizational activities.

A large problem faced by all organizations involves striking a balance between centralization and decentralization in decision-making. In part, this balance is determined by the history of the organization, but there are frequently opportunities for purposeful choices as to its nature. Any emerging group or association must decide whether to maintain a permanent staff of paid officials or to rely upon voluntary, nonpaid leaders. The choice is often based on how much securing greater leadership skills will cost the membership in increasing remoteness from the locus of decision-making. Members of large formal organizations always face the possibility that the leadership will become less responsive to their interests, in which case a major parameter of the leaders' decision-making problem is how to survive in their positions. It is just this phenomenon that leads to what Robert Michels called the "iron law of oligarchy."[24] This so-called law holds that, wherever organizations of scale occur, leaders become separated from members and, instead of responding to membership desires, direct the organization in their own interests regardless of the impact upon the members.

The issue of centralization versus decentralization usually results in a choice to rely upon either size or cohesion, at least for the time being. Decentralized groups have a tendency to better satisfy a diverse clientele and thereby generate larger memberships. Centralized groups ordinarily maintain closer control over the members and act in a more rapid and cohesive manner. The leadership and organizational capabilities of the group not only are independent sources of power but affect the building of other power resources needed for goal achievement.

Status

The social status of the individual members of the group, as well as the status of the group itself, has a significant effect upon the influence of the group. Leaders of virtually all groups attempt to persuade nonmembers that their demands are in the "public interest," and they are more likely to be believed if they are respected and deferred to by others in society. Groups frequently attempt to gain the endorsement of their programs by individuals of high status drawn from the worlds of entertainment, education, business, politics, and the professions. Such endorsements, even if they amount only to having prestigious individuals listed as "honorary" members of some committee, add legitimacy to the arguments of the group. Their names can attract social support for the group's goals and may reduce the ability of competing groups to activate a broad counter-response to those goals.

The status of the group is in part determined by the status of individual members. A good example is the very high group status achieved by the American Medical Association, which in turn is a function of the high status of medical practitioners.

The tactics of a group are in part dictated by its status. For example, the forces supporting the prohibition of alcohol in certain "dry" communities may include both ministers of certain religious sects and persons involved in the illegal sale of alcoholic beverages. In attempts to end prohibition, the religious leaders often become the overt leaders of the dry campaign while the illegal dealers play a more covert role by financing the campaign. It does not require much imagination to conclude that there would be a considerable reduction in the power and influence of the prohibition forces if these roles and activities were reversed. The forces of organized labor also find themselves in a paradoxical position: Labor's avowed support is necessary to a successful political campaign in some areas whereas in others the open endorsement of a candidate by organized labor is the political kiss of death. Such examples show the complex relationship between status and power.

Power can flow from status and status from power. One way to acquire high status is to develop power. The position of organized labor, patriotic groups, liberated women, or professors varies in power and status in different sections of the country. The status of the group is an important independent power resource that enhances the leadership's ability to gain the support of "fellow travelers" and to generate financial resources. In general, the higher the status of the group, the more easily it can identify its demands with the "public interest" and the more overt its tactics can be in securing access to policy-makers. Conversely, low-status groups must often act more covertly in seeking to influence the course of public policy.

THE SPIRAL OF POWER

While to some extent each of the factors discussed above is an independent source of group power, they are interrelated in complex ways. On the one hand, power resources are cumulative. The higher a group stands with respect to these several dimensions, the greater its total power and the stronger the probability that it will be able to acquire more of the same and other ingredients of group power. For this reason, power tends to flow to the powerful and away from the weak. To some extent, a group must already have some power in order to generate more of it. On the other hand, as we have noted, some power resources, particularly those of size and cohesion, tend to run in opposite directions. It is a task of leadership to calculate and strive for the achievable balance which maximizes the group's total power.

The development of new sources of power by a group often leads to attempts by the opposition to expand its own power base. Eventually all groups may have to keep raising their requirements for power simply to maintain their respective positions in the struggle. The spiral of power that one finds in the labor-management area illustrates this problem.[25] Successful claims by organized labor vis-à-vis management cause management to seek offsetting power. Organized labor and management have thus accumulated tremendous power for purposes of contending with each other. But the same power can be, and has been, turned with telling effect on other interests, such as consumers and unorganized workers. Wage claims by organized labor can be financed by business oligopoly through price increases which the unorganized are powerless to block.

From the point of view of group theory, however, the world is not divided into discrete groups such as unions, corporations, consumers, taxpayers, veterans, women, students, farmers, and so on. Individuals have many group affiliations. A woman, in addition to being a consumer and taxpayer, may be employed by a corporation in which she holds stock and which pays her tuition at night school. According to some interpretations of group theory, one's loyalty to any particular group is conditioned by *all* the group memberships which one holds. Multiple, or so-called overlapping, group memberships pull people in different directions on matters of public policy and decrease their intensity of support for any one group.[26] Actually, there is reason to believe that individuals tend to belong to groups with similar outlooks and orientations and thus that overlapping memberships reinforce policy preferences and intensity rather than the opposite. A full critique of group theory should be sought elsewhere.[27]

GROUPS AND
THE AMERICAN POLITY

America is frequently characterized as a nation of joiners. Although a very large proportion of Americans do not belong to any formal voluntary groups, a vast array of such groups exist to fill needs of many Americans. Some are small and transitory; others are large and quite stable through time. Some provide strictly social and recreational services; others press their demands upon the political system and thereby become political interest groups. Any of these groups have the potential to enter politics and will do so when such entry is deemed efficient. Entry can be at any level of government and directed at any agent of government. A large number of political interest groups first began as social or service groups only to become politicized later when it was determined that the interests of members and/or leaders might be protected by the intervention of a governmental authority. Conversely, some groups were organized with the explicit expectation of influencing the course of public policy. We have explained earlier why groups generally perform suboptimally when they are large, impersonal, noncoercive, and interested in securing public goods. As emphasized throughout, most political interest groups in the society play a dual role by providing directly divisible goods, services, and sociability for their individual members and by offering a means by which the interests of the members can be reflected in the political process. Thus, the life of society may be viewed as consisting in a diverse set of groups which are both large and small, highly organized and unstructured, powerful and weak, national and local in scope, primarily political and entirely nonpolitical.

These Vietnam veterans provide one example of an originally nonpolitical group which organized and politicized — in this case as an antiwar group— with goals of influencing public policy. *Steve Clevenger/BBM*

Interests, Political Structure, and Decision-Rules

The concern here is mainly with groups that make demands upon government. Although the range of political interests represented in the group process is broad, the chief political interest groups are usually organized around the economic interests of their members. Large and powerful interest groups represent the interests in the business, labor, and agricultural sectors and have an important impact upon the nature of public policy. They tend to be organized around the individual's *producing* rather than *consuming* role in the economy. Each major sector of the economy is characterized by diverse groups that support and advance the interests of different individuals. It is wrong to expect that all business interests will be arrayed against all labor interests in any situation; for example, some elements of business and labor are often united against ecologists and those who advocate unlimited foreign trade. Typically, the groups in each sector are less than unified on their respective policy posi-

Table 6-1. Characteristics of Selected Interest Groups.

Group	Membership	Staff	Local Units
Agricultural Groups			
American Farm Bureau Federation	2,000,000	65	2,878
Farmer's Educational and Cooperative Union of America	250,000	25	3,000
National Grange	600,000	26	6,000
Business Groups			
National Association of Manufacturers	12,000	250	N.A.
Chamber of Commerce of United States	5,000,000	850	4,000
United States JAYCEES	300,000	85	6,400
Conservation Groups			
Izaak Walton Leage of America	50,000	16	600
National Audubon Society	200,000	225	250
National Wildlife Federation	700,000	20	6,500
Sierra Club	135,000	90	42
Labor Groups			
American Federation of Labor and Congress of Industrial Organizations	13,500,000	600	N.A.
International Brotherhood of Teamsters	1,830,000	N.A.	805
International Union of Automobile Workers	1,500,000	N.A.	1,405
United Steelworkers of America	1,400,000	1,429	5,600
Patriotic Groups			
American Legion	2,700,000	301	16,604
Daughters of the American Revolution	194,364	150	2,939
Disabled American Veterans	377,000	160	1,972
Veterans of Foreign Wars	1,750,000	250	10,000

N.A. Not available.

Source: Compiled from *Encyclopedia of Associations,* 8th ed. (Detroit: Gale Research Company, 1973), Vol. I.

tions. Some will favor and others will oppose any given policy. Just as importantly, many of the groups in each sector will remain neutral and uninvolved in any particular conflict. This selective attention to issues, although one of the principal aspects of the political process, is frequently ignored in descriptions of the interest group struggle. The point becomes obvious, however, when we remember the presumption that entry into politics is a matter of rational choice, and that the costs and benefits associated with any resolution of any conflict will not affect all groups equally.

Although economic groups are very influential and visible in the political process, there are important groups which are not organized directly around the economic interests of their members. Other wants — for public virtue, solidarity, learning, uplift, charity, tradition, safety — are represented in the group process as well, although they are usually less enduring and less stable. Think of patriotic groups, such as the Daughters of the American Revolution; veterans' groups, such as the American Legion; professional groups, such as the American Economics Association; charitable groups, such as the March of Dimes; public interest groups, such as Common Cause; conservationist groups, such as the Sierra Club; revolutionary groups, such as Students for a Democratic Society. These and others make demands upon government to develop, alter, or maintain policies and programs promoting interests and points of view that are not always economic.

A strategic decision by group leaders to "go public" with group demands is made simultaneously with the tactical decision on precisely how those demands can be pursued most efficiently in the political order. The tactical problem is how to combine, organize, and coordinate the resources of the group so as to maximize its power vis-à-vis the larger society.[28] The presentation to the polity of a united front produces influence far in excess of that possessed by a similar number of like-minded but uncoordinated individuals. A team has greater power resources than do disconnected individuals. For this reason, group membership enhances the impact individuals may have upon the formation of public policy.

The group decision to enter the political process and the group's subsequent effectiveness are strongly shaped by the political structures and rules that define government. It cannot be emphasized often enough that the formal structures and decision-rules of the political system are rarely or never neutral in any given decisional situation.[29] They favor certain interests and place others at a disadvantage. To be effective, a group must take into account the rules of the game and choose its activities correspondingly. Even if one of its goals is the restructuring of the rules of the game, it must take the rules as given and fixed in the short run and come to grips with their implications for its own goals and tactics.

The decentralization of formal authority is perhaps the most significant aspect of the structure of government in the United States. It has been a weighty factor in the nature of the group process. The power to govern is divided both territorially and functionally. On the one hand, it is allocated to national, state, and local jurisdictions. In accordance with constitutional requirements and practical limitations, some governmental powers are held exclusively by one level while others may be exercised concurrently by any or all levels. In the latter case, the critical problem for a group may be which level of government is most likely to act in a manner congenial to its interests and which level has the capacity to deal effectively with its demands. Groups seek not only sympathetic but effective responses. On the other hand, power at each territorial level is divided among a large number of structures — legislative, judicial, and executive — as well as many independent boards and commissions. Frequently, a demand pressed by an interest group must be accepted by several or even all of these structures independently if group goals are to be achieved.

The fragmentation of authority, therefore, tends to favor groups that prefer the status quo and to work against groups that seek change. In many cases, to be successful a group that stands in a defensive position need only gain access to *one* of these authorities, while a group that desires something new must gain access to *all* of them. Thus, the rules guiding the governmental system protect existing groups from a serious erosion of their social positions and make it difficult for groups to improve their positions vis-à-vis other groups. Because they inhibit change, these rules have often been attacked for their conservative bias. Quite so, but they also serve to defend groups against a unified governmental authority, whether it is controlled by a majority or a minority. Tyranny of either sort is minimized as a possibility by the fragmentation of authority.[30]

Decentralization presents interest groups with a choice of points at which they may seek access. As just mentioned, the two primary criteria used in selecting points of access are the sympathy and the effectiveness of the authority in question. Much of the rhetoric about "states' rights" is related to these criteria, for example. Groups want authority placed in institutions that will provide them with the best access (i.e., institutions that will be both sympathetic and effective). Although it is now a dead issue, segregationists might argue that decisions concerning the admission of students to the public schools must constitutionally be made at the state level. The constitutional argument, based on the reserved powers of the Tenth Amendment, is not a trivial one. Conversely, those who oppose segregation might argue that the national government must intervene to enforce (other) constitutional provisions, such as the equal protection clause of the Fourteenth Amendment. Constitutional positions are often occupied for tactical reasons, and group leaders who argue for the independence of the states and for reserving a broad range of powers to the states believe that they are more likely to gain their goals at the state than at the national level.

The trend over the last several decades has been for more and more policy decisions to be taken at the national level, revenue sharing and other developments notwithstanding. One reason is that many interests have shifted their demands from local to state and finally to the national level in pursuit of their policy objectives. Current demands for returning power to the localities represent an effort to shift the priorities of government once again. To the extent that the demands for decentralization are successful, a different array of interest groups will be rewarded. Although the argument between states' rights and national power has an ideological component, it is primarily a dispute over which groups will control public policy.

A related dispute concerns the appropriate powers of national institutions — Congress, the president, the Supreme Court, and the independent regulatory agencies. Group leaders must calculate which of these entities controls the values they are interested in and what the probabilities are of achieving success by working through them. If the authority in control is unfriendly, group leaders may demand that power be lodged in some other, and more "appropriate," agency.

Tactical Access and Generalized Preferences

Group leaders must make tactical decisions in accordance with existing reality in the distribution of authority. If a particular agency controls some value, groups interested in that value must approach that agency if their immediate needs are to be accommodated. A case has to be submitted to whomever has jurisdiction, and whether the group approves or disapproves of the way jurisdiction is organized is not always important.

It is necessary to distinguish between a group's search for access within the existing rules and its generalized preferences or ideological orientation with respect to how power should be distributed among existing or inventible political institutions. Much of the controversy over the relative power of the Congress and the president, for example, arises from the distribution of influence between those institutions. Over the last few decades the generalized preferences of many groups interested in an expanded social welfare policy and other so-called liberal programs have been for an "indispensably" enlarged and strengthened presidency. Only the president was elected by all the people. Only the president could presume to speak for them. Only the president could confront the continuing crises of our time with logic, force, dispatch, effectiveness; certainly Congress, with its corruption, parochialism, fragmentation, procrastinations, could not do so. This particular metaphysic collapsed for the time being with the Vietnam policies of President Lyndon Johnson and the election of a conservative President Nixon who showed every willingness to accept the concept of a strong presidency, but on behalf of his and not always liberal preferences. Numerous erstwhile supporters of an ascendant presidency, having suffered convenient attacks of amnesia, now conclude that a strong presidency is imperial, dictatorial, remote, contrary to our traditions, a threat to freedom, etc., and have developed constitutional arguments to prove it. Actually, of course, many arguments that, on their face, concern constitutional delegations of power among the branches of government involve, at bottom, the ability of political interests to gain access to congenial and like-minded officials. This intellectual flimflam is not confined to the issue of presidential versus congressional power, of course.

Throughout most of our history, the Supreme Court, to cite another important case, has supported "conservative" interests and has often been attacked by liberal groups as an aristocratic element in an otherwise well-conceived democratic political system. However, a shift in the ideological stance of the Court in the late 1930s dramatically switched its defenders and detractors. From that period at least until the time of the Burger Court, liberal interests tended to view it as a protector of enlightened values against the forces of oppression and ignorance which at least occasionally control the rest of government. Conservatives charged to the contrary that the Court's nine old men had imposed a judicial tyranny on an otherwise republican society. Clearly, the debate over the "proper" powers of the Supreme Court has to do directly with the winners and losers in the group struggle before the Court.[31] This is not to say that constitutional issues like federalism and the separation of powers involve only efforts to shift or maintain the power of certain groups; such questions may have a purely philosophical dimension as well. Nonetheless, group interests are significant aspects of all these controversies.

Direct and Indirect Access

Interest groups may attempt to apply influence directly or indirectly. Tactics associated with direct influence include contacting public officials; intervening in political campaigns in support of, or opposition to, a candidate; and seeking to have sympathetic individuals appointed to public office. The purpose is to communicate group demands to policy-makers and to sway their judgments. Many groups have large permanent staffs to carry out these tasks, while others rely on ad hoc and unstructured means. The general purpose is to convince an official that a given policy decision is appropriate, sound, in the "public interest," *and* advantageous to the interests of the official and his political party. The direct approach has the particular advantage of being less likely to activate opposition groups. Covert techniques are most useful for groups in a favorable power position. The activation of a larger public is not always to their advantage because "he who controls the scope of conflict controls the outcome."[32]

The political interest group may influence public policy in a more indirect way if it can shape a supportive popular opinion. Affluent groups sometimes conduct expensive and sophisticated advertising and public relations campaigns to gain widespread support for a favored policy. A successful PR campaign communicates to the public official that decisions consistent with the group's goals will be supported by public opinion. The official may become convinced that there is political capital to be accumulated by choosing to support a given policy position. The indirect method may be an important option for certain groups, although it has the disadvantage of requiring the expenditure of substantial resources. PR campaigns may also arouse and mobilize the interest of many persons uninvolved in the issue, in which case a very different structure of power can result. The activities of the civil rights movement in the early 1960s and the antiwar movement of the late 1960s are examples of the application of indirect pressure to political decision-makers. In both instances widespread use of demonstrations, civil disobedience, the creation of martyrs, and other propaganda of the deed so altered public opinion that public policy shifted. Just as groups seek access to authorities who control important values, so do they try to make aware, involved, and sympathetic whatever portion of the public has interests compatible with a "proper" outcome. Those who find themselves with few power resources sometimes attempt to expand the number of persons interested in an issue in order to restructure power relationships. Groups such as the United Farm Workers or minor political parties fall into this category. Groups favored by current power alignments endeavor to guard against the extension of awareness and the mobilization of an enlarged opposition.

Large interest groups often attempt to use a balanced combination of direct and indirect techniques to influence decision-makers. More specific analysis of the techniques of interest groups, and an evaluation of their implications for the operation of the political system, must be made in relation to specific governmental agents and institutions. The present discussion is limited to the national government, but similar activities can be found at state and local levels. The process itself is not strikingly different at these levels, although the winners and losers in the process vary from region to region, from state to state, and from locality to locality.

The Group Imbroglio in Congress

Congress is the preeminent representative institution of the American government. Many expect it to be responsive and responsible to the "will of the people." It is therefore not surprising that Congress is a major object of interest group activity. The relations of groups with the legislative branch are the most obvious and frequently discussed aspect of pressure groups in the political process. The typical characterization of interest group activity, lobbying, describes it as a primary means by which groups try to influence members of Congress.[33] The nature and structure of the legislative processes provide many and significant points of access for interest groups. They also shape the precise kinds of activity that are likely to be successful and, in so doing, define the relative power of the groups that seek legislative intervention.

The organization of Congress affects the conduct of interest groups in several major ways. The two houses of Congress with their different sizes, terms of office, constitutional powers, bases of representation, and constituencies offer rather different patterns of access. The House of Representatives is based upon relatively small constituencies, and the social homogeneity of many congressional districts makes it likely that one or only a few interest groups will dominate a district and have direct access to the district's representative. Members of the Senate have larger and more diverse constituencies, so that generally a wider range of groups will be making demands on them. Moreover, substantially broader electoral coalitions are normally required to gain membership in the Senate than in the House. For this reason alone, the avenues of access to members of the two houses are quite different, and the result may be rather incompatible policy stances by House and Senate members. The fact that both houses must act upon a measure before it becomes law forces compromises between the divergent aggregate interests represented and disadvantages interests that seek to modify existing policy.

The rules of the two houses, discussed in some detail in Chapter 9, reflect their respective sizes and complexity. The much greater formality and dependence on the committee system in the House and the rule of unlimited debate in the Senate are particularly obvious means by which individual members of Congress can come to occupy strategic positions, access to which can be sought by interest groups to block innovation in the political system. The general situation is one of dispersed power, which makes concerted and expeditious action difficult at best. The costs of getting agreement in the Congress are consequently high. There is, however, an important offsetting benefit: Action that might injure particular interests is inhibited at the same time that innovation is stymied or delayed. In this connection, one very important matter must be discussed before we move on to the group process in other institutions.

Specialization is an informal congressional norm; a consequence of the committee system; a requirement, in a complex world, of intelligent decision-making; and a means by which power is allocated to those most deeply involved in some aspect of public policy. Specialization of function and its associated fragmentation of power give rise to **logrolling,** a process which bears on the understanding of group influence in policy-making. Logrolling consists in vote-trading and is usually, although not necessarily, accomplished tacitly. Members of Congress vote for each others' pet projects not because they would support such projects on the merits but because, by doing so, they ensure support for their own measures. It is easy to see that the outcome — the total, aggregate policy outcome — may be one which *no* interest group is concerned to support. Even more importantly, the process may give each interest represented in it most or all of what it wants, an outcome most group theorists would not want to defend. Contrary to the requirements of interest group theory, such an outcome is not produced by hard bargaining, compromises, and trade-offs. Not at all; there may be no real requirement for compromise and no effective control exercised by competing groups. One might conclude that logrolling profoundly undermines the assumptions of group theory and that the policy-making process in Congress is one in which interest groups control some aspect of public affairs without effective opposition. The protection of the "public interest" which some interest group theory seeks to ensure becomes skimpy indeed under these circumstances.[34]

Some people, therefore, believe logrolling is inconsistent with the normative basis of group theory. But there is a dialectic in these matters and there are limits to the damage to group theory just described. The intervention turns on the question of the *intensity* with which individual and group interests are held. If one supports the view that numbers alone should not determine public policy but that intensity of concern should be considered as well, it follows that the processes of decision must allow intensity of feeling and concern to influence the final outcome. How this goal might best be arrived at is a matter of continuing discussion, but it may well be that logrolling, by facilitating the incorporation of intensity into the decision process, works to achieve a more efficient recognition of interests and preferences in the society than would be possible without logrolling. Indeed, it can be argued that, rather than abolish logrolling (a dim prospect at best), it should be brought out more into the open, clarified, and made more efficient. In any case, there are some interests that probably should *not* be compromised, such as certain ones involving civil rights and liberties. Undeniably, the rules and organization of the Congress give differential access to intense over less intense and apathetic groups and interests. This is either an outrageous turn of events, a vaguely disquieting fact of life, or a positive good, depending on one's political theory. The authors would argue against the elimination of vote-trading until other techniques are discovered and developed which would be equally sensitive to the problem of intensity. No other practical techniques occur to us, however.

There are a number of lobbying tactics in general use by political interest groups that seek to have their intensities of concern felt in the legislative process. The classic idea of lobbying, as just implied, was that it was an illegitimate activity in which undue pressure was applied to members of Congress by special interest groups. There continues to be an aura of corruption and wrongdoing associated with the term and not always without reason. Still, it is not really accurate to picture the typical lobbyist as a sinister fellow attempting to bribe or coerce politicians into supporting his special and probably illegitimate interests. Nonetheless, the more skeptical view gets reflected in the periodic waves of demands for placing further controls over the activities of lobbyists.[35] Cases like those involving with such luminous and unsettling clarity former Vice-

President Spiro Agnew and some aspects of the Watergate episode suggest that the demands may be soundly based and more than the hysteria of individuals who believe that the morality of the political process should resemble the morality of the convent. What requires emphasis, however, is that the activities of lobbyists are more complex, more subtle, and less crass than is popularly supposed.

The role of the lobbyist is primarily one of persuasion. Interest group representatives frequently contact key members of the Congress and attempt to convince them to support or oppose certain policies and programs. This is normally done on the grounds that the policies of the group are compatible with, and even demanded by, the public interest and, coincidentally, the personal interests of the member of congress. Communicating this contention is a matter of high priority for the lobbyist. One of the ways of showing the coincidence of public and private political interest is through letter-writing and other propaganda campaigns designed to show that constituents strongly favor a given measure. Such campaigns can be quite effective if they are carefully formulated. Campaigns that are obviously controlled by a single group tend to be discounted by members of congress.[36]

To be persuasive, it is first necessary to gain the respect of the senator or representative. This may be done by providing information of a rare or technical nature about pending legislation. The lobbyist serves as an extremely important source of information, but whatever data are furnished must be factual and, when biased, identified as such if the desired effect is to be had. Similarly, intelligence on political matters may be provided by the lobbyist, but this is more biased and consequently discounted. The critical problem for the interest group representative is to gain the trust of the congressional member so that, on issues on which the group wants to exert influence, it will receive a "fair" hearing.[37]

The primary influence of the interest group on an individual member of Congress is related to the range of contributions or services performed by the group for him or her. When a dependent relationship develops between a strategically placed senator or representative and an interest group, the group has gained effective access.

Interest Groups and Policy Execution

During the last several decades the relative power of the executive branch has substantially increased. The activities of political groups attempting to influence the choices and patterns of behavior of executive officials have shifted and expanded in a like manner. The enhanced role of the president in developing policy proposals, and particularly in budget formation, dictates that access must be gained to the executive branch if many group demands are to receive a hearing. Similarly, the tendency in Congress to write legislation in more and more general form, with the understanding that "details" will be worked out in the administrative process, has enlarged the discretion which can be used by executive branch officials to aid or restrict the success of interest groups. The principle holds that interest groups focus their resources on officials who control values of most concern to the groups. So greatly has the power of the executive increased that lobbying activities before executive agencies now probably exceed those devoted to influencing legislation through direct contact with members of Congress.[38]

Activities of political interest groups attempting to influence choices of executive officials have expanded. Legion post spokesmen, for example, have recently endorsed or condemned political issues, especially those pertaining to the military. *Eugene Richards Photo*

The president is the only elected official with executive powers. The capacity of interest groups to intervene effectively in elections as a way of increasing their access is always problematical. However, the sheer importance of the presidency in policy-making leads many interest groups to try to influence presidential elections to some degree. Donations in kind, financial contributions, and endorsements of support are used as means of gaining access. Some groups have been known to make contributions to both major political parties in order to claim some basis for access regardless of which party wins. The larger, more powerful interest groups tend to be active in presidential campaigns, and the group coalitions formed on behalf of the winning candidate go a long way in setting the general public policy tone of the administration. Because of the president's necessarily very large electoral constituency, no single group can hope to dominate presidential policy decisions. Even so, many groups do attempt to play a helpful role in the formation of a winning coalition. The successful involvement of an interest group gives it some claim to be consulted in the policy proposals, appointment decisions, and budgetary recommendations of the president.

As discussed more fully in Chapter 10, many significant political actors are selected and appointed to key positions in the executive and judicial branches of government by the president. Among the most critical of these positions, from an interest group perspective, are cabinet posts, federal judgeships, and seats on the governing boards of the independent regulatory agencies. The appointment process is used to reward individual supporters of the president, but the rewards that accrue to groups as a consequence are more important politically. Interest groups have gained a near veto power over who shall be nominated to certain positions. But even though business interests always play a part in the selection of the secretary of commerce, organized labor in the selection of the secretary of labor, and agricultural interests in the choice of a secretary of agriculture, the particular groups that have the greatest power in this process vary with the party in power, the personality and interests of the president, and the exigencies of the time. For example, the American Farm Bureau generally dominates in the selection of the secretary of agriculture in Republican administrations while the Farmers Union has a much bigger role in the selection process in Democratic administrations.[39] Of course, the large and diverse executive departments harbor representatives of many interests which can coalesce behind certain policy lines or struggle among themselves for access to the cabinet secretary. The group whose policy the secretary chooses to advance is the winner. It comes then to this: that in most administrations the secretaries of the major clientele departments become little more than special pleaders for one or more interest groups. Much of the controversy that flares up from time to time over the Senate ratification of a person nominated to an important executive branch position reflects the interest group struggle. These points are expanded in Chapter 11.

The large number of independent regulatory commissions with responsibilities to regulate many aspects of the economy also provide targets for the activities of political interest groups. It can be greatly to their advantage to influence the process through which members of these commissions are selected. The commissions generally require technical expertise in the area in which they operate, such expertise being solely or most conveniently found among the regulated interests themselves. For this and other reasons, the agencies have often fallen under the control of the groups they were organized to regulate.[40] The result has been characterized as the regulation of an industry by an industry in the interest of the industry in the name of the public interest.

Many of the complex activities of the governmental departments and the regulatory agencies require cooperation between themselves and major clientele groups. In order to maintain and expand their power position, agency officials frequently try to develop clientele groups to support agency activities.[41] The dynamic underlying such attempts is explained in Chapter 11. The interaction between political interest groups and governmental agencies of the executive branch places certain of the former in an advantageous position in the political struggle. A symbiosis develops that allows governmental officials to maximize their agency budgets with the aid of interest groups and interest group leaders to gain some of their purposes through this exchange. Then, with the assistance of agency officials, new groups form, which make new demands upon the agency.[42] The Department of Agriculture played a critical role in developing the Farm Bureau, now one of the most powerful groups in the agricultural sector. "Poverty committees" were created as a part of the action programs of the now defunct War on Poverty, both to support the Office of Economic Opportunity in the budget process and to place new demands upon it.

Significant in the field of interest group activity is the emergence of highly influential firms of "political" lawyers in Washington.[43] They operate as lobbyists before the Congress but have come more and more to apply their skills on behalf of affluent interests in order to influence the activities of the administrative and regulatory agencies. A whole profession has grown up around the critical need of interest groups and individuals to have effective representation before such agencies. The firms use their legal talents in the representation of their clients and supplement their legal skills with a variety of techniques of political influence.

This section has only touched on a few of the ways interest groups attempt to gain access to decision-makers in the executive establishment. Some organized groups have acquired access of a highly effective, broad, and stable sort. The selection of agency officials, policy proposals of the executive and regulatory agencies, and the day-to-day decisions of these agencies as they apply and administer the law are objects of interest group involvement. The actual process of interest group concern and intervention is increasingly intense in the executive arena. However, the actions of interest groups and their leaders in this area tend to be more covert and are less frequently discussed in the press and academic literature than similar activities in the legislative branch. One outcome of the Watergate affair was to make public some examples of such activities. Their invisibility is a compelling reason why there was such a strong negative reaction to disclosures related to the milk fund and ITT contributions to the Nixon campaign and their alleged impact upon executive recommendations. These activities were not shown to have resulted in any illegitimate public policies or special favors not dictated by the nature of the law and other political forces, but the mere intervention at this level was enough to smack of corruption of the political process. Evidence that substantial contributions had also been made by the milk producers to members of Congress, including several on the House Judiciary Committee and its chairman, was much more compatible with politics as usual in the public mind and was therefore less shocking. As long as so many critical decisions that seriously affect core concerns of interest groups are to be made by officials in the executive branch of the government, they will be major objects of interest group pressure.

Interest Groups and the Courts

The judicial system makes decisions that are important to the goal achievement of interest groups. Therefore, it is not surprising that the courts are scrutinized by interest groups and that the latter try to influence judicial rulings. Certain features of the judiciary dictate tactics rather different from those used to influence decisions elsewhere.

The extreme formalism and rigid processes of the judicial system, as well as a widespread commitment to the myth that the courts are outside of the political process, tend to obscure the fact that the courts are participants in the interest group struggle. The peculiarity of the judicial process produces rather specialized interest group tactics where the allocations of values made through judicial decisions are concerned. Not all tactics vis-à-vis the judiciary are unique, however.

For example, groups seek access to the judicial system by attempting to influence the selection of judges.[44] Any vacancy in the judicial system, particularly on the Supreme Court, but even on district courts, activates many groups to try to determine who will fill that position. The intent is to seat judges who will make decisions favoring the interests and ideology of the group. The judicial role is so constituted that groups generally cannot argue acceptably or legitimately for or against candidates on the basis of how they are likely to vote as members of the court. Typically, arguments are framed in terms of a candidate's experience, judicial temperament, and legal competence. However, they tend to screen the real concern, which is the probable voting record if the candidate should become a judge. Because of the insulation of judges from overt lobbying activities, it may be critical for an interest group to have an "appropriate" judge on the bench.

Most of the means of influencing the decisions of judges must be embedded in legal forms. The two main devices used by interest groups are the amicus curiae brief and the class action suit. By the amicus curiae brief an entity not itself a party to a suit can present arguments before the court concerning the "proper" disposal of a case.[45] These arguments add strength to the position of the litigant, whose success will support the goals and interests of those providing such assistance. A group may appear before the Supreme Court as an amicus curiae or friend of the court; some groups have legal staffs to carry out this form of lobbying. The National Association for the Advancement of Colored People and the American Civil Liberties Union repeatedly use this technique of group intervention into the policy process.[46]

Groups may develop test cases to gain a constitutional interpretation of a law or issue that impinges upon their goals. These actions ordinarily take the form of class suits, or suits in which a remedy is asked not only for the parties of record but for all other persons who are "similarly situated." The class action suit is used extensively in the areas of civil rights and civil liberties and increasingly by those who are involved in issues of environmental quality. All of the above matters are discussed in Chapter 5.

Although public opinion per se may normally have only indirect effects on judicial determinations, professional legal opinions probably have a substantial and somewhat more direct impact. Interest groups may rely, consequently, upon the activities of bar associations and the publications of prestigious law schools as a means of communicating to judges the groups' perspective on the law.[47] A well-reasoned scholarly article on an aspect of law in which a group is interested may come to the attention of judges and influence their views on policy issues before them.

While there are real limitations to bringing group views before the courts, interest groups can be quite innovative in finding ways to use the courts to gain access to public and elite opinion and, thereby, to other centers of power. The fact that anybody can sue anybody else is not lost on the occasional publicity-seeking politician who, by suing an opponent or an opposition newspaper, is the subject of daily headlines and television film clips. Contemptuous and disruptive courtroom behavior — as exhibited, for example, by the Chicago Seven in their trial for conspiracy involving the violent disorders at the Democratic party's 1968 National Convention — is a means by which the judicial system can be used to dramatize an issue, sway some centers of opinion, and, perhaps, affect public policy.

SUMMARY

The above discussion of interest group activity in the different branches of government is illustrative only, and not a survey of all forms of actual conduct followed before Congress, the executive branch, and the courts. The general principles that emerge from this analysis are consistent with the presumptions about interest groups made in Chapter 2. Interest group leaders allocate their scarce resources among political and non-political activities so as to maximize the welfare both of themselves and of group members. The portion of group resources allocated to political activity is likewise distributed in whatever manner seems most likely to promote group welfare. Group leaders approach those officials who control values of interest to the group, who are thought to be most responsive to group demands, and who can be dealt with on "reasonable" terms. If two or more political arenas can yield the same favorable decision and offer the same probability of doing so, the arena requiring the smallest investment of group resources will be entered. The rules of the game, the structure of power in the polity, group interests, and group resources dictate both the objects of interest group pressure and the techniques and tactics used.

The history of political theory reveals an ongoing debate over the degree to which political power should be unified or divided in society. American ideology and political practice have been dominated by commitment to the wide scattering of authority. The commitment derives from the view that the concentration of political power is always and everywhere a threat to individual freedom. This perspective is reflected in the empirical theory of groups, the major paradigm of politics developed and supported by American political scientists over the last several decades.

Group theory makes the group the central unit of analysis in the study of politics. One's political behavior is seen as shaped by one's group memberships, and the political process as structured by the conflicts among organized groups. (This view has been amended in the present book by the presumption that group membership is a matter of rational choice by individuals who bring their preferences to the group rather than vice versa.) The assumptions of standard group theory are that no group will alone control all the outcomes of political conflict, that all outcomes will require compromise, and that the "public interest" will be served by the interplay of conflict and compromise. A central issue in empirical analysis concerns the power that is available to groups. Power is a relative concept, best measured in terms of who wins what at what cost and who loses what at what cost. Outcomes depend upon the varying distributions and interactions of power resources, such as size, cohesion, money, leadership, and status.

The stability of the group process is explained by a number of concepts which are themselves outside the general assumptions of the theory. One is that all participants in the group struggle share common democratic values and will attempt to maintain a political process that is free, open, competitive, and "fair." Acceptance of the rules of the game is really not explicable in terms of group theory, nor does it appear to be universal, given the destructive and revolutionary conduct of some groups in recent years. The ideas of potential groups and overlapping memberships are additional (and limited) ways of explaining stability in a process characterized by conflict. Group theory is limited in its capacity to explain some features of the political process, but it does focus attention on an extremely important set of actors, structures, and procedures operative in the American political system.

Interest groups seek effective access to positions of policy-making and use combinations of direct and indirect means in doing so. The rules by which decisions are reached in the polity strongly influence the points of access and tactics chosen by the group. Targets and tactics, to be efficient, must be adapted to the reality of the distribution of policy-making power in society. The rules are never neutral but function to inhibit the forces of change even while they protect all groups against assaults from others.

The problem of groups, free riders, and public goods (discussed earlier) indicates that the power of large and noncoercive groups in the political process will be less than optimal. Political activity for such groups is a spillover made possible when the group's leadership is able to provide immediate social values and tangible services to members and, having done so, to reserve some portion of group resources for political activity. The number of politically intense participants in the political process is minuscule relative to total group membership — and for reasons of rational individual choice.

NOTES

1. Gabriel L. Almond and James S. Coleman, eds., *The Politics of Developing Areas* (Princeton, N.J.: Princeton University Press, 1960), pp. 33–38; Gabriel L. Almond and G. Bingham Powell, Jr., *Comparative Politics: A Developmental Approach* (Boston: Little, Brown, 1966), pp. 73–97; and David Easton, *A Systems Analysis of Political Life* (New York: Wiley, 1965), pp. 128–152, have useful discussions of this activity.

2. See Richard R. Fagen, *Politics and Communications* (Boston: Little, Brown, 1966); Dorwin Cartwright and Alvin Zander, eds., *Group Dynamics,* 3rd ed. (New York: Harper & Row, 1968); and Elihu Katz and Paul F. Lazarsfeld, *Political Influence* (New York: Free Press, 1955).

3. An attempt to find ways of achieving unity and stability in the state is a central theme of *The Republic of Plato,* trans. by Francis M. Cornford (New York: Oxford University Press, 1945).

4. See Jean Jacques Rousseau, *The Social Contract and Discourses,* trans. by G.D.H. Cole (New York: Dutton, 1950).

5. See Bernard Bosenquet, *Philosophical Theory of the State,* 4th ed. (London: Macmillan, 1923); Johann G. Fichte, *Addresses to the German Nation,* trans. by R.F. Jones and G.F. Turnbull (LaSalle, Ill.: Open Court, 1922); and G.W.F. Hegel, *Philosophy of Right,* trans. by T.M. Knox (Oxford: Clarendon, 1942).

6. See Hannah Arendt, *The Origins of Totalitarianism* (New York: Harcourt, Brace & World, 1966); William Ebenstein, *Totalitarianism: New Perspectives* (New York: Holt, Rinehart & Winston, 1962); and

Carl J. Friedrich, ed., *Totalitarianism* (Cambridge, Mass.: Harvard University Press, 1954).

7. See J.W. Allen, *History of Political Thought in the Sixteenth Century*, rev. ed. (New York: Barnes & Noble, 1957).

8. Harold J. Laski, *A Grammar of Politics*, 4th ed. (New York: Humanities Press, 1964), and *The State in Theory and Practice* (New York: Viking Press, 1935), has useful statements of the pluralist position. Cf. the formulation of pluralism in Robert A. Dahl, *Polyarchy* (New Haven, Conn.: Yale University Press, 1971).

9. See Lord Acton, *Essays on Freedom and Power*. Cf. the arguments presented in A. Rogow and H.D. Lasswell, *Power, Corruption, and Rectitude* (Englewood Cliffs, N.J.: Prentice-Hall, 1963).

10. See Daniel J. Boorstin, *The Genius of American Politics* (Chicago: University of Chicago Press, 1953); and Louis Hartz, *The Liberal Tradition in America* (New York: Harcourt, Brace, 1955).

11. The most famous version of this argument, as noted earlier, is found in James Madison, *The Federalist*, No. 10. See Edward Mead Earle, *The Federalist* (New York: Modern Library, 1941). Cf. the analysis of these arguments in Robert A. Dahl, *A Preface to Democratic Theory* (Chicago: University of Chicago Press, 1956). See also John C. Calhoun, "A Disquisition on Government," in Richard K. Cralle, ed., *The Works of John C. Calhoun* (New York: D. Appleton, 1854), Vol. I.

12. See Pendleton Herring, *The Politics of Democracy* (New York: Rinehart, 1940).

13. See Dorothy B. James, ed., *Outside, Looking In: Critiques of American Politics and Institutions; Left and Right* (New York: Harper & Row, 1972), for a wide variety of selections representing this orientation.

14. The first thoroughgoing presentation of the group theory of politics appeared in Arthur F. Bentley's 1908 *The Process of Government* (Cambridge, Mass.: Harvard University Press, 1967). The major impact of the approach was not felt until it was reformulated in David B. Truman, *The Governmental Process* (New York: Knopf, 1951). This is clearly the most influential version of the theory and one of the most important books in the history of American political science. Also of great importance, and basic to the present analysis, is the work of Mancur L. Olson, Jr., *The Logic of Collective Action* (Cambridge, Mass.: Harvard University Press, 1965). The self-interest assumption is central to James Q. Wilson's comprehensive treatise on groups, *Political Organizations* (New York: Basic Books, 1973).

15. See Earl Latham, *The Group Basis of Politics* (New York: Octagon, 1965); and Truman, *The Governmental Process*.

16. Bentley, *The Process of Government*, argued, for example, that the group dynamics of the society explained completely all aspects of politics.

17. See Truman, *The Governmental Process*, and Latham, *The Group Basis of Politics*.

18. Ibid.

19. See, for example, Leo Weinstein, "The Group Approach: Arthur F. Bentley," in Herbert J. Storing et al., eds., *Essays on the Scientific Study of Politics* (New York: Holt, Rinehart & Winston, 1962), pp. 151–224.
20. See James G. March, "The Power of Power," in David Easton, ed., *Varieties of Political Theory* (Englewood Cliffs, N.J.: Prentice-Hall, 1966), pp. 39–70.
21. Truman, *The Governmental Process,* pp. 110–210.
22. One of the problems inadequately handled by the group theorists is finding ways to aggregate meaningfully these independent measures of power resources.
23. The Soviet doctrine of democratic centralism is a classic example. See Herbert McCloskey and John E. Turner, *The Soviet Dictatorship* (New York: McGraw-Hill, 1960), pp. 202–203.
24. See Robert Michels, *Political Parties,* trans. by Eden and Cedar Paul (New York: Collier Books, 1962).
25. An example is the development of large-scale labor and business organizations. For a useful description and explanation of this process see Seymour Martin Lipset, "The Political Process in Trade Unions: A Theoretical Statement," in Morroe Berger et al., *Freedom and Control in Modern Society* (New York: Octagon, 1964), pp. 82–124.
26. Truman, *The Governmental Process,* pp. 157–167.
27. See, for example, R.E. Dowling, "Pressure Group Theory: Its Methodological Range," *American Political Science Review,* 54 (March 1961), 944–954.
28. Easton, *A Systems Analysis of Political Life.*
29. Truman, *The Governmental Process,* pp. 501–537.
30. See David Riesman, Nathan Glazer, and Reuel Denney, *The Lonely Crowd,* rev. ed. (New Haven, Conn.: Yale University Press, 1964).
31. Clement E. Vose, *Caucasians Only: The Supreme Court, the NAACP, and the Restrictive Covenant Cases* (Berkeley: University of California Press, 1959).
32. See E.E. Schattschneider, *The Semisovereign People* (New York: Holt, Rinehart & Winston, 1967), which is very much a restatement of John Dewey's classic *The Public and Its Problems* (New York: Holt, 1927).
33. Perhaps the best example is Bertram Gross, *The Legislative Struggle* (New York: McGraw-Hill, 1953).
34. An influential source is Grant McConnell, *Private Power and American Democracy* (New York: Knopf, 1966).
35. Ibid., pp. 11–51.
36. Raymond A. Bauer, Ithiel de Sola Pool, and Lewis A. Dexter, *American Business and Public Policy* (New York: Atherton, 1964), p. 404.
37. See Lester W. Milbrath, *The Washington Lobbyists* (Chicago: Rand McNally, 1963), and Lewis A. Dexter, *How Organizations Are Represented in Washington* (Indianapolis: Bobbs-Merrill, 1969).
38. Ibid.
39. See McConnell, *Private Power and American Democracy.*

40. See Marver H. Bernstein, *Regulating Business by Independent Commission* (Princeton, N.J.: Princeton University Press, 1955).

41. Consult, for example, Norton Long, "Power and Administration," *Public Administration Review,* 9 (1949), 257–264.

42. An interesting reference is Theodore Lowi, *The End of Liberalism* (New York: Norton, 1969).

43. See Charles A. Horsky (himself a Washington lawyer), *The Washington Lawyers* (Boston: Little, Brown, 1952).

44. See David J. Danielski, *A Supreme Court Justice Is Appointed* (New York: Random House, 1964), and John R. Schmidhauser, *The Supreme Court* (New York: Holt, Rinehart & Winston, 1961).

45. See Samuel Krislov, "The Amicus Curiae Brief: From Friendship to Advocacy," in Gottfried Dietze, ed., *Essays on the American Constitution* (Englewood Cliffs, N.J.: Prentice-Hall, 1964).

46. See Fowler V. Harper and Edwin D. Etherington, "Lobbyist Before the Court," *University of Pennsylvania Law Review,* 10 (1953), 1172 ff.

47. See Chester A. Newland, "The Supreme Court and Legal Writing: Learned Journals as Vehicles of an Anti-Antitrust Lobby?" *Georgetown Law Journal,* 48 (Fall 1959), 105–143.

7 Political Parties and the Public Will

The political party is a unique kind of political interest group, members of which perform significant functions in the polity. In America, political party is a group that attempts to influence public choices by electing group members to official positions in the government.[1] The minimum goal shared (at least ostensibly) by party members is to capture whatever governmental decision-making positions are required in order to control the public policy of society.

A major difference in the activities and goals of the political party as compared with other forms of political interest groups is, then, that the farmer seeks to control government directly by seizing public office, while the latter are satisfied if they can influence the content of policy by more indirect means.

Another major difference is that political parties are vehicles for the representation of social interests that are unrepresented or underrepresented (and often unrepresentable) in the pluralistic or special interest

196

group struggle described in the preceding chapter. Many interests are essentially unorganizable in any authentic sense outside the political party system (although people who appoint themselves to speak for such interests often claim to represent and to have organized them). We have already explained why some groups perform suboptimally in the political process. Suboptimality is particularly typical of large, noncoercive groups concerned to secure increased public goods from government. The interests of so-called **categoric groups** — "liberals," "conservatives," mothers, Chicanos, midwesterners, senior citizens, "people of goodwill" — are vulnerable in this regard. Such interests are large, complicated, poorly defined, and lacking in self-consciousness; they do not control sanctions by which, if certain potential members were organized, others could be induced to join the group and to share in the costs of advancing its goals. Incentives for individuals to participate on behalf of these interests are meager. Simply stated, there are few inducements for members of categoric groups as such to participate very actively in the politi-

*"How would you like me to answer that question?
As a member of my ethnic group, educational class,
income group, or religious category?"*
Drawing by D. Fradon; © 1969 The New Yorker
Magazine, Inc.

cal process. The institution best situated to incorporate interests of this kind is the political party, through its candidates' search for votes. Party politicians, in reducing the complexity of the world to manageable proportions, find it useful to think in terms of categoric groups (the youth vote, "middle-of-the roaders," "workers," etc.), to seek out their support and, by so doing, give life, meaning, and representation to their collective interests. Without parties, such interests would be represented only weakly if at all in politics.[2] In our complex society, the successful political party must develop the support of a very diverse set of interests, organized and specific, as well as unorganized and categoric.

One traditional description of political parties is to be found in the writings of the English political thinker and politician Edmund Burke. Burke defined a political party as "a body of men united, for promoting by their joint endeavors the national interest, upon some particular principle in which they are all agreed."[3] From this book's perspective, Burke's definition is misleading if it requires, as it seems to, that all individuals who identify with a political party necessarily share some ethic or ideology in common. Probably most analysts of American political parties believe, on the contrary, that the central, if not the only, force binding individuals to a political party is a shared desire to win elections.[4] From an individualistic point of view — which asserts that the *content* of individual preferences must always be discovered and not presumed — perhaps only one inference can actually be drawn from the existence of a political party: Its members are in agreement that their coalition should continue for at least the time being. It is certainly true that most party leaders and members do associate their control of the government with the public interest; that the earnest and viable party, to retain its membership and support, must possess, or seem to possess, some probability of capturing control of the government either now or in the foreseeable future; and that, without such expectation, the coalition (party) will collapse entirely or become the fag end of the party system, consisting of a small number of individuals without serious chance of coming to power.

Nonetheless, the individuals who comprise the loose coalitions that we call American political parties are agreed on few abstract principles or ideological dimensions, including the proper function of the party. They become involved in party politics for many reasons: to win elections, find jobs, combat boredom, achieve policy preferences, acquire personal power, make friends, and fight injustice wherever it raises its ugly head. The desire to win elections is characteristic of most partisans, although frequently questions of ideological purity and consistency, or of which intraparty faction is to be dominant, are given a higher priority than winning.

The expression "He would rather be right than be President" describes a view which, under some circumstances, can become dominant in a party. The intraparty Republican factions that formed in support of Senator Goldwater in 1964 and the intraparty Democratic factions attracted by Senator McGovern in 1972 provide two dramatic examples. Supporters of these candidates were either more concerned to save the "soul" of their parties and prepared to radically reduce their chances of winning the current election to do so, *or* they were self-deceived about the nature of the American electorate and the operation of the party system. When such forces capture control of a major party and refuse to compete seriously for governmental power in the here and now, the result has been to install the other party in power with a landslide victory. A consistent pattern of this sort of behavior must lead to either chronic one-party rule, wild oscillations in party control and electoral landslides, or the emergence of a fragmented party system.[5] The last possibility is not unknown in American politics. A case in point is the Democratic party's control of southern politics (at the nonpresidential level) since the Civil War. The result has been a multifactional organization which, by obscuring lines of cleavage and by poorly structuring electoral choices, appears to aggregate and advance the diverse interests of the region rather inefficiently.[6]

Although there are historical exceptions to the rule, managers of the major American political parties can normally assemble loose coalitions of citizens able to work together, or tolerate one another, for extended periods of time. The Democratic and Republican parties are not fly-by-night outfits; indeed, they are the oldest political parties in the world! The hope of winning elections and sharing in the spoils and power is the cement that holds them together and little else.[7] A strong proof appears in the party platforms that are written and presented to the electorate every four years: They reflect the internal fragmentation of the parties and are efforts to develop and maintain winning coalitions of often strange bedfellows. American history provides many instances of odd coalitions. Think of Democratic party conventions of recent years in which civil rights militants and segregationists both participated, *and* influenced, party deliberations. Usually the competition between the two major parties is keen enough to provide alternative arenas in which the interests of a vast array of groups and individuals could meet in order to discuss, compromise, and coordinate differences and identify and debate a manageable range of potential policy positions. This narrowing of alternatives is a necessary condition for the making of rational choices by individual voters at election time.

THE TROUBLE WITH PARTIES:
TYRANNY AND CORRUPTION

Political parties are among the most frequently and harshly criticized institutions in the political system. Throughout American history there has been widespread distrust of parties and party politics, and many attempts have been made to restrict their development and power. The Founding Fathers themselves were fearful of the possibility of parties, believing that they would be destructive of the public interest. The Constitution makes no provision for political parties; its framers were clearly hopeful that parties would not emerge in America. Political parties were considered a dangerous form of faction which, if permitted, would promote private interests at the expense of the interests of all. Arguments on behalf of a factionalized society (by Madison, for example) rested upon the precondition that any given faction would be precluded from gaining total control of the government. The political party had the serious defect that it might produce a majority coalition which would impose its view of the public interest upon society. A grand majority coalition was seen as a threat to the checks and balances so artfully embedded in the Constitution. The logic of the constitutional system required, after all, that the separate institutional levers of power — the presidency, Congress, the Supreme Court, federalism — could not be controlled and orchestrated by the same coalition of interests. Political parties threatened a tyranny which might do just that. Like so many hopes, those of the framers of the polity were shattered in this regard almost immediately after the promulgation of the Constitution. By the election of 1800, party loyalty had developed to a point that the original scheme for the operation of the electoral college was made unworkable, and the Twelfth Amendment (1804) was added to the Constitution. The framers' fears were at least partly justified, inasmuch as political parties have become important mechanisms for integrating the several branches of government and for diminishing the cleavages installed by the separation of powers doctrine and the system of checks and balances.[8] However, probably most contemporary analysts tend to evaluate this result as a positive rather than negative effect of party activity, at least if they happen to approve of the policy lines of the dominant party.[9] If one disapproves of the dominant party, support for constitutional separations and adversary relationships presumably makes just as much sense.

The charge of corruption has also been made continuously against parties and party politicians. The terms *boss, machine, spoils, graft, deal, smoke-filled room, sellout, compromise,* and many others appear and reappear in the polemical and reformist literature bearing on the party system.[10] Many reform and "indignation" movements have focused recurring attention on such themes and have sought to limit the power, independence, and influence of political parties, all in an effort to "perfect" democracy. Alleged inadequacies of the party system ostensibly motivated many of those who sought to alter electoral processes and to extend increasingly "popular" control of the party system and the government. A number of those efforts succeeded; that is, they succeeded in weakening the party system. Whether the community has benefited is problematical. Some reform efforts are discussed later in this chapter.

FUNCTIONS OF PARTIES

Although often under attack, political parties have survived as important structures within the political system. Their durability is attributable to the fact that they contribute to the achievement of many concrete individual interests. The moment that no interests are served by their activities, parties will disappear. Traditionally, for example, political parties have supplied social services for individuals, including getting them jobs.[11] Providing social services directly through parties reached its high point in the late nineteenth and early twentieth centuries. This function has been reduced in importance with the development of public welfare systems and civil service reform, but parties still afford channels for the achievement of individual goals. The perpetuation of party support requires the existence of such channels.

An important activity of the leadership of political parties is the combining of the diverse interests in society and the development of programs that will satisfy a wide range of political demands.[12] This activity, undertaken to maximize support at the polls, works to frame a manageable number of political issues and policy alternatives for the individual electoral choice. The goals and values of diverse groups are often compromised within the party structure, and the party is instrumental in building majority acceptance of the resulting compromises. This vital process may broaden public support for policy proposals far beyond the capacity of other interest groups in the society to do so.[13] The conflict between parties sharpens the issues and tends to clarify the costs and benefits associated with various policies and programs. While individuals and groups may be able to articulate effectively a new policy, issue, or threat, the *major* shifts in governmental policy occur when innovations are approved by political parties and majority acceptance is generated through party propaganda.

A typical cycle of securing party support for successful innovation involves a series of steps: (1) A "need for governmental action in some area is asserted by some interest — individuals or the leaders of a group. (2) A policy proposal to meet the need is articulated by that interest. (3) One of the major political parties includes the proposal in its platform in order to gain the support of people who are pressing for the adoption of the proposal. (4) The proposal is adopted as an item in the political program of a party that wins an election, and that party is able to translate the proposal into effective public policy. (5) The opposition party is unable to make any political capital by attacking the program, or may lose support by doing so, at which time the matter ceases to be a significant public issue. A policy proposal generally arouses controversy when it becomes an aspect of serious party conflict; it ceases to be an issue when it is no longer a source of such conflict. There are, of course, many other ways in which political programs are instituted, and certainly not all proposals that are articulated are adopted. However, this series of steps does describe a typical pattern by which public policy evolves. Thus the party plays a critical role in linking the interests and demands of individuals and groups to the policy structures and decisions of government. The combining of political demands, the fabrication of politically viable programs, the development of adequate political support for innovation, the formulation and enactment of public policy, and the effectuation of the policy are activities in which the political party is highly instrumental. The weaker parties become, the less able they are to perform these functions. It is doubtful that such implications are always taken into account by agitators for party reform.

To be most efficient, the functions described above require the presence of another significant activity. Under some conditions, the party system can enhance the responsiveness and accountability of governmental agencies to interests in society.[14] The conditions involve competition for votes. The electoral competition between parties for political offices forces each party to try to develop positions on issues that will gain it the support of enough persons so that they can gain control of the government. Uncertainty and other factors may lead to failure in this regard, but the effort must be made. If the political party in power does not satisfy a majority of those who vote more than the opposition party is expected to do, it will lose the next election. People will support the party that best serves their interests, and they can always shift if their interests are not being met or if the opposition promises to meet them more fully. The conditions that inhibit and facilitate the shift of support from one to another party are discussed later in this chapter.

The single goal of winning elections is often criticized as unprincipled and vulgar pragmatism of the worst sort. That such a goal requires political parties in a free, democratic, and competitive society to respond to the desires of a majority of the electorate if they are to win the power to govern is, however, an important redeeming quality. The statement "All a political party cares about is winning elections" is the functional equivalent in a competitive electoral system with majority decision-rules of the statement that all a party cares about is responding to the wishes of the majority.[15] Of course, the party is not a mere passive agent in this process; it plays important leadership, propaganda, and educational roles in attempting to convince voters that its policies are right, proper, and just, even though these policies initially may not have been preferred by a majority. The use of persuasion is a necessary and widely accepted technique of democratic decision-making.

In a direct sense, the political party can be held accountable for failures when it controls the government. If it never gains control of the government, its policies cannot be tested and it can operate in an altogether nonresponsible manner. The existence of a serious opposition party is indispensable in developing and maintaining governmental responsibility. Without an opposition party, there is no viable alternative to the party in power and thus no competing object of support.[16] We emphasize again: It is the desire of political party leaders to win elections that forces them to play their most significant role in the operation of a democratic society. In large-scale societies, only political parties offer a means of making the government more or less accountable to rank-and-file citizens. Paradoxically, a party whose members and leaders do not "care" about winning elections has the greatest tendency to act in an irresponsible and capricious manner and makes the least contribution to popular and democratic government.

The ordinary citizen has limited time available to deal with political questions and few incentives to participate or distribute his or her scarce resources very lavishly in the political process. As difficult as it is for some political scientists to believe, politics is a minor element in the interests and activities of most people — and, as we have stressed repeatedly, for good reasons. To influence the political system at all, the average citizen needs some kind of mechanism through which individuals can seek to make government responsive to their needs at slight cost. The political party is one such mechanism. The costs for individuals in gaining enough information to make intelligent, self-interested choices on public issues and candidacies that affect their lives exceed any benefits that are likely to accrue from their efforts. Unwilling to allocate much time and resources to politics, a person may find in the political party a means of making expectedly beneficial choices within the limits of acceptable costs.[17] The party label attached to a candidate or program, by communicating a great deal of inexpensive information to a potential voter, allows the making of choices with a minimum of time and effort. To the extent that a voter is able to associate individual interests and needs with the history, reputation, policies, programs, candidates, and record of a given political party, the party identification of a candidate can be used to predict the probable orientation of the candidate vis-à-vis the voter's desires. For some voters, party labels are all that is required for their decision-making. Although the fragmented conditions of American political parties, their shifts in policy orientations through time, and the variable quality of their performance in office do produce an error factor in such predictions, there is enough continuity of policy positions and stability of coalitions of interests within the major parties to guide many citizens in making voting choices consistent with their own welfare. Obviously, voting choices are made under conditions of uncertainty and carry some risk, but the amount of time and information needed to make more informed choices on the merits of each issue and candidate exceeds acceptable limits for most voters.

According to the 1972 National Election Study conducted by the University of Michigan's Survey Research Center (SRC), some 10 percent of the nation's adults regarded themselves as "strong" Republicans and 15 percent as "strong" Democrats. In so-called normal times, this 25 percent of the population will find voting in some ways at least a very inexpensive act; a strong partisan must only ascertain the party affiliation of a candidate in order to decide how to vote. The problem of choice is presumably greater for the 13 percent who described themselves as "weak" Republicans or for the 26 percent who identified themselves as "weak" Democrats. For this large portion of the community (39 percent) a party label provides an initial point of reference but may need to be supplemented with additional information if the voter is to make an intelligent voting choice. Strong partisans are likely to vote and to remain loyal to their party in doing so. Weak partisans are less likely to vote and more likely to shift between parties.

Table 7-1. Party Identification of the American Electorate (in percentages).

Year	Strong Democrat	Weak Democrat	Independent	Weak Republican	Strong Republican	Other
1972	15	26	34	13	10	2
1968	20	25	29	14	10	2
1964	27	25	22	13	11	2
1960	21	26	23	14	14	2
1956	21	23	23	14	15	4

Source: Center for Political Studies of the University of Michigan; data made available through the Inter-University Consortium for Political Research.

Some 34 percent of the population in the SRC survey were self-classified as "independents." (This is a much larger proportion, incidentally, than the 23 percent who identified as Republicans and not all that far below the 41 percent who regarded themselves as Democrats.) One-third of the independents "leaned" to the Republicans, one-third "leaned" to the Democrats, and one-third viewed themselves as truly independent of the influence of party labels. The "leaners" receive at least some helpful information from party labels since they are slightly predisposed to favor one party over another. True independents receive almost no assistance from knowing the party identifications of candidates. For them, altogether different cues are required. This is a problem discussed at greater length in Chapter 8. As a group, independents have a lower rate of voting and a greater tendency than partisans to shift between parties: over 60 percent report having voted for presidential candidates from both parties.

Republicans, Democrats, and independents include almost all of the population. Those with no discernible political view at all, the apoliticals, number about 1 percent, and "others," identifiers with minor parties and those who refuse to say, constitute less than 0.3 percent of the population.

RECRUITMENT TO OFFICE

With few exceptions, elections above the local level are partisan in nature. A major party label is almost always a necessary (and sometimes a sufficient) condition for a candidate to win election to an important political office. Thus, the political party serves as a principal means of recruiting governmental leaders.[18] The party organization may induce individuals to become involved in the nomination of leaders; provides for the identification, socialization, and training of potential leaders; and makes available a career or mobility pattern for those who wish to obtain high-level positions in the government. The weak position of the Democratic and Republican parties' central leadership, occasioned by their decentralized organizational and ideological structures, somewhat limits the control of the parties over the process of political recruitment. Frequently an ambitious personality can gain enough political support through nonparty activities so that party leaders have strong inducements to nominate the person for some office even though he or she has made no traditional contributions to the work of the party. General Eisenhower is an example. Although it does not hold in Eisenhower's case, this pattern is particularly apparent in jurisdictions using the direct primary electoral system to select party candidates.

The party that succeeds in electing a majority of the members of the House and/or Senate has the power and responsibility to organize those bodies. A party preeminent in Congress, however, need not control the presidency. Since World War II, for example, the Republicans have controlled Congress for only two sessions (1946–1948 and 1950–1952), although they have, as of 1975, controlled the presidency for sixteen years. With divided control of government, it is not always easy to say which party, if either, is "responsible" for any particular state of affairs. Bicameralism, the separation of powers, and the state and local basis of party power have proved durable and disheartening obstacles to supporters of "responsible party government" who would like to see one or another party take charge of the whole of government and, by so doing, be made accountable by the electorate for whatever follows.[19] This conception has a certain tidy, albeit mechanical, attractiveness. That there are profound reasons of culture and interest for the existing decentralized "irresponsible" system is a fact either conceded grudgingly, overlooked entirely, or dismissed for obscure reasons as unimportant by the advocates of various and sundry reforms designed to create party government.

Fragmented as party power is, however, utter chaos does not reign. There is considerable structure to things as they are: One identifiable party *does* control the presidency and one identifiable party *does* control the House and/or Senate. While evaluating these complex contingencies is perhaps more difficult for the voter than evaluating the performance of a single responsible party, the task is not an impossible one. Besides, as pointed out in our discussion of factions, a system of divided rule protects all factions from the tyranny of others. A party's control of leadership positions in whatever branch of government forces it to compile a record of performance that may be evaluated, however roughly, by the electorate. Popular rejection of its record may result in capture of those positions by the opposition party in the next election. As we have said, some analysts argue that the uncoordinated and diffuse nature of authority in the national government limits the capacity of government to respond appropriately to the "needs" of society. It is all to the good, they say, if a political party can integrate the pluralistic institutions of government by staffing them with like-minded or at least cooperative-minded people, thus reducing the "negative" consequences of the Constitution's checks and balances. Control of government by a single political party lessens the chances of governmental stalemate and inaction.

Others might argue that the meaning of social "needs" is ordinarily confused to begin with, but, however defined, those needs are better met and protected from abuses if a divided government is maintained than if remedial action is facilitated by more unity in government. Whichever view one takes, the pattern of American politics, by allowing for the control of the legislative and executive branches by different political parties, lowers the capacity of the national government to develop and apply consistent policies.

It comes to this: Political parties occupy a paradoxical position in America. On the one hand, the party system is an indispensable instrument of self-government. A competitive party system is, indeed, a prerequisite of democratic rule in a society of any scale at all. The idea of democracy is widely supported in America. Without parties, government would be less responsive, less responsible, and less accountable to the people. Parties make democracy possible, although they do not, of course, guarantee it. On the other hand, political parties have been under attack throughout the history of the American polity as *threats* to rule by "the people." Barriers designed to restrict the efficacy with which the parties operate have been erected by various reforming impulses. This quixotic attitude toward parties stems from a generalized fear, distrust, and rejection of the concentration of political power, combined with a countervailing and contradictory propensity to rely upon government in achieving a wide range of individual wants. Thus the competitive party system is necessary for responsive democratic government, but American attitudes toward power seriously limit the capacity of the parties to perform effectively the tasks of mobilizing and advancing the interests of individuals throughout the society.

THE AMERICAN PARTY SYSTEM

The American party system is usually regarded as a two-party system, a characterization that implies several of its operational and organizational elements. The number of major parties in a political system suggests something about their internal attributes and how conflict between or among them will be structured.[20] In a general way, the operation of parties in the United States follows anticipated patterns for a two-party system, but some structural and attitudinal factors in the American polity substantially modify the behavior of parties projected from the ideal two-party model.

Each presidential election year the Republicans and Democrats hold huge conventions which are major events in the operation of the two-party system. *Camerique*

Party Fragmentation

At the national level, the president and vice-president are the only elected officials with a nationwide constituency. The two-party model is operative in national elections, and only in presidential elections does the American party system work at the national level in a manner that is mainly consistent with the expectations of most analysts of two-party systems. The Congress is based upon a large number of smaller constituencies (435 House districts and 50 states = 485 constituencies); given the largely local orientation of American politics, the separate party struggle in *each* of these constituencies determines its collective character. The national party and its policy concerns are nearly always subordinate to local officials and local issues. Integration between the national, or presidential, party (which is little more than a coalition of state parties brought temporarily together in presidential election years) and the local, or congressional, party is weak at best. The importance attached to party control of the presidency is the only important inducement for cooperation between local and national party leaders.[21] Congressional candidates from an area in which their party's presidential candidate is in disfavor may profitably dissociate themselves from the national party during an election. Thus, even though virtually all members of congress carry the label of one of the major political parties, the national party does not play a significant role in their selection nor does it always have an important impact on their behavior. State and local party organizations, operating quite independently of the national organization, serve more often as the point of reference for the congressional candidate. And too, in many constituencies the complete domination of the area by a single party (and hence lack of competition) may reduce the relevance of party activity in congressional elections to near insignificance. The politics of friends and neighbors replaces party politics of the competitive sort. Thus, even the most minimal coordination between national and local parties may lack a rational basis and is, for that reason, frequently nonexistent. Many congressional elections are marked by a total lack of party competition, and the elements of a "normal" two-party system are consequently not operative.

Party and Intensity

Compared to a system of many parties, a two-party system has the effect of diminishing *intensity* and *insecurity* in the polity. The less-than-polarized differences in the policy proposals of the two parties — required if they are to compete successfully for support from the same set of moderate voters — tend to reduce the importance and risk of failure in the electoral process. The existence of strident partisans with access to the media, college campuses, and the like obscures the fact that most American voters are not very frightened by the prospect of the opposition party's gaining control of the government. Conversely, they are not consumed with excitement if their party preference turns out to be successful or dread if unsuccessful. This lowering of the risk for the average individual makes the incentives to participate vigorously in the electoral process less attractive.[22] Of course, the "payoffs" from winning may also be insufficiently large to induce vigorous participation.

The drift to the center by both parties in a competitive two-party system causes people with the least political information and fewest ideological or policy commitments to conclude that there are scant practical differences between the parties. That conclusion further reduces the incentives for participation in either the party or the electoral process. Party leaders are forced to rely for active workers upon persons who have developed keen party identifications, intense ideological commitments, or concrete material interest in the outcome of elections.[23] Since for these persons it makes a considerable difference which political party controls the government, they are willing to contribute their energy and money to increase their party's chances at the polls. Some extreme partisans view every electoral choice as important and certain elections as life-and-death matters affecting the course of world history. Such intense feelings shade off to greatly muted concern if not indifference toward the modal position taken by voters on the conflicts structured by the parties.

The greater the number of persons who are intensely concerned about the outcome of an election, the more people there are who will sense the serious risk involved should the "wrong" party win. In all national elections, at least some people believe the outcome so vital that the society will not be worth living in if the choice of the electorate is "wrong." If such perceptions were sufficiently widespread, it would be utterly unacceptable to a significant portion of the population for one or the other party to take office. Fears of this kind are major incentives for undermining or subverting the electoral process itself.

Under normal operation of the two-party system, then, most people do not see high risk in the electoral process. Incentives to participate in electoral politics are therefore low, and stability and predictability of the electoral system are high.[24] The two-party system is thus a significant element in social stability. It is paradoxical that, by reducing the incentives to participate, the two-party system contributes to the maintenance of democratic processes. Furthermore, the parties are part of the "checks and balances" of the American polity. By denying power to rule-or-ruin ideologues, they are as important as any formal rule of the Constitution in limiting control of government by any intense hell-bent-for-election group, however large or small.

Party Ideology and Responsiveness

The often-heard description of American political parties as providing a nonchoice between Tweedledee and Tweedledum reflects a negative evaluation of the two-party system lodged most typically by persons with keen ideological or policy commitments who are unsatisfied by existing processes. There are recurring demands for the two parties to become more distinguishable ideologically so that voters can have "real" alternatives. Recent attempts by a major party to provide the electorate with a clearer ideological choice have produced *noncompetitive* elections in which the vast majority of the electorate found the party providing the "choice" emphatically unacceptable. Most voters perceived that these "ideological" elections provided them with no viable alternative except to vote for the party following the moderate coalitional tactics normally associated with the two-party system. Perhaps Americans do not really want ideological choices to be presented in election campaigns after all, particularly if those choices deviate very far from the centrist ideology held by most voters.

The rejection by either major party of the normal practice of coalition-building in favor of adopting ideologically consistent commitments always seems to allow the other party to preempt the middle of the political spectrum, which is precisely where most voters are to be found. A landslide election victory for even a moderate party has potentially destabilizing consequences. One of them is that the leaders of the winning party may claim receipt of a mandate not intended by many erstwhile supporters. If winning politicians conclude that they can afford to lose some of their support and still win the next election, they may not try to respond to the interest of many individuals who have newly joined the winning coalition of moderates.[25] Similarly, the winning party, having little need to broaden its base of support, can safely ignore the interests of those who supported the losing party. *The general outcome is to make the winning political party and thereby the government it controls less responsive to the demands and interests of both its supporters and its opponents.* The principle to be remembered is that any serious lessening of competition between the major parties lowers responsiveness to the electorate and hence the extent to which individual goals can be achieved through politics. An attempt by either party to provide a "real" choice not only tends to produce failure at the polls but reduces the efficiency of the polity's responsiveness and accountability to the broader community.

By its very nature, a two-party system cannot practically provide a clear ideological choice which would satisfy persons with well-integrated ideological preferences. Distinct ideological choices would be possible only if all or most people in the society were concentrated into two distinct homogeneous groups whose behavior was conditioned primarily by ideology. Such a situation would require a much greater interest in politics and much more similarity of individual preferences than actually exist in our large and diverse society. Moreover, it is doubtful that a society divided into two distinct ideological groupings could function democratically as a single political community for any protracted period. Ideological purity and intensity beyond some point are simply inconsistent with two-party systems. If both political parties were to adopt sharply conflicting ideological positions, the risk to the individual whose party lost an election would be increased. Incentives to accept an unfavorable outcome would be minimal and political instability thereby enhanced.

It is also highly unlikely that a government controlled by such an ideologically charged group would be willing to lay down the reins of power knowing that they would be picked up by its ideological antithesis. Such self-abnegation would require a strength of commitment to democratic processes not generally held by anyone, much less by ideologues who have discovered substantive Truth and Justice. The more likely result would be subversion of the most central of all democratic norms: that a governing party, having lost a free election, must peacefully turn over the power to govern to those who have won. A party that will not withdraw peacefully from power ceases to be an instrument of democracy and becomes an instrument of its denial.

The demand for a real ideological choice between the parties, if carried to its last extension, would, however, achieve one of the goals sought by the proponents of such change. The marginal concern and indifference toward party politics held currently by many people would probably be markedly reduced — and so would stability, predictability, governmental responsiveness, and democracy. A more perfect achievement of democratic values would not be realized; the destruction of constitutional democracy would be. This description is more than a parade of imaginary horrors. These actual patterns begin to form in embryo whenever the electorate is presented with "a choice, not an echo," and whether the choice is presented from the left or the right of the political continuum. There are ideologically intense persons in all societies, partisans with deep and earnest loyalties who believe that election of the opposition party will destroy all public virtue, hope, tradition, etc. They see any means as legitimate that will serve to expel or thwart the intolerable opposition. The decision of some of the "president's men" to covertly enter the Democratic headquarters which began the spiral of events collectively known as "Watergate" was probably at base an example of the operation of this phenomenon. Although that dimension of the problem has been little discussed, the belief of some of the more intense conservative partisans of President Nixon that the election of George McGovern would lead to the destruction of most of what is "good" in American institutions apparently justified (to them) the use of extraordinary and even illegal campaign tactics. The important issue is not whether Mr. McGovern posed such a threat but that strategically placed individuals believed he did. The costs of defeat were too large to risk total reliance upon traditional practices. Any major growth in the perception that one of the major political parties represents an unacceptable governing entity endangers the maintenance of basic democratic values and processes. Of course, such perceptions need not be paranoid. Some values of basic importance to at least some people are at risk in any election — even distinctly moderate ones. More radical choices simply expand the number of persons involved and the intensity of feeling that is likely to develop.

ONE-PARTY SYSTEMS

The functioning of a two-party system can perhaps best be understood through a comparison with other political party systems. Space does not allow for any complete discussion of other systems, but a brief treatment of the operation of one-party and multiparty systems will inform the reader about alternatives to two-party competition. By evaluating the two-party system in the United States in a somewhat broader context, we can shed more light upon its operation and performance.

One-party systems have generally been associated with authoritarianism, dictatorship, and totalitarianism.[26] However, the American experience reminds us that at least two (perhaps more) fundamentally different forms of one-party systems exist. The implications for the operation of a political system of each form are quite different. One type exists when the government is controlled by a single party and no other parties are allowed to compete effectively for, or to share in, the power to govern. Alternative parties may be proscribed completely or, less ruthlessly if no less effectively, may be permitted to operate as long as they have no real chance of capturing control of the government. The Soviet Union is representative of the first sort and Mexico of the second. In either case, critical public decisions are made within the higher circles of the ruling party, and party decisions are reflected directly in the laws and programs of the governmental system. In a very real sense, there is little distinction between the policy determinations of the ruling party and the government. Discussions of policy proposals involving bargains, negotiations, assertions, disagreements, or compromise go forward within the ranks of the party, if at all. Individuals without access to the party have no real voice in the operation of the polity or, typically, no viable way of creating substitutes for prevailing institutions. The party generally attempts to control and limit the admission of persons into its ranks and demands unswerving fidelity to its leadership and policies. The party is not (cannot be) used as a means of ensuring responsiveness or accountability of the government to popular interests. It is an instrument for controlling society and advancing goals which the party leadership considers, transcendentally, to be right, necessary, and proper regardless of the desires of other individuals. Leaders tend to be highly charged ideologically and to justify their monopoly of power on the grounds that they are the authentic interpreters of the public interest. For such Truth Bearers, to tolerate opposition would be to tolerate error and to make impossible the achievement of the good society.[27] This form of one-party rule has not developed at any point in American history, although we have had our share of moralists in possession of one or another brand of the Truth. The continuing constitutional problem, as Madison understood it, was to prevent any of these zealots from coming to full power.

Before growing too sanguine about these matters, however, we should note that many states and localities in the United States (although a declining number) have been and are subject to another form of single-party domination. These one-party regions are not organized in the manner just described. They are simply areas which, for complex historical reasons, have come to be dominated by one political party. Other parties are allowed to operate freely but remain unable to compete effectively with the prevailing party in the election of public officials. In one-party states, control of state government is actually decided within a decentralized but still single party in the process of nominating party candidates. Individuals who receive the party designation of the dominant party are always elected. The general election in such states is a (vital) formality with no choice available to the voters. The control of much of the South by the Democratic party in nonpresidential elections since the Civil War is the best known (if not unique) example.[28] The system of direct primary elections and the openness of party membership in the one-party American states, however, provide a measure of competition and popular access quite at variance with that predicted on the basis of the traditional one-party model. For another thing, the "leadership" of the parties, which in some states is not even prominent enough to be easily identified, has little control over the party policies, programs, and candidates put forward in one-party areas. This is far from the case in most non-American one-party systems. In America, the actual operation of a one-party system is controlled by personalities who owe their ascendancy to activities generally unassociated with the formal party organization.

The political conflicts of one-party areas tend to be unstable, involving fragmented issues and mere personalities. Issues that would be considered "important" by many political observers may not even be addressed in one-party systems. Party organizations are weak, and since the major decisions as to who will hold office are made within the party, the party label cannot communicate cues to the voter as to the probable policy orientations of the candidates for whom they vote. Since there is really no viable opposition at the general elections in one-party areas, voting turnout is low. The "stakes" of politics are simply not at risk in such elections, and there are, consequently, minimal inducements to participate. Of course, the voter need pay no costs of "making up his mind" either, inasmuch as no real choice is to be made. But other costs are likely to be extremely high: Lacking a viable opposition party, the party system cannot play any significant role in making the polity responsive, responsible, and accountable to the voters. The political party in one-party areas is little more than an agency for dispensing **patronage** and other spoils to party supporters and a quasi-public agency in the selection of officeholders. Under these conditions, parties are minimally involved in the achievement of democratic values.

One-party areas are marked by the same patterns of political behavior associated with nonpartisan elections. The voter usually has less political information available, less interest in politics and the electoral process, and fewer inducements to participate. It is little wonder that in such regions voting turnout is relatively low,[29] stable and important political objectives are relatively rare, and the possibilities for systematic and directed change are correspondingly narrowed. The American form of one-party rule is perhaps more accurately described as a "no-party" system which has the effect of reducing the capacity of the citizen to control the government.

MULTIPARTY SYSTEMS

Multiparty systems are those in which more than two important political parties compete for the power to govern. Generally, in such a system no single party can hope to gain complete control of the agencies of government in any single election, and the governing power is shared by two or more of the parties. Coalition government is the norm in a multiparty system. The individual parties tend to appeal to a much narrower range of interests and ideologies than do the parties in a two-party system and are more likely to take ideologically clear and coherent political positions. The number of parties is usually a rough measure of the degree of ideological fragmentation of the society, and the presence of ideologically oriented parties itself reinforces, intensifies, and *creates* ideological conflict. There are relatively few inducements to encourage the leadership of the several parties to compromise their policy positions in order to expand their support among the diverse interests in society. Seldom does a party attempt to broaden its base of appeal to include an absolute majority. The social and economic composition of the membership may be quite homogeneous, and the party may gain little from modifying its ideological or policy orientations to appeal to outsiders. The costs associated with losses in cohesion, unity, and intensity may be much greater than potential gains associated with expanded membership. The negotiations and compromises that are necessary for policy-making in any democratic society are ordinarily concentrated in interparty bargaining in the postelection period. This bargaining is carried on by the leaders of successful parties after the election rather than among the different factions within the party prior to the election, as is the typical pattern in two-party systems.[30]

   It is important to recognize that in multiparty parliamentary systems the coalitions formed to share in the power of governance are not subject to ratification by the voters. The nature of these coalitions cannot be known with any precision by the voter when he casts his ballot. Although the differences are more in degrees than in kind, it is somewhat more difficult for the voter in a multiparty system to predict the implications of his voting choice than it is for the voter in the two-party system.[31] Such uncertainty lodges greater discretion in the leadership of the party and requires voters to place greater trust in the party leadership than is the case in the two-party system. The policy positions of the party are more completely controlled by its formal leadership, and the direct accountability of the government to the people is reduced. In this type of system, the voter can be much more aware of and knowledgeable about the policy positions of the party but less sure of what actions will be taken by the elected representative in order to obtain and maintain a share of the power of governance. The large policy differences between and among the parties and their greater ideological consistency make it harder than in a two-party system for individual voters to shift from party to party to express their dissatisfaction with what the government is doing. Formal membership in a political party tends to be more important and developed in the multiparty system.[32] Factors, such as these, that reduce the voter's realistic choices narrow the mechanisms by which voters can effectuate a responsible and accountable relationship between themselves and their representative and, finally, with the government.

WHY TWO PARTIES IN AMERICA?

The formal organization of American parties has never borne much similarity to that found in multiparty systems. Among the important factors that have reduced the capacity of minor parties to be effective competitors in the American system are the importance to a party's success of controlling the presidency, the existence and nature of that obscure institution the electoral college, the system of single-member districts and plurality elections, the local orientation of most party structures, and the continental and cosmopolitan society within which the parties operate.[33] Even with such constraints, there are always more than two parties that put forward candidates for the presidency, and, not infrequently, elections at all levels in the polity are marked by the participation of minor parties. Third parties regularly emerge but have generally not been able to compete with the major parties for control or even a share in the power to govern.[34] Very few third or other minor parties can elect even a single member to the Congress, although locally based third parties have had some impact on the operation of some state governments for limited periods in American history.[35] The Progressive Era, so called, did see substantial effects of third parties in a few states, for example. Nonetheless, the complete domination of the national government by the Democratic and Republican parties makes for an accurate description of America as having a two-party system. However, third parties occasionally play significant roles in the political system, roles different from those performed by the two major parties and by parties in a multiparty system.

For one thing, minor parties in America do not generally expect or attempt to gain control of the government. Indeed, they seldom expect to gain even the smallest share in the formal power of government, although there are rare historical exceptions. The replacement of the Whigs by the Republicans as a major party just prior to the Civil War is a case in point. The more typical pattern is for the third party to try to modify the positions of the major parties and thereby implant their interests and policy preferences into the mainstream of the political process. The successful third party is one that gains enough strength on a limited range of issues so that it becomes advantageous to at least one of the major parties to take over the more salient of those issues as planks in its own policy platform. Astute calculations lie behind such "takeovers": It is virtually impossible for a third party to maintain its electoral support when a voter can shift to a more probable winner (the major party) that promotes the same policy objectives as the minor party. The nature of the two-party system promotes the responsiveness of the major parties to the concerns of any large identifiable group of voters. Thus, the successful third party is likely to be destroyed by its own success. The comments on this point by Norman Thomas, a respected four-time candidate for president on the American Socialist party ticket, are apropos. Thomas contended that his party had been very successful because, though its voting strength had declined since the early part of the century, the most significant planks of its 1932 platform had become law through the programs of the Democratic party and the New Deal. This is a graphic illustration of the phenomenon. More recently, an important effect of the presidential candidacy of Governor George Wallace of Alabama has been to modify somewhat the positions of both of the major political parties on several economic and race-related issues. Thus, "the" third party in the American context, whenever it has emerged, has not yet represented any movement toward the development of a multiparty system. It is, rather, an extension of the group process: Competing for office is a tactic through which persons discontented with the policies of the major parties can register a potentially effective protest.

When the number of persons showing support for a heretofore obscure, disreputable, or feared position grows to a significant block of voters, there is a substantial incentive for one or both of the major parties to modify its/their positions enough to compete for the support of the malcontents. Representatives of ethnic, racial, and ideological minorities often find this a means of coercing the attention of the major parties and thereby enhancing their chances of getting their demands translated into public policy.[36] The more intense the competition between the major parties, the greater the marginal value of winning the support of third-party voters and the more likely the major parties will attempt to bring such voters into the fold.[37]

Table 7-2. Third Party Candidates Receiving Presidential Votes in 1968 and 1972.

Party	Presidential Candidate	Votes
1972		
American	John G. Schmitz	1,099,482
People's	Benjamin Spock	78,756
Socialist Workers	Linda Jenness	66,677
Socialist Labor	Louis Fisher	53,814
Communist	Gus Hall	25,595
Prohibition	E. Harold Munn	13,505
Libertarian	John Hospers	3,673
America First	John Mahalchik	1,743
Universal	Gabriel Green	220
1968		
American Independent	George Wallace	9,906,473
Socialist Labor	H. A. Blomen	52,588
Peace and Freedom	Dick Gregory	47,133
Socialist Workers	Fred Halstead	41,388
Prohibition	E. Harold Munn	15,123
People's Constitutional	Ventura Chavez	1,519
Communist	Charlene Mitchell	1,075
Universal	James Hensley	142
Constitution	Richard Troxell	34

Source: Adapted from data in Richard M. Scammon, *America Votes 10* (Washington: Governmental Affairs Institute, 1973), pp. 12, 14.

CONGRESS AND
THE TWO-PARTY SYSTEM

The Congress of the United States has always been under the control of a majority party, and minor parties have seldom played any large part in the organization or performance of the Congress. However, many of the activities in the Congress resemble activities familiar in a multiparty system. The decisions reached often involve the kinds of bargains and compromises typical in parliamentary bodies controlled by coalitions of parties rather than in ones controlled clearly, if formally, by a majority party.[38] The congressional pattern of bargaining, compromising, and logrolling is based largely on the lack of power of the party leadership and the undisciplined, locally oriented nature of American political parties. Party discipline and responsibility, to be discussed later, are major influences in congressional behavior, although they are far less important than, say, in the two-party system of Great Britain. So while party loyalty and discipline help shape voting behavior in the Congress, the weakness of the party structures and their regional and ideological variations lead to considerable overlapping of voting patterns across party lines.

Frequently, critical issues of the day have supporters in both parties, and legislative majorities can be created only through bipartisan coalitions.[39] These "unholy" coalitions may be temporary, formed around a single measure, or they may be extremely stable and involve many issues. In either case, the majorities in the Congress do often exhibit features familiar in multiparty coalitions. The alliance between southern Democrats and midwestern Republicans in support of particular farm policies and a generally conservative orientation in a number of areas, especially civil rights, is perhaps the most frequently discussed example of an enduring coalition.[40] The community of interest between members of this coalition transcends the dictates of party regularity and reduces the usefulness of describing the houses of Congress as two-party legislative bodies. There is, however, one very significant difference between the multifactional United States Congress and legislative assemblies in multiparty systems. Bargaining in the Congress is carried out by individual members as they attempt to maximize gains and to minimize losses for themselves; bargaining in a multiparty system is conducted by party leaders, the ordinary members being more or less bound by the bargains that have been struck by the leadership. Thus, the Congress does show some signs of the fragmentation and coalitional politics associated with multiparty systems but lacks the powerful leadership structure by which they control the bargaining process. It should be remembered that on critical issues of electing officers of the House, controlling legislative committees, and other "organizational" matters the members do vote consistently along party lines.

The American party system conforms most closely to the competitive two-party model. Since localities are frequently dominated by a single party, politics in these areas occurs within what we could call a "no party" system, or one in which no serious competition for votes takes place. The discipline of American parties is often weak, and the policy stances of members of Congress are more influenced by local issues and orientations than by national party platforms and "principles." The fragmentation of political power is a major characteristic of the American polity. It dictates and flows from the nature of American political party organization.

PARTY ORGANIZATION IN AMERICA

The preceding discussion treats political parties as organic entities, as if the party *qua* party acts and performs functions in the political system. Actually, the term **political party** is only a label used to identify the patterned, institutionalized behavior of individuals in the polity. The label is a sort of summary concept to describe economically how the interactions of a very large number of persons get organized as they attempt to influence the operation of the governmental system in a manner compatible with their individual preferences. The concept of the political party does serve as a symbol toward which people adopt positive and negative attitudes, but more important is how the leaders and followers structure their actual behavior into forms that can be identified as party activity. It is well to know something about the persons who are involved in party activity, the reasons for their involvement, and the ways in which they coordinate and aggregate their preferences into an effective political force.

Membership

The nature and structure of a political party derive from the historical choices of many individuals as they developed and used their association to control the political system. These choices — concerning organizational style, procedures, and policy orientations — form the traditions that shape and define the behavior of party members and initiates as they interact in the political process. So, while the organization, procedures, and structure of American political parties are historically conditioned, they are of much more than historical interest to anyone who wishes to understand or influence the operation of the polity.

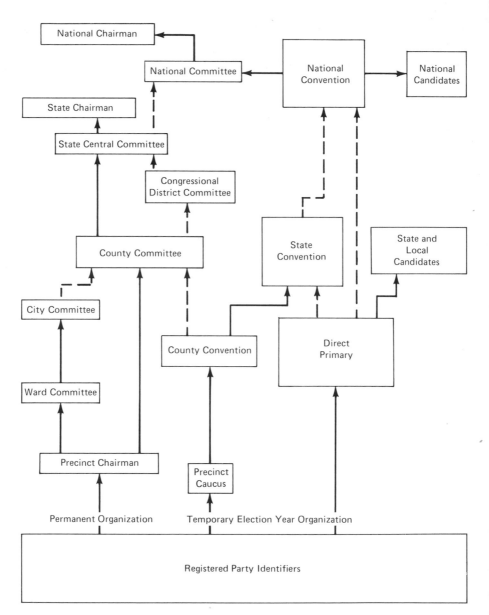

Figure 7-1. General Organizational Structure of American Political Parties.

Some combination of time, energy, skill, loyalty, money, and, ultimately, votes of millions of individuals determines the success or failure of the Democratic and Republican parties. The preferences and interests of these people must be served by the party in some minimal way if it is to survive and thrive as a viable social force. Serving those preferences is both facilitated and hindered by the general weakness of party structures in America, a fact reflected in the fragility of party "membership." Weak partisan identifications indicate that the parties do not occupy a very profound place in the everyday life of most members of society. In a strict sense, there is no concept of *formal* party membership. Americans do not formally join political parties; they undergo no initiations; they pay no organizational dues; they do not carry membership cards; they need not and seldom do attend party meetings; they do not swear any oath to support party programs or to accept and promote the election of candidates selected by the party. None of these commitments is required to be a full participant in party decisional affairs.[41]

The major criterion of party membership is self-identification. One may think of oneself as a Democrat or a Republican and, by so thinking, become such. As a result of election laws, it is true, a person who wishes to vote may have to register first with governmental officials and may be encouraged or required to indicate a party preference, particularly in party primary elections. Such registration guarantees to the individual the legal right to participate in the activities of the party. The party leadership cannot control admission to or exit from the party.[42] Nor can the organization require any of its members regularity of party activity or voting behavior. The legal requirement of secret elections is a crucial if overlooked factor limiting the capacity of the party to control members. The leadership may persuade, request, advise, cajole, or beg, but it cannot dictate or demand that individual party members behave in any particular manner in order to remain in good standing in the party. The party itself has almost no sanctions that it can impose on rank-and-file members to ensure party loyalty. Instead it must rely on moral incentives, on the occasional availability of material incentives (e.g., patronage), and, most importantly, on offering policy positions consistent with the self-interest of the voters.

Fundamental party decisions on whom to nominate and what stands to take on issues are made either directly by individual members in primary elections or by representatives or delegates to party gatherings. Delegates need not always have won their spurs as party workers or loyalists. Indeed, they may have only a tenuous and temporary attachment to the party and its long-term survival. Many delegates to the 1972 Democratic Party Convention, for example, had never previously had a hand in party affairs — a major source, it turned out, of intraparty conflict. As we have said, the most restrictive requirement for party membership is that a person must have registered to vote with a local government official and have stated his party identification. This simple action admits the individual as a full participant to the basic decision-making activities of the party, such as voting in primary elections, attending precinct meetings, and selecting delegates to party conventions. (In a few jurisdictions with so-called open primaries, even the registration requirement for party membership is lacking.) The growing reliance (now in some thirty-two states) upon the primary as a means of selecting presidential and other party candidates reduces the influence of the formal party leaders and maximizes the impact of the choices of individual members who may have weak and exceedingly transitory identifications with the party. As a result of choices made via the primaries, party leaders and party activists often find themselves obliged to support candidates and policies that are at great variance with their own preferences and with the traditional positions of the party.

Party Preferences and Activity

About two out of every three Americans hold at least a slight preference for one or the other of the major political parties, a proportion that includes independents who "lean" to either party. Approximately one-third of those indicating any perceptible preference strongly favor the party of their choice. Conversely, approximately one-third of American voters do not assert any party identification whatsoever, and a similar number have only a very weak or unstable orientation toward one of the political parties.[43] Party loyalty is certainly not very compelling in the life of most Americans. Moreover, most party members take a passive stance toward the organizational activities of the political parties.[44] For example, less than 10 percent report that they attend political meetings and rallies, and normally less than 50 percent of the registered members of the parties turn out to vote in party primaries. Even though the opportunity to participate fully in the decisional processes of the parties is readily available, a relatively small proportion of Americans see fit to pay the altogether minimal costs necessary to do so. Furthermore, some evidence suggests a trend toward less interest in and identification with political parties and a similar decline in the propensity of voters to follow party lines consistently in their voting decisions. The portrait drawn is one of a deep malaise at the roots of the party organization.[45] The weaker the party becomes, the less able it is to perform the functions described earlier in this chapter. A drop in party strength means either that these functions will be less adequately performed or that alternative — and probably less democratic — structures must be developed to perform them. It is ironic that many reforms designed to "democratize" the parties (e.g., primaries, delegate quotas, denial of patronage) may assist in destroying them.

The social composition of the American parties testifies to the fragmented competitive nature of the party system. Persons from virtually all occupations, educational levels, social strata, and cultural backgrounds can be found in both political parties. However, the *proportions* of members drawn from different groups are different for the two parties and would be more so in the absence of regional anomalies, such as the South. Republican party members are somewhat older, more secure financially, more often white Anglo-American Protestants, and somewhat more conservative than their Democratic counterparts. Conversely, a person who is a member of an identifiable racial or ethnic minority, a member of a labor union, or a political liberal is more likely to be a Democrat than a Republican.[46] Crosscutting memberships consisting of persons from all or most social groups lower the intensity of the conflict between the parties and explain, if only in part, the fact that the parties tend to espouse the same or at least not wildly dissimilar social values in their platforms and programs. Many debates — by no means trivial — between the parties turn on the question of how best to achieve particular social objectives rather than on which values should be pursued.

These factors enhance the influence of persons with only a marginal identification with a political party. Such persons may shift their votes between the parties whenever they become disenchanted with the current state of affairs. Efforts by each party to attract the support of these the median voters also explain the similarity of policy positions. The same factors, as explained above, increase the incentives for the individual to pass up the opportunity to vote since there is little real fear concerning the outcome of the election.[47]

Most voters gain their party identification from their family background, the structure of power in their local community, the people they associate with in occupational and friendship roles, and their evaluations of these and other associations in light of their own interests. For fully intelligible reasons, party identifications tend to be of low salience to the average person. If they are not reinforced for social or ideological reasons by active participation in party affairs, the individual's invest- ment in party identification can be overcome by social and political forces of both short- and long-term duration.[48] Loyal partisans face a much more difficult problem when circumstances place them in a position in which their personal preferences conflict with the choices made by the party. Political apostasy is a psychologically costly course, after all.

The modal party member's partisan activities are limited in scope, in- tensity, regularity, and personal significance. He or she maintains a pas- sive orientation toward the party, a low propensity to participate in its internal affairs, a record of infrequent voting in primary elections, a somewhat unstable pattern of voting choice, a general lack of interest in the development of a more effective party organization, and little if any commitment to preserve or adjust the policy positions of the party. Since the great bulk of members do not involve themselves vigorously or exten- sively in party affairs, the responsibility for and control of the party or- ganization are left in the hands of a relatively small number of self- selected personalities. The existence of elite or minority control is not ex- clusively or even mainly dependent upon any restrictive activities by party leaders. It flows, rather, from a lack of interest of the average party member. Rational disinterest makes possible the "capture" of the party organization and structures by small and earnest minorities who may wish to use the party as an instrument to achieve their own rather nar- row goals. In periods of intense political conflict, newly aroused persons with passionate concerns for the issues or candidates of the day are prone to enter and seize control of the party. A return to less frenzied conditions usually allows loyal traditional activists to regain their ascendancy in party affairs.

Normally, then, a few partisans control the day-to-day operation of the party. As one might expect, they display a strong identification with the party and a rather consistent ideological commitment. Frequently, they view the party as a means of achieving their personal goals. (Of course, most people have a remarkable capacity for showing that their personal goals are inseparable from the general good of society.) Party ac- tivity may be seen as a way to fight boredom and make friends; to obtain influence in the political order; to acquire elective or appointed office; to carry out a responsibility for public service and perform a civic obligation; to come to popular attention and scramble for celebrity status. Regardless of the motivation, and whether one wishes to characterize the activist as a latter-day Moses, a sophisticated politician, a good citizen, a fanatical ideologue, an unscrupulous demagogue, or a mere kook, those who are active in a political party tend to have more influence on the operation of the polity and the composition of public policy than do their more passive neighbors.

The organizational pursuits of the party can be divided into two broad categories. On the one hand, the party has several powers which are vitally important in a democratic political system. The power to choose candidates whose names appear on the ballot for election to public office is one. The development of a policy program which then focuses the debate in the campaign is another. On the other hand, the party undertakes to organize the electorate more directly in an effort to conduct a successful election campaign — by selecting delegates to nominating conventions, poll watching, knocking on doors, licking envelopes, collecting money, making phone calls, arranging itineraries, and driving voters to the polls. Some tasks — such as being a delegate to a national convention — are exciting and much sought after; others are boring, carry few rewards, and require a keen ideological commitment or a financial payment if they are to be performed. Contrary to some conceptions, both moral commitment and money are in short supply in large-scale campaigns. One who wishes to participate, therefore, need do no more than indicate a willingness to work. In general, party activities between elections are conducted by a handful of loyalists whose efforts are supplemented during election campaigns by the financially interested and/or sporadically concerned.

The Local Party

The local organizations are the core of American political parties.[49] The major decisions, responsibilities, duties, and powers of the party are concentrated at the local level. The basic, and sometimes merely formal, structure is the precinct organization. Each party seeks to provide a viable organization in as many local voting precincts or districts as possible. Its main and often critical responsibility is to assure that as many potential supporters of the party as possible are formally qualified to vote and to see that as many of these people as possible actually cast their ballot in general elections. Maximizing the voting turnout has much more bearing on the outcome of elections than attempts to change the preferences of voters toward candidates or policies. Thus the mobilization of the electorate is a major concern of the precinct organization. Many election out-

Volunteers at local Democratic headquarters at a country fair sell bumper stickers, a popular campaign tool which provides visibility to politicians and issues. *Daniel S. Brody/Editorial Photocolor Archives*

comes would have been reversed if the losing party had received a single additional vote in each voting district. This fact is stated and restated in precinct organization meetings.

The precinct organization carries out a large number of simple, often dull, and, by themselves, trivial activities. However, when aggregated across the entire electoral system, they are of great importance in determining the results of elections and the success of the party. The power of individual partisans at the local level is quite limited while their duties may be quite onerous. This combination of heavy obligation and minimal power scarcely encourages participation in local party work. The discouraging ratio of benefits to costs often makes it difficult/impossible to fill all of the positions available at the local level, particularly when the party is a clear and permanent minority in an area. Indeed, a local party organization is much more likely to mount a recruiting drive to find some susceptible individual to serve as a precinct official than it is to spend time screening potential candidates who aspire to the post. Formally, precinct and ward officials are elected in the primary or in precinct meetings, but there are seldom hotly contested races for these positions. Many of them are actually filled by appointment from above, as no candidate appears in the precinct meeting or primary. Occasionally, when the party is highly fractionalized or a new wing of the party is attempting to gain local control, there is some competition for a position. The chief means of recruitment of local leaders is still self-selection. Success usually flows from the willingness of individuals to volunteer their services rather than from any ability to gain support and confidence from voters in the district.

Precinct leaders receive no pay for their efforts, and few other opportunities for gain are attached to the position. Traditionally, in the context of the highly organized political machine, precinct leaders might be able to gain favors for themselves or their constituents from the machine and its officeholders. Granting jobs, fixing minor criminal or traffic cases, providing food to the needy were activities often directed by precinct leaders in the era of machine politics. But civil service reform and public welfare systems have dramatically reduced — indeed, have generally destroyed — such party organizations.

Party organizations in America need not involve meetings, interactions, face-to-face discussions in any serious sense. In fact, party voters in a precinct seldom meet as a group. The political education of voters through attendance at regularly scheduled precinct meetings has never developed as a major feature of American political parties. In some areas, however, the precinct voters may meet to choose those who will represent the precinct at higher levels within the party, and such meetings are important in states that still use the convention technique for picking delegates to the national convention or for nominating candidates. In these systems, frequently persons who wish to attend a presidential nominating convention must first be nominated by their own precincts. The growth of direct primary elections as a means of selecting delegates has drastically reduced the importance of precinct meetings and decisions, especially decisions on the platform planks that are to be included in the party's program at the state and national levels. Inducements to participate actively in precinct affairs have usually been meager enough — except during the heyday of the political machine — and now, with the extension of primary elections, are even smaller. With inducements to share power removed, only moral inducements remain. Precinct meetings are ordinarily attended by only a minuscule proportion of the qualified party voters in a precinct. Although the meetings are open to all qualified electors of the party, it turns out that a very few persons can normally gain control of the precinct organization. Increased attendance may occur when heated intraparty conflict develops. Persons who as a rule do not participate may become agitated by an intense attachment to a political personality or an ideological position and enter party affairs as a consequence. However, large turnout at this level remains sporadic and rare.

The State Party

Beyond the precinct, the political party is organized at the ward, city, or county level, where the activities of the precinct organizations are coordinated. Ward and equivalent organizations are charged with the strategic problem of developing ways and means to win elections in their areas. They work with precinct-level party members in promoting the party, its candidates and platforms, and attempt to organize the electorate for successful election campaigns. They are normally made up of representatives from the precincts and frequently select delegates to participate in organizational meetings at higher, often state, levels in the party organization. Proposed platform planks for the state party may also be selected at this level, as are, occasionally, platforms designed to guide the programs of local government. However, the emphasis is on linking the precinct and state organizations, at least formally and sometimes actually.

Because of weakness at the precinct level (for reasons already explained) and because of the sometimes formal character of the connection between precinct and "higher" party organization, the party tends to be relatively weak and to exhibit a fragmented leadership structure at the state level. Power in the state organization is distributed among the state chairman, national committee members, a state committee, and periodic state conventions. The state organization works to acquire, maintain, or expand party control of the state and to assist the national party in gaining state support in national elections. The state party seeks candidates, leads registration drives, provides some aid to the local parties, and raises money. The traditional practice was for state conventions to select the nominees of the party for statewide offices, but, again, the direct primary has generally supplanted this function. In only isolated areas does the state party organization play a major role in choosing nominees for public office. The state convention in about half the states still controls the selection of delegates to the national convention. The state party organization may also have a part in the dispensing of patronage when the party controls the government at either the national or state level. These caveats aside, the state party organization, generally weak, has been made weaker by various electoral reforms and the elimination, by government, of traditional party social service functions. It consequently plays only a minor role in the determination of candidates and the platforms upon which they will run.

The National Party

The national party organization has a not very strong permanent structure and an ad hoc structure that operates in presidential election years. The most significant decisions at the national level involve the selection of candidates for president and vice-president and the development of the policy positions which the nominees, at least ostensibly, will espouse. These decisions are taken by a national convention called for such purposes. Delegates attend from all of the states, having been chosen by state parties under the laws of the several states as interpreted by guidelines of the national committees. The basic orientations of national convention delegates rest on state and local systems of power, ideology, and organization. The national convention is really an arena for bargaining and exchange among the plurality of groups in the party and not a meeting of like-minded activists. When the bargaining is conducted efficiently, it broadens the appeal of the party and brings about at least a papered-over unity among the competing factions in the party.

Bargaining is a process that often allows the intense concerns of threatened or apprehensive minorities to be influential in the collective decision-making. The growth of primaries and other means of binding delegates to specific candidates reduces the amount and efficiency of bargaining that is possible, however. Recent conventions have done little more than formally ratify already made decisions as to which candidates will be supported by which delegates. The result is a growing incapacity for the party convention to allay the frustrations of minorities at the convention — minorities that have given considerable social and electoral support and may desert the party on election day, as happened with the Democrats in 1972. Bargaining is largely restricted to the erection of the party platform, which, while more than a symbolic undertaking, is less crucial than the decisions on candidates. The platform that is developed in a committee is generally accepted, beyond an occasional "floor fight" on specific issues, by the convention. Limited debate on the platform is dictated by the fact that the nominee is often obvious and the platform committee must have a policy document that is compatible with the interests and desires of the probable candidate.

The broadness — and vagueness — of the platform is an effective measure of the groups that have power in the party and the interests to which the party wants to appeal. The platform, after all, is an attempt to appeal to a coalition of individuals and groups that will lead to a successful election campaign. After the nominating and platform functions, perhaps the main problem for the convention is to develop enthusiasm for the upcoming campaign throughout the nation and among all segments of the party. The convention is an announcement to the general electorate that a campaign is beginning and is designed to direct interest, concern, and support to the party's nominee. The convention leaders seek to induce persons throughout society to undertake the manifold tasks involved in a modern campaign. A successful party convention unites the party activists, achieves positive publicity, and promotes public interest in the election. Failure to achieve these goals is likely to lead to a defeat in the ensuing election campaign.[50]

The party's permanent national organization is accountable to the national convention and involves, mainly, the national committee. Representatives of the state parties hold membership on this committee and are picked by the independent state organizations. The committee is chaired by a person who is technically selected by the committee but is actually chosen by the presidential nominee of the party. The committee may change this person after the election campaign and frequently does so on its own volition after an unsuccessful campaign. If the party controls the presidency, the president determines who will head the national committee; the person serves primarily as an organizer, a fund raiser, and a noncontroversial representative of party views and is not normally a potential candidate for high office. The national committee and its chairperson have significant duties and responsibilities in developing a successful party organization but very little power in their own right.

The primary contributions made by the permanent national organization are housekeeping and organizational in nature; it plays few significant roles in the polity.

There have been periodic attempts to add to the power of the permanent organization by making it a source of policy proposals and assigning it the duty of speaking for the party out of power. However, the basically local and diverse nature of the party militates against such schemes. The permanent organization is comprised of persons with relatively little personal prestige, with low national public visibility, and with scant if any control over the platform or candidates of the party. Under these conditions, the shrimp will learn to whistle before genuine power will come to be lodged in the permanent national organization. We emphasize: The decentralized, fragmented, often chaotic, and even impotent formal structure of our political parties is both a cause and an effect of two significant parameters of American political life: (1) the lack of responsibility and discipline associated with the parties and (2) the growing propensity of candidates to build their own campaign organizations and to give correspondingly less attention to the formal organizations of the party. Factors such as these, which are related to the weak condition of American political parties, tend to weaken the parties even further.

The fact is that there is very little basis upon which the national party's formal leadership can sanction, discipline, or reward members of the party. Persons who carry the party label in campaigns usually do so quite independently of the desires of its formal leaders. Individual candidates build their own sources of support which are often unrelated to the party organization. The primary election is a particularly significant element in this process since whoever carries the election wins the party's nomination whether the party regulars approve or not. Party regularity is generally not a very telling factor in being able to win a primary election. The victor may or may not support the traditional principles of the party and cannot be compelled to accept the party platform. Except in a few states with highly organized local parties, most candidates cannot realistically be said to owe their position on the ballot or their election to the formal organization of the party. Thus the party usually can claim little control over the behavior of the elected official who holds nominal membership in it. Rather, it will probably find itself in a subordinate role, supporting the candidate who is most likely to win so that the party leaders can maintain some claim to access to the elected official. The success of its efforts result in limited influence for the party leaders over public policy. The relationships between officeholders and party leaders found in well-disciplined party systems do not broadly obtain in the American system.

THE PARTY AND THE POLITY: AN EVALUATION

America's much-maligned two-party system is a central feature of democratic rule. It performs functions critical to the maintenance of a democratic polity. However awkwardly, it provides voters with alternative public choices and, thereby, with a means of collecting and combining individual preferences into viable public policies. The social bargains and compromises that are so essential for the survival of democratic rule in a large, complex, and heterogeneous society are carried out to a significant (if not exclusive) degree within the framework of the party system. The political parties provide a necessary if imperfect instrument through which government may be made more accountable and responsible to the individual members of the electorate than it would or could be otherwise. Democracy cannot exist in the absence of an effective competitive party system. In a two-party context the parties are forced to compete for the support of the median voter, to take reasonably similar positions on most issues. Competition, paradoxically, diminishes the ideological purity and consistency within the parties but consequently lowers the risk of losing elections by promoting general acceptance of the outcome and increases stability.

The historically endemic fear of political power in American society, combined with the excesses that have marked some periods of party activity, has dramatically reduced support for the party system in the United States. Reform movements have frequently, if often naively and mistakenly (in terms of their own declared objectives of furthering democratic rule), attacked the political parties. Success of these movements has often meant further weakening of the power and influence — and hence accountability and responsibility — of the political party. Democracy has not been strengthened as a result. On the contrary, social decisions have simply been made through less organized, and hence less accountable, processes. In addition, the prevailing local orientations of American politics have operated to keep the central organs of the political parties from gaining much effective power, a fact which further impairs the party organization as an instrument for the integration of public choices. These considerations strike deeply at the capacity of the parties to discipline and control their candidates and members, and lack of power in the formal party structures inhibits the development of a fully responsible party system which, arguably, is such a useful mechanism in a democratic polity.[51] The basic values and practices of the American party system are much too deep-seated for us to argue that a responsible party system on the English model — itself in some current disarray — should be developed in the United States. Inducements to do so are insufficient, and the costs would be astronomical, particularly in view of problematical success. Those who speak of fundamental party reform are really talking about fundamental changes in society, which is a prerequisite for party reform. Nonetheless, anyone concerned with the effective operation of the polity and the furtherance of democratic values might consider carefully ways in which the strength of the party system could be enhanced. A dim view should be taken of "solutions" designed to meet transitory and often merely alleged problems; they may permanently impair the capacity of the parties to operate competitively, responsibly, and accountably. With inducements — both moral and material — to participate already at a low ebb, a deaf ear should be turned to proposals which, in their consequences, will further depress active, sustained involvement in party affairs.

In the absence of strong parties, innumerable unorganized interests, the so-called categoric groups in America — consumers, taxpayers, the old, blacks, college students, rightists, leftists, to name a few — will inevitably be denied effective access to the councils of government. The dispersed character of such interests and the minimal inducements for individuals in such social categories to formally organize themselves mean that they will — without parties — be far less than optimally represented in the public process. Categoric groups often bear the costs of policy decisions made to benefit organized pressure groups, as when taxpayers pay subsidies to maintain some inefficient but well-organized interest, yet have no way to organize themselves to contest the decisions. As noted at the outset of this chapter, the problem of free riders and the costs of organizing, which plague all interest groups, are particularly acute for categoric interests: Only through the political party can such interests be advanced, if they are to be advanced at all.[52] The enterprising politician, in search of the support of the median voter, often finds it convenient to take categoric interests into account when developing a campaign strategy.

NOTES

1. See V.O. Key, Jr., *Politics, Parties, and Pressure Groups*, 5th ed. (New York: Thomas Y. Crowell, 1964), for a thorough discussion of the nature and functions of political parties.
2. See David B. Truman, *The Governmental Process* (New York: Knopf, 1951), for the most complete description of the strategies and tactics of political interest groups. The party politician as a representative of categoric or collective interests is developed in Richard E. Wagner, "Pressure Groups and Political Entrepreneurs," *Papers on Non-Market Decision Making*, 1 (1966), 161–170.
3. Edmund Burke, *Works*, 1862, Vol. 1.

4. See Pendletom Herring, *The Politics of Democracy* (New York: Rinehart, 1940), for a discussion of this position.

5. These and related issues are discussed in Walter Dean Burnham, *Critical Elections and the Mainstream of American Politics* (New York: Norton, 1970). A good criticism of Burnham is James F. Ward, "Toward a Sixth Party System?" *Western Political Quarterly,* September 1973, pp. 385–413.

6. See V.O. Key, Jr., *Southern Politics* (New York: Knopf, 1949).

7. See Everett Carl Ladd, Jr., *American Political Parties* (New York: Norton, 1970), and Wilfred E. Binkley, *American Political Parties,* 4th ed. (New York: Knopf, 1963), for extended treatments of the history of American political parties. See also James L. Sundquist, *Dynamics of the Party System* (Washington: Brookings, 1973).

8. See Binkley, *American Political Parties,* and Henry Jones Ford, *The Rise and Growth of American Politics,* 2nd ed. (New York: Macmillan, 1967).

9. For example, see Frank J. Sorauf, *Party Politics in America* (Boston: Little, Brown, 1968).

10. See Blaine A. Browness and Warren E. Stickles, eds., *Bosses and Reformers* (Boston: Houghton Mifflin, 1973); James Bryce, *The American Commonwealth* (New York: Macmillan, 1910); H.F. Gosnell, *Machine Politics: Chicago Model,* 2nd ed. (Chicago: University of Chicago Press, 1968); M. Ostrogorski, *Democracy and the Party System in the United States* (New York: Macmillan, 1910); W.L. Riordon, *Plunkitt of Tammany Hall* (New York: McClure, Phillips, 1905); and Lincoln Steffens, *The Autobiography of Lincoln Steffens* (New York: Harcourt, 1931).

11. See Frank J. Sorauf, "Patronage and Party," *Midwest Journal of Political Science,* 5 (May 1959), 115–126.

12. See Gabriel A. Almond and James S. Coleman, eds., *The Politics of the Developing Areas* (Princeton, N.J.: Princeton University Press, 1960); Gabriel A. Almond and G. Bingham Powell, Jr., *Comparative Politics: A Developmental Approach* (Boston: Little, Brown, 1966); and David Easton, *A Systems Analysis of Political Life* (New York: Wiley, 1965).

13. See Truman, *The Governmental Process.*

14. See A.D. Lindsay, *The Modern Democratic State* (London: Oxford University Press, 1943), and Henry B. Mayo, *An Introduction to Democratic Theory* (New York: Oxford University Press, 1960).

15. See Anthony Downs, *An Economic Theory of Democracy* (New York: Harper & Row, 1957), for a treatment of individual preferences and voting behavior. Cf. N. Frohlich, J.A. Oppenheimer, and O.R. Young, *Political Leadership and Collective Goods* (Princeton, N.J.: Princeton University Press, 1971).

16. Consult Easton, *A Systems Analysis of Political Life.*

17. Downs, *An Economic Theory of Democracy,* presents the most complete argument of this question. Cf. William H. Riker and Peter C.

Ordeshook, *An Introduction to Positive Political Theory* (Englewood Cliffs, N.J.: Prentice-Hall, 1973), Chapters 11, 12.

18. See Maurice Duverger, *Political Parties,* 3rd ed. (London: North, Barbara & North, 1969), and Lester Seligman, "Party Recruitment and Party Structure: A Case History," *American Political Science Review,* 5 (1961), 77–86.

19. See as examples of the vast literature on "party responsibility" the famous 1950 publication of the American Political Science Association, "Toward a More Responsible Two-Party System," and James MacGregor Burns, *The Deadlock of Democracy* (Englewood Cliffs, N.J.: Prentice-Hall, 1963). For a critique of the thesis, see Evron M. Kirkpatrick, "Toward a More Responsible Two-Party System: Political Science, Policy Science, or Pseudo-Science?" *American Political Science Review,* 65 (December 1971), 965–991.

20. For an influential treatment see Duverger, *Political Parties.*

21. David B. Truman, *The Congressional Party* (New York: Wiley, 1959); Julius Turner, *Party & Constituency: Pressures on Congress,* rev. ed. (Baltimore: Johns Hopkins Press, 1970); and Frank J. Sorauf, *Party and Representation* (New York: Atherton, 1963).

22. See Downs, *An Economic Theory of Democracy.* Cf. B.R. Berelson, P.F. Lazarsfeld, and W.N. McPhee, *Voting* (Chicago: University of Chicago Press, 1954).

23. See Lester W. Millbrath, *Political Participation* (Chicago: Rand McNally, 1965).

24. See Downs, *An Economic Theory of Democracy.*

25. Cf. William H. Riker, *The Theory of Political Coalitions* (New Haven, Conn.: Yale University Press, 1962).

26. See Duverger, *Political Parties,* and Sigmund Neumann, ed., *Modern Political Parties* (Chicago: University of Chicago Press, 1955).

27. See Carl J. Friedrich and Zbigniew K. Brzezinski, *Totalitarian Dictatorship and Autocracy* (New York: Praeger, 1956).

28. See Key, *Southern Politics.*

29. Ibid.

30. See Duverger, *Political Parties.*

31. Downs, *An Economic Theory of Democracy.*

32. See Duverger, *Political Parties.*

33. See Burns, *The Deadlock of Democracy.*

34. See H.P. Nash, Jr., *Third Parties in American Politics* (Washington: Public Affairs Press, 1959).

35. Sundquist, *Dynamics of the Party System.*

36. The development of *La Raza Unida* to speak for the Chicano community of the Southwest is an excellent example of this process.

37. Walter F. Murphy, *Elements of Judicial Strategy* (Chicago: University of Chicago Press, 1964).

38. See Bertram Gross, *The Legislative Struggle* (New York: McGraw-Hill, 1953).

39. See Grant McConnell, *Private Power and American Democracy* (New York: Knopf, 1966), for a useful treatment of logrolling.
40. Ibid.
41. See Sorauf, *Party Politics in America,* pp. 129–186.
42. See Duverger's discussion of the cadre party in *Political Parties.*
43. See A. Campbell, P.E. Converse, W.E. Miller, and D.E. Stokes, *The American Voter* (New York: Wiley, 1960).
44. See Millbrath, *Political Participation.*
45. See Burnham, *Critical Elections and the Mainstream of American Politics.*
46. See Campbell et al., *The American Voter.*
47. See Berelson et al., *Voting.*
48. See V.O. Key, Jr., *The Responsible Electorate* (Cambridge, Mass.: Harvard University Press, 1966), and Sundquist, *Dynamics of the Party System.*
49. See E.E. Schattschneider, *Party Government* (New York: Farrar & Rinehart, 1942).
50. See Gerald Pomper, *Nominating the President* (New York: Norton, 1966).
51. See James W. Davis, *Presidential Primaries* (New York: Thomas Y. Crowell, 1967).
52. This argument is developed in E.E. Schattschneider, *The Semisovereign People* (New York: Holt, Rinehart & Winston, 1960).

The People Choose: Suffrage, Elections, and Voting Decisions

Modern democratic theory rests upon the premise that all legitimate government flows from the consent of the governed.[1] In a fully democratic polity the public policies pursued by government have been ranked and chosen by the ordinary members of society. Direct participation in, and control of, all public choices by all members of the society acting collectively and following some unanimously accepted decision-rules would characterize political democracy in its purest form. Although democracy in America is based upon a variant of this popular principle, day-to-day public choices are made by much more specialized sets of actors who follow exceedingly complex rules. However, the policies selected by these actors — elected officeholders, bureaucrats, and judges, in the main — are legitimized through a systematic linkage — real or imagined, between those choices and the preferences of individual members of the polity. As all modern democracies are *representative* democracies at best, one of their most significant problems is developing, maintaining, and strengthening democratic connections between the people and their representatives.

Unlike the citizens of the ancient Greek city-state, Americans are not governed by a leisure class that spends most of its time debating current issues and making day-to-day governmental decisions. The bulk of the waking time of most people is consumed in earning a living, performing domestic duties, and discharging communal responsibilities. Politics must compete with recreational, entertainment, and cultural opportunities for their limited leisure time. Even with recent expansions in leisure time, politics is not a very effective competitor for attention, and political activity is never likely to be the national pastime.

Moreover, the sheer size of the population, combined with the insistence that all have an equal right to participate in governmental affairs, leads to a rejection of "pure" or direct democracy even as a goal in the polity. The idea of a great "town meeting" to formulate policies in a society composed of over 200 million persons is absurd. The growing complexity of the society demands that most policy decisions be made in arenas unsuitable for direct participation by all its members. As a matter of fact, unless one is willing to accept the formalistic participation of plebiscite democracy (as in Hitler's Germany or de Gaulle's France), in which the people occasionally vote yes or no on proposals formulated by government and are given no real alternative, full participation is not consistent with practical democratic governance. Short of the fantasies, made possible by the technological age, in which every citizen has a household computer to record preferences on every issue of the day, the main policy-making activities must continue to be conducted through representative political institutions.[2] Americans have chosen, as have all other democratic societies, to rely upon representatives for the primary management of public affairs.

The "rulers" in a modern democracy are the relatively few persons who conduct formal governmental affairs. Regardless of philosophy, basic decisions in *all* governments are actually made by a small segment of the population, a small elite.[3] But a democratic polity differs from other systems of government (1) in the ways in which the members of the elite are selected for, and removed from, public office and (2) in the mechanisms through which the needs, values, and interests of individual citizens can influence public policy. Public policies are responsive to the needs and aspirations of the population to the extent that viable mechanisms for indirect citizen influence can be constructed and maintained. Popular rule understood in this sense places an extremely high premium upon the perfection of the process through which public officials are chosen and held accountable for their actions. A fundamental question in any modern democracy involves the relationship between that process and the general population. Although Americans use many techniques to influence government, the periodic elections in which leaders compete for their support are probably the most significant, — indeed, indispensable — aspect of democracy. The rules and practices that define and shape the electoral process are important in evaluating the nature and extent of democracy in the polity. They largely determine the degree of fit between the values and goals of individual citizens and the values embodied in the public policies that flow from the governmental system.

A number of ways in which citizens can shape the activities of government are discussed throughout this volume. Our present task is to describe and evaluate participation in electoral choice. In this task, it is necessary to consider the nature and significance of the rules that control the process, the factors that induce individuals to participate or not to participate, and the determinants of the political choices of those who do participate.

VOTING RIGHTS AND AMERICAN DEMOCRACY

The right to vote in competitive elections is equivalent to being included in the body of self-governing people in a society. Those who are excluded from the suffrage are defined, by implication, as incapable, for practical or moral reasons, of governing themselves or of sharing in the governance of others. The importance that supporters of democracy place upon the periodic election as a means for making public officials responsible and accountable to "the people" indicates that, when they speak of government "by the people" and the "consent of the governed," they are talking about control by the electorate. The regulations specifying the inclusion and exclusion of individuals in or from the electorate are critical aspects in any democracy. Full participation of "the people" has one meaning in a society in which the people turn out to be the privileged few and quite a different one where virtually all persons are included in the electorate. The rules that determine inclusion in the electorate in the United States have changed through time, and there has occurred a concomitant shift in the conventional understanding of democracy.

The original Constitution left the very significant issue of defining the electorate to the member states of the new federation. Although there was some variation among the states, the general pattern reflected the ideas that were dominant in English society of the day. Revolutionary America did not choose to revolutionize the definition of the electorate. The states followed what would now be regarded as quite restrictive rules controlling admission to the electorate. The prevailing view was that only those with the capacity to choose wisely and those with the greatest stake in the society (i.e., who held property or paid the requisite taxes) should be granted the power to determine the course of public affairs.[4] The right to vote required personal ability and social perspective and was not to be granted lightly to any group in society; it was generally restricted to white male adults. Children, blacks, and women should be represented in voting by those who, by nature, were better qualified to choose wisely. This paternalistic sentiment was so dominant that almost no one argued against it. Some states also required a voter to be a member of the appropriate church or, alternatively, of "good moral character." However, few serious attempts were made to enforce such rules and they rapidly fell into disuse.

Ideally, eligible voters should cast their ballots in furtherance of the public interest and should not try to promote their own narrow interests in the process. In fact, voting was generally conducted in public, in order to deter use of the vote in a self-serving manner. Under these conditions, the admission of dependent classes to the electorate would dilute the quality of public choices, giving undue influence to those with little or no stake in society and with little capacity to act prudently with regard to the fortunes of others.

But these beliefs were not to last. American history has been marked by periodic demands that the electorate be made more inclusive. As a result, one or another heretofore excluded group has been granted the right to participate fully in the electoral politics of the nation. The demands frequently flowed from members of the disenfranchised classes who were able to gain the sympathy of significant elements of the electorate or from politicians seeking to expand their popular support. Of course, those who sought the right to vote always had to convince those who already had it to share their political power. Since any change in the rules defining the electorate was a matter more or less controlled by people who had a right that others lacked, the latter were unable to participate fully in the process through which final disposition of the question would have to be made. The many expansions of the suffrage that have occurred in American history reveal the diverse factors leading to an agreement by the "old" electorate to share power with a "new" electorate.

The ideology of equality, particularly as political equality requires universal suffrage, has been frequently invoked to mobilize support for broadening the electorate. As in so many circumstances, the ability to attach a political demand to a widely held value system can be an extremely useful political tactic. But although ideology has played a role in the expansion of the suffrage, political and partisan considerations have been involved as well. It is more than coincidental that many people who for moral reasons have advocated an expansion of the right to vote have also believed that such an expansion would strengthen their own political positions by adding new and grateful voters to the party. Similarly, some efforts to enlarge the electorate are directly related to the hopes or predictions of activists that the new voters will provide the indispensable margin necessary to bring about desired changes in public policy. In short, decisions to change rules governing membership in the electorate have often been influenced by various benefits that were expected to flow to those who already held power, as well as to the new participants.

Removal of Property Qualifications

There have been recurring appeals to the ideal of "universal" suffrage as a justification for expansion of the electorate. The actual meaning of this concept has changed through time, as has the definition of the right to vote. The first major effort to achieve universal suffrage defined universality very narrowly by modern standards. The demand was for the acceptance of full and complete white manhood suffrage. The property qualification for voting was the major obstacle to this goal. The movement received its heaviest backing from the development of Jacksonian democracy and the leveling influence of the frontiers on social relations. The mood of equality in the western states gave support to the ideological premise that every man was competent to participate freely in the political processes of the nation. The spread of the franchise movement was facilitated by the emerging Democratic party's desire to consolidate its position by attracting new supporters. The chief object of the drive, the abolition of property qualifications for voting, was in fact achieved for most elections in all of the states by the time of the Civil War. However, some states did substitute limited taxpaying requirements or property requirements in all elections, and in many states property taxes had to be paid before one could vote in local elections involving increases in property taxes. Tax payment requirements for voting in city, school, and special district elections survived in a number of states into the 1960s.

The growth of "universal" suffrage before the Civil War was related to an improved view of the capabilities of the common man. There was no basic change in the idea that voting rights should be exercised to promote the public interest and that individuals should not vote to advance their own narrow self-interest. The expansion of the suffrage by removal of property qualifications was marked by the enactment of numerous specific legal requirements designed to preserve the integrity of the electoral process. Many states, for example, denied soldiers, sailors, and students the right to vote. Such individuals might inordinately influence the outcomes of local elections in a community in which they had at best only a transitory interest. The lack of a permanent identification with the locality might lead to the casting of votes in an irresponsible manner. Consequently, formal and often relatively long residency requirements and various standards of citizenship were established. The insane, and convicted criminals were specifically denied the right to vote, and poll taxes and literacy tests began to emerge. During this period, demands that blacks and women be granted the vote began to be made. Some states, for the first time, passed laws formalizing the long-standing custom that only white men could vote. (True, a handful of states did give blacks the suffrage before the Civil War, although all of these were in New England where there was virtually no black population in any case.[5]) The idea was to preserve the purity of the electoral process in view of the "threats" to that process from so-called universal manhood suffrage. Previously property qualifications were generally considered sufficient to achieve this goal, and its modification required new rules that would guarantee responsible behavior by a broadened electorate. Attempts were again made to ensure that only those committed to social stability and those fully responsible for their own acts would be granted the right to vote. Most of the rules developed in the pre–Civil War period survived for well over a century. While the Fifteenth Amendment (1870) eliminated race as a basis for restricting the electorate, the ancient practices of property requirements, poll taxes, and literacy tests continued with the same effect. Major changes have occurred in the last two decades and have consisted in removing and modifying the limitations upon the right to vote that were instituted then.

Black Suffrage

Since the Civil War, the national government has played a much greater role in defining the rules which control admission to the electorate. For almost a century, the states were allowed independently to define the right to vote. Then national governmental actions increasingly limited that authority. The process of national governmental intervention began with the adoption of the Fourteenth Amendment to the Constitution in 1868. This amendment was designed primarily to guarantee the full rights of citizenship, including the right to vote, to persons who had been freed from slavery by the Civil War and the Thirteenth Amendment. Any state denying black persons the right to vote was to have its representation reduced. This incentive to the states to extend the suffrage was hampered by the fact that the provision containing it was never acted upon by the Congress. Actually, then, it was decades before the equal protection clause of the amendment was made effective in the area of voting rights. In recent years this clause has become a significant legal basis for judicial and legislative action to achieve equality of voting rights for all Americans. The indirect means relied upon in the Fourteenth Amendment were soon replaced by more direct measures, with the adoption of the Fifteenth Amendment in 1870. It specifically guaranteed the right to vote regardless of race, color, or previous condition of servitude and empowered the Congress to enact legislation to secure this end. Congressional responsibility in this area was exercised effectively only in our own time. The voting right for blacks was protected in the post–Civil War South only about as long as federal troops were maintained there as part of the reconstruction policy.

The commitment to equality as well as a desire permanently to install the Republican party as an effective force in the South resulted in the formal extension of the suffrage to black Americans through the civil rights amendments. The presence of federal troops and the disqualification of white voters secured this right during the period of reconstruction. Blacks voted rather extensively in the South at that time, and a large number of them were elected to local, state, and national offices from this region. A majority of all black persons who have ever been elected to the Congress of the United States came from the South between the end of the Civil War and 1900. The first black representative from a northern district was not elected until 1929.

The end of reconstruction was marked by a reversal of this trend toward black suffrage. Southern states began to enact a series of rules designed to bar blacks from the electoral process and to return virtually total white dominance to the South. Legislatures and election officials were quite innovative in devising techniques to restrict the suffrage which did not, on their face, violate prevailing interpretations of the Civil War amendments and supporting legislation. This was the first but not the last period of massive regional resistance to national rules demanding equality for blacks in the South. The poll tax was adopted in a number of states, many forms of literacy tests were developed — frequently administered in a discriminatory fashion — and long residency requirements were established. Although these provisions were clearly meant to limit the number of blacks who could vote, they also disenfranchised many poor whites. The legal rules were often reinforced by extralegal tactics such as economic and physical threats and reprisals against black persons who attempted to exercise rights guaranteed to them under the Civil War amendments.

A 1921 decision by the United States Supreme Court involving the enforcement of a corrupt practices statute held that primary elections were not a part of the formal governmental process but part of a party process. It provided a legal rationale for one of the most effective means of denying blacks a voice in politics in the South.[6] The South emerged from reconstruction as a one-party region in which all elections came to be dominated by the Democratic party. Usually the general election (which of course was a governmental matter) would be won by a Democratic candidate who had no opposition. Thus, if blacks were excluded from Democratic primaries, they would effectively be prevented from participating in any election of significance. The development of the so-called **white primary** provided a constitutional means of restricting the suffrage for over four decades. Although certain procedural requirements had to be changed as a result of several Supreme Court decisions in the late 1920s and early 1930s,[7] it survived as a legal concept and an instrument of discrimination into the 1940s.[8] Even with the end of the white primary, most black persons in the South were denied the right to vote until a series of affirmative actions was taken by the national government to guarantee voting rights in the 1960s. The history of this matter illustrates the difficulty and slowness with which formal rules influence behavior when they conflict with deep-seated attitudes and traditions.

Women's Suffrage

Before the Civil War, the demand for women's suffrage was often associated with the demand for black suffrage. The issue of women's suffrage was debated politically and philosophically throughout the nineteenth century. Women were first allowed to vote in all elections in Wyoming territory in 1869, a right included in the constitution of that

The Nineteenth Amendment was adopted in 1920 granting women the right to vote. The preadoption banner aptly describes New York suffragettes' sentiments on this issue. *Culver Pictures*

state when it was admitted to the Union in 1890. Women had won the right to vote in eleven western states before the adoption of the Nineteenth Amendment in 1920, which granted voting rights to women in both state and national elections. The extension of voting rights in the western states was part of the philosophy of equality that developed on the frontier. It was also perceived as a means of enticing more women to a society with a large surplus of males. The Nineteenth Amendment was adopted amid demonstrations, civil disobedience actions, and expansive claims of the positive moral consequences of admitting women to the voting booths of the nation. On the one hand, women's suffrage was to be a means of ending all manner of corruption in the American political system and in American life. It would end prostitution, drunkenness, gambling, boss rule, and crime in the streets. On the other hand, if women were given the right to vote, the American family would disintegrate and the "fairer" sex would lose both its virtue and the protection of the male members of society. Conflict, family strife, and child neglect would increase throughout the land as women neglected domestic responsibilities and engaged in the nasty business of politics. Although the more dramatic claims of each side seem not to have come to pass, the Nineteenth Amendment did formally end the last major aspect of paternalism that had marked the definition of the electorate from the early days of the republic. It brought the greatest increase in the size of the electorate of any change ever made in the redefinition of the electorate. With its adoption, universal suffrage had become constitutional law on a nationwide basis. Few new rules concerning the nature of the electorate were to be enacted for over a generation.

Full Universal Suffrage

In the past two decades activity to change the effective exercise of the franchise has been more vigorous than in any other period since 1920. Many legal barriers to equal voting rights for all adult members of the society have been washed away by judicial decisions, constitutional amendments, and legislative actions. The national government has intervened in the definition and control of the suffrage in an unprecedented fashion. From the standpoint of the formal rules, universal suffrage has been fully achieved. For the first time in our history, there is no significant movement in the United States to extend the suffrage to any major group. The political decisions of recent years have permanently changed the original configuration of the electorate and completed the ancient trend toward universality of citizenship (if children, the certified insane, and felons are not regarded as citizens).

Table 8-1. White and Black Voter Registration in Southern States.

Year	White	Black
1960	61%	29%
1964	74	36
1969	80	65
1971	65	59

Source: Statistical Abstract of the United States, 1973, p. 378.

Recent expansion of the suffrage was based upon a rising interest in civil rights and a broadened conception of equal protection of the law. The Constitution has been amended to restrict the use of the poll tax for voting in federal elections (1964), to extend the right to vote in presidential elections to residents of the District of Columbia (1961), and to lower the voting age in state elections to eighteen years (1971). The Supreme Court has found that poll taxes in state elections,[9] taxpaying requirements for voting in local and municipal elections,[10] restriction of the right to vote by soldiers stationed in an area,[11] and long residency requirements[12] all violate the equal protection clause of the Fourteenth Amendment. By invalidating them it has substantially enlarged the electorate.

In an important and related area, the equal *effectiveness* of the vote has been decreed in a long series of cases bearing on the apportionment of political districts. All legislative bodies and voting districts throughout the country (except the U.S. Senate, which is specifically excluded by the Constitution) must be apportioned in accordance with population under a "one person, one vote" rule based upon judicial interpretations of the Fourteenth Amendment.[13] The determination that apportionment involved the issue of equality of voting rights was an indispensable link in the chain of events that led to the constitutional requirement for the **reapportionment** of districts for the House of Representatives, state legislatures, and many units of local government.[14]

The Congress has also worked to expand voting rights in recent years. A series of civil rights acts was passed between 1957 and 1970. The dominant component of almost all of them was the guaranteeing of equal voting rights for black Americans. Most significant perhaps are the Voting Rights Act of 1965 and its extension by the Voting Rights Act of 1970. Finally included are effective means of overcoming the legal barriers to black voting in the South. The acts provide for national intervention in the voting registration in states in which less than half of the adult population has voted in the preceding presidential election. This intervention allowed for the suspension of all methods by which the rights of black persons to vote in the southern states had been restricted.

The 1970 act also extended the right to vote in federal elections to persons between the ages of eighteen and twenty-one years. It limited residency requirements for voting for president and vice-president and suspended the use of literacy tests throughout the country for five years.[15] The force of these rules, when added to those made by the courts and relevant constitutional amendments, is to guarantee virtually all arguably adult members of the society the right to vote.

At present, rules governing voting are fairly clear, and very permissive by historical standards. A person may be required to register to vote and to be a resident for thirty days of the locality in which he or she intends to vote. The restriction is justified as a means to forestall corruption in the voting process. A voter may be required to be at least eighteen years of age and a citizen of the United States. Persons who are in jail on election day, are convicted felons, or have been formally adjudged insane or mentally incompetent may be excluded from the electorate. The long history of property qualification, racial discrimination, sex discrimination, and local biases have been fully rejected as legal means of restricting the suffrage. The fact that some aspects of these restrictive rules remain in the informal electoral practices of the society is reflected in the differential voting rates for different groups in the potential electorate. In an important symbolic sense, the thrust of the modern period has been to include virtually everyone in the society within the legal definition of the electorate and hence within the definition of "the people" to whom elected representatives are to be formally accountable and responsible; their consent is necessary to the legitimacy of the policy decisions of American government.

Popular conceptions of democracy in the American polity have shifted along with the broadening of the suffrage. The ideal that only the "better" elements of society should be allowed to choose our rulers has been replaced by the idea that all citizens are capable of determining for themselves what political choices are in their own interest. Each individual must be allowed to participate directly in the selection of those who will represent the people in the government. The notion of dependent classes, whose real interests can best be taken care of by others, has been rejected. The view is widely accepted that the voting act can and should be used to serve the perceived needs, aspirations, and goals of the individual voter. Expansion of the suffrage, with its consequent inclusion of many voters with little interest in elections, has also produced new laws and practices to protect the right of the individual to choose freely and to maintain the integrity of the voting process: the secret ballot, numerous corrupt practices statutes, and a variety of limitations upon the financial and electoral activities of candidates. Such regulations ensure that individuals can cast their votes as their own judgment dictates and shield them from undue influence or control by other members of the society. The search for ways to protect the integrity of the electoral process is a continuous one, intensified recently by the Watergate scandals. Demands for tighter controls over campaign spending, better and more complete public reporting of campaign contributions, and a larger role for public financing of election campaigns have brought rule changes that promote somewhat greater equality and fairness in the electoral system. These formalistic actions are at best poor substitutes for more basic changes in the level of popular awareness and in political attitudes and practices. A fair, universal, and efficient electoral system is an essential feature of democracy as now conceived. By allowing all to participate in the process, it is a genuine public good.

POLITICAL PARTICIPATION IN AMERICA

The above account of the evolution of voting rights in America supports the contention that universal suffrage has become a reality. Traditional legal barriers to voting have been eliminated. Changes in electoral rules have broadened the number of persons who have the formal right to influence public choices through periodic elections. Obviously, however, the formal rules only set the boundaries within which electoral participation may take place; the actual extent of voting is determined by the choices of millions of individuals as to whether they will exercise their right to vote. The level and distribution of voting participation in America result from complex interactions among the formal rules, individual values, and social and political circumstances.

Voting Turnout

The long, sometimes intense struggle for universal suffrage might lead one to believe that everyone entitled to this very significant right would be delighted to use it on all possible occasions. This conclusion is not borne out by the facts. The rate of turnout in elections in the United States is not impressive. The largest turnout can usually be expected in presidential elections, in which only about 60 percent of persons of voting age cast ballots. Thus, over one-third of all adult Americans do not vote in the single most popular event in the entire electoral system. The propensity to reject electoral participation is even more marked in other kinds of elections. Usually, less than half of the voting-age citizens vote in off-year congressional and state elections. Local and city elections are marked by even smaller turnouts. Only about 20 percent of adult residents cast ballots in most municipal elections. Many elections involving significant public policies — school budgets, municipal improvements, water supply, and other activities of special districts — draw less than 5 percent of the eligible voters to the polls.

A rather clear pattern emerges from a study of American voting activities. National elections are likely to draw the most voters to the polls; state elections, the next highest number; and local elections the fewest. Elections held to select officials who are "closest" to the people mobilize the smallest proportion of voters. A great many Americans vote only in presidential elections and (occasionally) in particularly salient state and local elections. This disinclination to vote is an object of interest and concern to scholars and activists alike, particularly because the major burden of conducting and influencing electoral politics falls upon so few people, who contribute time and funds to the candidates and parties of their choice or try to get others to be active in election politics. But while the low level of participation is universally recognized, the reasons for it are very much in dispute, as are the evaluations of its meaning for democracy. The following discussion identifies the major factors in the individual's decision to vote or not vote and evaluates their significance for public policy and for the course of democracy in America.

Table 8-2.   Participation in Election of President and House of Representatives, 1952–1972.*

Year	President	House of Representatives
1952	61.6%	57.6%
1954		41.7
1956	59.3	55.9
1958		43.0
1960	62.8	58.5
1962		46.1
1964	61.8	58.1
1966		45.4
1968	60.9	55.2
1970		43.5
1972	55.7	51.0

*Percentage based on total number of voting-age persons.

Source: Statistical Abstract of the United States, 1969, p. 368; 1973, p. 380.

Table 8-3. Individuals Reporting Different Acts of Political Participation.

Report regularly voting in presidential elections	72%
Report always voting in local elections	47
Have attempted to persuade others to vote as they were voting	28
Have ever worked actively for a party or candidates during an election	26
Have attended at least one political meeting or rally in last three years	19
Have ever given money to a party or candidate during an election campaign	13
Belong to a political club or organization	8

Source: Adapted from Sidney Verba and Norman H. Nie, *Participation in America,* (New York: Harper & Row, 1972), p. 31.

Reasons for Voting and Nonvoting

The reasons why people do not vote even though they are formally eligible to do so fall into two broad categories. First, many people fail to vote because of conditions that are beyond their control. They are ill on election day; weather conditions and work assignments interfere with their getting to the polls; they are traveling; they cannot meet the very minimal residency requirements which still exist. Although estimates vary somewhat, probably almost one-half of those who do not vote in presidential elections are prevented by such factors.[16] There is no reason to believe that these factors affect any greater number of persons in state and local elections. Therefore we can conclude that there are substantially more who *choose* not to vote in the latter elections. Little can be done to increase the turnout under these circumstances, except possibly by expanding absentee voting.

Second, a great many people who fail to vote in presidential elections, and an even greater number who do not vote in state and local elections, simply choose not to exercise the franchise available to them. Some must be characterized as habitual nonvoters. Somewhat more than 10 percent of adult citizens report that they have never voted in any election.[17] Others decide for one reason or another not to vote in particular elections. Obviously, this number fluctuates from election to election. The major issue to be addressed here concerns the causes and significance of that nonvoting which is a consequence of the free choice of individuals.

One obvious explanation of nonvoting is that the act of casting a ballot is not worth the cost involved in doing so. A favorable balance of expected benefits over costs to be gained from voting would induce one to exercise the right to vote. A negative balance would be reflected in nonvoting. Any attempt to increase the amount of voting by people who make such calculations would require a more positive balance of costs and benefits, either by an increase in the value of the vote to the individual or by a reduction in the cost of voting. The balance between expected costs and benefits is an outgrowth of the interaction of complex political, social, and psychological factors that figure in the calculus of the individual as he or she attempts to decide whether to vote in any given election. A large margin of expected benefits over costs provides a strong incentive actually to vote and even to participate in other ways in the electoral system. Negative evaluations tend to result in withdrawal from the voting process, while rough equality of costs and benefits is likely to produce indifference to the voting act or, at best, only phlegmatic participation. Most individuals do not, of course, actually weigh and rank all possible aspects of the election, as the above description might indicate. The point is that, implicitly or explicitly, many factors determine whether the individual will choose to cast a ballot in any given election. As a matter of fact, some minority of voters do engage in endless attitudinizing and calculations in arriving at a decision to participate or not.

Voting is not a costless act as sometimes supposed. There are at least the usually trivial costs in time and energy to get to the polling place and to exercise the voting act. Long lines, complex ballots, rude officials, bad weather, and poor transportation systems may increase these costs. Present rules generally try to reduce them. Voting machines, the short ballot, simplified and standardized ballots, the dispersion of voting and registration points, and the secret ballot all help to lessen these inconvenience costs. Although the manifest purpose of many electoral reforms has been to make elections more honest, they frequently have a latent consequence of lowering or raising the cost imposed upon the individual voter. Thus any changes in voting regulations should first be examined in terms of their impact upon the costs to the voter. A new electoral rule that makes registration procedures and/or voting actions easier will at least marginally increase the number of voters; one that is more complex will remove some marginal voters from the electorate. As mentioned earlier, the extension and simplification of rules governing absentee voting deserve particular attention by those who wish to increase voting turnout in America.

Forming Preferences

How the individual forms a preference for an issue or a candidate at election time is a serious question in political science. Very few persons will assume the costs in time and energy of going to the polls merely to pull levers or mark boxes on a piece of paper randomly. Voting generally depends upon the formation of a preference for some alternative or set of alternatives advanced in the election. The more important the value attributed to the preferred outcome, the greater the probability that the individual will be willing to pay the costs. Intense preferences are related to a high propensity to vote. These preferences may be negative or positive; that is, one may go to the polls strongly wanting someone to be elected or keenly wanting someone to be defeated. Any reduction in the intensity of preferences will result in a lowered inclination to vote. Of course, the process through which preferences are formed and then found to be related or unrelated to the electoral process is itself costly to the individual, a point we shall return to directly.

Any activities that intensify preferences add salience to the voting act and promote participation in the election. Hence the common tactic of partisans who argue that the election issues are stark and simple and the outcome is critical to the survival of the nation. Candidates have a way of calling the instant election the most important event in the history of the country or Western civilization or even the human race. Claims of this sort are important instruments in seeking to increase voting turnout. In a sense, the objective of any political campaign is to increase the relevance of the issues and/or the candidates in order to get potential supporters to the polls. A highly criticized (and soon removed) television spot used in the presidential election of 1964 illustrates this technique. The Johnson campaign presented a picture of a small child picking flowers who was then consumed by a mushroom cloud attributed to the election of Barry Goldwater. The message was simple: Choose Goldwater and you choose nuclear war. Cast in these terms, if believed, it simplifies the issues; increases their pertinence; reinforces the likelihood of voting by those who believe it; and, by discrediting the opposition, may attract new support from the opposition's normal voting base.

PARTICIPATION AND GROUP IDENTIFICATION

Identification with a political party or political interest group can give a forceful impetus to participation in the electoral process. Intense identification increases the probability that an individual will vote and otherwise become involved because choices take on greater importance and the costs of getting information about an election, the issues it deals with, and his or her stake in it are lower.[18] Endorsement of a candidate by a respected reference group may provide adequate and cheap information useful in making a voting choice and may magnify the perceived differences between the available alternatives. Intense identification with a single group also allows the individual to focus attention on a narrow range of issues in forming preferences. Group and party commitments, then, promote voting by providing a more favorable balance between the benefits expected to accrue from winning the election and the costs associated with the voting act.

Political party loyalty is strongly related to the propensity to vote. The devoted partisan needs little information to make a choice between candidates. The party label of the candidate is sufficient. It provides useful information to all voters, not only the partisan. It is of decreasing utility, however, as the importance of party identification decreases. The party label may even be helpful to the "pure" independent, or one who does not lean toward either political party. It supplies a cue as to who should be rewarded or blamed for prevailing economic or social conditions. The party label provides, then, significant information to the voter at very low cost. It is the most important datum in the electoral process. It tells partisans enough so that they can develop a preference, inexpensively, and be lured to the polls. This partisan factor is, of course, absent in nonpartisan elections and in party primaries. The lack of inexpensive cues to rational choice in nonpartisan and primary elections explains to a degree why their rate of participation is almost uniformly lower. Persons with intense political preoccupations and those with special relationships with the candidates are most likely to vote in primary and nonpartisan elections. This is the reason such elections so often select candidates who are viewed as ideologically extreme by the typical voters in partisan elections.

Partisanship also plays a role in increasing the perceived stakes in any given election. Highly partisan people usually believe that very different benefits and costs will flow from the election of different candidates: great benefits, secured at very low costs, if a member of their party wins office; great burdens, dangerous risks, and few improvements if the opposition wins. This sort of view provides incentives to participate actively in the electoral process. Generally, persons with weaker loyalties are less certain of the cost-benefit ratio associated with the success of either party. For them to judge, more information than party label is required, and the party label remains at best a small incentive for participation. Recent trends, which point to an apparent decrease in party identification in the United States, may indicate a lowering of the voting turnout in many elections.

Formal membership in, or psychological attachment to, any social group that attempts to gain policy objectives through political action also increases the tendency to vote. Like party affiliation, it enhances the importance attributed to an election outcome and supplies additional reasons for participation. The statements and actions of the leader of the group, by associating the group's objectives with the issues in the election, supply members with useful information. The formal endorsement of a candidate by the leaders may be enough to activate the individual to cast a ballot for the candidate. The stronger the identification with a group, the greater the confidence that the leadership's choice is correct and the more likely the individual is to vote. As with political party allegiance, group identification and loyalty simplify the process of securing the information necessary to establish and act upon a sensible preference. Intense group identifications, therefore, tend to be positively related to active participation in the electoral process. If identification with the group is weak, the member will need data from other sources before forming an electoral choice. An individual who receives contradictory cues from two or more respected organizations, or from other favored sources of information of near equal significance, is cross-pressured, a state that complicates the electoral decision, and may not vote.[19] The decision costs of resolving contradictory political recommendations from respected sources are often disproportionate to the likely risk or gain associated with the outcome of the election. Political listlessness is the rational response.

PARTICIPATION, CANDIDATES, AND ISSUES

The short-run conditions that are unique to any election may have an important impact on the overall level of turnout in an election. The candidates (their personalities, character, experience, family life) and policy issues in a campaign induce some persons who usually do not vote to do so and even to become active in other ways. The same factors convince others to "go fishing" and ignore that particular election. A position taken on a momentous issue or a personal idiosyncrasy of one of the candidates may raise the stakes of the election in the mind of a traditional nonvoter to the point that a threshold of interest is passed and participation results. The Goldwater campaign in 1964 and the McGovern campaign in 1972 were both based to some degree on the mistaken belief that a substantial number of nonvoters could be activated by "principled" stands on specified issues. The results of these two elections indicate the limited effectiveness of the strategy. Still, the composition of the electorate can be marginally influenced by such appeals. Similarly, a judgment that both candidates in an election are unacceptable, or at least equally distasteful, may lead some traditional voters away from the polls. In 1964 and 1972 many moderate Republicans were alienated by Goldwater and many moderate Democrats by McGovern. In brief, short-term factors have some impact upon turnout but are not normally the most critical determinants of decisions to vote or not to vote.

While of transitory significance, short-term factors are the major sources of the somewhat uneven patterns of participation from election to election. Either positive or negative reactions to one of the candidates can cause individuals to take part in or be repelled by the election. Intense emotional attachment to a candidate may be based on nothing more than the magical qualities imputed by the voter to the candidate. The political motivation generated by such psychological relationships has generally not been the dominant feature of the American electoral system. The reaction of many voters to candidates' positions on the war in Vietnam is an example of the way a single issue can influence participation while the reaction to the attractive personal characteristics of President Eisenhower shows how a candidate can trigger strong emotional identifications among many people.

PARTICIPATION AND CIVIC DUTY

The expectation of receiving specific material gains and losses as a result of a given election provides one of the bases for political activity. However, more generalized cultural values, involving the significance imputed to the voting act itself, may offer another incentive. The extent to which individuals consider that it is their civic obligation to vote, or believe that self-government is dependent upon universal citizen participation in the election system, may be a factor in the decision to vote. A commitment to democratic values as ends in themselves increases the probability that the individual will expend the energy necessary to acquire a position on the issues of the day and to cast a ballot.[20] Therefore, well-designed campaigns to convince people so committed of the value of voting to the maintenance of democracy would cause nonvoting to decline.

The manifest thrust of civic education programs (especially in the schools) is toward getting individuals interested and involved in public affairs. People are urged to be active in the political process, particularly in the electoral choices of the polity, as a matter of duty. Attempts are made, often ineptly, to convince them that they can and should influence the direction of public policy by voting in all elections. A frequent throwaway line on this theme is "If you don't vote, you don't have any right to complain" when public officials are acting irresponsibly or ineffectively. There are many sources of such hortatory rhetoric: civics, social studies, and political science courses in primary and secondary schools and many classes at the college level. The idea is to expand interest in politics, to strengthen feelings of political efficacy, and to inculcate the belief that one has a civic obligation to participate in politics. Perhaps there is some cumulative effect, since we know that the more education individuals have (and hence the more they have been exposed to such exhortation) the more likely they are to have attitudes consistent with these norms.

Newspapers, radio, and television convey messages in most elections emphasizing that all persons have the right, the privilege, and the responsibility to vote regardless of their political views. Nonpartisan groups conduct appeals directed to increasing participation in the political system. The League of Women Voters is perhaps the best known of the organizations pressing for broader exercise of the franchise through public persuasion. These appeals do not, however, reach all members of the population uniformly, and their effects vary among those who receive the messages. Nevertheless, although it is difficult to be precise in this matter, there is absolutely no doubt that individuals who (1) have the greatest interest in and awareness of politics, (2) have the strongest feeling that voting is a part of their duty as citizens, and (3) have formed impressions of their political effectiveness are most likely to participate consistently in electoral politics.[21]

But there is another side to the story. Certain elements in the civic education system can diminish the inclination to vote. The "duty to vote" argument is frequently wedded to the proposition that one must be highly informed on the candidates and issues in order properly to fulfill that duty. Furthermore, the voter is supposed to vote not for the party but for the "best" candidate. Choice should be made after careful study of the positions of the candidates on the issues of the day. The potential voter, it seems, is expected to spend a great deal of time and effort in reaching a conscientious decision — to incur substantial information costs. The individual who actually believes that all possible alternatives in relation to issues and candidates must be weighed before a legitimate vote can be cast may find such heroic standards too high to be met. The upshot may well be withdrawal from the situation.

Consider also the fact that the reformist bias in much of the political socialization process tends to characterize politics as a dirty business conducted by officials whose honesty and integrity are problematical at best. The pervasive view that political promises are meaningless and that politicians care only about being reelected leads to distrust of politicians and the political system. If all politicians are thought to be crooks, electoral choices will obviously seem irrelevant, and indifference or hostility to political forms promotes nonvoting.[22] There is evidence of a growing political cynicism which may produce an even lower level of participation in electoral politics in the future.[23]

The impact of civic education and political socialization in the United States upon voting behavior thus cuts two ways. Individuals who come to believe that they have the opportunity, duty, information, and ability to take part meaningfully in the electoral process have a heightened propensity to vote. Conversely, the belief that a great amount of information is a precondition for proper voting, or the growth of political cynicism, clearly reduces participation in elections. Personal attitudes formed in the political socialization process serve as screening devices through which the individual views the political world and through which political information must flow. They condition the cost-benefit calculations of voters and nonvoters alike.

PARTICIPATION AND SOCIETY

There are certain social facts that influence the choice to involve oneself in or withdraw from electoral politics. Being active in the electoral system entails some minimal costs of information and participation. Any factor that reduces these costs is likely to bring more persons into the electorate, and each additional reduction produces its increment of new voters. These "new" voters tend to be less politically concerned than the "old" voters. They usually have less political information and other political resources than those who had voted when costs were higher. Any simplification of voting rules or processes, any increases in party or group loyalty and identification, any newly important issues, any more attractive candidates expand the electorate. Elimination of both the direct costs of participation and the indirect costs associated with forming a political preference would induce almost all to vote who were not completely indifferent to the alternatives available. Although very few people are totally apathetic or indifferent, many are unwilling or unable to assume the costs that prevail at present.

A belief that participation is valuable makes for a greater willingness to bear its costs and, consequently, increases voting turnout. But we have not yet considered who exactly is likely to have that belief. Any political polarization of the society into "left" and "right" will increase participation unless the alternatives presented are so extreme and so unacceptable that they leave moderate members of the community indifferent. Conversely, total polarization occurs when conditions have forced everyone to choose; in that event, however, electoral politics is already dead and the political struggle is over the regime itself, as in Spain in the 1930s.

Characteristics of Voters and Nonvoters

The perceived cost-benefit ratio is not sufficiently favorable to cause most Americans to vote in most elections. It is crucial to remember that persons who choose not to vote are not evenly distributed throughout all groups and classes. The active electorate is not a perfect microcosm of society. There are significant differences in the social, economic, and personal characteristics of those who most frequently and those who least frequently participate in electoral politics. The uneven distribution of voting behavior across social groups creates a situation in which some

Drawing by D. Fradon; © 1973 The New Yorker Magazine, Inc.

groups have substantially more power in the electoral system than would be predicted from their numbers in the society; others have substantially less influence than would be expected on the same basis. For example, a study has shown that while wage earners represented 37 percent of the potential voters in 1960 and persons in professional and executive positions comprised only 18 percent of the population each group contributed 26 percent of the actual votes cast in the election.[24] This pattern of voting and nonvoting is reflected to some extent in the allocation of benefits and costs to various groups by government. A brief description of the social patterns of participation is necessary before an evaluation of the significance of nonvoting for the development of public policy can be presented.

Most Americans choose to vote at least occasionally, and some voters move into and out of the electorate depending on the election. Those who are habitual nonvoters (approximately 15 percent of the eligible population) and those who are only occasional voters share certain traits that distinguish them from more consistent electoral participants.[25] The most obvious difference between voters and nonvoters is one of attitudes and has already been discussed: Nonvoters are consistently less interested in politics, are less aware of candidates and issues, have less intense identifications with one of the major political parties, and attribute less importance to electoral outcomes. Lacking political interest, they have very little incentive to pay any significant costs in order to participate in an election. Candidates and chance events may entice the marginal voter to the polls in any given election. The marginal voter is the most likely to shift from party to party because no habitual political responses have been developed. Ironically, the shifting about of poorly informed marginal voters is often taken by journalists to represent the current political "mood" of the country.

There is also great consistency in the social and demographic characteristics that distinguish citizens with the strongest and weakest voting records. The propensity to vote tends to increase to some point as the individual gets older; then it weakens. The lowest voting rates are to be found among the youngest voters. The best voting record is to be found among those between the ages of forty-five and sixty-four years. Older people participate less after the age of sixty-five. Thus politics does not compete very favorably with the activities of the young, who are preoccupied with families, jobs, and establishing a stake in society. As people become more integrated and secure, they generally have more time to act politically, and a habitual political response pattern develops which reduces decision costs to them. Party, group, and class interests firm up, and they become more aware of ways to protect or advance those interests politically. After retirement, some withdrawal from politics is likely.

There is still a slight difference in male and female participation in electoral politics. Men vote slightly more than women do. This apparently is a holdover from the traditional view that politics is a man's business. It is probably related, too, to the fact that fewer women are in the work force and women receive less information concerning occupational and other interests and voting alternatives. The growing demands for equality of women as well as shifts in employment patterns will undoubtedly reduce the margin of difference between the sexes as political participants.

Most important of all are the profound differences in voting participation among socioeconomic groups. The most habitual voters are those who are college graduates, who receive relatively high incomes, who have professional status. The pattern is consistent: Individuals with more educa-

Table 8-4. Participation in Presidential Elections by Population Characteristics (in percentages).

Characteristic	1964	1968	1972
Male	72	70	64
Female	67	66	62
White	71	69	65
Nonwhite	59	58	52
Age			
18–20 years	39	33	48
21–24 years	51	51	51
25–34 years	65	63	60
35–44 years	73	71	66
45–64 years	76	75	71
65 years and over	66	66	64
Education			
8 years or less	59	55	47
9–11 years	65	61	52
12 years	76	73	65
More than 12 years	85	81	79
Family income			
Under $3000	53	54	Data
$3000–4999	63	58	not
$5000–7499	72	66	available
$7500–9999	78	73	
$10,000 and over	85	80	

Source: Statistical Abstract of the United States, 1969, p. 371; 1973, p. 379.

tion participate more than those with less education; those with higher incomes participate more than those with lower incomes; those in more esteemed occupations participate more than those in less esteemed occupations. Voters are proportionately more frequently white than black; more likely to be Episcopalians and Jews than Catholics or Baptists; more often northerners than southerners. Thus, higher-status persons participate more than lower-status persons according to most standards by which status is measured. There are many reasons for this.

One important reason is that the stakes of politics are more apparent to higher-status people, who, because of education and broader experiences, have greater insight into their social and political interests than others. More information is available to them, and their intellectual sophistication enables them to understand and assimilate that information as it relates to their self-interest. Higher-status persons are more likely to have been recipients of the messages designed to arouse a sense of civic duty. They are more effective personally in their occupational and other social roles and hence in their political activity. They have greater resources of all sorts, some of which they can allocate to politics at a lower marginal cost than can others. The closer one lives to the margin of survival, the more costly it is to contribute time or energy to the often abstract problem of political choice, especially when political success is judged to be a remote prospect at best.

Social Significance of Nonvoting

There is continuing and often impassioned debate in American political science over the social significance of nonvoting. On the one hand, the argument is that substantial nonvoting is solid evidence of health in the polity. High levels of voting are held to be associated with great intensity, divisiveness, and crises.[26] When total populations are aroused, social stability is threatened. Antidemocratic opportunists and demagogues appear. The democratic virtues of tolerance, adjustment, and forbearance may be wiped away. Any large increase in voting would signal heightened political conflict and would tend to be destructive of social order and democratic practice. The nonvoter is considered to be basically satisfied with the external costs and benefits accrued by the political participation of others.

On the other hand, there is the view that nonvoting, because it is mainly characteristic of the "have-nots" of society, cannot be a sign of a wholesome social condition. Nonvoters are the most disadvantaged, the most ignored, the most withdrawn, the most dissatisfied, the most anomic, the most cynical. Their social mobilization would generate a radically different distribution of indulgences and burdens. Their participation is held to be essential if the goals of equality and justice are to be achieved in America.[27]

As a matter of fact, there are both complacent and alienated nonvoters, although the social traits of most nonvoters are very disquieting to advocates of democracy. However regarded, nonvoters are unwilling to pay the costs of voting. In some cases, they feel that things are going fine without their participation and that leaving electoral choices to others involves very little risk. They are free riders, receiving the benefits of a democratic polity without absorbing any of the participation costs. In other cases, individuals may consider that political choices have no impact upon their life and that things will go badly regardless of the outcome of elections. In such a situation, voting would be absurd. The traditional nonvoter may fall into either of these categories. If the stakes are not relevant, or if victory is improbable, political abstention may be chosen. Some reformers see a remedy in offering nonvoters relevant alternatives in elections; others, in inculcating the participation norms of the democratic culture and increasing turnout through moral suasion.

It is true that a rapid rise in voting turnout would probably be associated with growing intensity and intransigence in the political system. The activation of many new voters, often easily swayed by ephemeral and poorly understood impulses, might produce considerable instability as long as their social and personal characteristics remained unchanged. On the other hand, participation accompanied by improvements in the educational and economic positions of the new voters could probably be accommodated without major disruption to other groups. But wherever the truth may lie on this issue, no major shifts in current patterns are likely until the perceptions of nonvoters concerning the relevance of politics to their basic needs are changed or until participation costs are reduced. The increases in black voting in the last two decades provide an important illustration of how such changes may come about. The civil rights movement communicated the belief that the condition of life for black persons could be changed through mass voting, which could have an impact on public policy. The emergence of black leaders who identified group goals with the Democratic party provided a means through which black voters could easily make a rational choice as to the expectedly best candidate for them. These developments reveal a typical pattern in American politics by which ethnic groups have come to form more or less stable political identifications. First, it was perceived that substantial benefits could be secured through political mobilization, particularly voting. Second, voting could be increased by the elimination of restrictive voting rules. Third, voting could be increased still further if group goals were connected to a party label, thus lowering information costs to the individual voter. Such an analysis must be qualified by the apparently growing doubt about the political system's capacity to solve many group problems, a doubt which could reduce the participation of some citizens.

THE VOTING CHOICE IN
AMERICAN ELECTORAL POLITICS

The voting act involves a process through which individuals acquire a preference for a candidate of sufficient strength to motivate them to register that preference at the polls. A number of factors influence the nature and strength of voting preferences. The decisions on whether one should vote and how one will vote are interrelated. The above discussion focuses on this relationship, emphasizing the basic decision whether or not to participate in any given election. Here attention is directed at how the person who decides to vote acquires the positions he or she will support on election day.

The Voting "Package"

Everyone has needs, aspirations, values, and expectations which may be advanced or thwarted by the public policies made by government. Direct participation in all decisions of government would allow the individual to support preferred positions on all public issues. The only problem would be to identify the relationship of a policy proposal with individual goals. Mistakes due to ignorance could be made, but the dictates of rationality could be met by ranking all alternatives in such a way that the benefits and costs were equal at the margin. Such calculations would be immensely costly in terms of time and energy; we cannot all be Director of the Office of Management and Budget in Washington, D.C., nor would we all want to be. The election of representatives to make these decisions for us both simplifies and complicates the problem of maintaining a connection between what we want and our positions on policy issues. A vote cast for any candidate includes support for a very broad and diffuse set of policy positions, and individual voters, at least by implication, vote in favor of the whole set when they cast their ballots for a particular candidate. The voter must choose one or another main course; there is no picking and choosing as at a smorgasbord. All candidates will have some policy positions at variance with the preference structure of any individual. Voters are thus unable to vote specifically on all policy issues that interest them. They will necessarily "lose" on some issues regardless of how they vote. On the other hand, they do not have to (cannot) absorb the decision costs of casting decisions on all issues. Let such costs be borne by the representative.

Moreover, some positions taken by the candidates may be a matter of indifference to an individual voter. If one has only a limited range of issues, the decision problem is simplified. In the simplest case of all, a voter would be so intensely committed to a single issue that all other positions held by the candidates could be ignored. Single-issue orientations do occur, but more typically a range of issues is involved. Individuals must seek information until they believe they have enough to make a rational choice — that is, until further search would be more costly than any likely benefits therefrom. Usually, any further items of information will be redundant — and inefficient if they impose any costs on the individual. The likelihood of redundancy is reinforced by the tendency to obtain additional information selectively, so that it supports the original choice. The greater the importance attributed to the election and to voting, the more information the voter may need to make and reinforce the voting decision. If little value is attached to the voting act, and if the issues are of low priority, trivial data may be sufficient to reach a decision. Voting for the candidate with the most sex appeal is not irrational if the candidates are seen to be equally satisfactory or unsatisfactory on all other dimensions.

The voter must choose grossly a total set of conditions and prospective outcomes when he or she chooses to cast a ballot for one or the other of the candidates.[28] The personalities of the candidates and their positions on issues will appeal differentially to different voters, and the same candidate will be supported for very different reasons. Thus it is difficult to determine exactly *why* a candidate was elected and even more difficult to interpret the nature of any "mandate" for action given to him or her. The individuals who voted for the winning candidate can be said to prefer the state of affairs they predicted would prevail if this candidate were elected over what they believed would follow from the election of the other candidate. These predictions, however, vary so much from voter to voter that the aggregate prediction is more mystical than real. A package of issue positions, personal characteristics, and a partisan label is purchased by the voters. A few voters may prefer every aspect of the package; others will be indifferent to some aspects and interested in others; and some voters will prefer certain elements of the package and find some elements distasteful. What the voters "really" want or have "really" voted for is usually obscure. It is the very ambiguity of the relationship between individual and collective choices that provides the elected politician such latitude on many occasions, a point made more precisely in the discussion of congressional voting in Chapter 9.

The Issue of Self-Interest

From the voter's point of view, the question is: "Which candidate has the most favorable net balance of preferred positions in terms of my own interests?"[29] The answer establishes the voting preference. If there is no perceived difference between candidates, the voter is likely to abstain from voting or to turn to some external, nonpolitical rule to make the voting decision.

The political party of the candidate, we have noted, may enter into the individual's calculus in several ways.[30] The intense partisan who identifies completely with a political party will usually vote that preference in all elections. The informational flow to the voter will be conditioned by his or her party affiliation, and information will be interpreted from a party perspective. It is very difficult to convince such persons that a candidate of another party is more compatible with their individual interest. Intense party identification has developed at least to some extent out of observations that one party will support policies and programs that are consistent with the individual's interest more than another. Only when a preferred party takes clear and obvious issue positions that are unacceptable will the partisan cast a vote for the opposing candidate. Even then, abstention from the election is more likely than a switch in party allegiance. A sequence of unpopular party actions will of course weaken the individual's identification with the original party and ease transition to the opposition party. The party label provides a simple and inexpensive means to summarize the positions of the candidates and to make predictions about the balance of negative and positive components in their programs. These factors may well produce a lag in electoral behavior, and party loyalty may continue for a period even after the chosen party has dramatically shifted its basic positions or the interests of the individual have changed.

The weak partisan or the independent who leans toward one of the parties makes somewhat less use of the party label. The party label does furnish some information helpful in reaching a decision, but it is generally not sufficient to culminate in a voting choice. Candidates and issues of the campaign are also important. Clear preference for the policy position or personal characteristics of a candidate is likely to move this voter across party lines but, in the absence of strong reasons for voting for the opposition, party preference will determine the choice. The true independent receives virtually no information from the party label and must find other grounds upon which to form a judgment. The information costs of decision-making increase as one moves from the intense partisan to the independent, inasmuch as the most readily available piece of information, party label, becomes less decisive. This is, as already noted, one reason why the independent votes less frequently than the dedicated partisan. The position of the independent is simplified, however, by the fact that this voter is usually less interested in politics and attributes less significance to the voting act than the partisan. The independent is thus able to make a choice on meager information gathered from the mass media or on the basis of very limited exposure to the candidates and their programs.

The party label has another significant contribution to make. The party provides a focal point for responsibility for the operation of the political system. The party in power tends to be held accountable for the state of the nation and quality of life in the society.[31] Between elections a mood of general evaluation of how things are going in the society develops. A negative evaluation may lead many independents and weak partisans to believe that a change in control of the government is in order. That change can most readily be brought about by rejecting the party in power and shifting voting support to the opposition party. Thus, the performance of the party in the immediate past is an extremely important influence upon the decision-making of numerous members of the electorate. In the American system it is generally accepted that the government is responsible for maintaining a satisfactory quality of life. Any major decline in social conditions is likely to be attributed to those who have been in control of government, whether or not there was any meaningful governmental contribution to the perceived deteriorating state of affairs. The historical record of the American political parties seems to be a much more dependable guide to behavior for most voters than the promises that are made in election campaigns or the proposed programs embedded in party platforms.

In consequence, one or the other of the parties usually bears a heavier burden of convincing the electorate that it is worthy of support in any given election. The positions of the Republicans after the economic collapse in the late 1920s and again after the Watergate scandals forced a Republican president to resign and of the Democrats after the Korean and Vietnam wars illustrate these shifting burdens. But even in the most massive landslide election the losing candidate is usually able to hold the voting loyalty of a majority of the members of his party. The losing margin in such elections is due to almost unanimous rejection by the members of the opposition party and a sharp loss in the ranks of voters who hold no clear identification with either of the parties.

Table 8-5. Vote by Political Party in Presidential Elections, 1952–1972.

Year	Candidates	Democrats	Independents	Republicans
1952	Stevenson	77%	35%	8%
	Eisenhower	23	65	92
1956	Stevenson	85	30	4
	Eisenhower	15	70	96
1960	Kennedy	84	43	5
	Nixon	16	57	95
1964	Johnson	87	56	20
	Goldwater	13	44	80
1968	Humphrey	74	31	9
	Nixon	12	44	86
	Wallace	14	25	5
1972	McGovern	67	31	5
	Nixon	33	69	95

Source: Compiled from data included in *The Gallup Opinion Index,* March 1974.

Distribution of Party Affiliations

The importance of party identification warrants a brief discussion of the factors leading toward the distribution of party identifications. It has been said that all Americans are born either little Democrats or little Republicans. This obvious overstatement can be justified only by the fact that most Americans do cast their first vote for their parents' party. In the majority of cases this first vote establishes a pattern that is generally followed throughout life (although it may now be in some decay). Family background is perhaps the main source of party identification, particularly in a home in which both parents are firm supporters of the same political party. The informal socialization process within the family results in the internalization of positive orientations toward one party. In politically aware families, magazines, books, selected television programs, and other material around the home are likely to reinforce informal discussion in which the merits of one party and the deficiencies of the other are emphasized. Friends of the family tend to be persons similarly placed in the social structure and to possess the same party loyalties. Peer and friendship groups acquired in the process of maturation generally uphold the preconception of politics developed in the family. Typically one assumes a role in society of similar status to that of one's parents, thereby sharing the same general economic and other interests. Thus informal interpretations of the world to which the child is exposed create a political bias that can be fitted more perfectly to the bias of one party than another. This almost casual process results in a relatively systematic intergenerational transfer of political party identifications and political interests and attitudes.

The individual who matures in a home in which politics is of low salience and there is little identification with a political party tends to internalize this outlook. Similarly, the child of parents who hold competing political identifications will probably be exposed to less clear stimuli and not develop a firm party loyalty. The upshot will be less interest in politics and more random political behavior.

Individuals who change position in the social structure may find themselves in a situation in which all immediate stimuli encourage a shift in party identification. Thus, the party system tends not to alter more rapidly than the society as a whole, and social stability is associated with only small changes in the composition of party identification. Current trends point to a lessened intensity of party identification, with more and more persons claiming to be independents. This movement has been particularly significant in reducing identification with the Republican party over the last several years. Such a tendency diminishes the importance of the political party in providing inexpensive guides to individual choice. Without party labels to organize and inform voters' decisions, voting may become more capricious and less sensible in the future. Perhaps this is an alarmist view, but it should alert one to a potential danger.

Republicans and Democrats

Recent presidential elections have fluctuated from the landslide victory for the Democratic candidate in 1964 to the landslide victory of the Republican candidate in 1972. These very large swings have submerged but not destroyed the traditional patterns of voting among most social groupings in the United States. The margins have shifted dramatically but the basic orientations have considerable continuity.

The Democratic party maintains its strong appeal to the nonwhite population. Democratic support for civil rights and social welfare programs has consolidated that support in recent elections. Occupationally, the Democrats' greatest strength lies in the working classes. The blue-collar worker and trade union member are among its more consistent supporters. Paradoxically, Democratic party policies in the areas of civil rights and some welfare programs have somewhat weakened the party's position with this group of voters. Events have placed a strain on the Democratic party coalition as the demands of one element in it — nonwhites — are vigorously opposed by many members of the occupational groups that comprise the traditional strength of the party. The Democratic party maintains a greater appeal for Catholics than for Protestants, for younger voters than older ones. Persons who have the least amount of education are also more likely to support the Democratic party. Now rather old, the Democratic coalition forged in the years of the New Deal still holds, although badly undermined by the campaign of 1972.

Republican voters are more frequently drawn from the more prosperous groups in society. They usually have higher incomes, are older, and have completed more years of schooling than Democrats. They are more often Protestants and white than are Democratic voters. Their general interests fit well with the generally more conservative and business-oriented policies associated with the Republican party outlook.

These data must be looked at only as inclinations rather than as definite stratifications in the society. There is a tendency toward a class basis for the political parties, but remember that large numbers of each group consistently vote for the candidates of a party other than the one associated with their social and economic characteristics. A good many people in most social groupings move to the opposition party in elections if the positions advocated by the party for which they usually vote seem to them incompatible with their interests or their view of appropriate social policy.

Table 8-6. Vote by Groups in Presidential Elections, 1960–1972 (in percentages).

	1960		1964		1968			1972	
	Kennedy	Nixon	Johnson	Goldwater	Humphrey	Nixon	Wallace	McGovern	Nixon
Sex									
Men	52	48	60	40	41	43	16	37	63
Women	49	51	62	38	45	43	12	38	62
Race									
White	49	51	59	41	38	47	15	32	68
Nonwhite	68	32	94	6	85	12	3	87	13
Education									
College	39	61	52	48	37	54	9	37	63
High school	52	48	62	38	42	43	15	34	66
Grade school	55	45	66	34	52	33	15	49	51
Occupation									
Professional and business	42	58	54	46	34	56	10	31	69
White-collar	48	52	57	43	41	47	12	36	64
Manual	60	40	71	29	50	35	15	43	57
Age									
Under 30 years	54	46	64	36	47	38	15	48	52
30–49 years	54	46	63	37	44	41	15	33	67
50 years and older	46	54	59	41	41	47	12	36	64
Religion									
Protestants	38	62	55	45	35	49	16	30	70
Catholics	78	22	76	24	59	33	8	48	52

Source: Adapted from *The Gallup Opinion Index*, March 1974.

SUMMARY

The American polity is organized as a representative democracy. Control of the public policy of the society by the general population is dependent upon institutions through which the representatives can be made responsible and accountable to the people. One important institution is the periodic election through which citizens may freely choose individuals to make the substantive policy decisions of the government.

In a society that relies upon elections as a means for influencing public policy a critical question is who shall be granted the right to vote. The formal rules delineating membership in the electorate also define in a sense the people to whom government, in democratic theory, is responsible. The dominant trend in the United States has been a broadening of the suffrage, and at present the law clearly states the ideal of universal suffrage. Virtually all adults can vote. The extension of the suffrage has stimulated the enactment of rules to maintain the integrity of the electoral process. They are, paradoxically, one basis for the relatively low turnout in most elections.

The formal rules have defined the electorate in a very broad manner, but many individuals do not see fit to participate in electoral politics. The largest turnout of voters can be expected in presidential elections, while smaller turnout is associated with state and local elections. The primary reason many eligible voters choose not to vote is that the costs of participation are equal to or greater than the expected benefits from participation. The costs involve the time and energy required to engage in the voting act and, more importantly, the effort required to form a preference of sufficient strength to motivate action. Higher expected benefits from voting, derived either from increasing the stakes of election contests or from increasing the general evaluation of the importance of voting, would reduce nonvoting. Rules and processes that lower the decisional costs in voting also raise the propensity of some persons to vote. Nonvoters tend to be concentrated in the disadvantaged classes in society, and the mobilization of this group could conceivably bring significant shifts in the composition of American public policy.

The voting choice is dictated by the balance of positive and negative results that are expected to flow from any given electoral outcome. The candidate's political party, positions on the issues of the day, and personal characteristics all enter into the individual voter's ultimate choice. The party label plays a central role in this process because it provides ready and free information to the voter. The partisan voter is more strongly influenced by party than are others, but the party provides at least a focus of attention for all voters seeking cues as to how to make their choices in an election. There are substantial social differences between the voters who support the two major parties in the United States. Each party is comprised of a stable, basic coalition that supports the party in all elections, but each election sees shifts in the actual voting choices of some members of the electorate.

NOTES

1. This position is deeply integrated into the belief system of most Americans. See Louis Hartz, *The Liberal Tradition in America* (New York: Harcourt, Brace, 1955), for a classic treatment.
2. See Gordon Tullock, *Toward a Mathematics of Politics* (Ann Arbor: University of Michigan Press, 1967), for an attempt to describe a means of evading the representation problem.
3. The importance of this point is emphasized in Harold D. Lasswell and Abraham Kaplan, *Power and Society* (New Haven, Conn.: Yale University Press, 1950).
4. See Kirk H. Porter, *History of Suffrage in the United States* (Westport, Conn.: Greenwood, 1969), for the development of this argument.
5. Ibid.
6. See *Newberry v. United States,* 256 U.S. 232 (1921).
7. See *Nixon v. Herndon,* 273 U.S. 536 (1927), and *Nixon v. Condon,* 286 U.S. 73 (1932). Cf. *Grovey v. Townsend,* 295 U.S. 45 (1935).
8. See *Smith v. Allwright,* 321 U.S. 649 (1944), and *Terry v. Adams,* 345 U.S. 461 (1953).
9. *Harper v. Virginia Board of Elections,* 383 U.S. 663 (1966).
10. See *Phoenix v. Koladziejski,* 399 U.S. 204 (1970), and *Cipriano v. Houma,* 395 U.S. 701 (1969).
11. *Carrington v. Rash,* 380 U.S. 89 (1965).
12. *Dunn v. Blumstein,* 405 U.S. 331 (1972).
13. See *Reynolds v. Sims,* 377 U.S. 533 (1964).
14. See *Avery v. Midland County,* 390 U.S. 1114 (1969).
15. See *South Carolina v. Katzenbach,* 383 U.S. 307 (1966), and *Katzenbach v. Morgan* 384 U.S. 641 (1966).
16. Elmo Roper estimated that nearly 20 million of the 37 million adult Americans who did not vote in 1960 were precluded from voting for some reason other than their own choice. James Barber, *Citizen Politics* (Chicago: Markham, 1969).
17. See William H. Flanigan, *Political Behavior of the American Electorate* (Boston: Allyn & Bacon, 1968), pp. 15–25.
18. See Bernard R. Berelson, Paul F. Lazarsfeld, and William N. McPhee, *Voting* (Chicago: University of Chicago Press, 1954); Lester W.

Millbrath, *Political Participation* (Chicago: Rand McNally, 1965); and Sidney Verba and Norman H. Nie, *Participation in America* (New York: Harper & Row, 1972).

19. Paul F. Lazarsfeld, Bernard Berelson, and Hazel Gaudet, *The People's Choice* (New York: Columbia University Press, 1948), Chapters 6–7.

20. See William C. Mitchell, *Why Vote?* (Chicago: Markham, 1971), pp. 8–28.

21. Angus Campbell, Phillip Converse, Warren Miller, and Donald Stokes, *The American Voter* (New York: Wiley, 1960), Chapter 5.

22. A useful study of political perceptions is Dan D. Nimmo, *Popular Images of Politics* (Englewood Cliffs, N.J.: Prentice-Hall, 1974).

23. Lack of confidence in political institutions was reflected in public opinion polls during 1973 and 1974. For an interesting discussion of this trend by five members of Congress, see "Congress and the People," *Congressional Quarterly,* 32 (March 9, 1974), 600–604.

24. R. Joseph Monsen and Mark W. Cannon, *The Makers of Public Policy* (New York: McGraw-Hill, 1965), p. 71.

25. See Flanigan, *Political Behavior of the American Electorate,* pp. 45–68.

26. See Berelson et al., *Voting,* Chapter 14.

27. See E.E. Schattschneider, *The Semisovereign People* (New York: Holt, Rinehart & Winston, 1960).

28. See Anthony Downs, *An Economic Theory of Democracy* (New York: Harper & Row, 1957), pp. 36–50.

29. See Stanley Kelley, Jr., and Thad W. Mirer, "The Simple Act of Voting," *American Political Science Review,* 68 (June 1974), 572–591, for an interesting empirical analysis of this matter. It shows that very considerable predictability results from obtaining the voters' balance between favorable and unfavorable responses to candidates.

30. See Campbell et al., *The American Voter.*

31. The most useful example of this view is V.O. Key, Jr., *The Responsible Electorate* (Cambridge, Mass.: Harvard University Press, 1966).

9

The Congress: Rules of Collective Choice

Legislative bodies are the central feature of all representative democracies. It is primarily through them that the will of the people is expected to be expressed in the public policies of the society. The legislature provides a mechanism through which many competing interests can be brought together and aggregated into public choices. The resulting policies are usually considered legitimate because they represent the choices of "the people" as made through their elected agents. The legislature is expected to establish the direction and general value content of the public policies of the society. Legislators are expected to represent competing goals and provide a means for including these in governmental actions. The legislative process is expected to afford an arena in which the conflicting interests can be accommodated in a fair and equitable manner. This elaborate set of linkages makes the legislative body a major agency for negotiation, bargaining, and compromise — the hallmarks of a democratic polity. It is an indispensable element in developing the legitimacy of public policies.

Under the Constitution of the United States, legislative power is placed in the Congress. That power is divided between the House and the Senate in a manner which requires duplication of efforts in the two houses and demands substantial consensus before major affirmative actions can be taken. The chief substantive powers delegated to the national government are lodged in the Congress in Article I of the Constitution. Virtually all public policies require some action by the legislature before they become binding on the individual members of the polity. Even in periods in which extraordinary discretion has been granted to the president and the executive branch, at base all public policies can be traced to some generalized authorization made by the Congress. Similarly, the Constitution places the Congress in a position to be able to remove all other officials of the national government through the process of impeachment. In the final analysis, the Congress is supreme in the American system of government. In a very formal, legal sense, the extent to which the people rule in a democratic society depends upon the operation of the legislative system.

The Congress is the preeminent representative institution in the polity, reflecting as it does the pluralistic character of the American people. The contentiousness and seeming disarray of the Congress stem from competing values and diversity in the society. The inability of the Congress to act with dispatch — so frequently criticized — mirrors the uncertainty and confusion that flow from the competing demands of the population. The Congress and its members can play a very significant leadership role, but the process of education, persuasion, and articulation which is necessary to gain consensus in the country takes time as the Congress searches for some means of aggregating varied social demands into acceptable public policies. The system places priority on compromise and the generation of consent before major policy innovations can be activated. Criticism of the Congress is really criticism of a democratic society in which the interests of different persons are considered to have equal legitimacy and an equal right to be represented. The process seems inefficient if not degenerate to those who know the Truth and would like to impose it upon their fellows.

CONSTITUTIONAL RULES AND THE CONGRESS

Article I, Section 2 of the Constitution requires that a census of the population be taken every ten years in order that each state's representation in the House of Representatives will be based upon the size of its population (except that each state must have at least one representative). The first House had 65 members, or roughly one for every 30,000 people in the country. Following the first national census in 1790, the House was reapportioned and expanded to 105 members. By 1800 there were 141 members; by 1850, 234 members. Finally, in 1911, the House reached its present size of 435 members with each member representing some 212,000 people. Today, each member represents nearly 500,000 people.

Since each state is entitled by Article I, Section 3 of the Constitution to two senators, and eleven states had joined the Union when the First Congress met in March, 1789, there were twenty-two members in the first Senate.

Inasmuch as members of the House are all elected for concurrent two-year terms, a new House is elected every two years. In the case of the Senate, however, the Constitution provides for staggered six-year terms, with one-third of the seats up for election every two years, and makes the Senate a continuing body.

A member of the House must be at least twenty-five years old, an American citizen for at least seven years, and an "inhabitant" (the definition of which has never been settled) of the state from which she or he is elected. A member of the Senate must be at least thirty years old, a citizen for nine years, and, when elected, an inhabitant of the state from which she or he is chosen. No member of Congress may hold any other public office (the definition of which remains unclear) simultaneously, presumably because other public duties might conflict with those of a national legislature. A number of immunities are granted to members of Congress. Except on charges of "treason, felony, and breach of the peace" (now means: any indictable crime), no member may be arrested while going to or returning from a session of Congress. No member may be questioned elsewhere (e.g., in a court of law) for any statement made in Congress; this is one of the few constitutional rights which has been held to be virtually absolute as long as the internal house rules governing the terms of debate have been obeyed.

"All legislative powers . . . shall be vested in a . . . Senate and House of Representatives," according to the first words of Article I of the Constitution. In fact, however, the powers of Congress extend beyond those involving legislation. Houses of Congress also, on occasion, propose constitutional amendments, influence public opinion, count electoral votes, receive the State of the Union address from the president, conduct investigations, pass on nominees to high office, and assist constituents in their business with the government. All of these congressional functions are important, although, in social terms, questions of legislation (which is by far the most crucial activity of Congress), investigation, and impeachment are perhaps most important. These, and the role of the political parties in Congress, are discussed below.

RULES GOVERNING THE LEGISLATIVE PROCESS

With respect to its legislative powers, the Constitution states that the Congress can, among other things, impose taxes (but only uniformly throughout the country), borrow money, regulate commerce, coin and regulate money, establish inferior courts, declare war, raise and support military forces, and provide for the suppression of insurrections and invasions. Moreover, it may make all laws "necessary and proper" for executing these various powers.

Of course, history has not been entirely on the side of Congress in its constitutional primacy with respect to legislation. Over the years, the courts, the presidency, and the bureaucracy have all gained power in the formation of official public policy. Judicial decisions, executive orders, and administrative regulations often have all the import of legislation passed by Congress, although Congress has by no means been deprived of its legislative prerogatives whenever it has chosen to assert them.

The fact is, however, that being a representative institution Congress has members with very different social philosophies, political ambitions, and interests. They acknowledge no clear hierarchy of interests or values and have no united point of view on any subject except continuation of their own offices. One should not be surprised, therefore, when Congress fails to act consistently or decisively on all policy matters. Because of its internal dynamics and decision-rules, it has been known to pass contradictory laws, to procrastinate in the face of crises, and to adopt ineffective means in pursuit of some goal — even when individual members are acting sensibly in terms of their own personal interest.

If Congress attains sufficient internal agreement (which may be neither possible nor desirable), only amendments to the Constitution can limit its legislative powers. As it is, the courts cannot rule on congressional action nor may the president exercise a veto *until* Congress has legislated. Conversely, Congress may overturn by legislative action decisions made by the other branches of government. An internally united

Congress, however, would be one altogether unrepresentative of the ideological and political diversity of our pluralistic society and perhaps is more to be feared than hoped for. The specific rules by which legislation is processed are crucial to an understanding of Congress and of legislative action.

Congress is a committee itself divided into two committees, the House of Representatives and the Senate. They share equally in making of public policy and in discharging tasks assigned by the Constitution or assumed over the years. Because of the different sizes of the two bodies (435 members in the House compared to 100 members in the Senate), however, they have different rules for the making of collective decisions. As we shall see, the House has elaborated and codified its rules to an advanced degree while the Senate's rules are fewer and more flexible. The individual member of the House must usually surrender to the rules, having less opportunity to manipulate them to his own advantage than does his counterpart in the Senate.

In the House, for example, a representative may not speak for more than one hour on any bill, whereas in the Senate unlimited debate is normally allowed. Individual House members also have less chance to get a bill called up for a vote than does any senator.

Any member of the Congress may propose legislation on any subject. In recent years, over 20,000 bills have been introduced in each congressional session. Since only about 10 percent of them are ever signed into law, the reader will understand, accurately, that many of the 20,000 measures are never intended to pass into law at all. Members of Congress are, for the most part, worldly and intelligent people who are usually alert to the political advantage of "introducing a bill at the next session" which will set right all manner of presumed injustices, deprivations, and oversights. Whether the panacea is believed to consist in a return to the gold standard, or the elimination of the income tax, some legislator can normally be found who will be pleased to design and introduce a bill to achieve it. Even knowing that the measure is doomed, the introducer has nonetheless provided the bill's supporters with a definite psychic return: The polity is seen to have accorded them a democratic legislative hearing, and, after all, one must expect occasional losses in a democracy. In this manner the support of constituencies is secured or retained, and it may be important on subsequent occasions.

Many bills are also presented whenever a notable substantive proposal is being debated in Congress. If the administration is seeking major

Table 9-1. Congressional Bills, Acts, and Resolutions, 1955–1972. (Excludes simple and concurrent resolutions.)

Item	84th Cong.	85th Cong.	86th Cong.	87th Cong.	88th Cong.	89th Cong.	90th Cong.	91st Cong.	92nd Cong.
Period of session	1955–56	1957–58	1959–60	1961–62	1963–64	1965–66	1967–68	1969–70	1971–72
Measures introduced	17,687	19,112	18,261	18,376	17,480	24,003	26,460	26,303	22,969
Bills	16,782	18,205	17,230	17,230	16,079	22,483	24,786	24,631	21,363
Joint resolutions	905	907	1,031	1,146	1,401	1,520	1,674	1,672	1,606
Measures enacted	1,921	1,854	1,292	1,569	1,026	1,283	1,002	941	768
Public	1,028	1,009	800	885	666	810	640	695	607
Private	893	845	492	684	360	473	362	246	161

Source: Statistical Abstract of the United States, 1973, p. 373.

legislation in the health care system, or if school busing has become a socially contentious issue, publicity-seeking members of congress often find it personally expedient to introduce their own bills on the subject, even when they differ only marginally from existing proposals or, if very different, have absolutely no chance of passage. Indeed, they may introduce bills which they themselves do not want passed and which they hope will be defeated. In addition, there are certain so-called private bills, designed to relieve personal problems of one sort or another and having little significance for public policy. For the most part, however, legislative proposals of importance have emerged from the executive branch and get introduced by a representative or senator at the behest of the administration. Housekeeping measures, although cleared by the Office of the Presidency, are often presented at the initiative of the executive agencies. Still other measures, sometimes rather important ones, may be introduced on behalf of interest groups. Rules by which Congress manages these many bills are crucial politically.

During the two centuries of its existence, Congress has evolved a set of formal and informal practices and rules that govern the conduct of its business, and no member who has not achieved minimal mastery of the rules can aspire to sustained legislative influence. So complex is this body of rules that it is quite impossible to identify here more than a few of them.[1]

CONSTITUTIONAL RULES AND THE CONGRESS

Article I of the Constitution, we have observed, provides the framework for organizing the legislative power. It specifies that there shall be a House and Senate, how their members shall be elected (the Seventeenth Amendment, 1913, provided for the popular election of senators), how old they must be, how vacancies will be filled, who the president of the Senate will be (the vice-president of the United States, who is to be voteless except in case of a tie vote), and how other officers of the Senate should be selected. Article II allocates the power of impeachment to the House and the power to try all impeachments to the Senate; a two-thirds vote of those present is stipulated as necessary to remove an impeached president from office. Congress is required to meet at least once a year and to keep a journal of its proceedings (now the *Congressional Record*), and neither house is to adjourn for more than three days without the consent of the other.

Sections 7 and 8 of Article I are important to the legislative *process* as opposed to the structure of the congressional institution. Revenue bills must originate in the House of Representatives, and both houses must concur in a bill before submitting it to the president. The president may either sign the bill or return it, with objections, to the house in which it originated. Two-thirds of those present in each house are required to override a presidential veto. Any bill left unsigned and unreturned by the president for over ten days passes into law unless Congress has adjourned in the meantime, in which case it does not. It is Section 8 that specifies, albeit in broad language, the major constitutional power of the Congress (although the Thirteenth through Twentieth and the Twenty-third through Twenty-fifth amendments all affect its authority in various ways, as do Articles II, III, IV, and V). There is little to be gained from enumerating here all those powers; a reading of the Constitution will serve that purpose. Conflict over the precise meaning and scope of Congress's powers has often been resolved through the judicial process.

Especially important to an understanding of legislative policy-making is Section 5 of Article I. It states that a simple majority of each house constitutes a quorum to do business and that each house is free to *determine its own internal rules.* Struggles over what these rules are or should be account for a good bit of congressional conflict, not only because the rules partially determine what public policy is to be but because they also allocate status and power to individual members of Congress. This conjunction between private aspirations and public consequences must be kept constantly in mind in studying the Congress.

CONGRESSIONAL COMMITTEES

The power of the strategically situated House Rules Committee, for example, has been notably expanded and contracted four times in the last quarter-century. During the Truman and Eisenhower years, a conservative coalition dominated the committee and kept much social welfare legislation from reaching the floor for a vote. Although the Rules Committee cannot block taxation and appropriation bills and cannot itself initiate legislation, it can, by failing to issue a so-called special rule, block major legislation which has been reported out favorably by the standing committees. The committee can also set the conditions for the length and content of debate on legislation which is submitted to the full House. The administrative requirement of this "traffic cop" function is clear, if only because the 435 members cannot be expected to debate extensively all of the measures passed out of the committees. Moreover, the committee has often performed a service to the leadership and members of the House by refusing to issue rules to measures that face obvious defeat (thus conserv-

The Joint Economic Committee is one of the many committees created by Congress. Above, members of the press cover proceedings. *Editorial Photocolor Archives*

ing the energy of the House) or to measures so whimsical or pernicious as to embarrass or undermine the authority or prestige of the Congress. This latter "cooling out" function is as institutionally important as the "traffic cop" function. Both are highly political. What is to one member a healthy derailing of outrageous and dangerous proposals is to another an antidemocratic usurpation of popular sovereignty.

Upon recapturing control of the House in 1949, the Democrats weakened the Rules Committee by providing an alternative — a rather tortuous one — by which a bill could reach the floor. Previous practice was reinstituted by a conservative coalition of both parties in 1951. In 1963, under prompting from the Kennedy White House, the committee was enlarged, thus enabling additional liberals to be appointed. And in 1965, the 1949 rule was restored and extended. All these debates over the Rules Committee were about "neutral" rules alone. Yet nobody was deceived; the continuing issue was who would have power and whose political interests would prevail. Similar dramas can be witnessed whenever "abstract" or "neutral" decision-making rules are discussed in any political setting.

The interpenetration of personalities, rules, and resources determines the content of public policy. It is often charged, for example, that conservative personalities dominate the Congress. This situation is said to be a function of the rules allocating (1) committee seats and chairships to the most senior, often conservative, members of Congress and (2) decision-making power to the committees and not to the Congress as a whole. While the point must be greatly qualified, no doubt this is partly the case: Some three-fourths of committee presiding officers are from safe southern and conservative districts whenever, as for the last quarter-century, the Democrats control the House. Conservative Republicans have dominated the committees when their party has organized the Congress.

The Constitution makes no mention of committees; they are creatures of Congress alone and are sustained by the forces of tradition, American pluralism, and the power and interests of those currently benefited by the committee system (who, as we shall see, are at least a majority in each house). It was not always so. In the earliest days of the republic, bills were first considered on the floor and referred to temporary committees for further study. Several hundred ad hoc committees were appointed for such purposes in each early Congress. The practice was abandoned as members gained experience in the new institutions and as an emerging informal legislative power structure demanded increased order, permanence, and official recognition. The fragmented nature of American society, occasioned by federalism, regionalism, and economic and cultural diversity, encouraged the development of a legislative system with specialized, diverse, and only roughly coordinated parts. Congress is not to be viewed as a legislative system governed by a monolithic conservative elite of elders who have managed to defeat the actuarial odds. It is more appropriate to say that the seniority system works to produce a multiplicity of elites who constitute a ruling coalition only in the sense

Table 9–2. Congressional Standing Committees (92nd Congress).

Committee	Number on Committees	Number of Standing Sub-committees
Joint Committees		
Atomic Energy	18	7
Congressional Operations	10	0
Defense Production	10	0
Economic	20	8
Internal Revenue Taxation	10	0
Library	10	0
Printing	6	0
Reduction of Federal Expenditures	12	0
Senate Committees		
Aeronautical and Space Sciences	11	0
Agriculture and Forestry	14	6
Appropriations	24	13
Armed Services	16	11
Banking, Housing and Urban Affairs	15	6
Budget	16	0
Commerce	18	8
District of Columbia	7	3
Finance	16	0
Foreign Relations	16	9
Government Operations	18	4
Interior and Insular Affairs	16	6
Judiciary	16	10
Labor and Public Welfare	17	10
Post Office and Civil Service	9	3
Public Works	16	5
Rules and Administration	9	7
House Committees		
Agriculture	36	10
Appropriations	55	13
Armed Services	41	4
Banking and Currency	37	7
Budget	25	0
District of Columbia	25	5
Education and Labor	38	7
Foreign Affairs	38	9
Government Operations	39	7
House Administration	25	4
Interior and Insular Affairs	38	7
Internal Security	9	0
Interstate and Foreign Commerce	43	4
Judiciary	38	5

(continued)

Table 9-2.   (continued).

House Committees (continued)		
Merchant Marine and Fisheries	37	5
Post Office and Civil Service	26	7
Public Works	37	6
Rules	15	0
Science and Astronautics	30	6
Standards of Official Conduct	12	0
Veterans Affairs	26	N.A.
Ways and Means	25	0

N.A.   Not available.

Source: Compiled from information presented in *Guide to the Congress of the United States* (Washington: Congressional Quarterly Service, 1971), pp. 232a–261a.

that they have agreed to *leave one another alone.* This may well be the first rule for congressional success. The system is further refined by the existence of subcommittees, in which norms of reciprocity function in much the same way as in the committees proper.

In 1946 the Legislative Reorganization Act brought some order out of an altogether rampant organizational diversity by reducing Senate standing committees from thirty-three to fifteen (there are now seventeen) and House committees from forty-eight to nineteen (there are now twenty-two). In addition, there are several committees with representatives from both houses (e.g., Atomic Energy Defense Production, Economic, Internal Revenue Taxation, Nonessential Expenditures). All in all, roughly 1,000 assignments are available either to be contested for or avoided. In the House, committees on Rules, Ways and Means, Appropriations, Banking and Currency, Agriculture, Armed Services, and Foreign Affairs have traditionally been viewed as the most important, with a total of 233 seats to be allocated among 435 members. Lately the Education and Labor Committee and Budget Committee have assumed a stature. Lesser committees (such as District of Columbia, Merchant Marine and Fisheries) are ordinarily if often unsuccessfully avoided by new members. There is usually little effort to match committee assignments with the constituency or personal interests of new members. The black congresswoman Shirley A. Chisholm from New York City was first assigned to the Veterans' Affairs Committee, although, untypically, her protest was successful and she was reappointed to the Education and Labor Committee.

The death or retirement of a member of an influential committee sets off a reshuffling of committee chairs. Securing a favorable committee assignment and getting, retaining, and extending personal influence in their committees is a constant preoccupation with most members of Congress, particularly in the House of Representatives where the possibility of achieving national prominence outside the institution is statistically remote. In the House, the route to power is through the committee system. The Senate may offer more individual opportunities, but playing the committee game in the Senate is, for most members, also an absolute requirement for getting institutional power.

If the search for influential committee assignments is critical, a number of rules work to reduce the anxiety of older members. Party representation on committees reflects roughly party strength in either the House or the Senate and, excluding those rare occasions when the party composition of Congress changes dramatically, a committee assignment, once secured, can be held permanently even though assignments are formally the responsibility of the party caucuses of each house. Ascending to a position as a committee presiding officer is almost entirely a matter of sheer political and biological survival, although informal processes have long been invoked by the leadership and/or the members of relevant committees to encourage the resignation of incompetent or senile chairpersons. The resignation of Wilbur Mills as chairman of the powerful House Ways and Means Committee after his highly publicized involvement with alcohol and a burlesque dancer is a case in point. These informal means of circumventing the rigidity of the seniority rule render criticism of that rule either misplaced or tendentious when it is based upon the presumed senility of congressional leaders. Many elderly committee chairpersons are cagey in the extreme and use their great parliamentary skill in the service of their own views of appropriate policy. It is their political ideology that is really at issue when the seniority system is discussed and not, usually, the keenness of their intellect or productivity. Even this criticism is mistaken if it assumes that unrepresentative and obstructionistic heads of committees tyrannize over a fearful, powerless, bur right-thinking committee majority. The extent to which the seniority system places somewhat more conservative members in important leadership roles does justify complaints by those who would like to see a more liberal bias in the legislative process.

At present the seniority system is under extreme attack, and recent rule changes have made possible the challenging of its operation in individual cases before the party caucus. The beginning of the legislative session in 1975 was marked by one of the most vigorous and successful attacks. In the context of panic for reform, new members of Congress deposed four influential chairpersons from major committees in the House.

However, the general pattern was that the second most senior person assumed the vacated post. This shift does indicate a modification of the seniority rule, but hardly its abandonment. When the present wave of reform passes, the normal operation of the seniority system will probably resume. Those who believe that the seniority rule is the cause of inaction in Congress are likely to find that this is the result not of the operation of the rule but of the very nature of the Congress as a representative institution in a diverse society. Destruction of the seniority system may lead to the reduction of expertise, the development of even more poorly formulated legislation, and a growth in the administering of legislation at the discretion of the executive branch. The goal of increasing the relative power and efficiency of Congress that is presented as a justification for removal of the seniority system may actually recede to the extent that the seniority rule is destroyed.

RULES AS THE MANAGEMENT OF LEGISLATION

Although a minority which includes a committee head has many ways to obstruct majority action, a *determined* committee majority is almost always able finally to work its way if it chooses. Often a "majority" wishes to give the impression that its position cannot prevail while actually preferring that no vote be taken! This is far from an unusual situation. In the House, for example, there is a device, Calendar Wednesday, which enables those chairing committees whose business is being "held up" by the Rules Committee to call up their own bills for a vote. Alternatively, the Speaker — who is the presiding officer of the House by virtue of receiving first a *majority* vote from his party caucus and then a *majority* vote of the full House — may recognize at any time a committee chairperson whose business has been before the Rules Committee for at least twenty-one days. Still further, on the second and fourth Monday of each month a *simple majority* of 218 members may submit a signed discharge petition to compel consideration by the House of any measure before a committee within seven days. And on the first and third Mondays, an extraordinary majority of two-thirds may suspend the rules for the immediate consideration of any measure. Finally, a committee head may be deposed by a majority of committee members following a reform adopted in 1973. Power in the House is further distributed by other rules. For example, anyone who is chairing a full committee cannot chair more than one subcommittee of that committee; no member can be presiding officer of more than one legislative subcommittee; and no member can serve on more than two committees with legislative jurisdiction.

The fact that discharge petitions rarely secure more than a few signatures is clear evidence that frustrated majorities are not typical in the House. "Frustrated" members of Congress or political activists may point to the Rules Committees as the source of their grief over the obstacles to the democratic process. By failing to mention the democratic rules by which the House conducts its business, they avoid contamination both with the truth of the matter and with the contradictions in their positions. The main points are these: (1) The House leadership is democratically elected by simple majority rule and can, if it chooses, move any measure before a House for a vote. (2) Even if the leadership refuses to act, a simple majority of House members may require a vote on any issue.

The situation in the Senate is somewhat different. There, bills must be introduced formally from the Senate floor and may be cosponsored (in the House they may not). As in the House, the presiding officer refers bills to the appropriate standing committees. When committee jurisdictions overlap, or can be made to appear to overlap, the referral process may be crucial to a bill's fate, depending upon the personalities of the people serving on various committees. Indeed, bills can be written so as to ensure that they are referred to one committee rather than another. Portions of one of the most important bills passed in this century, the Civil Rights Act of 1964, were written so as to be referred to the Commerce Committee because the constitutional authority for the bill was to be the commerce clause of the Constitution. Ordinarily, civil rights legislation might have been referred to, and predictably delayed by, the Judiciary Committee chaired by the unsympathetic Senator Eastland of Mississippi.[2]

Bills reported out of Senate committees for floor action receive, formally, uncomplicated treatment. In the House, a bill reported out by the Rules Committee may be given a "closed" rule (which prohibits amendments) or an "open" rule (which can limit amendments to those stipulated by the Rules Committee). Senate bills are quite unencumbered. True, discussions are supposed to be "germane" to the substance of a bill, but this term is given generous definition. Remotely related "riders," otherwise unpassable through ordinary committee procedures, are sometimes successfully attached, since the germaneness rule does not extend to amendments except in the case of appropriations bills. Five appointees of the majority leader, the leader himself, and three ex officio members (all

Democrats) constitute the Democratic Policy Committee, which, in seem-ingly permanent control of the Senate, schedules bills for the Senate. Un-like the House Rules Committee, this committee arouses little objection to the way it uses its power to prevent action on pending legislation. In-deed, since any senator can demand recognition, receive the floor, and move a vote on legislation, obstruction from the leadership is not possible. *However,* this formal simplicity of procedure is only the tip of the iceberg; informal norms limit the anarchy which the absence of formal rules might be expected to encourage.

The House is large and, like all durable formal organizations, has pro-cedures to sustain its durability. The rules governing the manner in which legislation normally reaches the floor for a vote, for example, serve to reduce if not eliminate the opportunity for disruption of settled politi-cal agreements and compromises. Tax legislation, for instance, invari-ably reaches the floor under a closed rule — which prevents individual amendments — because tax bills constitute extremely important and more or less accepted sets of bargains and shared understandings among sectors of society and cannot acceptably be written by a committee of 435 members. Most people in Congress respect these agreements, as well as the formal rules that prevent individual members from upsetting such fragile coalitions on the floor. The House's "gag rule" could in fact be re-moved quickly enough if a majority of the representatives were interested in doing so. But most of them fear disruptive and disagreeable amend-ments more than they do the power of the Rules Committee. They consent to be "gagged" by their formal rules in the interests of stability and pre-dictability. Informal arrangements for reaching these ends are not possi-ble in the House because of its size.

In the Senate, however, face-to-face relationships and hence informal management of the problem of stability are possible. The formal simplic-ity of the Senate's procedures are deceptive, therefore, because it rests upon a host of complex norms that minimize the legitimacy of unpredict-able conduct. Essentially, the scheduling of a measure for consideration on the floor is worked out informally by the majority leader in consulta-tion with the minority leader as well as all other senators strongly in-terested in the measure. The majority leader brings matters before the Senate for action, often by asking unanimous consent to do so; such con-sent is normally granted, all senators recognizing that informal agree-ment among interested parties has already been reached. Debate on a pending measure may be brought to an end by (after informal consultation) unanimous consent, which again is generally forthcoming, and the orderly processing of legislation is thereby facilitated.

RULES FOR EXTRAORDINARY MAJORITIES IN THE CONGRESS

The Senate, however, is famous for Rule XXII, which permits debate to continue almost indefinitely. Unless three-fifths of the membership vote to limit debate, the **filibuster** (dilatory "debate" which frustrates the voting process) is allowed. But just as important as the formal rules are the informal norms that govern the management of filibusters and **cloture** (or the manner in which debate can be forced to a close). The extraordinary majority rule required to limit debate has, of course, been considered "undemocratic" by those who, although rarely specifying their reasons, regard simple majority rule as indispensable to the democratic process. Until 1917, limiting debate in the Senate was not possible at all; no procedure existed by which a majority, no matter how large, could force a senator to yield the floor. The three-fifths rule, adopted in 1975, was a relaxation from the previous requirement that a two-thirds vote of those present and voting was necessary to end debate. A two-thirds majority is still required to change the rules under which the Senate conducts its business.

The difficulty of successfully invoking cloture in the Senate is well known. The basic reason is obvious; it is simply harder and costlier to get more rather than fewer people to agree on anything. Putting together a coalition of two-thirds or three-fifths in support of some proposal is manifestly more problematical than putting together a coalition of one-half plus one. No matter how much grousing reformers both within and without the Senate may do about the existence of extended debate, most senators of all ideological outlooks prefer Rule XXII to any radical alternative. Undoubtedly the rule inhibits action and hence maintains the status quo. But this fact alone does not indicate very much, since a change in the status quo can be damaging to all sorts of interests, liberal as well as conservative. Democratic liberals from the North are as likely to find that unlimited debate will advance their cause as traditional southerners. Circumstances determine the interests that can be advanced or thwarted by Rule XXII, which cannot be said to be either "conservative" or "liberal." The filibuster, or the threat of filibuster, is a potential weapon in the arsenal of any political concern represented in the Senate. As such, the mere existence of Rule XXII influences the whole institutional life at the Senate. Any Senate member or group can use it to defend threatened minority interests. In a world where senators, like everyone else, cannot predict what the issues of the future will be, it is a comfort to know that Rule XXII is in reserve, ever available for protection if need be. Therefore the Senate is not likely to change the rule significantly.

The extraordinary majority required under Rule XXII is, of course, by no means an aberration in a polity otherwise governed by simple majority rule. On the contrary, extraordinary majorities are a traditional and accepted way of handling many matters in American government. The Constitution requires a two-thirds vote in both houses of Congress before a constitutional amendment can be submitted to the states, three-fourths of which must ratify if it is to be accepted; two-thirds of the states are required to call a convention to amend the Constitution, and three-fourths must agree to any changes. No state can be deprived of its equal representation in the Senate without its consent (an interesting constitutional instance of the unanimity rule). A two-thirds vote in either house of Congress is necessary to expel an individual member. A two-thirds vote in each house is necessary to overturn a presidential veto. A two-thirds vote in the Senate is necessary to ratify treaties. A two-thirds vote in both houses is required to remove a president for reasons of physical disability when the president asserts that no disability exists but when the vice-president and a majority of cabinet secretaries contend that one does. A two-thirds vote of the Senate is required to convict a president on articles of impeachment brought by a majority of the House of Representatives. What all of these matters have in common is their *importance* to the formal distribution of power among political institutions. Rule XXII in the Senate, like all the rules mentioned above, serves to protect minorities against majorities.

One defense of extraordinary majority rules is that they tend to moderate social cleavages. Since it is difficult to assemble a two-thirds or even a three-fifths majority, the advocates of a contentious proposal must increasingly temporize their position until weak and marginal supporters are satisfied that its more severe features have been eliminated or moderated. Only then will the marginal supporters enter the coalition. Or marginal supporters will enter the coalition only when the keen supporters of the proposal have agreed to back the less keen on some other occasion. In this way extraordinary majority requirements facilitate vote-trading or logrolling, which, notwithstanding the criticism it arouses, is often an efficient way to accommodate the views of intense minorities by damaging only *apathetic* majorities or minorities in the process.[3] We hasten to add that logrolling can also produce aggregate outcomes which no majority or even intense minority would support. Thus, whether it is socially desirable is always an empirical question.[4] Of course, a simple majority rule may also produce logrolling and the moderation of demands that could otherwise be objectionable to large numbers of decision-makers. Rule XXII further enhances these tendencies, however, inasmuch as any proposal for change forces senators "to plan their legislative strategies and tactics carefully, and to anticipate some objections which may be intense."[5]

Critics of American political practice may not be satisfied with the theoretical justifications for Rule XXII or the several constitutional rules that allow intense (if still rather large) minorities to stifle or delay actions of a majority. But in Congress, as in other political institutions, Americans have chosen a system which imposes high decision costs (by making it difficult to get agreement by requiring large majorities) but minimizes the prospects of bearing burdens imposed without the consent of nearly all interested parties. The fear of minority *and* majority tyranny makes support for rules requiring extraordinary majorities sensible. In any case, the origin of decision-rules is to be sought as much in experience as in ideology. Whether "democratic" or not, they exist because real interests are served by them. The cultural and political pluralism of American society means that on specific issues alignments and coalitions may shift considerably. Majorities are not stable over all important policy questions. If socioeconomic class were the only salient cleavage in society, more or less enduring majorities and minorities might form. In America, where the social structure is more complex than in any other society, there are many politically important cleavages, some of them overlapping, others sharply divergent. Race and class tend to overlap, even though, for example, there are many lower-class whites and some middle-class blacks. Religion and class diverge more significantly; there are rich and poor Protestants and rich and poor Catholics, even though Protestants have tended to do better economically. Regionalism, especially between the North and the South (which is as much cultural as geographical), bears some relationship to class and race. But, more obviously now than when racism was viewed as a uniquely southern phenomenon, it may have an independence in social affairs of its own. These social cleavages are represented in the Congress and in the rules its members agree on and fight over.

American politics involves a plurality of groups. Security of group interests rests on the availability of tactics by which particular majorities may be "cooled out" and established statuses maintained. The rule of extraordinary majorities is accepted precisely because it provides formally for this effect. The possible alternative is disorder and, more importantly, tyranny — or at least many groups have so feared. And something that is thought to be real *is* real in its effects. Again, the avoidance of tyranny has been central to major groups in America and hence in the Congress, sentimental and ahistorical conceptions of democracy notwithstanding.

RULES RECONCILING HOUSE AND SENATE DIFFERENCES

The Constitution and common sense both require agreement of House and Senate on bills to be submitted to the president, and the resolution of differences between the houses follows both formal and informal rules. Normally, particularly in routine transactions, one house acquiesces to changes in a measure introduced in the other house. For the sake of efficiency, this is a convenient practice because bills passed in both houses usually differ according to variations in personalities, rules, and bargaining circumstances and because the system of coordination between the houses is weak.

On important issues especially, however (addressed by perhaps 10 percent of all bills passed), disagreement between House and Senate is transformed into agreement through ad hoc (or temporary) **conference committee.** Such a committee provides further opportunities to display the considerable skills with which American politicians manipulate rules to reach their objectives. The conference committee is a vital institution in the legislative process. Its membership and the rules under which it operates comprise, in some ways, a "third house of Congress."[6]

In broad outline, an ad hoc conference committee includes three or more members from each house and is appointed by the Speaker of the House and the president of the Senate whenever either house will not agree to changes in a bill added by the other. A majority of each house's delegation is drawn from the political party that controls the house. Ordinarily included are the more senior members of the standing committees originally concerned with the legislation in question. A simple majority of each house's delegation is necessary to resolve differences between bills, and both houses remain free to reject (but not to amend) any agreement reached by the conference committee (a right seldom used). In rare but sometimes important cases the conference committee may fail to reach agreement. The deliberations of conference committees are secret, and members are usually free to negotiate any agreement they choose; occasionally, however, the conferences are instructed not to negotiate on certain issues. A conference report is guaranteed early consideration in both houses. For these reasons, conference committees are extremely powerful.

A bill first passed in the House is sent to the Senate, where, normally, it is referred to a standing committee or, if even one senator insists, is put on the calendar for floor action. In either case the bill is likely to be altered to some degree. The Senate may then either request a conference on the changes or send the altered measure back to the House for action. If the House refuses to accede to changes made by the Senate, it may, in turn, request a conference. At this point strategic opportunities are available to politicians concerned to avoid "normal" legislative procedures. It so happens that bills once passed by the House, amended by the Senate, and returned to the House for action need *not* be referred back to the appropriate standing committee and Rules Committee for consideration before being sent to the floor again. The Speaker, with the support of a simple majority, may thus bypass the normal committee structure in the House, and, in particular, the Rules Committee.

Recall also that there is no rule of germaneness in the Senate concerning amendments. The Senate can, therefore, radically alter a House-passed bill and send it back in the hope that the House committees (substantive and Rules) will not have an opportunity to work their often more conservative wills on what is effectively a new bill. Persistent use of this tactic, however, is not really possible. House majorities in favor of bypassing their own committee system would be difficult to form if the Senate were suspected of abusing a rule designed to expedite business so that it would have the upper hand over the House. Excessive indulgence in this tactic would probably cause the House to revert to its pre-1965 rule, under which unanimous consent was required to bypass normal committee procedures.

A bill originally passed in the Senate is, upon submission to the House — and assuming that no similar measure is already set for floor debate — sent to a standing committee in the usual way. Upon House passage, either the bill, if amended, goes back to the Senate, where it is put directly on the calendar, or a conference is requested. The latter strategy is used if Senate agreement with House changes is not anticipated.

Whether or not agreement is likely is a matter of judgment by experienced politicians. Not the least of the factors to be considered is Senate Rule XXII and the possibility of a filibuster by which congressional action might be prevented or delayed.

RULES AND CONFLICT RESOLUTION

Logrolling and compromise are characteristic features of American politics. Politicians are, for the most part, motivated more by pragmatism — a prudent recognition of realistic opportunities and limitations — than by ideology or "principle" in seeking the resolution of conflict. It follows that the rules and institutions of the political system make bargaining and compromising possible. The way Rule XXII in the Senate encourages "moderation," or temporizing with intense minorities, was discussed earlier, but many more examples could be cited.

Congress consists of 535 members, and face-to-face negotiations among a group of that size are impossible. The need for organization, rules, and a division of labor is reflected in the committee system for, unlike most other parliamentary bodies in the world, Congress does not exist merely to ratify the proposals of the executive.

The committee and seniority systems can be justified on many grounds. The membership of congressional committees is remarkably stable, thereby providing consistency in congressional outlook vis-à-vis the executive branch and its stands on public policy. To abolish committees, or to reshuffle their membership frequently, would enhance the ascendancy of the executive over the legislative branch. A few senators or representatives who have extensive familiarity with a limited range of problems may be more effective in checking and balancing the executive than a large group (the House or Senate itself) trying to inform itself on all issues. The same can be said of the seniority system. If new and inexperienced members were placed in control of important committees, their surveillance over issues with complex historical and technical dimensions would probably be inadequate to limit the legislative imperialism of the executive branch.

From the point of view of democratic theory, it may also be noted that the committee system, by providing for the trading off of various interests held with different degrees of intensity, can improve the general welfare. As it happens, congressional committees tend to consist of members from districts or states that have strong interests in the activities of those committees. For example, the House Agriculture Committee is controlled by representatives from predominantly agricultural areas, who view agricultural problems with understandable concern. This representation is refined further: The Agriculture Committee's subcommittee on cotton is controlled by members from cotton districts. Agricultural interests are not monolithic but diverse and often contending (e.g., large versus small farmers, corporate versus family farming, subsidized versus unsubsidized farmers, and farmers divided by crop specialization); they are brought together on the Agriculture Committee.[7] Thus farm interest checks farm interest, and any congressional farm policy that emerges is one in which those deeply concerned have bargained and compromised their way to some agreement. This is not to say that all interests are represented in the committee system, or that all those represented have proportionate weight in the legislative process. But the outcome has been forged by a multiplicity of interests and accommodates intense minorities whose views, in any other process, would be overlooked or neglected.

CONGRESSIONAL INVESTIGATIONS

An important source of Congress's influence derives from its investigative power.[8] While congressional investigations, by either standing or select committees, must be technically related to the legislative function, they also inform or prepare public opinion on issues and may achieve personal renown for a member of Congress. Other devices are available for these purposes, of course: debates on the floor, particularly in the Senate, and maverick or demagogic behavior which attracts the mass media, interested as it is in conflict and colorful personalities. Publicity secured through the investigative process, however, has additional attractions. For example, the investigators, having received their charters from the House or Senate, are cloaked with the prestige and power of Congress. Hostile or friendly witnesses may be summoned; interrogations featuring virtuous members of congress and representatives of sinister interests can be stage-managed for the benefit of the television cameras.

The benefits which may accrue to those active in investigations are many. The need for, or mere enjoyment of, favorable publicity may call forth investigations into any number of things, with alleged profiteering, corruption in high places, organized crime, and subversion being favorite topics. Senator Nye's famous inquiry into the munitions industry following World War I made his name a household word. Harry Truman's investigation of defense contractors during World War II won him enviable notoriety. Senator Kefauver's piercing look at the pharmaceutical industry launched him as a serious presidential candidate. Senator Joseph McCarthy's investigation of alleged Communists in government provided him with a national constituency and considerable power. Senator Ervin's chairmanship of the Senate committee appointed to investigate irregularities in the 1972 presidential election (i.e., "Watergate") established him in the public mind as a fearless defender of constitutional principles.

During periods of inflation or recession, members of congress can be counted on to investigate any politically vulnerable interests that can be made to seem the real source of the crisis. Wall Street, the oil industry, automobile makers, the railroads, the airlines, "middlemen," "speculators," foreign despots, and union "bosses" are favorite targets of congressional inquiries, normally guaranteed to win popularity for the investigator. Pet hates and hobbyhorses may also lead to the undertaking of investigations of various sorts, whether of the banking system, cotton prices, public housing, or the Chicago commodity exchange. The search for power and publicity may, therefore, motivate self-serving investigations of real or imagined problems. Nevertheless, such investigations do not necessarily serve merely personal political ends.

The social consequences must also be considered. Investigations may assist Congress in its legislative responsibilities by uncovering administrative bungling, social and political scandals, and important new facts and relationships, and by giving interested parties an opportunity to express their views. Investigations may also help in maintaining supervision over the executive branch and in informing and educating the public to necessary sacrifices or new dangers. However, the history of congressional investigations is by no means impeccable.

The oversight of the executive bureaucracy has always been an important if disputed function of Congress. Congress has viewed its powers to secure information from the executive as extensive. Each standing committee is authorized by each house to undertake virtually any sort of investigation and to compel testimony from all witnesses within its area of jurisdiction. Special committees have often been established also to inquire into administrative conduct, beginning in 1792 with the defeat of General St. Clair by the Indians. Since 1921, however, the major source of congressional control over the executive agencies has been through the committees on appropriations. More recently, nonstatutory controls imposed by the appropriations process have been refined. Although there are formal rules that prohibit attaching riders to appropriations bills, such rules are circumvented by understandings with agency officials stated less formally through hearings, committee reports, floor debates, and informal meetings.[9] It is not enough, therefore, merely to examine the statutes in ascertaining the contribution of Congress to the policy process.

The oversight function of the Congress is now one of its more significant contributions to the operation of government. The growing complexity of legislation and the social conditions giving rise to complicated legislation demand that Congress write more and more of its laws in general and ambiguous terms. This necessity is enhanced by the difficulty of building a majority coalition when far-reaching legislation is framed in very precise form. Thus executive agents have to fill in many details and give the legislation precision in its administration. This broad discretion of executive agents allows for substantial shifts in the impact of the legislation and may result in policies quite at variance with the intentions of the legislators. Overseeing the enforcement and interpretation of the laws is necessary if Congress is not to forfeit much of its control of public policy to the executive departments. Congressional committees may inquire into the application of congressional policy and, either by exposing departures from congressional intent or by formally changing legislation, guide its administration back to congressionally approved directions. The investigations of the domestic operations of the Central Intelligence Agency in 1975 provide an excellent example of a congressional attempt to see that executive agents follow the dictates of the Congress in carrying out their responsibilities.

IMPEACHMENT POWERS

The removal from office of the president, vice-president, and all "civil officers of the United States" is possible through congressional action. Although the Constitution states that **impeachment** (by a simple majority in the House) and conviction (by a two-thirds vote in the Senate) can be only for "treason, bribery, or other high crimes and misdemeanors," the content of those terms has never been fully settled. This openness of meaning was quite evident in the discussions of the House Judiciary Committee as it considered the possible impeachment of Richard Nixon. Some authorities argue that impeachment and conviction must be based upon the commission of a crime which is indictable under existing statutes; others, that broadly defined official misconduct is sufficient even though no criminal act has been committed. Actually, given the vagueness of the constitutional criteria and the political nature of the Congress, impeachment and conviction are necessarily acts in which political as well as legal issues are operative. In fact, of the dozen or so instances in which the House has passed articles of impeachment (usually involving federal judges) all but two included charges of a nonindictable nature. The allegations against President Nixon contained both indictable and nonindictable charges. Of course, his resignation ended the consideration of possible impeachment, and the pardon granted by President Ford precluded any judicial determination of his guilt or innocence.

The House alone is empowered to impeach. No appeal is possible from its decision. In the Nixon case, the House Judiciary Committee, composed of twenty-one Democrats and seventeen Republicans, first investigated the president's alleged involvement in the Watergate affair as well as other, more obviously partisan, claims of misconduct, before the issue was referred to the full House. The committee did adopt articles of impeachment, which were joined in by all of its members after the disclosure of the contents of the tape recordings ordered released by the Supreme Court. However, the resignation of the president was used by the House as a means of avoiding formal consideration of the matter. From a legal standpoint, there is no reason why the resignation would necessarily end the impeachment process, but for many political reasons the continuation of the process would not be considered efficacious.

Impeachment proceedings may be initiated in several ways: A House member may introduce a resolution; the president may forward a message; a grand jury may submit a report. Any impeachment resolution is privileged and allows its proponent one hour of debate at the time it is introduced. Normally, the resignation of a person who may be impeached ends the impeachment proceedings (although it need not), but criminal process may still be invoked. This, rather clearly, was the intent of the framers of the Constitution vis-à-vis the presidency, as Alexander Hamilton asserted in the *Federalist Papers*.

Any impeachment action recommended by the Judiciary Committee is considered by the full House, which may adopt the majority or minority report, table the report (which kills it), or ignore it altogether.

If the House adopts articles of impeachment, individuals are appointed by the Speaker or elected by the House to manage the case before the Senate. The Senate, upon receipt of the impeachment articles, appoints a committee to recommend procedures for the trial. Although all members of the House may attend the trial, only its managers are represented officially in the proceedings.

The Constitution is very brief concerning the role of the Senate in impeachment and trial proceedings, stating only that the Senate "shall have the sole power to try all impeachments," shall do so "on oath or affirmation," and that the chief justice must preside in cases involving the president. The *Senate Manual,* however, contains rather specific rules for trials of impeached officials. After the trial, which is conducted very much like normal court proceedings, a separate vote is taken on each article. Conviction by a two-thirds vote on any impeachment article results in the conviction and removal from office of the official.

In the impeachment proceedings against President Nixon, the importance, high drama, conflict, and anguish of impeachment politics were made manifest. Complex and compelling legal arguments were developed on both sides, statesmanship and partisanship were displayed, evenhandedness and prejudicial opportunism were observed, public regardfulness and personal ambition were juxtaposed. Societal unanimity in such momentous matters is not to be expected. But widespread agreement on the procedures by which impeachment and trial decisions are made reduces antagonisms engendered by the substance of the decisions themselves. For many people, it is just as important that justice is *seen* to be done as it is for justice to be done in fact.

INDIVIDUAL DECISION-RULES IN CONGRESS

The formal and institutional rules that govern behavior in the Congress tell one nothing about the rules individual members of Congress follow in making their voting decisions. The formal rules provide a framework of constraints and opportunities within which personal aspirations are pursued. By presumption, winning and keeping elected public office is the primary political goal of the normal American politician.

For example, Congressman X (or Senator Y) is subject to many influences in judging how best to achieve this objective: his constituency and its perceived reaction to his behavior, including his voting record; his colleagues, who may or may not accord him increased deference and power; interest groups, which control electoral resources, information, and access to the media and other opinion leaders "back home"; the administration, which can trade favors or not, depending upon his support for its program; the leadership of his political party, which hopes for loyalty on party issues; his staff; etc.

Of these social influences, according to an interesting study of the House, the most important (most members asserted) are one's fellow representatives, one's constituency, and interest groups. For very few members, however, were even these factors determinant. Indeed, the majority felt they were of minor consequence or not important at all.[10] Of course, their weight varies greatly among members and across issues.

For instance, it appears that on *civil rights* issues, constituency attitudes *determine* Congressman X's vote; he acts as an "instructed delegate," and deviation from the constituency's instructions may well bring him defeat at the next election. On matters of *social welfare,* he is a quasi representative rather than a delegate; he can consider factors other than constituency preferences in making decisions. Finally, on *foreign policy,* he is a true representative, although his tendency to defer to the president in this area means that his independent judgment on the issues may not be formed in fact.[11]

One study revealed strong statistical correlations between the representative's voting choices and the positions taken on the issues by constituents, House colleagues (who form an important institutional reference group), interest groups, and staff members. Correlations for party leadership (.57) and administration (.56) were lower but by no means insignificant.[12]

Within the formal institutional rules and the field of forces applied by other political actors, the member of congress must make decisions on how to maximize personal interests and minimize personal risks. The interests involve, mainly, retaining the present (or securing a greater) public office and taking full advantage of the opportunities it offers.

These decisions follow certain rules, and political scientists have sought to state them. Professor Kingdon's elegant statistical model suggests that, on any issue, several questions will arise.[13] First, "Is it controversial?" If it is not, no problem exists; one simply votes with the "herd." Second, if there is conflict, the question is "Are the actors in contention relevant to *me?*" A representative from a conservative Republican district may pay no attention to the Committee on Political Education of the AFL-CIO, while a person from a liberal inner-city district may show little concern for ideologically conservative groups. If the conflict is irrelevant (in the above sense), the vote will be cast in a manner consistent with the member's own "field of forces": personal policy preferences and those of constituency, party peers, staff, interest groups.

If there is conflict involving only one or two actors in the field of forces, the member normally votes against that faction. More serious conflict in the field of forces enlarges the decisional problem. Uncertainty is increased, rules of thumb are unavailable, and complex and problematical judgments are required. Under these conditions, miscalculations and "mistakes" may well occur. The opposition has an opportunity to seize the initiative and, if the mistake is sufficiently notorious, the member may be vulnerable at the next election.

A well-known and sophisticated study of the Senate by Professor Donald R. Matthews states the most important but unwritten decision-rules followed by senators who aspire to power and effectiveness in that body.[14] A senator who is interested in maximizing institutional advantage will, above all, approach the institution with some deference and humility. Although times are changing, the new senator will serve a proper apprenticeship — ideally respecting seniors, seeking advice, listening much, and talking little. But popular demands from constituents and interest groups, and consequently the need to present an image of vigorous and effective advocacy, sometimes make it impossible to indulge this institutional rule. The not unfamiliar first-term publicity-seeker and demagogue who flouts Senate norms may do so out of a need to make a splash back home. The senator with presidential ambitions may similarly violate institutional standards in pursuit of national attention. Other important expectations — to work hard on committee assignments, to specialize and develop expertise rather than flirting with many policy areas, to reciprocate favors (by compromising, trading votes, showing tolerance for colleagues with different outlooks and political problems — are met by those who desire to maximize their power in the Senate. Such norms are disregarded by the few members who view them as immoral, unprincipled, or unhelpful to their needs for popular attention or to their presidential campaigns.

PARTY POLITICS IN CONGRESS

The division of the Congress into the House and the Senate is only one of the many cleavages that run through our national legislature. Others are those of region, of ideology, of race, and of political party. Only the political party has a permanent, institutionalized relationship with the formal organization and operation of Congress. Efforts to organize formally along other lines have never been successful, although certain congressional groups, such as the Black Caucus and the liberal Democratic Study Group, have done their best in this direction.[15] Of course, informal blocs of interests form around particular issues. They can be discerned through the analysis of voting patterns.[16] Because of its importance, however, it is the political party organization in Congress to which attention is now directed.

Political Organization in the Congress

The electoral process determines which of the two major parties will "control" the Congress. (Since the influence of party membership upon congressional behavior is not always easy to measure, the word *control* must be used cautiously.) For over twenty years now, the Democrats, by electing majorities in each house, have organized both House and Senate, a condition that shows little sign of changing in the foreseeable future. Earlier we discussed the decentralized, locally based nature of the American

"You're just what we need in Congress, Dawson: young blood."
Drawing by Gauerke; © 1975 National Review.

party system. That discussion need not be reiterated here except to say that party discipline has profound limits in Congress just as elsewhere in the political system. The national political party convention and the policy platform developed by it have little relevance to members of Congress. The national conventions and the national committees of the parties are recognized in Congress for what they are: instruments of presidential, not congressional, politics. Presidential and congressional parties are different organizations and respond to different constituencies and different pressures.[17] Still, when the same party controls the presidency and the Congress, a greater measure of coordination and cooperation is possible than when control of the two branches is split between Republicans and Democrats.

Each party in each house is organized formally into a "**caucus**" (or "conference"), which theoretically, makes united action on legislative matters possible. In fact, incentives by which the party caucus might encourage united actions of all members are few, and party loyalty varies greatly across issues. On some issues, however, tight party loyalty does exist, including, most importantly, the question as to which party will organize the house by electing its members to leadership posts (the Speaker of the House, the president pro tempore of the Senate, all committee chairpersons) and by forming majorities on all committees. The election of floor leaders by the caucus is similarly important. The desire of most members to rise through the legislative machine to senior committee and leadership positions is sufficient inducement to compel party loyalty on these organizational questions.[18]

Party integration is complete at the organizational level: All House Republicans are members of the Republican Conference; all House Democrats are members of the Democratic Caucus; all Republicans and Democrats in the Senate are members of their respective conferences.[19] Each party group has a chairman and a secretary and each nominates candidates for election to certain House and Senate offices; the majority party invariably wins. Voting decisions within the party caucuses normally follow the simple majority rule.

Party Influence in Congress

To observe that the parties in Congress are undisciplined except on organizational questions is not to say that parties are uninfluential on all other matters. But no real sanctions exist to compel adherence to party positions. On some issues, party cohesion is high even though no punishments are levied against deviationists. Disciplined parties and cohesive parties are not quite the same thing. Party loyalty is nearly perfect on organizational questions, high on some kinds of policy issues, moderate on other issues, and low or nonexistent on still others. Across all or most issues that come before either house, party membership is the best single predictor of how a member will vote.[20] But on *some* issues party affiliation is not a good predictor at all.

Professor Aage R. Clausen's study of the relationship of party membership and voting on policy questions is perhaps the best on this subject.[21] Clausen found that specific policy issues could be grouped (by members of congress themselves) into broad areas having to do with civil liberties, international affairs, social welfare, agricultural assistance, and government management. In both the House and the Senate, the correlation between party membership and voting was low with respect to civil liberties and international involvement. That is, merely knowing whether a member is a Democrat or a Republican is not much help in ascertaining how the member will vote. On the other hand, party affiliation was a good predictor on issues concerning social welfare, agricultural programs, and government management. That this is the case in both houses of Congress suggests that political parties do, to some extent, integrate our bicameral national legislature.

Of these three policy areas, government management was most closely related to party membership. Government management included such things as "business-government relations, the level of public spending, and the public versus the private development of our natural resources."[22] In fact, if one knew only a member's political party, one could predict correctly about 90 percent of the time how that member would vote on such issues.

Whether party membership *causes* voting decisions is another question, but it is altogether reasonable to conclude that the American political parties do play a key role in congressional behavior.

SUMMARY

The Constitution vests the legislative power in the Congress. The House consists of 435 members elected concurrently for two-year terms; the Senate, of 100 members elected for six-year staggered terms. The Constitution assigns other powers to the Congress as well; it is authorized to prepare constitutional amendments; to count electoral votes; to elect the president when the electoral college fails to do so; to impeach and try the president, vice-president, and other civil officers; and to conduct investigations.

Each house of Congress follows formal and informal rules and institutional and personal rules in performing its legislative and other tasks. The House, because of its large size, conducts its business more formally, is more hierarchically structured, and allocates power less evenly among its members than the Senate. By and large, the House is also more conservative than the Senate, and House members have less prestige and visibility than senators.

As a bicameral committee made up of people with very different personalities and philosophies, Congress is able only on occasion to act consistently, harmoniously, and with dispatch. Congress is also subdivided into standing committees, joint committees, and, from time to time, special committees which review legislation, recommend appropriations, and make investigations and whose recommendations carry great weight in both houses. The investigative power has been both an instrument of intelligent social policy and a weapon of abuse when directed against various despised individuals and groups. The committee (and seniority) system, conventional wisdom to the contrary notwithstanding, is established by democratic rules and sustained by the popular preference of the vast majority of members of congress. Not only can intense congressional majorities always control the committees, but the committee system offers a forum in which the concrete interests of various groups can be heard effectively, including those of minorities who otherwise would be forced to submit to a tyrannical majority.

The two major parties maintain party caucuses in each house. The power of party membership in the legislative process is a matter of continuing discussion. Party discipline exists only with respect to organizational questions, but tight party cohesion is also apparent on certain kinds of issues. Members of congress vote on "scope of government" issues on party lines and rather closely on a party basis on issues of social welfare and agricultural policy. In other important areas, such as civil rights and international affairs, congressional voting bears little relationship to the members' party affiliations.

NOTES

1.   A full treatment of congressional decision-rules will be found in Lewis A. Froman, Jr., *The Congressional Process: Strategies, Rules, and Procedures* (Boston: Little, Brown, 1967).

2. Ibid., p. 102.

3. The problem of intense minorities in a democratic polity is taken up in Robert A. Dahl, *Preface to Democratic Theory* (Chicago: University of Chicago Press, 1956).

4. See William H. Riker and Steven J. Brams, "The Paradox of Vote Trading," *American Political Science Review,* 67 (December 1973), 1235–1247.

5. Froman, *The Congressional Process,* p. 122.

6. An enlightening analysis of the conference committee is found in Richard F. Fenno, Jr., *The Power of the Purse* (Boston: Little, Brown, 1966), Chapter 12. See also David J. Vogler, *The Third House: Conference Committees in the United States Congress* (Evanston, Ill.: Northwestern University Press, 1971). A useful study of conflict between the two houses is Jeffrey L. Pressman, *House Vs. Senate* (New Haven, Conn.: Yale University Press, 1966).

7. Charles O. Jones, "Representation in Congress: The Case of the House Agriculture Committee," *American Political Science Review,* 55 (June 1961), 358–367. There are a many good studies of various congressional committees, including Stephen Horn, *Unused Power: The Work of the Senate Committee on Appropriations* (Washington: Brookings, 1970), and James A. Robinson, *The House Rules Committee* (Indianapolis: Bobbs-Merrill, 1964).

8. See M. Nelson McGeary, *The Development of Congressional Investigative Power* (New York: Octagon, 1966).

9. An interesting study of this matter is Michael W. Kirst, *Government Without Passing Laws: Nonstatutory Techniques in Appropriations Control* (Chapel Hill: University of North Carolina Press, 1969).

10. John W. Kingdon, *Congressmen's Voting Decisions* (New York: Harper & Row, 1973). Also see Aage R. Clausen, *How Congressmen Decide: A Policy Focus* (New York: St. Martin's, 1973), who suggests that congressmen first consider the facts of a proposal, categorize the proposal, and then choose a decision-rule to follow in voting on it.

11. Warren E. Miller and Donald E. Stokes, "Constituency Influence in Congress," *American Political Science Review,* 57 (March 1963), 45–56. See also Julius Turner, *Party & Constituency,* rev. ed. (Baltimore: Johns Hopkins Press, 1970), and Lewis A. Froman, Jr., *Congressmen and Their Constituencies* (Chicago: Rand McNally, 1963).

12. Kingdon, *Congressmen's Voting Decisions,* p. 20.

13. Ibid., pp. 230–234. Kingdon's model accounts for 89 percent of the variance in his data.

14. Donald R. Matthews, *U.S. Senators and Their World* (Chapel Hill: University of North Carolina Press, 1960).

15. There are very few serious studies of efforts in Congress to organize along other than conventional party lines. See Mark Ferber, "The Democratic Study Group: A Case Study," unpublished Ph.D. dissertation, University of California, Los Angeles, 1964; Alan Fiellin, "The Functions of Informal Groups in Legislative Institutions: A Case

Study," *Journal of Politics,* 24 (February 1962), 72–91; and Kenneth Kofmehl, "The Institutionalization of a Voting Bloc," *Western Political Quarterly,* 17 (June 1964), 256–272.

16.   See Duncan MacRae, Jr., *Dimensions of Congressional Voting* (Berkeley: University of California Press, 1958), and William H. Riker and Donald Niemi, "Stability of Coalitions on Roll Calls in the House of Representatives," *American Political Science Review,* 56 (March 1962), 58–65. An oddly neglected topic in political science — the breakup of coalitions — is analyzed by roll call analysis in Malcolm E. Jewell, "Evaluating the Decline of Southern Internationalism Through Senatorial Roll Call Votes," *Journal of Politics,* 21 (November 1959), 624–646.

17.   A provocative elaboration of this point is James MacGregor Burns, *The Deadlock of Democracy: Four Party Politics in America* (Englewood Cliffs, N.J.: Prentice-Hall, 1963).

18.   The cost in terms of committee assignments of deserting one's party is described in Ralph K. Huitt, "The Morse Committee Assignment Controversy: A Study in Senate Norms," *American Political Science Review,* 51 (June 1961), 313–329.

19.   There are many excellent studies of political party behavior in Congress, including Randall B. Ripley, *Majority Party Leadership in Congress* (Boston: Little, Brown, 1969), and Charles O. Jones, *The Minority Party Leadership in Congress* (Boston: Little, Brown, 1970).

20.   Julius Turner, *Party & Constituency.*

21.   Clausen, *How Congressmen Decide,* Chapter 5.

22.   Ibid., p. 99.

The Presidency: Leadership and Policy Exhortation

All political systems have rules, we have repeatedly noted, which allocate power and authority among the population and its institutions. In the United States, formal and informal rules abound concerning the operation of the presidency, the political institution discussed in this chapter. The major formal rules applicable to the presidency are found in the Constitution itself, although the first words of Article II ("The executive Power shall be vested in a President of the United States of America") are so vague as to be, an eminent authority once said, of "uncertain content."

The uncertainty comes from not knowing, as the same scholar said, whether the "executive power" was meant to be a "grant of power or a mere designation of office."[1] Whatever the case may have been in earlier years, modern presidents and many modern commentators have come to regard Article II as a grant of power. This evolution in expectations has in some ways transformed the American presidency into one of the most powerful — and attacked — political institutions in the world.

The framers of the Constitution seem to have had no common image of the office they created. The earliest executive power in America had reposed in the governors of the royal provinces, who, while subordinate to the crown, had significant political authority, including power of appointment to public office, of military command, of control over public spending, and often a determinant voice in legislative matters. By the end of the colonial period, however, the legislators had managed (largely because of the control over appropriations they had exercised during the French and Indian War) to accumulate power at the expense of the executive and had begun to look upon the executive power with considerable trepidation, a fear born in part of George III's relative domination at that time over the other elements (the Houses of Lords and Commons) of Parliament. Following the American Revolution, most of the new state constitutions stripped the executive of most real power and assigned it largely ceremonial functions. To this day, many states maintain what is by now an ancient office, that of the "weak governor," although it is not so weak as that of some of the first state governors who were annually elected by the legislature and had no role of any importance at all in legislative matters. Even so, there were intimations in some state constitutions of respect for an executive capable of exercising leadership and of acting with forcefulness and dispatch should the need arise.

In 1784, for example, Pennsylvania's constitution was interpreted as entrusting all power not specifically granted to either the legislative or the executive to one or the other branch "according to its nature," and the New York governor was granted unusually extensive powers.[2] The ambivalence of many Americans in fearing a powerful central authority while recognizing the necessity on occasion for prompt and vigorous action is a pervasive theme in our history and has never been more troublesome than in the present generation. The demand for popular liberty and for checks upon potential despotism is countered by the demand for a political authority capable of integrating and mobilizing a large, heterogeneous society with worldwide responsibilities and an intensely disputed domestic agenda.

Neither conservative nor liberal ideologies provide clear guides to an appropriate stand on the question of presidential power. During the 1950s the democratic left criticized the alleged weakness and incoherence of the presidency. Its nostalgic despair was based, perhaps, upon the dynamic innovations and extensions in the social services and the regulations placed upon business enterprise on the initiative of the executive in the 1930s — actions that were consistent with the policy positions of many American liberals at the time. By the late 1960s, these same ideological sectors had reversed themselves somewhat: Unhappy with the Vietnam war (a particularly despised aspect of which came to be called the executive's "arrogance of power"), they often viewed the White House as being out of constitutional control; if democracy was to survive at all, the executive had to be brought to heel by an aroused, united, and responsible Congress. Liberal uneasiness continued into the 1970s, with the excesses of Watergate taken as proof by some that presidential power had reached intolerable proportions. Congress was again tapped by some commentators as the appropriate entity to shape policy, direct events, and maintain the initiative in social improvement. That the Congress had often been thought by the same people to be *incapable* of such responsibility, unity, and vigor was conveniently forgotten. Many conservatives have been no more consistent on the matter of presidential power.

For most political activists, the question of the desirability or undesirability of a strong presidency cannot be separated from the concrete interests which are being either assisted or hindered by the use or lack of such power. An abstract discussion of the virtues or dangers of a vigorous executive provides no information at all concerning the specific interests presidential power will or will not address. A generalized advocacy of a weak or strong presidency should normally lead one to seek out which interests would probably be served by that kind of political institution.

An awareness of the relationship between interests and ideology led the historian Charles A. Beard to write his famous *An Economic Interpretation of the Constitution* (1913). Its thesis was that the eighteenth-century American power elite, unchecked by popular preferences, wrote the Constitution to serve its own economic interests. The public interest rhetoric in which their work and results was shrouded served merely to disguise the betrayal of the public interest by this elite. Beard's position has been both attacked and restated in one form or another frequently since that time, and recent research has undermined the precise force of his "economic" argument. Several of the most important constitutional framers (e.g., James Madison) owned no lands or "personalty" (titles to wealth), and many of them controlled only insignificant amounts.[3]

In a larger sense, however, Beard was right in conception if wrong in execution. An explanation of the Constitution's content is to be sought not only in discussions of allegedly universal political principles — though this is one possible interpretation — but in the political preferences of the delegates to the Philadelphia Convention of 1787 and of those who were influential in securing ratification of their work. They had insistent and immediate personal and social needs to be met through political action, and their positions in debate can be viewed as strategic behavior in pursuit of those needs. That Beard may have erred in not taking a sufficiently broad view of these preferences is unfortunate, but, in debunking the mystique that had grown up around the Constitution over the decades, Beard provided a useful corrective. While the framers were doubtless influenced in their decision by the writings of Montesquieu, Locke, and Blackstone on executive power, their product evolved from the historical circumstances in which, as individuals, they found themselves in 1787. This is a story we have dealt with in Chapters 3 and 4.

The framers of the Constitution managed their anxieties over executive power by clever if not fully satisfactory logic. Providing what Hamilton called "energy in the executive" with checks against the emergence of "murdering Janizaries" (soldiers in the old Turkish infantry) in a *single* office was no easy task. Hamilton solved the problem to some extent by sleight of hand, when he argued in *The Federalist,* No. 70 that combining the executive power in *one* person was safer than diffusing it among several or many people; the "jealousy and watchfulness of the people" could be more easily concentrated upon one than upon multiple objects.[4]

But if the executive the framers created turned out to be a strong one — Lincoln's Secretary of State Seward once said that Americans "elect a king for four years, and give him absolute power within certain limits, which after all he can interpret for himself" — constraint was to be applied by other political institutions, mainly the Congress. The Senate particularly was to share in the executive function by approving major appointees, and Congress's control of the spending power would constitute a forceful check upon presidential willfulness. Whatever the outcome of the Philadelphia Convention concerning the presidency may be thought to have been, many of today's quarrels over its powers and limitations have their antecedents in several political clashes that arose not long after the adoption of the Constitution. To personalize the issue historically, Alexander Hamilton favored a strong executive, or had what Corwin calls a "quasi-monarchical" conception, while Thomas Jefferson and, to a lesser extent, James Madison, adhered to the "ultra-Whig" preference for a weak executive.[5]

ATTITUDES OF PRESIDENTS
TOWARD POWERS OF THE OFFICE

Thomas Jefferson

The cleavage between the **Hamiltonian** and the **Jeffersonian** philoso-phies of government, of course, transcended differences over the presi-dency. Nonetheless, their alternative conceptions of centralized power best illustrate their contending philosophies, philosophies that remain in conflict even today.[6] Jefferson feared an energetic executive with broad powers; Hamilton preferred it. In one sense, all Americans are Hamilton-ians or Jeffersonians in political disposition, whether they like it or not. Such is the power of culture. Our first two presidents, Washington and the elder Adams, adhered to the first conception. The facts of Jefferson's presi-dency are complex. Historians disagree as to whether Jefferson enfeebled the presidency (as his ideology required) or strengthened it. His unilateral action as president, with no apparent constitutional authority, in making the Louisiana Purchase from France is sometimes said to illustrate a gap frequently observed in politics between ideology and practice. In the abstract, it is said, Jefferson may have been opposed to presidential vigor, but when *personally* in office, he exploited its potentialities to the utmost, at least on important questions. Perhaps. Yet Jefferson undertook to sub-ordinate presidential office to congressional power. By acting more as a party leader and less as a chief executive, he coordinated the legislative activity of his party's membership in the Congress. True, the unity of congressional purpose which resulted furthered Jefferson's immediate policy aims but it also produced a powerful cohesive congressional entity, the party caucus. Later called the Congressional Caucus upon the col-lapse of the Federalist party, the caucus was able to control the sub-sequent nominations and/or elections of Presidents Madison, Monroe, and Adams. The longer-term, perhaps unintended, consequence of Jefferson's relative neglect of presidential prerogatives was to produce, as Corwin put it, "a presidency in commission" and a Congress whose power has never since been equaled.[7]

Andrew Jackson

Andrew Jackson's election in 1828 brought to office a man whose charac-ter and ideology were incompatible with the Whig conception of executive power. His forceful personality, an admiring public, and a capacity to build new political institutions led to the reversal of two decades of congressional predominance. Jackson rationalized (he by no means invented) the powers of his office to reward his followers. The **spoils system** was the major device he employed. The intelligent use of selective material incentives, patronage, or "jobs for the boys" enabled him to secure the services of loyal and devoted lieutenants. The effective utilization of spoils, Jackson thought, was necessary if men were to be moved to create the institutions he desired and to bestow on him the personal rewards of power and status he so obviously cherished.[8]

The national presidential nominating convention created by Jackson became the institutional machine (spoils was a large part of the fuel) by which the overwhelming power of Congress vis-à-vis the presidency was broken. Another part of this book (Chapter 7) discusses the nominating process. But, with the power of Congress to control presidential nominations destroyed, the autonomy of the presidency was reasserted and strengthened, particularly because the party which the president headed had strength at the grass roots of society. The power provided by their political parties has enabled succeeding presidents to appeal for support, often but not always successfully, to popular opinion directly, over the heads of members of Congress. Jackson was the first president to use this tactic but, of course, he was by no means the last.[9]

Between Jackson and Lincoln

Another important feature of the presidency — its inability in some circumstances to deal with issues requiring the delicate balancing of diverse social and political forces — is well illustrated by the history of the office between the presidencies of Jackson and Lincoln. In 1846 the question of slavery in the territories came to dominate all other political problems. This issue, volatile and highly charged in its own right but doubly so in terms of what it represented (e.g., the future of slavery in the South, the future relationships between northern and southern economic elites, the growth of southern nationalism), was not susceptible to resolution through vigorous and unilateral executive action.[10]

For most influential people at the time, presidential action in the face of uncertainty was not thought to be required. The need was for conciliation among groups with known preferences and clear policy positions and not for a strong presidency. The logical forum for conciliation was the Senate, where "satisfactory" bargains and compromises of a subtle and intricate sort might *conceivably* be managed and stability preserved. The post-Jacksonian, pre-Lincolnian conceptions of the presidency are illustrated if not entirely typified by William Henry Harrison, who said in 1838:

If elected, I will:

1. Confine my service to a single term.

2. Disclaim all right and control over the public treasury.

3. Eschew any attempt to influence elections.

4. Exercise due regard for laws passed by representatives of the people, and, within specified limitations, limit my exercise of the veto power.

5. Never suffer the influence of my office to be used for a partisan purpose.

6. If requested, I will furnish the Senate my reasons for removals from office.

7. Never suffer the executive "to become the source of legislation."[11]

What some people will not agree to in order to be elected president! Of course, Harrison succeeded, but whether in spite of or because of his pledge is not known. Harrison, the Whig, received 53.1 percent of the popular vote in 1840 compared to the Democratic incumbent Van Buren's 46.9 percent. Unfortunately, Harrison died a month after his inauguration. As we know, the attempted pre-Civil War compromises failed in the Congress. Whether the issues were indeed irreconcilable and the war was inevitable is an argument best left to historians; in point of fact no enduring bargains were struck, and the worst social hemorrhage in American history began in 1861.

Abraham Lincoln

The extraordinary historical circumstances in which Lincoln found himself, his undeviating objective (preservation of the Union), and his powerful personality and towering ambition combined to produce the largest
and most innovative expansion of the office by any president until at least
Franklin Roosevelt's second term. Lincoln's concern for the Union's stability and his analysis of the gathering crises made him suspicious of congressional maneuverings and indecisiveness on the main points of conflict. If the Union was to be saved, a new understanding of political
authority, given the failure of the old, was necessary. Lincoln found it in
the Constitution, which he came to regard as a nearly inexhaustible source
of legitimate presidential power. As commander in chief, as one with
the duty to "take care" that the law be implemented, Lincoln came to im-
pute virtually unlimited "war powers" to his office. Beyond question, his
conduct greatly expanded and strengthened the presidential office.[12]

Lincoln's willingness to act decisively on the basis of presumed constitutional power in order to save the Union contrasted sharply with his
predecessor's conception of presidential power. On December 3, 1860,
James Buchanan, in a message to Congress, argued that while it was unconstitutional for states to secede from the Union (South Carolina had declared its intention to do so) it was similarly unconstitutional for the president (or any other branch of government) to use force to prevent them
from doing so. In Buchanan's view, not only did the president lack legitimate power to prevent the dissolution of the Union by whatever means
might prove necessary, but no democratic state could resort to force and
survive: "The fact is that our Union rests upon public opinion, and can
never be cemented by the blood of its citizens shed in civil war. If it cannot
live in the affections of the people, it must one day perish."[13]

After the Civil War

But perhaps presidential power is more a function of events than
philosophy, a possibility suggested by the history of the office between
Lincoln and the recent strong presidents. Throughout the post-Civil War
era, the presidency under Hayes, Garfield, Arthur, Cleveland, Harrison,
and McKinley was dominated by lassitude and, consequently, by Congress (to the extent that Congress was itself not dominated by the main

centers of economic power) on the central issues of the age: economic development and territorial expansion.[14]

The Early Twentieth Century

The United States in this century has confronted many problems, but two of them — national security and economic stability — in conjunction with the personalities of the men who have held presidential office, account for the nature of the modern presidency. Those who first brought to the office a vigorous conception of the president's role during America's emergence as a great world power were Theodore Roosevelt and Woodrow Wilson. Together they dominated American politics during the first quarter of the century. Each was "a very fair specimen of the genus Americanus Egotisticus."[15] The genus is not extinct, for which we may be thankful or despondent, depending upon our inclination. Circumstances were ripe and personalities predisposed for an expansion in presidential power.

Roosevelt was the first to take an active role in international politics. The establishment by the United States of an "independent" Republic of Panama through which the Panama Canal was built gave both symbol and substance to America's growth as a world power. On one occasion, Roosevelt said his action in Central America was "carried out in accordance with the highest, finest and nicest standards of public and governmental ethics." That those standards may have been none too high by normal ethical standards was suggested by Roosevelt on another occasion: "If I had followed conventional conservative methods, I should have submitted a dignified State Paper of approximately two hundred pages to the Congress and the debate would have been going on yet, but I took the Canal Zone and let Congress debate, and while the debate goes on the canal does also." As a counterpoint to Roosevelt's image as one who delighted in the exercise of force, it should be (but rarely is) remembered that he won the Nobel Peace Prize upon arranging a settlement of the Russo-Japanese War and was extremely active in other efforts at international reconciliation. His domestic trust-busting activities, directed against the "malefactors of great wealth," were based in part on his view that large fortunes were "needless and useless." "Why is it," he said, "that everytime I mention the Eighth Commandment there is a panic on Wall Street?"[16]

Woodrow Wilson shared Roosevelt's energy and expansive view of the presidency if not his style and precise ideology. Wilson's presidency

President Theodore Roosevelt was the first to take an active role in international politics. Here he meets with officials before inspecting the Panama Canal in 1906. *OAS*

further supported the proposition that the general history of the office has been one of aggrandizement. History has tended to defeat the hopes of the agrarians, headed by Jefferson, that the executive would be made subordinate to the legislature.

A qualification to this conventional view was put forward by Lawrence H. Chamberlain, who studied the legislative history of ninety statutes enacted between 1882 and 1940 in the areas of agriculture, banking and currency, business, government credit, immigration, labor, national defense, natural resources, railroads, and tariff.[17] He then assigned credit for these statutes to either presidential or congressional power (or both) and concluded that the legislative process is truly a joint one. More importantly in terms of the present discussion, he could find no tendency toward increasing presidential domination of the legislative process. Of course, presidential power in domestic affairs may have increased dramatically since 1940; in any case, Chamberlain's study included the expansionistic presidencies of Wilson and the two Roosevelts.

Chamberlain does agree that the executive has been enlarged in other ways throughout this century, a process set in motion less by the power-seeking impulses of our presidents than by the pressures imposed by social, economic, and international crises. Presidential initiative, if not utter supremacy, in legislative matters has become the normal pattern. Theodore Roosevelt was probably the first president to assert (if not win) the point of executive dominance in legislation. Wilson sought, somewhat successfully, to strengthen the office through the exercise of party leadership, and during the 1930s Franklin D. Roosevelt's dynamic personality, prompted and assisted by the disastrous economic situation, gave him optimal opportunity for the exercise of legislative leadership.

The study of presidential power is in large measure the study of shifting relationships between president and Congress and of endless efforts to find more "satisfactory" ones. Clearly, what is thought satisfactory by various publics, interests, and scholars depends upon the issues and circumstances of the time. One painfully contrasts political commentator Arthur M. Schlesinger, Jr.'s 1965 tribute to John F. Kennedy's efforts to exert and extend his presidential powers with his altered view of less than a decade later that the presidency's powers had grown to fearful, indeed imperial, proportions.[18] The suspicion is inevitable that Schlesinger and similar publicists more or less approved of Kennedy's policies and more or less disapproved of the foreign policy of Lyndon Johnson and the tone and domestic policies of Richard Nixon. Still, positions on presidential power may be based on more than mere personal reactions to the changing events of the day. One noted authority has detected a certain constancy of interest on the point, arguing that, over time, it is the more privileged sectors of American society that fear the election of a strong, independent executive. In Wilfred Binkley's view, the evolution of the strong presidency is occasioned by a search for a "tribune of the people," one who might seek and speak authoritatively for "the public interest" and who would not be overly constrained by the conflicting interests and sordid compromises characteristic of parliamentary bodies.[19]

But precisely who are the "people" and what is the "public interest," if these are not merely high-sounding phrases invoked by propagandists to elicit a desired response? More empirical assertions concerning the growth of presidential power have been made by other scholars who, less certain of the meaning of such terms, have been interested in the political tactics presidents use in pursuit of their objectives.[20]

Franklin D. Roosevelt

The hiatus of the 1920s in presidential activity during the tenure of Harding, Coolidge, and Hoover was reversed when Franklin D. Roosevelt came to power. The extent to which FDR was able in his second term to transcend in power virtually all prior presidents was due in good part, of course, to the unprecedented economic crisis of the 1930s and the consequent popular (and congressional) willingness to acquiesce in the program of a strong leader. But it was also a function of Roosevelt's charisma. Rexford Tugwell, one of FDR's advisers, put it this way:

> No monarch, . . . unless it may have been Elizabeth or her magnificent Tudor father, or maybe Alexander or Augustus Caesar, can have given quite that sense of presiding, of gathering up into himself, of really representing a whole people. He had a right to his leeways, he had a right to use everyone in his own way, he had every right to manage and manipulate the palpables and impalpables. . . . He had touch with something deeper than reason. . . .[21]

Not only did FDR have the personality and opportunity necessary for extending presidential power; he was convinced that he had the constitutional right to be as vigorous as he might choose. Threatening in effect not to enforce an act of Congress involving agricultural policy during wartime, if it were not repealed, he said: "The President has the powers, under the Constitution and under Congressional acts, to take measures necessary to prevent a disaster which would interfere with the winning of the war. . . . When the war is won, the powers under which I act automatically revert to the people — to whom they belong."[22] The effect of this assertion was to claim, it has been noted, a royal prerogative, or the power to act for the "public good" with or without the sanction of law.[23] And FDR was rarely reluctant to invoke what legal authority he did clearly possess: Cunliffe tells the story that FDR cautioned his aides to look out for any congressional legislation he might veto simply to remind Congress that it was being watched.[24]

John F. Kennedy

Since 1936 at least, it has been obvious that energy in the White House — the "vital center" — has characterized the presidency. Whether or not we have entered upon the age of the Caesars, FDR, Truman, Johnson, and Nixon all applied their power in the Jackson-Lincoln tradition. Eisenhower, although imbued with a more restricted conception of his role, never retreated to the Buchanan concept of limited discretion.[25] Kennedy, given the brief two years and ten months of his term, is rather more ambiguous in this regard, although his attitude toward the powers of the office was clearly an expansive one. Kennedy believed that a dynamic and autonomous presidency was required in the 1960s and in some cases (e.g., the steel price increase of 1962) he adopted an unequivocal stance against those who challenged his political preeminence.[26]

It has also been suggested that Kennedy's reluctance to assert presidential power on certain other occasions (e.g., the two-and-one-half-year delay before initiating — in June 1963 — what was to become the Civil Rights Act of 1964) did not reflect his preferences concerning where power should lie in the American system but his sense of where it resided in fact. Acutely conscious of his extremely narrow victory over Nixon in 1960, Kennedy concluded, some contend, that he lacked a mandate for vigorous intervention in social — meaning racial — relationships.[27] By the same token, Kennedy opted in 1962 and 1963 for an interventionist solution to the economic stagnation of the 1950s. In doing so, however, he chose not to invigorate the economy by expanding social services as de-

sired by his more liberal advisers. Instead he decided on a general tax reduction, which, his liberal critics charged, served to exacerbate the
paradox of alleged private opulence amidst alleged public privation.[28]

By 1962 Kennedy had grown skeptical of his previous standards for
evaluating presidential conduct and refused the request of the eminent
historian, Arthur Schlesinger, Sr., to rank the presidents from "great" to
"failure." "A year ago I would have responded with confidence," he wrote,
"but now I am not so sure. After being in the office for a year I feel a good
deal more study is required to make my judgment sufficiently informed."
Later he remarked, "Only the President himself can know what the real
pressures are and his real alternatives are. If you don't know that, how
can you judge his performance?"[29] Kennedy was acutely aware that the
"mysterious institution" of the presidency was in many circumstances
hemmed in by congressional, judicial, bureaucratic, and other forces, an

John F. Kennedy, though only in office for less than three years, had an expansive attitude toward the powers of the presidency. *Pictorial Parade/Editorial
Photocolor Archives*

observation that may have led him to take a cautious view of his own opportunities. Kennedy's admonition is a wise one: A fully informed assessment of presidential behavior would include the president's own assessment of what it was possible to do, the resources to be commanded, and the probabilities of success associated with each policy alternative.[30]

As a practical matter, however, Kennedy's wisdom is relevant only in an academic sense. In fact, voters must evaluate presidential performance even if the data they possess are muddled and limited. But whatever one's view of Kennedy's performance, there would seem to be no need to resort to the embarrassing hyperbole of perhaps his closest adviser, Theodore Sorensen, who wrote two years after the president's assassination:

> One of John Kennedy's most important contributions to the human spirit was his concept of the office of the Presidency. His philosophy of government was keyed to power, not as a matter of personal ambition but of national obligation: the primacy of the White House within the Executive Branch and of the Executive Branch within the Federal Government, the leadership of the Federal Government within the United States and of the United States within the community of nations.[31]

This breathtaking conception of the president as Chief Magistrate of the Known Universe is not only a curious view of contributions to be made to the "human spirit" but a travesty upon Kennedy himself. There is no evidence that he thought of himself or his office in such preposterous terms.[32] That there is no constitutional basis for such a philosophy goes without saying.

Actually, with the exception of Kennedy's confrontation with Khrushchev during the Cuban missile crisis[33] and his behavior in facing down "Big Steel," Sorensen has difficulty in pointing to instances in which Kennedy exercised forceful and independent presidential power. Sorensen's examples to prove the opposite seem trivial — even pathetic — in retrospect: a $250,000 grant from Kennedy's "emergency fund" for guidance counselors in a campaign against school dropouts and an executive order increasing the distribution of surplus food to the needy.[34] Nonetheless, Kennedy was in office for less than three years, and many of his larger objectives might well have been achieved had his term run its normal course. Comparing recent with more remote presidents is dangerous business. Franklin Roosevelt, now often championed as the great emancipator of American labor, was notoriously lukewarm toward its enabling legislation, the Wagner Act, until its passage by Congress became a foregone conclusion.

In fine: If President Kennedy acted with restraint *merely* because of his narrow electoral victory, he could not have been aware of the definition of his office given in the Devil's Dictionary: "President, *n*.   The leading figure in a small group of men of whom — and of whom only — it is positively known that immense numbers of their countrymen did not want any of them for President."[35] Of the forty-seven presidential elections held between 1789 and 1972, thirteen put in office men who failed to receive a majority of the popular vote: Adams (1824), Polk (1844), Taylor (1848), Buchanan (1858), Lincoln (1860), Hayes (1870), Garfield (1880), Cleveland (1884), Wilson (1912, 1916), Truman (1948), Kennedy (1960), and Nixon (1968). Ford became president in 1974 with no election at all. And many presidents who have won a majority of the popular vote have done so only by the narrowest of margins. Presidents without majorities have often been activists in office, apparently undaunted by journalistic and scholastic references to their lack of a popular "mandate."

Lyndon Johnson

Lyndon Johnson's attitude toward the presidency was as expansive as that of any occupant in history. His great personal victory in 1964 assisted in the election of a reform-minded Congress which allowed full sway to his expansionistic biases and his willingness to trade on his popularity in order to secure his policy objectives.[36] The Great Society and War on Poverty programs were his effort to complete the agenda of social welfare reform begun in the 1930s by LBJ's hero (FDR "was like a daddy to me") but interrupted by World War II, reconversion, Korea, and the political respite of the 1950s. His greatest achievement — securing passage of the Civil Rights Act of 1964 with its sections on voting, employment, and public accommodations — illustrates the social benefits that a vigorous and united presidency can occasionally secure (but always in concert with other institutions) for Americans. And of course there was more; a voting rights bill in 1965, Medicare, and federal aid to education are major examples.

But by March 31, 1968, Johnson was impelled to announce that he would not seek reelection. His consensus was shattered, his popularity at an all-time low, his Vietnam policy under concerted and growing attacks. In Johnson's case, disillusionment with the bloody and seemingly open-ended and interminable military commitment in Vietnam brought his presidency to a sad and bitter conclusion. The history of America in Vietnam cannot be told here, but it is instructive on one point; correctly or not, the Vietnamese war was viewed increasingly as a *presidential* war, entered into without the full endorsement of Congress. To some extent, this is a meretricious argument: Congress, after all, had passed the Gulf of Tonkin Resolution empowering the president to use whatever force might be necessary to repel attack. Moreover, military appropriations to support the war were voted regularly. But the larger point is that the *procedures* for securing congressional consent presented a public image of deviousness and indirection altogether foreign to the solemnity of the undertaking. Nothing in American political history is clearer than the inability of any one of the three coordinate branches of government to force major policy commitments without the active, visible, and legitimate agreement of the others. Johnson undoubtedly knew this intellectually but, for whatever reason, proceeded with insufficient support, unable to pull back, sinking further into the quicksand of Asia.[37] He overestimated the power and authority of his office; in testing its outer limits he overextended it. The lesson seems plain: Determination by the incumbent to expand the discretion of the presidency is not enough. Acquiescence and support of others in powerful positions are also required, as is a favorable mass public in the longer run.

Richard Nixon

Another ambitious, determined president, Richard Nixon entered his second term with a 1972 victory as huge and convincing as Johnson's in 1964. He triumphed, at least temporarily, on many fronts in foreign affairs. The United States was extricated from Vietnam, détente was initiated with the Soviet Union, agreements were reached in the Strategic Arms Limitation Talks, European tensions were reduced, relations with China were restored, military disengagements in the Middle East were negotiated. Major domestic initiatives were proposed (e.g., sharing of federal revenues with state and local governments, universal health insurance, a guaranteed annual income to replace the old welfare system) and taken (e.g., imposition of wage and price controls, the devaluation of the dollar), many of which were somewhat startling to Nixon's more conservative supporters.

But within a year of his historic defeat of George McGovern, Nixon's presidency was crumbling. Within another year, impeachment proceedings were under way against a president for only the second time since the founding of the republic. By July 1974 the House Judiciary Committee had reported out three articles of impeachment (involving obstruction of justice, abuse of power, and, less plausibly, contempt of Congress) for consideration by the full House. By August the president had resigned following his admission that he had participated in an effort to deflect the investigation into the break-in at the Democratic Party National Committee headquarters in June 1972. With Nixon's resignation, Gerald R. Ford became the first nonelected president in American history. The ultimate significance of these traumatic events will not be fully understood for years, but at the very least it has again been made apparent that the presidency is a developing, not a finished, institution. Another president intent on using every leverage of power available had been brought to ruin; the disclosure not only of the Watergate scandal but of an entire catalogue of both specific and general abuses and indiscretions gave rise to such widespread discontent that the legitimacy of the Nixon presidency was drained away.

Whatever the truth or falsity of the many charges leveled against the president turns out to be, a principle of presidential power is clarified by all the Watergate-related events. Nixon, like Johnson, but for altogether different reasons, had exceeded the limits of presidential authority, a concept which is more psychological than legal. The presidency is an elastic institution but it cannot expand unilaterally, without popular approval and the agreement of other constitutional institutions. It is ironic that Richard Nixon, in seeking approval of his application to the New York bar, expressed clear awareness of this fact, for he wrote, "The principles underlying the government of the United States are decentralization of power, separation of power and maintaining a balance between freedom and order."[38] These have been and remain the most fundamental operational rules of the American polity; we have explicated their meanings in two previous chapters (3 and 4) on the Constitution and its interpretation.

There are myths, childlike but potentially mischievous, that in a dangerous and uncertain world only the president can visualize our problems, attack them before they destroy us, arouse the moral sense of the nation, inspire confidence, integrate diverse cultures, and generally get us back on the road to the New Jerusalem. Some otherwise sensible and hardheaded scholars have believed some of these things; indeed, all of these things are partially true. But a political institution touted and accepted as the fount of all energy, wisdom, and salvation must, when it fails to reduce all tensions, eliminate all problems, provide universal prosperity, and allocate perfect justice, become an object of suspicion and contempt. Lowering social expectations of the presidency — and that alone — can place the office in realistic (and constitutional) perspective.

THE SELECTION OF PRESIDENTS

Millions of Americans have passed the three constitutional tests neces-sary to qualify for the presidency: One must be a natural born citizen, at least thirty-five years of age, and a resident of the United States for at least fourteen years. Of these millions of potential presidents, of course, only a handful ever become serious candidates for the office. Obviously, then, many rules in addition to the constitutional ones work to limit ac-cess to the office to particular social types. These informal rules vary con-siderably in explicitness and bindingness.

For example, one rule of thumb is that a serious presidential hopeful must have a "political base from which to operate." Thus Richard Nixon's future presidential aspirations were thought by many (including himself) to be irretrievably shattered when he lost the 1962 election for governor of California. We know, of course, that the rule was "broken," and that Nixon was nominated and elected in 1968. Adlai Stevenson was governor-of Illinois when nominated by the Democratic party to run against Gen-eral Eisenhower in 1952, but he did not hold public office when he ran again in 1956. Perhaps, then, the rule should be amended to say some-thing like this: "It is best for a presidential hopeful to hold major public office when seeking the nomination; if that cannot be arranged, it is help-ful to have been the nominee on a previous occasion; but it is indispens-able to have held major office (not always elective) at some point in one's career." Thus the rule has become very cumbersome. However, we can state some norms with considerable accuracy, given historical hindsight. Historically, people who are in any one of the following categories have been ruled out of serious contention by an informal social rule: (1) females, (2) non-Caucasians, (3) non-Gentiles, (4) admitted homosexuals, and (5) the elderly.

Obviously the field is narrowed down. Still, there have been some re-cent adjustments. Until John F. Kennedy's election in 1960, one could have added "non-Protestants" to the list. In 1971 Senator Edmund Mus-kie, in discussing his campaign hopes before a group of black leaders, said that if he were to select a black politician as his vice-presidential running mate "we would both lose," an observation later denounced by President Nixon as a "libel" on the American people. Historical practice gives the edge to Muskie in this matter; the rule has been followed undeviatingly for 200 years. The rule requiring prior public office has been violated only twice. In 1872 Horace Greeley received the Democratic nomination (as well as that of the Liberal Republicans). Greeley was at the time the editor of the now defunct *New York Tribune*. In 1940 Wendell Willkie, a lawyer for a utility company, was nominated by the Republicans. Both Greeley and Willkie lost, but whether the violation of the prior public office rule contributed significantly to their defeat one cannot really say. Willkie's nomination was in any case a historical fluke: The German aggressions in Europe had produced a sudden shift in public opinion to internationalism. The major Republican candidates were identified with an isolationist foreign policy and found themselves suddenly alienated from dominant opinion.

Nearly all other informal rules have lower levels of probability than those involving ethnicity, sex, religion, and age. And the incidence of violations has increased in recent years. Let us cite a few of these.

It was once said that the ideal candidate should be a state governor at the time of nomination.[39] From 1900 to the present, a good many state governors have received presidential nominations: Woodrow Wilson (1912, 1916); James M. Cox (1920); Alfred E. Smith (1928); FDR (1932, 1936, 1940, 1944); Alfred Landon (1936); Thomas E. Dewey (1944, 1948); Adlai E. Stevenson (1952, 1956). Of the nineteen presidential elections held in this century, former governors have been major-party nominees in thirteen. Of course, in six of these elections the former governor had also been the former nominee of the party, which position counts as a more important credential perhaps than having been a governor. Thus the rule is a weak one at best. Indeed, between 1960 and 1972, no governor received his party's presidential nomination, although certain governors continue to be prominent possibilities for future nominations. Recent candidates have been drawn from the Senate, particularly for the vice-presidency. Think of Truman, Nixon, Johnson, all of whom received the presidential nomination after serving as vice-presidents. All had experience in the Senate as well, as did McGovern in 1972. One of them, of course (Johnson), was selected for the presidency by an assassin's bullet; another (Truman), by Roosevelt's failed health.

Political observers' conventional reasons for the old gubernatorial rule were essentially twofold: It was thought that governors, given their presumed control of their states' delegations to the nominating conventions, were in a better position to assemble convention support than those without similarly strong bases in state politics. As explained in Chapter 7, the state party, not the national one, is the locus of party strength in American politics. Moreover, it was thought that governors, having been involved in only local issues, could enter the nominating convention unopposed by major national enemies. Having (if ambitious) never announced themselves on divisive national questions, they had alienated no voting bloc essential to electoral success. Finally, a state governor had had experience as a chief executive, which was transferable to the management of the presidency.[40]

A traditional rule also asserted that a candidate from a large "swing state" was to be sought. This still has significant, if declining, effect but is observed more in the breach than in the observance. The precise qualities of a swing state are not clear, although they include large populations and genuinely competitive political parties. Thus New York, California, Ohio, and Illinois are apparently swing states; Pennsylvania is not, because throughout most of the century it has voted predictably Republican. And no Pennsylvanian has ever received the nomination of the Republican party. New York, on the other hand, has had six residents (seven, if Nixon is counted) nominated, and Ohio has supplied three candidates. The small states, however, have provided some nominees: Bryan of Nebraska (1900), Landon of Kansas (1936), Goldwater of Arizona (1964), McGovern of South Dakota (1972). The big-state rule presumed that some portion of a large state's voters would, out of local pride, vote for a person from their state regardless of other aspects of the election. The rule has little respectability; of all defeated candidates since 1900, only William Jennings Bryan (1908), Charles Evans Hughes (1916), Thomas Dewey (1948), Goldwater (1964), and Humphrey (1968) won in their home states.

A rather effective rule has operated against southern aspirants to the presidency. Wilson, while born a southerner, spent his career years in the North; Lyndon Johnson of Texas was regarded (and claimed to be) as much a westerner as a southerner. One historical explanation of the rule is simple and tactically sound. Democrats were assured of the southern vote in any case and had no reason to offend northern black voters by nominating someone who was anathema to them on civil rights. Republicans, similarly, had no reason to offend black supporters in the North, although they succeeded in alienating them in so many other ways that Lincoln's party of emancipation had virtually no strength at all among black voters a hundred years later. A tacit bargain between North and

South, by which presidential power was allocated to the former and congressional power (through the seniority system) to the latter, provides another explanation for the rule against southerners. That rule may be weakening to some extent although the test is still to come. Growing Republican strength in the South, especially in presidential politics, may induce the Republican party to pay greater heed to southern potential candidates.[41]

In a pluralistic society, a serious presidential contender must usually appear to be supportive of all legitimate interests, contradictory or not. Some presidents, it is true, have been loved for the enemies they made — FDR, for example. But securing popularity through confrontation can be risky politics.[42] The dynamics behind this rule are discussed fully in Chapter 7 on political parties; here we need only comment that presidential hopefuls should not offend any interests which, in coalition, are necessary for electoral success. Juggling contradictory issues is difficult, but the politician who insists upon campaigning on a consistent and "principled" platform has forgotten a crucial rule of presidential politics. It is not that voters are themselves unprincipled but that many different, even incompatible, principles coexist in a heterogeneous society.

There are also obscure but powerful rules covering how candidates should present themselves to the public, rules governing their style, their personality. The appearance of defeatism, flightiness, irresolution, or gullibility is taboo. So are illicit sex, drugs, and mysticism. A stable, ostensibly harmonious family life is desirable. If all of these rules were followed perfectly, of course, few candidates would qualify. They are not absolutes, but rough guides to decision which may, in a specific context, take on pronounced importance, be deemphasized, or get pushed aside or forgotten entirely. Pragmatism, not the idealization of rules, is the prevailing theme of presidential — indeed, most American — politics.

ON GETTING ELECTED PRESIDENT

Contenders for the presidency do not usually start on an equal footing. An incumbent president who is a candidate begins with substantial resources. Just or not, they are inherent in incumbency if the first term was not calamitous. The incumbent occupies a revered social role and basks in its reflected glory. This halo effect is augmented by mass recognition. There is no need to seek or establish popular familiarity; it has already been achieved; everyone knows the president. An incumbent president can not only speak but act: make policy, allocate opportunities, indulge interests. To many interests, actual payoffs are better than the promised payoffs of the opposition — a bird in the hand is worth two in the bush. Inevitably, the president's decisions have affected millions: Many of those favorably affected will offer support come what may, and even those not favorably affected may prefer known deficiencies to the untested talents of the opposition. Voters will want not only to maximize their benefits but to minimize their losses. A less risky, second-ranked choice may be selected over a more risky first-ranked choice.

Moreover, the president's achievements in office confront opponents with difficult tactical problems. If they criticize presidential programs, they will offend those who benefit from them; if they promise to continue them, they will be charged with me-tooism and lack of imagination; if they ignore them, they will arouse concern and insecurity among people receiving benefits and dark suspicions among voters who want to put an end to the programs.[43]

Other burdens must sometimes be borne. The legislative record of the challenger's own party may be essentially negative, having been built by opposing the president's initiatives. The president, who is normally re-nominated without opposition, heads a united party; any opponent has probably emerged through a rough-and-tumble, contentious, and inter-nally divisive party struggle. A party in disarray — as were the Demo-crats in 1968 and even more so in 1972 — is a poor beginning for a suc-cessful general election campaign. To appeal to erstwhile opponents is to sell out the candidate's long-suffering supporters; not to do so is to ad-vance with a disorganized party.

But challengers to incumbent presidents also have resources. Chal-lengers may be irresponsible; they are free to assert, to oversimplify, to publicize instances of alleged corruption and dereliction of duty that have occurred somewhere in the current administration for which the incum-bent is responsible. They are free to make more promises than they can possibly keep, to challenge the callous indifference of the incumbent, to exploit the cultural bias against persons who have exercised political power.

> Whatever a President does faces the hostile scrutiny of the op-position party bent upon dragging him from his great office at the next election. Unfriendly factions in his own party may manipulate against him. Some of the most formidable pres-sures upon the chief executive may be unloosed from Congress,

where legislators may harass the President with speeches, investigations, parliamentary maneuver, and public outcry.[44]

And, in the background always, as Hyman observes, is "the ancient superstition that when the old King dies and the young prince ascends the throne, by that event alone, everyone will become beautiful and rich."[45]

Another set of burdens and opportunities accrues to a candidate who is not the incumbent but is a member of the incumbent president's party. In 1960 Richard Nixon was in this category, as was Hubert Humphrey in 1968. Both lost. Indeed, since 1900 only Taft and Hoover have carried such candidacies to victorious conclusions. (Theodore Roosevelt, Coolidge, Truman, and Johnson came to office through the deaths of incumbents.) In this case candidates lack the mystique which only the presidency itself can bestow yet must accept some responsibility for the weakness of the incumbent's record. One must walk a narrow line: To criticize the incumbent's record is to show disloyalty and opportunism and to offend the incumbent's many supporters; to defend all aspects of the incumbent's performance is to accept enemies it may have made and to demonstrate servility unworthy of a president. Even to advance new ideas is dangerous: Why were your schemes not recommended previously to the president? The resources of such a candidate may not be disproportionate to those of the out-party's candidate, although some small share of credit may be taken for whatever achievements were scored by the incumbent administration.

CALCULATIONS IN OFFICE

Once a president is in office, we are informed by virtually all past presidents who have commented on the subject, any innocence concerning the orderliness and essential simplicity of the presidential decision-making process is immediately dispelled.[46]

Ordering their own priorities, taking stock of their resources and opportunities, organizing a personal staff and appointing persons to policy-making positions to assist them in applying their resources efficiently to the achievement of their priorities — these are tasks which presidents must undertake in the face of great uncertainty.

Among their most difficult jobs is to decide how to decide. He might be advised to follow that principle which most people regard as the sine qua non of democracy: Serve the interests of the majority. Such advice is not necessarily helpful, if only because majorities of the body politic do not exist on most specific public problems, problems which, after all, can get terribly complicated, abstruse, and remote from immediate interests. And even if a majority could be located on some occasion, *it* might consist mainly of people who were in the opposition on election day. Which majority is to be served? Simplistic majoritarian guides to presidential decision-making obviously will not do, except as analytical exercises. They are stated without full recognition of the types and nature of the issues that come before the president, of the president's goals — which may have less to do with "democracy" than with keeping the country together — and of the requirements of politics and the president's own welfare.

Partisan politics is important. Presidents have some idea of the kinds of people who supported them on election day. If the president is a Republican, significant supporters probably (and only probably) were women, older voters, Protestants, whites, suburban and rural dwellers, the college educated, professional and business people, nonunion groups, higher-income people. If the president is a Democrat, support came disproportionately from men, younger voters, Catholics, Jews, blacks, city dwellers, the noncollege educated, the unemployed, skilled and unskilled laboring groups, unions, lower-income people.

Now if these electoral coalitions were stable, and they are not, the problem would be simplified: The president could merely make choices designed to please the coalition that assured the election. However, the winning coalition begins to decay the day after the electoral victory is celebrated. Moreover, events pile up that require the rejection of numerous sympathizers, even when the president would much prefer not to reject them. Presidents who place more importance upon preserving peace than indulging the war hawks within their own party may allow their coalition to weaken in the interest of a goal higher than reelection or short-term party advantage. President Nixon was not unaware of the shock and rage his trip to Peking precipitated among many conservative Republicans, for example. But even in less dramatic circumstances, support may decrease when events, rules, and institutions force the president to acquiesce in a minority's veto. The rule that major social decisions in America must await the building of overwhelming consensus can be stated differently: Minorities are normally entitled not only to a voice in the government but to a veto over the positive action of a majority. The rule of minority veto has often been overturned or ignored in our political history, of course, sometimes with profound consequences. The ultimate unwillingness of our society to accept a southern minority's veto over issues of civil rights — manifested in the Civil War and the civil rights struggles of the 1960s — is a case in point.

The electoral coalition is unstable because it is contradictory. For the president to indulge one interest will anger another; to do nothing will anger them both; to do what events require will irritate or alarm previous supporters. To favor a majority — which may contain traditional opponents — may offend the party faithful; to favor a minority — as events will perhaps require — may offend a majority (usually bad politics). Regardless, therefore, of the decision-rule the president chooses to invoke, the outcome is problematical; often the fidelity of the electoral coalition and even avid partisans will be tested severely. Whatever a president does will be wrong in the eyes of some, and with each specific decision made, with all the indulgences and deprivations decisions carry for specific individuals and groups, the president becomes less and less the speaker for those interests and voters who contributed to the election!

> If he leads, he is a dictator. If he follows he is a weakling. If he appoints old friends to high places, he governs by crony. If he gets rid of them when they prove unequal to their new places, he uses people. If he speaks directly to the nation he is a demagogue. If he waits for a proper moment to disclose bits of news, he witholds vital information a free people must have if they are to make wise decisions. And so on.[47]

Whether or not there is a strategy that would enable a president to maintain popular or majority support is a nice theoretical question. Hypothetically, in a democratic political system with two parties, each of which has the winning of elections as its major goal, presidents are unwise to alienate any majority. Therefore, on all occasions calling for decision, a hypothetical poll is conducted and the will of the majority, if there is one, followed.[48] That is fine as far as it goes, but it may not appear a useful endeavor when the president knows more about a real and dangerous situation and its implications than the public does. Nonetheless, the reason presidents often do the popular thing can be explained by such calculations. But why do presidents in a democratic two-party system sometimes do the *un*popular thing? Mass publics, Walter Lippmann believed, can be "destructively wrong at the critical junctures."[49] At such junctures presidents have been known to suppress thoughts of party political advantage and deal with the crisis at hand on its own terms. Of course, presidential decisions can be destructively wrong too.

Whether presidents act to satisfy majorities or minorities, they must appear to act legitimately. Consequently, all presidents are prepared whenever possible to invoke constitutional authority to justify their conduct; if available, legislative authorization and judicial decisions can also be cited. A president who believes it necessary to act but lacks obvious authority from constitutional, legislative, or judicial sources may choose to act anyway, on grounds several presidents have deemed acceptable: that results count more than justifications and that justifications can be found later in any event.

If an immediate crisis is met quickly and successfully, legal justification ("words") can normally be found which will not be closely examined except in obscure legal periodicals. Justification can *always* be found or rationalized in legal terms, for if the "written Constitution" of 1789 with its later amendments does not provide the authority, some elements of the "unwritten constitution" can be made to do so. The unwritten constitution consists of legislation, judicial decisions, and, just as importantly, precedents. The precedents for presidential initiatives are not codified anywhere; they are scattered about in biographies, letters, speeches, history books. When they are pasted together by astute assistants, and covered by a veneer of support from the written Constitution, presidents can *manufacture their own guides to action*. There are limits to this maneuver, but the ability occasionally to write the rules as one acts is an important source of power. Without doubt, the major problem is to succeed in the undertaking; a failed action with meager legitimate underpinnings can destroy a president.

INDUCING COOPERATION FROM CONGRESS AND THE COURT

More than once we have stressed the need to build broad agreement among diverse centers of authority before launching major policy changes in America. The consensus-building process can be led by a president but it cannot be commanded to any great degree. Although legal justification, however tendentious, can always be found by an inventive presidential staff, legal support for important policy decisions is not sufficient. The president is but one of several actors whose cooperation is necessary if they are to be sustained.

It is well, therefore, to examine the most important resources which the president may deploy to encourage cooperation from other participants in the political process. The inducements extended to the voters generally by competitively elected officials — policy stances favorable to whatever intense majorities or minorities exist in the electorate — yield returns to the successful politicians as well. Holding legal office is itself a crucial political resource. Once elected, the official may use the powers of office to help make decisions on many policy questions the electorate is generally apathetic or ignorant about.

But whether seeking to redeem a campaign promise or to decide a question having little public visibility, the president must often proceed in harmony with other political entities. The Congress is one of them.

Congress

The president can order the Congress into special session and recess it when its two houses cannot agree but beyond that cannot compel it to do anything on any occasion. Nonetheless, skillful management of certain constitutional prerogatives vis-à-vis the legislative process can in some cases extend the president's sway over Congress. The authority to set the main agenda for the national policy-making process, one of the most crucial of all political powers, is made clear in Article II, Section 3 of the Constitution: "He shall from time to time give to the Congress information of the State of the Union, and recommend to their consideration such measures as he shall judge necessary and expedient." The legislative initiative has been the president's since the Square Deal of Theodore Roosevelt and the New Freedom of Woodrow Wilson. Think also of FDR's New Deal, Truman's Fair Deal, Eisenhower's Great Crusade, Kennedy's New Frontier, Johnson's Great Society. Still, many important presidential proposals get shipwrecked in Congress.[50]

Congressional-executive relationships are always uneasy, mildly to intensely suspicious, with each side maintaining jealous watch over its own domain. With some qualification, Congress and recent presidents have agreed that neither would seek total dominance over the other; that, specifically, the president's role in foreign and national security affairs should not be seriously diminished while Congress's (largely negative) powers in domestic affairs should be respected by the executive. Sickles is correct in observing that interaction between Congress and the president takes place when each expects some gain, not when one is likely to win all at the expense of the other. The relationship, to use Sickles's term, is "businesslike."[51] Bargains are negotiated in that pragmatic atmosphere which experienced American politicians find most congenial. Of course, there are "outsiders" in Congress who, because of conviction, frustration, or ambition, adopt a highly critical moral stance toward such a bargaining relationship. And some presidents, whether out of pique, genuine alarm, or miscalculation, have overplayed their hands in congressional relations. So, at times, the public impression — fostered by media attention — is one of confrontation between president and Congress; things are much more dramatic that way.

Powers are shared between the two institutions in many ways: Each house and the president must normally approve legislation — a requirement that opens up the possibility of institutional trade-offs *across* issues. For example, President Johnson received initial backing on his Vietnam policy from many congressional liberals because of his staunch support of civil rights and social welfare measures.

A president may prod Congress — call, or threaten to call, it into special session, threaten to or actually veto some measure (which only a two-thirds majority in each house can override); eliminate recalcitrant members' access to the White House on all occasions, not only on those when they oppose the president; refuse (sometimes) to spend funds appropriated by Congress; issue executive orders rather than seek legislative authorization, thereby bypassing Congress entirely; conclude executive agreements with other countries, thereby bypassing the Senate's constitutional authority to approve all treaties; appeal over the heads of Congress to mass opinion, as Truman did in 1948 in denouncing the "do-nothing" Eightieth Congress; refuse to assist Congress by claims of "executive privilege," as asserted by President Nixon upon the demands from the House Judiciary Committee for tape recordings and documents of interest in its impeachment proceedings.

These largely negative efforts to induce congressional cooperation may fail as often as not and are usually entered into only as a last resort. More productive are positive appeals and material inducements: pleas for party loyalty, patronage, access to the White House, being taken into the president's confidence, campaigning (or not campaigning, President Nixon's painful choice in the congressional elections of 1974) for members' reelection, yielding on matters of keen interest to a member but of marginal concern to the executive, maintaining an appearance of respect for the Congress.

Moreover, success or failure in other relations will affect the president's capacity to deal with Congress. An unsuccessful effort ("blunder") in foreign affairs, such as Kennedy's in the Bay of Pigs or Johnson's in Vietnam, may diminish a president's power and prestige in Congress. So may domestic troubles: a faltering economy, disorder in the ghettos, cultural drift. Conversely, success in the great world can bolster a president's position with Congress. President Nixon and his supporters pointed continually at his successes in foreign affairs as he fought against impeachment and removal from office.

The Supreme Court

The normal relationship between president and Supreme Court is discreet detachment and tacit cooperation. Some issues and personalities in American history, however, have replaced this norm with one of ideological antagonism, setting the institutions at cross-purposes and usually endangering the legitimacy of both in the process. Such confrontations have also been painful and unrewarding with respect to the immediate issues in dispute. As a consequence, a kind of historical learning has taken place: Each institution follows the unwritten rule to respect the other and to defer to its decisions whenever possible. The rule was not established without conflict. President Jefferson's aborted scheme to impeach all the Federalist members of the Supreme Court was one of the earliest, and perhaps the most serious, of all presidential attacks on the Court's authority. Jefferson failed because members of his own Republican party in the Senate refused to help him dismantle the Court. Never a person to give up easily, two years later Jefferson sought the impeachment of Chief Justice Marshall upon his dismissal of the charges of treason against Aaron Burr. In the same cases, Marshall twice subpoenaed the president to provide evidence and was twice resisted. Earlier, in *Marbury* v. *Madison,* Marshall had seized greatly expanded power for the Court — the power of judicial review — but had refrained from issuing an order to Jefferson which would surely have been ignored. Professor Sickles sums it up admirably: "The lesson the judiciary and executive bequeathed one another was that each could be a formidable adversary, proud and vindictive. The demonstrated costs of conflict were enough to induce most presidents and Court majorities to adopt a respectful live-and-let-live attitude toward each other in the generations that followed."[52]

Not for another hundred years did executive-court relations diverge so sharply. President Franklin Roosevelt's legislative program was blocked by a Court sympathetic to a previously dominant ruling coalition and fearful of the expansion of governmental power and activity pursued by the president and a compliant Congress. As one after another of FDR's proposals fell to the constitutional ax wielded by the Court — the National Industrial Recovery Act and the Agricultural Adjustment Act being the most important — the president retaliated by proposing, after his landslide reelection in 1936, that the Court be expanded (or "packed," as his opponents understood it) to improve its "efficiency." The president lost — congressional and public opinion was negative — but so did the Court. Two members of the Court, perhaps alarmed at the institutional confrontation, began to temporize and to swing to the erstwhile minority, thereby creating a new majority broadly supportive of the executive's initiatives. As Professor Dahl has shown, presidents have normally had op-

The relationship between president and Supreme Court has varied from cooperation to antagonism. During Franklin D. Roosevelt's first administration executive-court relations diverged sharply. His relationship with the public, however, was more amicable, as the above photo indicates. *Camerique*

portunities earlier in their terms to appoint judges likely to support their legislative programs and thus to avoid such conflicts.[53] In Roosevelt's case, the times, the personalities, and the actuarial tables conspired to force a conflict.

The Supreme Court has learned to be wary of provoking presidents, who may react in several ways: by subverting a judicial decision by proposing new legislation, by refusing to enforce or appearing reluctant to enforce a judicial decision, by influencing the climate of public opinion toward the Court. The doctrine of judicial restraint (see Chapter 5), when followed, minimizes the probability of institutional confrontations; so does the Court's presumption of constitutionality of presidential actions. By the same token, judicial activism increases the probability of conflict with the president. Judicial activists must rely on the Court's prestige and, less reliably, presidential self-abnegation when choosing to thwart or limit presidential action. The Court is also adversely affected relative to the "political" branches in its inability to "go public" on vital issues. It must suffer in silence when, for example, presidential candidates run against the Court on account of its past decisions. President Nixon, in running for office in 1968, promised, if elected, to appoint "strict" constitutionalists to the Court who would supposedly be less inclined to intervene in matters of social policy (e.g., school busing, school prayer, rights of the accused). However wounding such attacks may be, the Court cannot respond; paradoxically, it would probably be further damaged if it did so. Credibility would accrue to the charge that the Court was simply writing its own political opinions into law. Nonetheless, the Court's informal powers (its prestige, primarily) and its formal powers (judicial review, in the main) can be strong weapons against a presidential adversary. Both institutions have their strengths and vulnerable points; each can do damage to the other. No hierarchy exists between them.

By the same token, few mechanisms are available for adjusting disputes informally. Members of the Court have been criticized for acting as presidential advisers; the Court does not give legal opinions to the president on *proposed* courses of action. The bargaining that occurs is normally tacit, uncoordinated, and vague; the potential for confrontation is consequently high. President Nixon's troubles with the judiciary in the Watergate affair will provide considerable grist for scholars interested in the executive-judicial relationship. The president did accede to the Court's ruling that executive privilege, national security areas aside, cannot be asserted in criminal matters. On the other hand, the Court for the first time stated that executive privilege is constitutionally based.

The Executive Office

In the next chapter attention is directed to the departments and agencies of government that implement, modify, and, as we shall see, make public policy. Officials in the agencies often have great power, stemming from their inside knowledge, technical skills, personal and institutional prestige, job security, and other resources. None of the agencies, however, has constitutional status. All are legally subservient to constitutional officials, most particularly to the president, who possesses the "executive power" under the Constitution. In relating to the executive agencies, and for that matter to other audiences as well, presidents have come to rely increasingly upon an enlarged and rationalized group of staff assistants comprising, collectively, the Executive Office of the President (EOP), which was first established in 1939. The main contemporary components of the EOP consist in the White House Office, the Office of Management and Budget (OMB), the Council of Economic Advisers (CEA), and the National Security Council (NSC), and, under President Nixon, the Domestic Council.

The White House Office includes the president's most intimate staff assistants, although not always the president's closest or most influential confidants. Its role is to serve as an extension of the president's person: to advise, inform, follow through, coordinate, plan, organize, initiate, hire and fire, and, most importantly, protect the president's interests on all occasions. The intimacy of the president and these closest advisers poses dangers which not all presidents have recognized or acted upon in time. President Truman persisted out of misplaced loyalty in defending General Vaughan in the face of stories about his petty corruption. President Eisenhower was ill served by the indiscretion of his chief of staff, Sherman Adams, who accepted favors from an individual with business relations and legal problems pending with the government. To Eisenhower's credit, he did not waste time in defending Adams. Exaggerated loyalty on the part of staff assistants can be not only unedifying to the spirit of republicanism but harmful to the president. President Kennedy's principal assistant and speech writer, Theodore Sorensen, made a pompous and unrealistic assessment of both Kennedy and the presidency — referred to earlier — that in our view had neurotic overtones. Jack Valenti once delivered an appraisal of President Johnson's talents that was so unbalanced it left his audience gasping with embarrassment. President Nixon's two most intimate assistants, H. R. Haldeman and John Ehrlichman, failed him with disastrous consequences in not acting forthrightly in the Watergate affair and in engaging in other conduct that was actually or potentially illegal and destructive of Nixon's authority. Loyalty is a virtue in politics as elsewhere but it has limits and has often become perverted into sycophancy, conspiratorial self-righteousness, and corruption.

More remote, more bureaucratic, and more important than the White House Office to the continuity and stability of presidential management is the Office of Management and Budget. With a rather small staff for the magnitude of the task (500 people or so), the OMB must assemble the annual budget requests from the agencies, analyze them, and, within the constraints of fiscal policy, make recommendations to the president concerning them. In government as anywhere else, questions often get reduced or translated into money terms, and the budgetary process, in which OMB is a central actor, is crucial to, if not coterminous with, the political process itself. The OMB also has management and review functions which, with the executive budget, comprise the president's main sources of surveillance and control over the executive agencies.

The NSC and the Domestic Council (the latter is not yet well established) plan, coordinate, seek out alternatives, follow through, in the areas of national security and domestic policy. The CEA advises the president on economic policy.

In the following chapter, the executive establishment — the bureaucracy — is discussed, along with the president's and Congress's access to and control over the bureaucracy.

SUMMARY

The Constitution allocates vast, uncertain, yet restricted powers to the presidency. The men who created the office did not themselves possess a consistent view of its powers and prerogatives. Those who have filled the office, and the exigencies of the times, have given it substance and definition. Ideology is an uncertain guide in assessments of a "strong" or "weak" presidency. The modern "strong" (i.e., active and forceful on policy matters) presidency was created during times of crisis and responsibility and, occupied by liberal presidents, has been seen by their supporters as a vital, necessary institution for serving the public interest. Conservatives have normally feared a strong executive, one capable of successfully confronting private centers of power and other institutions of government. Some conservatives have viewed the strong executive as a threat to liberty, rights, and other values more likely to be protected by parliaments than presidents. But this is not a law of nature: Many liberals regarded President Nixon, a strong conservative executive, with alarm, even though he filled an office they had helped to create. And just to compound the confusion, many conservatives expressed fears that Nixon's critics would "weaken" the presidency, an outcome for which, earlier, the same conservatives had fervently hoped.

In the American political culture numerous rules of thumb (occasionally breached) serve to eliminate most of the adult population from being considered for the office. For example, no president has been female, non-Caucasian, non-Gentile, or admittedly homosexual. Other, less compelling and perhaps shifting, rules are also at work: No Catholic had been elected president until John F. Kennedy in 1960; southerners have often been considered ineligible.

In an election campaign, tactics are strongly conditioned by the candidate's current political status. Incumbent presidents have resources, mainly the capacity to act as well as speak, which their challengers lack. On the other hand, incumbent presidents running for reelection have records in office which can be attacked. They cannot be attacked too sweepingly, however, inasmuch as any president has benefited some people and their support will not flow to a candidate who threatens their gains. A challenger who belongs to the incumbent's party must walk a narrow line between uncritical support for the president's record and innovative proposals that depart too far from that record. All incumbents are vulnerable to the cultural bias against authority and the myth that if the "right person" can be found a new and brighter day will dawn for all.

Once in office, a president must make complex calculations in the midst of great uncertainty involving, among other things, the mass public, the diverse groups within the society, and other political institutions. With respect to the Congress and the Supreme Court the president may use a variety of formal and informal sanctions to induce their cooperation. In addition, a large staff, the Executive Office of the President, is of assistance in these relations as well as dealings with the departments and agencies of the executive establishment. Like some other agents in the American system, the president has great power but is limited by the most fundamental of all rules in the American polity: It is not enough to act alone, over time and on major questions, without the support of broad social and political majorities. Presidents may participate in building these sweeping coalitions and in neutralizing the veto groups that often restrict the positive action of a majority, but presidents cannot for very long pursue any policy line not based on such a coalition.

NOTES

1. Edward S. Corwin, *The President: Office and Powers, 1787–1957,* 4th ed. (New York: New York University Press, 1957). This magisterial book is recommended for all those seriously interested in the presidency.
2. Ibid., pp. 6–7.
3. See Charles Beard, *An Economic Interpretation of the Constitution* (New York: Macmillan, 1935). Keen opponents of Beard's thesis include Forrest McDonald, *We the People: The Economic Origins of the Constitution* (Chicago: University of Chicago Press, 1963), and Robert E. Brown, *Charles Beard and the Constitution* (Princeton, N.J.: Princeton University Press, 1956).
4. Numbers 66 to 77 of the *Federalist Papers,* all written by Alexander Hamilton, still provide rewarding reading for anyone interested in the contemporary debate over the actual and desirable powers of the presidency.
5. Corwin, *The President,* p. 17.
6. The thesis that the lines of conflict in America continued on these and related issues is stated in V.L. Parrington's great study, *Main Currents in American Thought* (New York: Harcourt, Brace, 1927). Stability in the organization of conflict is also a major theme in the interesting book by S.M. Lipset, *The First New Nation* (Garden City, N.Y.: Doubleday, 1967).
7. Corwin, *The President,* p. 19.
8. On the first point, see Leonard D. White's administrative history of the period, *The Jacksonians, 1829–1861* (New York: Macmillan, 1954). Readers interested in the American public bureaucracy in other periods should consult White's two other volumes: *The Jeffersonians, 1801–1829* (New York: Macmillan, 1951) and *The Republican Era, 1869–1901* (New York: Macmillan, 1958). On the second point, see the eminently readable book by Arthur M. Schlesinger, Jr., *The Age of Jackson* (Boston: Little, Brown, 1945).
9. In many ways, particularly with respect to legislation, Jackson was not an activist president. Some historians believe that he was interested in power more for its own sake than for policy reasons.
10. An excellent guide to historians' inconclusive discussion of the causes of the Civil War is J.G. Randall and David Donald, *The Civil War and Reconstruction,* 2nd ed. (Boston: Heath, 1961).
11. Freeman Cleaves, *Old Tippecanoe* (New York: Scribner, 1939), p. 326 (more recently, Port Washington, N.Y.: Kennikat, 1969).
12. Lincoln's message to Congress of July 4, 1861, contains his views on the exceptional authority of the presidential office in times of internal crisis. It is readily accessible in Robert S. Hirschfield, ed., *The Power of the Presidency* (New York: Atherton, 1968), pp. 76–78.
13. For the full text, see ibid., pp. 65–69.
14. See, for example, Fred A. Shannon, *Economic History of the People of the United States* (New York: Macmillan, 1936).

15. D.H. Elletson, *Roosevelt and Wilson: A Comparative Study* (London: John Murray, 1965), p. xv.
16. Roosevelt's quotes from ibid., pp. 43, 46.
17. Lawrence H. Chamberlain, *The President, Congress and Legislation* (New York: Columbia University Press, 1948).
18. Schlesinger's first view is advanced in *A Thousand Days* (Boston: Houghton Mifflin, 1965); his second, in *The Imperial Presidency* (Boston: Houghton Mifflin, 1973). The first has been called the "textbook" view of the office by Thomas E. Cronin, "The Textbook Presidency and Political Science," in J.F. Fiszman and G.S. Poschman, eds., *The American Political Arena* (Boston: Little, Brown, 1972), pp. 294–308.
19. Wilfred Binkley, *President and Congress* (New York: Knopf, 1947).
20. Two studies focusing upon *how* presidents have used their power, the sources in which they discovered it, and with what consequences for the office are a fine volume by George F. Milton, *The Use of Presidential Power, 1789–1943* (New York: Octagon, 1965), which analyzes how several "strong" presidents (Washington, Jefferson, Jackson, Lincoln, Cleveland, Theodore Roosevelt, Wilson, and Franklin D. Roosevelt) managed power; and Richard Neustadt's well-known *Presidential Power: The Politics of Leadership,* 2nd ed. (New York: Wiley, 1960). A highly readable book concerning the calculations of presidents is Robert J. Sickles, *Presidential Transactions* (Englewood Cliffs, N.J.: Prentice-Hall, 1974).
21. Quoted in Elmer E. Cornwell, Jr., *Presidential Leadership of Public Opinion* (Bloomington: Indiana University Press, 1965), p. 90.
22. Quoted in Marcus Cunliffe, *American Presidents and the Presidency,* (New York: American Heritage, 1972), p. 235.
23. Ibid.
24. Ibid., p. 320.
25. A study which seeks to explain the alternating periods of presidential (and political system) energy and of inertia and deadlock is James L. Sundquist, *Politics and Policy: The Eisenhower, Kennedy and Johnson Years* (Washington: Brookings, 1968).
26. Grant McConnell, *Steel and the Presidency, 1962* (New York: Norton, 1963). See Neustadt's gracious but studied assessment of the Kennedy presidency in *Presidential Power.*
27. See H. Golden, *Mr. Kennedy and the Negroes* (Greenwich, Conn.: Fawcett, 1964).
28. This alleged paradox provides the thesis for John Kenneth Galbraith's *The Affluent Society,* 2nd ed. (Boston: Houghton Mifflin, 1969).
29. Recounted in Schlesinger, Jr., *A Thousand Days,* pp. 671–685.
30. The pessimistic implication of this observation for the evaluation of political decision-makers is pursued in James M. Buchanan, *Cost and Choice* (Chicago: Markham, 1969).
31. Theodore Sorensen, *Kennedy* (New York: Harper & Row, 1965), p. 389.

32. For Kennedy's own modest assessment of his opportunities and power, a good source is his December 1962 television discussion with several commentators. A transcript may be found in Edmund S. Ions, ed., *The Politics of John F. Kennedy* (London: Routledge & Kegan Paul, 1967), pp. 157–165.

33. See Robert Kennedy, *Thirteen Days: A Memoir of the Cuban Missile Crisis* (New York: Norton, 1969).

34. Sorensen, *Kennedy,* p. 390.

35. Quoted in Cunliffe, *American Presidents and the Presidency,* p. 172.

36. An interesting study of popularity as, sometimes, an important presidential resource for change is Stuart Gerry Brown, *The American Presidency: Leadership, Partisanship and Popularity* (New York: Macmillan, 1969).

37. One explanation, for those interested in psychological interpretations of politics, is implicit in James David Barber, *The Presidential Character* (Englewood Cliffs, N.J.: Prentice-Hall, 1972). Barber views Johnson and Nixon as "Active-Negative" Personality types: aggressive, compulsive, irascible, and stubborn. Townsend Hoopes, *The Limits of Intervention* (New York: McKay, 1969), is an engrossing account of the policy of gradual escalation in Vietnam written by a disillusioned participant and internal critic.

38. Quoted in Barber, *The Presidential Character,* p. 366.

39. See, in connection with the following discussion, Sidney Hyman, "Nine Tests for the Presidential Hopeful," in F.M. Carney and H.F. Way, Jr., eds., *Politics, 1960* (Belmont, Calif.: Wadsworth, 1960), pp. 88–95.

40. On the president's role as manager, see Louis W. Koenig, *The Chief Executive,* rev. ed. (New York: Harcourt Brace Jovanovich, 1968).

41. Kevin Phillips, *The Emerging Republican Majority* (New Rochelle, N.Y.: Arlington House, 1969). Phillips's book advances a logic underlying a "Southern Strategy" for the Republican party which makes a certain tactical sense.

42. Brown, *The American Presidency.*

43. This and the following "types" of candidates are developed in Sidney Hyman, *The American President* (New York: Harper, 1954), pp. 16–30.

44. Koenig, *The Chief Executive,* p. 334.

45. Hyman, *The American President,* p. 22.

46. Most twentieth-century presidents who survived their terms in office have published memoirs: Theodore Roosevelt, Coolidge, Hoover, Truman, Eisenhower, and Johnson did so, and Taft wrote widely on the presidency.

47. Hyman, *The American President,* p. 56.

48. Anthony Downs, *An Economic Theory of Democracy* (New York: Harper, 1957).

49. Quoted in Sickles, *Presidential Transactions,* p. 149.

50. A vivid account of one such shipwreck may be found in Daniel P.

Moynihan, *A Guaranteed Income: The Nixon Administration and the Family Assistance Plan* (New York: Random House, 1973).

51. Sickles, *Presidential Transactions,* pp. 112–113.
52. Ibid., p. 101.
53. Robert Dahl, "Decision-making in a Democracy: The Supreme Court as a National Policy-maker," *Journal of Public Law,* 6 (Fall 1957), 279–295.

The Bureaucracy: Generating Goods and Services

$\mathbf{A}$t the beginning of this century, about 4 percent of the labor force worked for government at all levels in the United States; in 1970 some 15 percent of all workers were so employed, excluding the military services. If one looks at the total payroll of government relative to the payroll of private business, it turns out that nearly 20 percent of the national payroll now goes to public employees. Thus, public employees — 15 percent of workers — get a disproportionate 20 percent of total payroll. The main reason is that many are skilled technicians or professionals whose education and talents often can command similar if not higher salaries in private enterprise. \ Governments at all levels now purchase annually over 20 percent of all goods and services produced in America. In addition, the federal government allocates, by rough 1975 approximation, another $120 billion for **transfer payments** (so-called non-resource-exhausting activities). Transfers involve taking resources from' some people through taxes and redistributing them to others (farmers, vet-

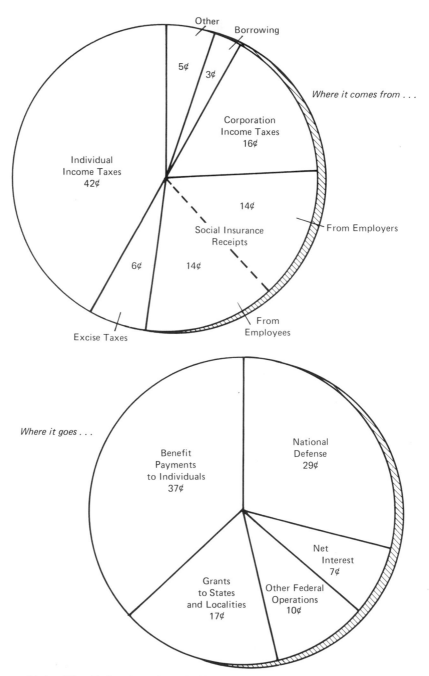

Figure 11-1.   The Federal Budget Dollar, Fiscal Year 1975 Estimate. *Source: Budget of the United States Government, Fiscal Year 1975*, p. 2.

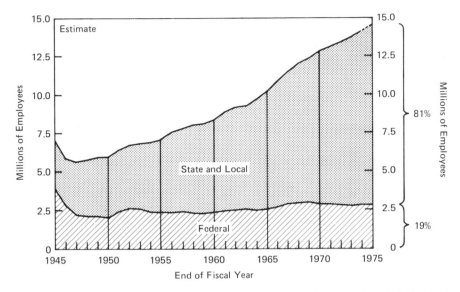

Figure 11-2. Government Civilian Employment. *Source: Special Analysis, Budget of the United States Government, Fiscal Year 1975*, p. 105.

erans, welfare recipients) and to the servicing of public debts. In these cases, government does not specify which particular goods and services are to be consumed by the recipients.

Is this too small a government? Too large? Just about right? Really the question cannot be answered so simply. Asking how large American government should be is like asking how long a piece of string should be. It all depends on the parcel. And, of course, a parcel containing over 210 million people with all of their varied wants is large in both absolute and relative terms. Only the Soviet Union, India, and China have more inhabitants. Such scale means that American government is unavoidably large. On the other hand, many countries devote a larger share of their national income to the public sector than does the United States. West Germany, Austria, France, Sweden, Italy, Britain, Norway, the Netherlands, Finland, and Belgium all have higher ratios of governmental spending relative to gross natural product (GNP) than we do.

FACTORS IN THE GROWTH OF GOVERNMENT

It is not difficult to isolate the political issues that so dramatically increased the scope of government in America in this century. They are (1)

Table 11-1. Domestic Transfer Payments by Federal Government (in billions of dollars).

Fiscal Year	Total	Retire-ment and Dis-ability[1]	Hospital and Supple-mentary Medical Insurance	Food Stamps	Veterans Benefits and Insurance	Unem-ployment Benefits	Other
1960	20.6	13.1			4.4	2.7	0.4
1961	23.6	14.4		*	4.6	4.2	.4
1962	25.1	16.4		*	4.6	3.6	.5
1963	26.4	18.0		*	4.8	3.1	.5
1964	27.3	19.1		*	4.6	2.9	.6
1965	28.3	20.2		*	4.7	2.5	.8
1966	31.8	23.9		0.1	4.7	2.1	1.2
1967	37.2	25.3	3.2	.1	5.3	2.1	1.2
1968	42.7	27.9	5.1	.2	5.5	2.2	1.8
1969	48.5	32.0	6.3	.2	6.2	2.3	1.6
1970	54.8	35.5	6.8	.6	6.9	3.0	2.0
1971	67.4	42.4	7.5	1.5	8.0	5.6	2.3
1972	75.8	47.8	8.4	1.8	8.8	6.6	2.4
1973	86.8	58.5	9.0	2.1	9.7	4.8	2.7
1974 estimate	102.5	69.6	11.4	2.9	10.4	5.0	3.2
1975 estimate	120.7	83.0	13.3	3.8	10.3	6.5	3.7

*Less than $50 million.
[1] Includes black-lung benefits and supplemental security income benefits.
Source: Special Analysis, Budget of the United States Government, Fiscal Year 1975, p. 13.

the welfare state versus individualism and (2) the security of the "free world" (the most prominent member of which is the United States) versus "international communism." Forces demanding more government action have dominated both these issues. Previously the resolution of political problems — no matter how they were resolved or in whose favor — did not usually require a massive increase in the size of government relative to the rest of society. A distinguished American historian made an effort to sort out the major political problems that have confronted our society historically.[1] While recognizing that none of these problems has been "solved," they have tended to impinge upon the polity most severely at different times. The issue of the American Revolution — withdrawal of allegiance or continuing loyalty to the crown and Great Britain — was followed in rough chronological order by intense struggles over the adoption of the Constitution, the extension of voting rights, slavery, regionalism versus nationalism, individual liberties, immigration, and corporate giantism. An interesting thing about this list is that most of the

Table 11-2. Selected Major Federal Subsidies—Costs: 1971 and 1972 (in millions of dollars, for years ending June 30).

Program and Item	1971	1972 est.	Program and Item	1971	1972 est.
Agriculture:			*Natural resources:*		
Feed grain production stabilization	1,504	1,060	Tax subsidy on excess of percentage over cost depletion	980	985
Wheat production stabilization	874	877	Construction grants for waste water treatment works	1,200	2,080
Cotton production stabilization	917	824	*Commerce and economic dev.:*		
Expensing and capital gains for farming	820	840	Urban renewal and neighborhood development	1,031	1,000
Food:			Investment tax credit	910	1,800
School lunch	535	797	Corporation capital gains tax credit	425	380
Food stamps	1,559	2,066	Individual capital gains tax	(NA)	5,600
Commodity distribution	596	680	Tax credit for excess bad debt reserves of financial institutions	380	400
Medical care:			Expensing of research and development expenditures	540	545
Deductibility of medical expenses	1,700	1,900	Corporate surtax exemption	2,000	2,300
Medical insurance premiums and medical care, tax deductions	1,450	2,000	Exclusion (tax) of interest on life insurance savings	1,050	1,100
Medicare: Health insurance	2,035	2,240	U.S. Postal Service	2,183	1,772
Medical assistance program	3,374	4,051	*Other:*		
Manpower, vocational rehabilitation:	502	560	Tax deductibility of charitable contributions	3,550	3,200
Education:			Tax exemption of interest on state and local debt	2,300	2,600
Veterans educational assistance	1,527	1,939	Net tax exclusion of pension contributions for employees	3,075	3,650
Additional tax exemption for students	500	550			
Housing:					
Owner-occupied homes:					
Deductibility of interest	2,800	2,400			
Deductibility of property taxes	2,900	2,700			
Interest subsidy for rental assistance	(NA)	(NA)			
Low-rent public housing loan insurance and debt service payments	(NA)	1,470			

NA: Not available.

Source: Statistical Abstract of the United States, 1973, p. 393.

items could be managed with only an incidental or temporary increase in the physical growth of government. The social mobilization that occurred at the time of the Revolutionary War was rather small, total war having not yet been invented. The American Civil War was the first great modern war in history but even it only temporarily distorted the size of the public sector; the vast armies assembled to fight it were quickly demobilized following Appomattox. Issues involving the new Constitution, voting, trust-busting, industrial regulation, and immigration policy did not center directly on the scope of government as measured in physical terms. For example, questions of participation could be met by political decisions; industrial organization and immigration policy, by small administrative, regulatory and prosecutory agencies.[2]

By the same token, the historic functions of government — physical protection of persons and property, development of natural resources, financial management, local services — have been carried out with a more or less constant and by no means overwhelming share of the social product. True enough, some of these, particularly education, have received new emphasis and additional resources in recent years. But the massive extension in the size of the public sector witnessed in this century has been occasioned by efforts to confront the problems of national security and social distress. Of course, demands are placed upon government for all manner of other things as well: subsidies for the arts, recreation, clean air and water, to name a few.

SECURITY PROBLEMS

Take national security issues. For over a quarter of a century now, between 6 and 11 percent of the gross national product (GNP) has been allocated directly to national defense; it is now declining from a Vietnam high of some 9.5 percent. This amounts to about 29 percent of federal spending. These proportions can be manipulated — and often are — depending on the point one wishes to make: It has been claimed that as much as 70 percent of all federal expenditures bears some relationship to national security expenses if debt accumulated during wartime veterans' programs, and mutual security activities are included as well as direct military support programs.[3]

Consider social distress. Since the 1930s, any number of public programs have been instigated to lessen individual risks with respect to all sorts of actual or potential calamities. Government has established public

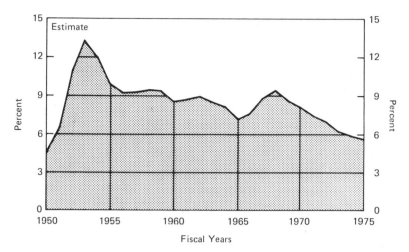

Figure 11-3.   Defense Outlays as a Percent of GNP. *Source: Budget of the United States Government, Fiscal Year 1975, p. 61.*

insurance schemes insuring: depositors in banks and savings and loan associations as well as American investors overseas; farmers against crop loss; financial institutions against defaults on housing and educational loans; veterans, who may purchase life insurance very cheaply; industries, which are protected from foreign competition in various ways through tariffs, quotas, and surcharges; industries, by means of tax advantages reducing the risk of doing business; workers, who receive limited insurance against unemployment; the elderly, whose incomes are insured through social security and Medicare; and the poor, who are assisted through public welfare and other programs. The public's safety is further insured through laws as diverse as traffic regulations and food and drug acts. The conduct of public business is to a very large extent all about *security,* either the physical security of the nation as a collectivity through national defense or the physical and financial security of the individual through police protection and insurance schemes of all sorts.[4]

Each generation faces different issues of security. But, however different the political issues of the contemporary period are, they share at least one feature with those of all other ages: They are complex, profoundly important, and in some degree intractable. Fully successful governments are rare; indeed, from somebody's point of view *all* governments are incompetent, biased, or debased. The existence of varying ideas on what the issues before the community "really" are, or should be, means that even the most efficient and enlightened governments, cannot escape a certain

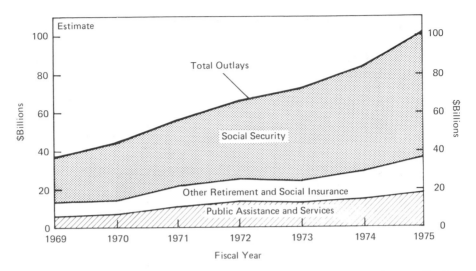

Figure 11-4.   Income Security Outlays by Federal Government. *Source: Budget of the United States Government, Fiscal Year 1975,* p. 126.

measure of public rage, contempt, and disappointment. The elimination of *relative* poverty, for example, by definition entails a redistribution of income. This necessity does not, and perhaps should not, disturb most serious advocates of greater income equality in America. But it is predictably disturbing to those who believe that their current tax burden is unconscionably high and that the progressive income tax is an attack upon the traditional American values of independence and self-reliance. The point is that almost any issue cuts at least two ways and many more besides in our complex society. Inflation, energy problems, the status of women, educational quality, health costs, environmental pollution, poverty, racial conflict, unemployment, urban decay, crimes against persons and property, terrorism and civil disobedience, prison conditions, population pressures, clogged courts, regional wars, the arms race, the balance of payments, the credibility of government, corruption of public officials — all these and more are said to be the unprecedented crises, piling one on another, that confront America today.

Some of these (and other) problems are remediable in varying degrees. All are real problems, and our political system has made efforts, however inadequate in the eyes of critics, to cope with them. To establish effective control over them requires powerful, competent, well-organized political institutions. And of course some matters defy solution. It is

Jobless men and women line up at a New York unemployment office to file claims. Unemployment has become an increasingly widespread problem confronting Americans in this decade. *Russell Reif/Pictorial Parade*

obscurantism of the worst sort to demand a rollback in the power of government and at the same time berate the political authorities for not devoting additional resources to social welfare.[5]

POLITICAL DEMANDS

So there is little mystery attached to the question "Why has our government gotten bigger and bigger?" Various individuals and groups have made claims upon the polity for the allocation of resources. Whether particular claims have arisen from pressing needs generated by the dislocations of social change, from the impulses of ostensibly generous ideologies, or from something else is an interesting question. From the point of view of those who staff and command the polity, an academic explanation of the origin of political demands is always less important than their existence and whether or not they can be coped with. Of course, the assessment of a specific political need — how genuine it is, how perva-

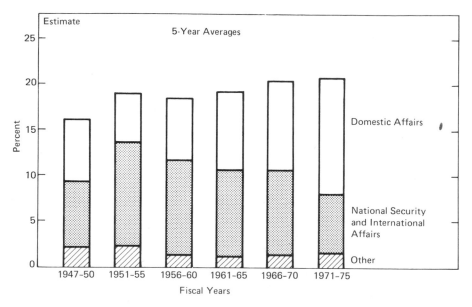

Figure 11-5.   Federal Budget Outlays as a Percent of GNP. *Source: Budget of the United States Government, Fiscal Year 1975,* p. 54.

sively it is held in the community, how deeply it is felt by those concerned — varies with the interests, ideologies, and responsibilities of the politician or bureaucrat who is called upon to act, react, or "solve" the problem. Widely held demands are sometimes passed off as emanating from a few agitators only. On the other hand, the demands of a vocal few may be interpreted as those of whole social types — youth, middle America, "the media."

It is instructive to read any debate in the Senate or House of Representatives over legislation involving a value or relationship of political importance. The participants in the debate almost always either *understate* or *overstate* the social consequences of proposed legislation. Thus, many southern senators during the early and mid-1960s, asserted that demands for civil rights legislation emanated from a few fanatics, agitators, or misguided and sentimental do-gooders seeking to coerce the community into changing its long-established and democratic social and political patterns. The extent to which the civil rights movement actually reflected the deeply felt aspirations of large numbers of Americans is now of course widely conceded.

On the other hand, proponents of the Civil Rights Act of 1964 (and of

1965) frequently understressed what they were in fact about, namely, the fundamental and permanent transformation of racial and class relations in the United States. To have been entirely candid about the revolution they were proposing might have alienated potential supporters who could be made to believe that the whole question was merely one of a few intransigent southern politicians intent upon denying black citizens a few inconsequential legal rights. In this particular case the consequences of the legislation were not so dramatic as the advocates had perhaps hoped, but in very important ways the economic opportunities, political influence, and social position of millions of black citizens have been improved. Here again the powers of the federal government were extended significantly to control and regulate social relations.

Expansion of the polity can proceed, thus, in many nonphysical ways. A duly enacted law may expand state power by (1) giving support to citizens and officials who want to do what the law requires but who have been deterred from doing so by local values and practices; (2) providing a legal threat which those who benefit from the law may use to encourage the compliance of potential violators; (3) encouraging everyone to accept, over time, the legal statement as the proper or natural way of doing things.[6]

If the law is eventually assimilated into the moral code of the community, social convention and formal requirements become one and the same. In this event, how are we to speak of the scope of government? Has the state gotten larger or smaller? Or have polity and society merged so that they are no longer distinguishable? Perhaps we should leave these questions to the philosophers and turn our attention to the social forces that have in our day, either transparently or plausibly, produced a measurable increase in the size of the American polity.

JUSTIFYING PUBLIC ACTIVITY, GOODS, AND SERVICES

In the minds of many Americans, governmental bureaucrats are thought to be unproductive, self-seeking, and expansionistic. This view is not entirely incorrect, although the criticism applies with the same force to nongovernmental workers as well. Nonetheless, it is far from the whole truth: Many public officials are productive and efficient by any reasonable standard, and some are even occasionally self-abnegating in their work. Skeptical attitudes toward government abound. Not only are Americans traditionally suspicious of government; they have tended to look askance at those not directly involved in the *competitive* production or sale of things of physical value. The view that the business of America is business is by no means obsolete. Public employees do not, for the most part, produce goods and services that can be bought or sold efficiently in the marketplace. The most important reasons are mentioned below.[7]

Population Increase

The Census Bureau concluded its constitutionally required 1970 census with the publication of millions of facts about millions of Americans. There were now some 215 million people in the United States. Each new citizen who survives beyond infancy will inevitably place demands upon educational, health care, transportation, sanitation, safety, and other public services. The economist Barbara Ward has suggested that, just as responsible parents of an expanding family defer expenditures on less essential amenities in favor of increased expenditures for education, insurance, housing, health, and so forth, so will politicians, faced with a deluge of new citizens, commit greater community resources to similar ends and away from less important consumer goods.[8] By the mid-1970s a declining birth rate in the United States held out some hope that the population would stabilize in the early twenty-first century. Demographic projections, however, are notoriously unreliable, and it is too soon to know whether demands for social services would stabilize even with population stability. The point is that young families require not only housing — financed largely by themselves but with varying degrees of public assistance — but streets, water, sewage systems, police and fire protection, hospitals, education, and other publicly provided amenities which, notes Ward, "help to turn four walls and a roof into a functioning unit in a civilized community."[9]

Not only must this new social capital and services for new people be formed but the social capital that inevitably deteriorates over the years must be replaced. Moreover, the social services may have to be augmented to offset consumption deferred during austere periods (the Great Depression, World War II).

The Income Effect on Levels of
Public Activity

As the American people have as a whole become more affluent, they have demanded more goods and services of all kinds, from both public and private institutions. This so-called **income effect** is self-explanatory and very important. It does not, however, explain the fact that the demand for publicly provided goods and services has increased at a faster rate than the demand for privately provided goods and services. In 1902, for example, government spending was 8 percent of GNP. It had risen to 21 percent by 1936, reached an extremely high 52 percent in 1944 (due to the war, of course), and fell back to about 31 percent in 1975 (still high by historic patterns). The impact of increased incomes on the demand for goods and services varies not only with individual tastes and preferences but across income ranges as well.[10]

Interestingly, the greatest effective demand for increases in the public services may come not from the lowest (and certainly not from the highest) income groups but from those in the middle-income strata.[11] For very low-income people, primary concern is not with politics but with survival — with securing food, shelter, and clothing from *existing* patterns of distribution.[12] As incomes rise, however, demands for education, roads, health and sanitation, income protection, recreation, and so forth increase relative to increased demands for the old bare "subsistence" goods and services. Once survival needs are met, energy can be diverted to political actions which, in responsive democracies, may achieve some success. But with still further increases in income the relative (remember: not the absolute) demand for public as opposed to private goods begins to fall. That is, once "satisfactory" levels of public goods have been successfully demanded from the political system (and once taxes necessary to provide them have been imposed), relatively greater demands are made for privately provided amenities of all sorts. You may compose your own list as to what sorts of choices will be (are) made by affluent people. A vacation in Europe may be desired more than an improvement in health care or the local schools. Health and education are not ignored, but other things are wanted as well.

One authority suggests that in the aggregate — that is, putting all the individuals of all income groups together with all their diverse, sometimes contradictory preferences and with their very different degrees of access to political decision-makers — the income effect in the 1960s was virtually constant. As incomes rose, the proportion of "new" income allocated to public and to private goods remained about the same as the proportion of "old" income.[13]

If this is the case, and if the assumptions about the importance of the income effect on demands for public activity across income groups are roughly correct, what about the distribution of decision-making power in America? Other things being equal, there would seem to be a sort of standoff between the groups that want public spending to *increase* proportionally and the groups that prefer a proportionate *decrease* in the public sector. Interesting as this question may be, it is purely speculative. As we know, choices for private and public goods are made in different ways: They are aggregated differently and follow different decision-making rules. Consequently, to understand the way the polity has increased in scale and social importance in this century, we must know a good deal about the rules by which our public choices are made. That is why this book has discussed decision-rules at such length.

Inflation

A characteristic feature of the economy for some years now has been **inflation,** the erosion in the purchasing power of money. By the mid-1970s, two-digit inflation had occurred for the first time in memory. Its effects are numerous and, in the view of many (not all) authorities, particularly damaging to the less privileged and economically vulnerable segments of the population (e.g., those on pensions, unorganized workers, small unsubsidized farmers). Another consequence of inflation, however, is that it surreptitiously increases the size of government. The following major effects occur: (1) Individuals whose incomes are increased by employers in order to keep them abreast of inflation are shifted into higher tax brackets. They thereby pay a higher proportion of their incomes in taxes, even though their real incomes have not increased at all. Government has captured a larger portion of community income without *formally* increasing taxes at all. (2) Pressure on always tight public budgets is decreased since government may service its obligations with cheap money, thereby releasing resources for other public activities.

There is no way of knowing precisely how much of government's expansion over time has been facilitated by inflation but, again, the cumulative impact of inflation on the scope of government is undoubtedly

*"Mrs. Dodsworth, I'm happy to report that you
do not have a persecution complex. Everybody's
added costs really are passed on to you."*
Drawing by Alan Dunn; © 1974 The New Yorker
Magazine, Inc.

significant. Confusion is enhanced by the tendency always to attribute government's growth to some specific, plausible cause — say, organized labor's demands for more educational opportunities even though greater educational services were made possible less by such demands than by the increased public revenues made available by inflation. Which factor, trade union demands or inflation, "caused" the public expansion? Clearly, both did. The specific decision to expand education was made by the political authorities over other and competing claims; the opportunity to do so was made possible by inflation.

There is another literature which attributes the growth in the public sector to still other insidious influences. This literature is often serious, just as often self-indulgent and lamenting, and it argues that the increases have occurred at the expense of more socially redeeming purposes. Many sources are cited by various writers as responsible for the alleged misallocation of community resources: the top military, government, and business officials;[14] a governing class;[15] the "military-industrial complex";[16] fear;[17] and biology.[18] There are others; moralizing journalism is a seedbed of alternative theories about who "really" has the power or what "really" determines government decisions.

Public Goods

Government provides certain indivisible benefits to the community, or public goods. The logic underlying this service has been covered previously. What remains to be said is that pure public goods — such as national defense — are rare. More typically, government-supplied goods are "mixed"; that is, they contain both divisible and indivisible benefits. An individual is *privately* advantaged by public education, but the public is advantaged as well; a better-trained, better-informed citizenry is in everyone's interest. Normatively, there are good reasons, therefore, for the government to pay at least for the share of public benefits generated by education. Where the line might be drawn is difficult to say, but the principle is clear. The provision of one public good, national defense, accounts for a large portion of the increased size of government in recent decades. No one can be excluded from national security once it is provided; but no one would "buy" some degree of national security if it were sold on the open market. Only a coercive institution (government) can supply, through its power to tax, whatever benefits accrue from national defense activity. The Department of Defense, the army, the navy, the air force, the military academies, the Veterans' Administration, the Central Intelligence Agency, the National Security Agency are only a few organizations that provide services in this area. The burdens imposed on the community by war and the threat of war have been very great. In 1975, some 29 percent of the federal budget was allocated directly to national defense. Adding other international activities, veterans' programs, and servicing of the national debt (accumulated in large part to pay for wars entered into since 1941) would increase this proportion considerably. The average annual proportion of GNP allocated to defense purchases between 1945 and 1972 was a little less than 9 percent; it rose slightly during the height of the war in Southeast Asia. To say that the Vietnamese war directed resources away from more important projects of social reconstruction at home is not entirely accurate. The fact is, sadly, that the diversion of resources from productive to destructive uses occurred much earlier, roughly in 1951 with the outbreak of the Korean war following a demobilization between 1947 and 1950 when direct defense expenditures fell to about 5 percent of GNP. There are many domestic agencies allocating security which, if not provided by government, will not be provided at all. The reader could compile her or his own list: the Federal Bureau of Investigation, the State Highway Patrol, the city police force, and so on.

Redistribution of Income

If the marketplace distributes income in a pattern unacceptable to the political process, only government can alter existing patterns. *Part* of the job of the Internal Revenue Service is to apply public redistributive policy by administering the tax laws, some of which are progressive. Other agencies that share this task are the Social Security Administration, Medicare, the Department of Housing and Urban Development (in part), the Department of Health, Education and Welfare (in part), and so forth. Subsidy programs of all sorts — in education, agriculture, the maritime industry, public transit — redistribute resources in ways not possible through marketplace decisions. The redistributions are justified by the political process, if not always by arguments for economic efficiency or social justice.

Until well into this century, money incomes of people in America were of two main kinds. First, there was (and is) income from earnings received as workers and proprietors. Second, there was (and is) income from property, in the form of rent, dividends, and interest. In 1929, for example, about three-quarters of all personal income in the United States was earned income, and nearly all the rest (some 23 percent) was income from property. The remaining portion (only about 1 percent) consisted of money income received from national, state, and local government in the form of **transfer payments.**

Over time, the share of transfer payments as a proportion of total personal income has steadily grown. They now constitute some 8 percent of personal income from all sources. For millions of people, recipients of public assistance, veterans' pensions, and social security, the receipt of transfer payments is crucial to their survival.

As much as 30 percent of the total income received by all people sixty-five years old or older is now provided through social security. This amounts to about 5 percent of GNP; public welfare involves some 1.5 percent of GNP. These are by far the largest of the *direct* income-providing programs of government, although there are others: veterans' educational allowances, farmers' subsidies, for example. With respect to some of these programs, such as public welfare, it is relatively easy to determine just who — the needy or the not so needy — are being aided by governmental action. A "means test" certifying that one is needy is required of recipients on public welfare, a program which surely does therefore redistribute income from the taxpayers to the poor. Social security payments to the elderly are less clear in their redistributive effects. Recipients have contributed to the program during their working years, and many elderly people receive both social security income and income from investments and other pension schemes that remove them from any reasonable category of need.

Or consider agricultural subsidies. Payments in this area are made not on the basis of need but on the basis of crops grown. Both poor and rich farmers grow cotton, rice, wheat, tobacco, peanuts, and other subsidized crops. The more affluent farmers get a larger proportion of the subsidy than the smaller farmers, merely because they have more land under cultivation. Incidentally, nearly everyone agrees that agricultural subsidies are probably inefficient social policy; they have recently been reduced in some cases or eliminated.

Veterans' educational allowances may or may not be redistributive, depending on how one views them. If they are payments for services rendered, they are not redistributive but merely part of the government's wage bill.

Figuring out the net redistributive impact of government action is very difficult, especially because much governmental **assistance** is **in kind**, not in money. The maintenance of educational institutions is a case in point. It has been argued that state universities provide subsidized education to the affluent, who enroll, at the expense of less wealthy taxpayers, who do not.[19] This assertion is true at one level. However, since many more poorer students are now attending college than in the past, higher education may turn out to redistribute income from the affluent to the poor over time — that is, across generations. In other words, the impact of governmental programs cannot be viewed in static terms alone.

Such analytic problems make it impossible to state precisely the net effect of government on the distribution of income.[20] Some programs redistribute income from the poor to the rich and some from the rich to the poor. And redistribution takes place within income groups as well. But clearly the government does serve in some degree to redistribute resources from the better off to the less well off. The poor would be poorer still without governmental assistance.

Apart from personal income taxes, we do not know just how the tax burden is distributed among income groups. Corporation taxes, for example, may be shifted to workers (lower wages), consumers (higher prices), stockholders (lower dividends), or to some combination of these. Property taxes and sales taxes are proportionate across income groups only if the same proportion of everyone's income is spent on taxed goods. This is not the case (the poor spend more of their income on untaxed food than the rich, and the rich, because they save, spend a smaller proportion of their income on taxed commodities than the poor). We cannot go further into these complex matters here except to reiterate that the problem of determining who really pays for and who really benefits from public programs continues to bedevil political economists.

The problem is compounded in that public decisions have secondary effects which also influence the distribution of values in society. Consider one example: A public housing authority may allocate $5,000,000 raised through taxation to provide housing for 500 people. Mere knowledge about the taxpayers who supplied the resources and the individuals who received the housing is not enough to answer the question "Who gets what and who pays for it?" One would need to know, among other things, the impact of the public housing on the schools, libraries, transportation systems, and quality of life in the community where it is situated. Local property taxes might need to be increased to provide additional school classrooms, sewer lines and treatment plants, and community amenities, for instance. The increased use of environmental impact reporting, which seeks to answer such questions before a project is approved, may improve our social accounting and induce public officials to be more aware of the full range of costs and benefits associated with their decisions.

Regulation of Monopolies

Natural monopolies — natural gas lines, telephone service, electrical power, some transportation systems, for example — are not subject to market competition and hence would be able, if not controlled by government, to restrict production and set prices by arbitrary decisions. Monopolies in any sector of the economy would have the same power. The Interstate Commerce Commission, the Federal Reserve Board, the Federal Power Commission, the Federal Trade Commission, the Federal Communications Commission, the Securities and Exchange Commission, the Civil Aeronautics Board, and the Antitrust Division of the Justice Department function in whole or in part to regulate or prevent monopolies and other practices in restraint of trade, in industry, commerce, and finance. Similar organizations exist at the state level.

External Costs and Benefits

Some decisions taken by private individuals have effects on people who were not consulted in the decision-making process. Buyers and sellers of automobiles impose costs in the form of air pollution on others in the community. Manufacturers may damage others by discharging wastes into rivers and streams. A municipality may reduce the water quality of a city downstream by maintaining an inefficient sewage treatment plant. If these external costs are to be taken into account, it must be done by government. Those who impose external costs on others will not mend their ways unless they are induced or coerced to do so. For example, taxes can be adjusted until they alter their behavior, or fines and jail terms can be levied against them if it is illegal. In either case, government's involvement in society is increased by efforts to "internalize" such costs (i.e., to consider the full costs associated with various decisions, not just those that go into the establishment of market prices).

The same reasoning applies to external benefits not supplied in optimum amounts by private markets. The social benefits of good city planning may not be considered by private developers. Integrated and balanced transportation systems bestow benefits which private markets either cannot do or have not done. Governments often intervene in such areas in order to capture and allocate benefits that would not otherwise exist.

Furthermore, modern governments manage activities which it has been decided should be *insulated* from the rigors of marketplace competition. The price of labor, for example, can in fact be established through market forces the same way prices are established for divisible physical goods. The political process, however, has restrained these forces with regard to labor. Minimum wage laws, collective bargaining, and other requirements protect some portion of American labor from the free play of market conditions.[21]

Such diverse agencies as local zoning commissions, state planning agencies, the Environmental Protection Agency, the National Labor Relations Board, and the Children's Bureau all seek, in one degree or another, to consider the full costs associated with public and private decisions. So do some natural resource agencies — the Corps of Engineers, the Bureau of Reclamation, the Tennessee Valley Authority, for example. The latter agencies are or have often been assigned tasks when the job in view was too risky or too large or the amortization period too long to attract private capital. To obtain the most benefits possible, government involvement is altogether sensible as long as the costs incurred are not excessive and more meritorious projects are not being slighted.

Economic Stability

Since the 1930s, all national administrations have acknowledged responsibility for providing economic stability — that is, for reasonably stable prices, acceptable employment levels, and economic growth.

Demands for stability are among the most pressing of all on political decision-makers. The economic nightmare of the 1930s lingers in the consciences and family histories of millions of people. The prospect of unemployment is altogether frightening. The specter of inflation is an acute concern to those who see their incomes and savings eroded by rising prices.

To control the economy, government maintains agencies to keep tabs on economic performance. Statistical sections in the Commerce and Labor and Treasury departments, the Census Bureau, the Federal Reserve Board, the Council of Economic Advisers (CEA), and the Office of Management and Budget (OMB) monitor economic activity. The "troika" (Treasury, CEA, OMB) share responsibility for recommending compensatory action when economic stability is threatened. Other less obvious agencies also provide stability and assist in growth: the Federal Home Loan Board and the Federal Deposit Insurance Corporation, for example.

The *techniques* chosen to maintain or restore stability usually involve expanded governmental control over society; entire new institutions have been created or grafted onto existing ones in efforts to control the economy. Taxes and subsidies can be adjusted to stimulate or dampen demand; interest rates are manipulated; bonds are offered at attractive rates; "jawboning" (appeals to business and labor on price and wage policy) is tried; variations in public expenditures are made; antitrust laws may be extended or more adequately enforced; industries may be nationalized; or direct wage and price controls may be imposed.

Demands for stability are so pervasive and unrelenting that government would try just about anything, whatever its alleged political principles, to rein in an economy lurching out of control. Not that governmental effort, however strenuous, can necessarily "solve" all economic problems. In a world of scarce, even diminishing, resources it manifestly cannot.

Many of the activities described in connection with attempts to redistribute income (welfare, social security, subsidies, tax schemes, and so forth) serve as well to stabilize the business cycle. Income maintenance programs, by guaranteeing people some level of income (unemployment insurance is a good example) can help ease the anguish created by a business slowdown, rising unemployment, and reduced government revenues. Policies to redistribute income may bear on policies to maintain economic stability. The obverse is also true.

Housekeeping and the Public Domain

Certain central governmental agencies provide services for, and surveillance over, the operating agencies of the government. The General Services Administration, the Government Accounting Office, the Civil Service Commission, the Office of Management and Budget build and maintain physical facilities (GSA), audit agency expenditures (GAO), recruit staff for agency positions (CSC), and review agency budgets, programs, management systems and proposed legislation (OMB).

Natural resource agencies — the Department of the Interior, the Forest Service, the Bureau of Land Management, for example — manage the public domain. Most of their activities are managed through nonmarket agencies: "Collecting taxes, granting licenses, enforcing laws and regulations, keeping records, operating the courts, carrying on diplomacy clearly are not directly productive of things which have value in the sense that one could put a price tag on them, even though they have indirect value because production and commerce could not flourish — perhaps not continue — without them."[22]

Society and Bureaucracy

It is one thing to say that government *should* respond to needs generated by larger populations, or supply public goods in appropriate degree, or redistribute income, or regulate monopolies, or internalize external costs and benefits, or stabilize the economy, or manage the public domain efficiently. It is quite another to suggest that governments do such things because they find it either nice or necessary. Governments enter into these matters less for reasons of logic than for reasons of politics. External threats and the rise to political influence of the organized working class, newly empowered ethnic minorities, mass middle-class "public interest" movements (e.g., conservation, consumer, and peace groups), and business and trade associations have all contributed to new demands being placed upon the polity. Many traditionally quiescent interests have become increasingly well organized, self-conscious, and politically skillful. Their claims upon society frequently involve an extension of state activity. Organized labor has favored increased expenditures in the fields of education, health, pensions, and the social services generally. Ethnic minorities have sought an expanded polity by calling for enhanced support in the areas of welfare, job and career training, compensatory education, and improved local services (e.g., public safety, sanitation, transportation, housing). Conservation groups have demanded more governmental surveillance of the environment and comprehensive control over private action affecting the environment and the exploitation of natural resources. Consumer advocates have urged the creation of new and powerful governmental agencies to protect the interests of consumers, to ensure product safety. Major public action on these demands does not always occur; but sometimes it does. All the small accretions of governmental expansion over time have combined to enlarge the polity significantly, especially in the last half-century.

Bureaucracies, therefore, not only provide collective or merit goods of the sort described above which are consumed by very broad sectors of society. Modern society consists of specialized parts, and the political interests in the community are just as diverse. The pluralistic nature of American society is reflected in the programs undertaken by government and in the size and composition of the bureaucracies that carry them out. All sectors of public administration are affected — including the sectors charged with providing public goods. (The police in some areas are known to distribute their powers differentially, for instance.)

Interest Groups and Bureaucracy

However, the importance of narrow interest groups in shaping the bureaucracy is more obvious in other areas, as in the regulatory field, for example. Although the practice appears to be weakening, agency heads have normally had, before assuming office, close and supportive affiliations with the groups they are charged to regulate. The American Medical Association is listened to attentively when the post of assistant secretary for health and scientific affairs in HEW is to be filled. Scientific elites, through the National Science Board, have wielded an effective veto over the appointment of the director of the National Science Foundation. The American Bar Association's role in "clearing" presidential appointments to the Supreme Court has been influential on many occasions. The secretary of the interior is usually from west of the Mississippi; the attorney general is always a lawyer; the secretaries of labor, commerce, and treasury are always individuals known to be sympathetic to the dominant members of their new constituencies.[23] Interestingly enough, the association between the types of bureaucrats who staff particular agencies and the publics with which they deal is even closer as one *descends* the typical agency hierarchy.[24]

Under and assistant secretaries usually come from more limited social and political backgrounds than do cabinet secretaries. As Seidman notes, "Sub-Cabinet appointments tend to mirror the diverse clientele groups, dependencies such as defense contractors, construction companies, educational institutions, and professional organizations which constitute an agency's constituency."[25] For example, among President Nixon's first appointments were David Packard, deputy secretary of defense and former chief executive of a major defense contractor, the Hewlett-Packard Co.; Russell E. Train, undersecretary of the Interior Department and former president, Conservation Foundation; J. P. Campbell, undersecretary of agriculture and former commissioner of agriculture in Georgia; Robert Siciliano, undersecretary of commerce and former president, Pacific Maritime Association; Charles P. Walker, undersecretary of the Treasury and former vice-president of the American Bankers Association. At the assistant secretary level, the tendency is just as marked, if not more so. To cite but one example, the original assistant secretaries in the Department of Agriculture in the Nixon administration included a former vice-president of the U.S. Feed Grains Council, a former dean of agriculture at Michigan State University, and a former director of agriculture for the state of California.[26] No doubt such appointments are meant in part to reassure major political interests that decisions which harm them will not be made or that, whatever happens, room at the conference table has been reserved for someone who speaks for them. There is more than symbolism to it, however. Not only do political executives with "appropriate" backgrounds reduce anxiety but they also represent real and powerful interests who seek more than emotional therapy.

Political interests are insinuated into the bureaucracy in order to achieve, maintain, or extend material advantages. In some cases the values of business enterprises are accepted in agencies that depend upon the good will of the business community. The Federal Housing Authority (FHA) — which provides a main mechanism Americans can use to become homeowners — has apparently followed the success standards of private home mortgage finance institutions. By pursuing a policy of minimizing defaults on guaranteed loans (an objective it has achieved), the FHA has been led to neglect the housing needs of the poor — not because they were poor but because, being poor, they were bad credit risks. The result should surprise no one: FHA officials have the goal of business efficiency and do not conceive of themselves as soldiers in the war against poverty.[27]

The Forest Service recruits its professional personnel from the universities' schools of forestry, which, to a remarkable extent, share the same understandings and values.[28] The multiple-use philosophy of the Forest Service (that its resources should be managed to exploit recreational, aesthetic, industrial, agricultural, and other possibilities at the same time) has proved resistant to those single-minded groups (e.g., some logging interests and some conservation groups) that pressure it to acquiesce in their particular land-use philosophy. The ideological schizophrenia of the Forest Service reflects the nation's cultural schizophrenia toward its resources; it wants exploitation and preservation of the same resource at the same time. Since such conflicts cannot be resolved to everyone's satisfaction, the tensions within the Forest Service as it tries to adjust to contending constituencies are of a permanent character. So too are the tensions of many other agencies.

Consider the Farm Credit Administration, which seeks to assist poor farmers. It cannot follow standard banking requirements involving interest rates, collateral, and so forth. But if it were to violate "sound" banking procedures, it would soon, under the terms of its charter, be insolvent and able to help no one. The Office of Education in HEW endeavors, on the one hand, to make low-interest loans available to needy students; if its terms are unconventionally generous ("pay us back whenever you like"), the repayment rate will suffer and the pool of financial and political resources necessary for the program may dry up. The Office of Economic Opportunity's criterion of "maximum feasible participation" of the poor was established to help the poor develop community programs and institutions; resulting inefficiencies damaged it politically.[29] Public works programs designed to stimulate the economy may go not to the communities with the greatest need but to those with the expert staffs who have produced well-designed proposals.

Virtually all public agencies must adjust to this pushing about. Sometimes a final agency decision is biased toward a professional interest — engineers in the case of public works projects; lawyers in the case of the regulatory agencies; bankers in the case of government loans, insurance, and finance; scientists in the case of research programs; doctors in the case of public health. Sometimes the bias is directed crudely toward a powerful external entity, such as an important business interest — an aircraft manufacturer, a railroad company, an agricultural interest group.

Allocating Public Goods

The net result of the multiplicity of interests directed at public decision-making and administration is the American bureaucracy as we find it: a pluralistic, tenuously organized coalition of entities, which vary so greatly in resources, activity, sentiment, and scale that only the most heroic generalization can encompass it.[30] As someone once said, the only thing American civil servants have in common is the color of their paychecks.

Thus, the provision of public goods, transfers, and stability is not a neutral business. Perhaps it should not be, a view argued by many sophisticated political theorists.[31] After all, the robust activity of special interests offers useful avenues through which individual needs can be heard, other avenues of making needs known being exceedingly cumbersome (as elections) or unreliable (as when matters are left to the good will of the decision-maker). An insight into the sheer number of *formal national* organizations in America is available in the 1,467 pages of Volume I, *National Organizations of the United States* of the *Encyclopedia of Associations*.[32] They range from the Abrasive Grain Association to the Zirconium Association among trade, business, and commercial organizations; from the Chicago Area Agricultural Advertising Association to the Wool Associates of the New York Cotton Exchange among agricultural organizations and commodity exchanges; from the International Association of Industrial Accident Boards and Commissions to Women in Public Service among governmental, public administration, military, and legal organizations; from the Acoustical Society of America to the Society of Systematic Zoology among scientific, engineering, and technical organizations; from the Society for Academic Achievement to the International Christian Youth Exchange among educational and cultural organizations; from the Actors Fund of America to the YWCA among social welfare organizations; from the American Board of Abdominal Surgery to the Water Pollution Control Federation among health and medical organizations. This is without mentioning any organizations in the public affairs, veterans, fraternal, foreign interest, nationality, and ethnic fields, or any religious or labor associations.

In a society as complex and noisy as ours, great effort, cohesive organization, access to the mass media, and sophisticated leaders are required for an interest to be heard above the din of contending bids and claims. The "tracks" of successful groups can be found in the programs, budgets, staffs, and authority of the agencies of government.

Political tactics that seem odd or extreme can often be understood as efforts to attract the attention of political authorities — policy-making bureaucrats as well as elected officials — preoccupied as they are with bringing order out of the surrounding chaos and unable to listen to everyone at once. Moreover, there is every personal incentive to listen closely only to groups that are seen (by the politician or bureaucrat, not by the detached scholar, agitated social critic, or ideological journalist) to be politically relevant in the short run. Groups given to sermonizing rather than to organizing and strategic thinking are rarely taken seriously in America. All of these forces are part of the very fabric of the bureaucracy. The character of the bureaucracy and that of the society are near mirror images.

Nor is the picture a static one. As society changes, so does the bureaucracy. As old forces and interests fade from social relevance, the bureaucratic entities charged with ministering to them are hived off from the center of political concern. The declining agency may hang on in a formal sense while budgetary decisions deplete its effectiveness, or it may get shoved down the bureaucratic hierarchy by a decision to reorganize, or it may lose its distinctiveness altogether by a merger of its collapsing functions with those of some more vigorous bureaucratic unit.[33]

It is not entirely true that, once established, bureaucracies go on forever. They go on only as long as some external social impetus makes decision-makers maintain them. Nostalgia, tradition, and inertia exist in the political system, just as elsewhere. But American policy-makers are not famous as sentimentalists. They rarely shrink from taking resources from a politically declining program and diverting them to where the claims are louder or more intense. It should be clearly understood that the relationships between government agencies and social interests are frequently so concrete as to be formally institutionalized; we are not speaking of amorphous relationships that are merely assumed. In fact, most significant federal agencies (and some insignificant ones as well) which dispense federal funds have formal (but unofficial) lobbies in the centers of final decision (the Office of Management and Budget, the White House, the Congress). The National Association of Soil and Water Conservation Districts can be counted on to take up any struggle on behalf of the Soil Conservation Service; the National Reclamation Association does the same for the Bureau of Reclamation; the Rivers and Harbors Congress protects the interests of the Corps of Engineers; and the National Education Association is normally in alliance with the Office of Education. Indeed, agencies sometimes seek to establish favorable organized groups where none existed; the Department of Agriculture's fostering of the Farm Bureau is a case in point. These relationships between bureaucracy and clientele group are apparent throughout the entire structure of government, in virtually all agencies and concerning all programs.

Agencies that allocate generalized public goods are less able to encourage the organization of their beneficiaries to effectively support their activities than are agencies with specific, tangible, divisible benefits to bestow upon selected beneficiaries. Even the military, which is often alleged to play the political game astutely, is not immune. Defense contractors and the service associations (the Navy League, the Air Force Association, for example) organize to advance the interests of their respective components of the national security establishment. But the larger clientele — the public as a whole — cannot be mobilized effectively because of the familiar problem of free riders and public goods. The National Park Service must make its facilities available to all citizens, but its broad constituency is never fully mobilized. A fire department must respond to all alarms, not just to those of members of some group interested in the quality of fire protection. It is relevant to observe in this connection that high-quality fire protection is ensured not by the political influence of groups sympathetic to the mission of fire departments but by the monetary interests of the fire insurance underwriters. If quality declines, fire insurance rates go up. And consumer protection agencies, to cite a final example, are notoriously incapable of generating sustained large-scale external support.[34]

The Advocacy Function

Agencies are advocates; anyone who fails to understand that fact will fail to understand how public choices are made in America. Before the Congress or the presidency undertakes to advance or amend major policy proposals, the bureaucrats who best know the issues involved must, out of sheer prudence, be consulted. To readers who have not personally observed high-level administrative decision processes in the government, we must emphasize how extensive and detailed most bureaucratic reviews of policy proposals actually are.[35] If analysis fails to meet the idealized standards of truly comprehensive and integrated decision-making norms, the product is nonetheless frequently impressive. It is not, however, disinterested. While the norms of the civil servant and the scientific scholar are much alike — each aspires formally to precision, objectivity, and truth — neither quite reaches such standards. And the bureaucrat, much more than the scientist, is a person of the world. The bureaucrat is, at high levels, invariably caught up in the issues of the age, exposed to the raucous claims of contending interests, disputatious politicians, and the prying and impertinent media. Moreover, all bureaucrats have policy preferences of their own which they seek to advance. They also have their own careers to think about: Will an expansion in their agency's mission create a new bureau which one of them might head? If the new proposals are defeated, will the hated assistant secretary move on and a more pliable personality be appointed? The bureaucrat would be less than human if his or her decisions were not influenced by the question: How will this policy affect me — my values, power, future?

Implementing Policy

From the perspective of the political system's constitutional officers — members of congress, the president, the Supreme Court — it is clearly one thing to have the legal power to enunciate a policy and quite another thing to implement it. The gap between the policy positions of elected policy-makers and their achievements in office is due to many factors, of course: Resources, even when used efficiently, are not equal to the task at hand; old intentions get forgotten and new and contradictory ones take their place; the achievement of one promised policy makes others absurd or impossible. But suppose the formal policy-makers have (1) clear and consistent policy intentions which they are determined to realize, (2) command over sufficient material resources to make that determination effective, and (3) constitutional or other legal authority to act. In American political life, such conditions alone will not enable us to predict whether the policy-makers' intentions will be pursued and implemented.

The reason is not difficult to fathom: Political decisions rely for their implementation upon human beings (bureaucrats) who are very much like the authors and readers of this book. They are themselves engaged in making strategic calculations in a more or less uncertain environment. They have personal preferences and politically applicable resources. The success of formal policy-makers in securing their objectives requires cooperation from the often faceless civil servants who staff the executive branch of government. Their control over information, their job security, their ability to obstruct, delay, reinterpret, "play the waiting game" all combine to make them full partners in any effort to implement public policy.

Consequently, the relationship among the decisions of policy-makers, the response of bureaucrats, and the achievement or failure of policy objectives is an important practical topic not only for academics but for politicians and administrators as well.[36]

To reiterate: The starting point is the realization that the "government" is not a monolithic, homogeneous entity at all but a social creation that is nearly as complex, contentious, and contradictory as the society that produced it. At one level, this is not a unique insight; everyone is aware of the constitutional separation of powers, checks and balances, and federalism. Nor need we be reminded that our political institutions — Congress, the judiciary, state legislatures — contain personalities of conflicting social preferences. For some poorly understood reason, however, we tend not to recognize that the same social pluralism that produces fragmentation in all other political institutions in America also produces (and sustains) pluralism in public bureaucracies. Depending upon one's interests and political philosophy, this may be either a deeply frustrating or a profoundly reassuring fact of life.

What are the implications for public policy? (1) It is not always enough to win a favorable formal decision from the constitutional authorities; one must have it implemented as well, and thus still further decisions must be won from the bureaucracy. (2) By the same token, a case lost before the formal political authorities does not always signal the end of the game; there may be a chance of retrieving the situation in the administrative arena.

ADMINISTRATIVE
DECISION-MAKING

We have now considered how an individualistic approach to government might justify certain types of government activity. Only government can supply most public goods, or redistribute income, or consider *all* the important effects of private action, or achieve economic stability, or regulate monopolies, or administer the public domain, for example. If these things are not done by government, or if they are done in insufficient degree, a misallocation of scarce resources will result. A misallocation will also occur, of course, if government's involvement in such matters is too great. The optimal, or most efficient, level of government activity is difficult or impossible to state precisely but is always a goal to be sought.

Yet government mirrors society with all of its diverse interests and conflicts. The political process, not an abstract view of what government "ought" to do, or would do if things were in proper working order, determines what government will do in fact. Thus, it would be purely coincidental if what the government did in fact resembled what an individualistically based normative model asserts that government should do.

This book presumes that government officials are concerned less with social efficiency, or the general good, than with maximizing their personal welfare. Efficiency or general welfare may be the *consequence* of official decision-making but it is not the usual motivation. From a practical point of view, it is critical that means are provided for aligning the self-interests of public officials with the aspirations and needs of persons in the society. This matching of self-interests is a much more important technique for achieving responsive government than is railing against the untrustworthiness of public officials. The actual calculations made by officials in the executive branch in recommending, making, or applying public policy and the decision-rules they follow are, therefore, very important concerns.

Administrative Rule-Making

This book has stressed the role of decision-rules in guiding behavior and in allocating goods and services and power and legitimacy in the political system. The point must now be reiterated concerning the rules, both formal and informal, that guide bureaucratic behavior. Contrary to some modern authorities, we have emphasized the traditionally understood importance of *formal* rules in the policy process (e.g., the Constitution, its interpretation by the judiciary, rules governing elections, the internal rules of Congress). American public officials are controlled, of course, by the Constitution, by statutory law, and by the Code of Federal Regulations which they both promulgate and obey. The latter is a codification of the general and permanent rules published in the Federal Register by the agencies of the federal government. These rules usually turn out to have the full force of law and, under the law, must be "judicially noted" in court proceedings.[37] The code concerns matters of procedure and substance for those doing business with the federal government and constitutes the administrator's effort to "fill in the gaps" in unavoidably vague statutes passed by Congress and to apply very generally stated laws to specific cases.

Rules of bureaucratic origin can have far-reaching significance. In 1974, to cite just one case, the Office of Civil Rights (OCR) in the Department of Health, Education and Welfare proposed new regulations concerning sex discrimination in the nation's schools and universities. The OCR asserted that the rules would implement the less precise amendments to the Education Act passed by Congress in 1972. OCR's rules would bar sex discrimination of almost any kind in public schools and in public and private universities under threat of court action or the cutting off of federal funds. Sexual discrimination in school admissions would be barred; schools would have to conduct annual surveys to find out what sports students wanted to participate in, so as to provide "comparable" opportunities for both sexes; segregation by sex in class (including courses in physical education but perhaps excluding sex education) would be prohibited; teaching practices that treat children differently by sex (e.g., male versus female spelling bees) would be ruled out; rules for men's and women's dorms would be the same. OCR did refrain from requiring a purge of "sex stereotyping" in textbooks, a general phenomenon we have attempted, as a matter of personal judgment, to avoid in this book. According to the *Wall Street Journal*, "HEW argued that First Amendment prohibitions against interfering with freedom of speech prevented them from tampering with the educational process."[38] This is an interesting example of the way constitutional rules (in this case the First Amendment), statutory rules (1972 amendments to the Education Act), and administrative regulations (those of OCR) interrelate. It also vividly shows the power of bureaucrats in the policy-making process.

Reconciling such bureaucratic power with democratic norms is difficult. Indeed, at least one prominent political scientist views the problem as central to the contemporary "crisis of authority."[39] Trends toward administrative discretion (and hence power) have been justified on several grounds: (1) Only agency specialists can deal intelligently with complex technical problems; (2) the Congress should not be "bogged down" in petty details but should deal with "broad" policy questions; (3) flexibility is increased by allowing administrators to develop rules on a case-by-case basis. In Professor Lowi's view, the result is anomalous: "The more government operates by the spreading of access, the more public order seems to suffer. The more public men pursue their constituencies, the more they seem to find their constituencies alienated."[40] Lowi suggests a remedy: a rule making "invalid and unconstitutional any delegation of power to an administrative agency that is not accompanied by clear standards of implementation."[41] Administrators would still make general rules for society but only in close collaboration with Congress.

Lowi's complaints are only among the most recent in a continuing tradition. Agency rule-making had expanded to such an extent and in the absence of clear guidelines that Congress passed the Administrative Procedures Act of 1946. The act imposed several strictures on administrative power by requiring rule-making agencies to identify themselves, state the legal basis of their authority, publish their procedures and their rules, give interested parties an opportunity to comment before a rule is put into effect, and consider petitions from those who want a change in the rules.

Administrative Rule Adjudication

Not only do the executive agencies make and apply rules; they adjudicate disputes over them as well. This quasi-judicial power is delegated to the agencies by Congress and, in a complex society, is a necessary one. The formal judicial system is unable to accommodate the many and often extremely technical disputes arising in an agency's share of authority (although cases originating before the agencies may eventually enter the judicial system). Moreover, an agency can initiate cases to compel compliance with its rules, a power which the courts do not have (remember: under the Constitution, the judiciary can respond only to cases brought before it). Agencies having quasi-judicial power include administrative courts (such as the Tax Court, Court of Claims, Court of Customs and Patent Appeals); the independent regulatory commissions (especially); some elements in the line departments (such as the Food and Drug Administration in HEW); and department heads (on occasion).

In response to charges that rule adjudication often followed arbitrary procedures established by thinly disguised political partisans, the Administrative Procedures Act of 1946 laid down due process requirements to be followed by the agencies.[42] The act requires (1) that the agency examiners who hear cases be classified civil servants (and thus insulated to some extent against "political" forces in the same manner as judges); (2) that examiners' responsibilities not include investigative or prosecutory functions; and (3) that the hearings be conducted by timely and well-ordered procedures. Under the act, the judiciary's power to review agency decisions was broadened, although it remains true that, normally, court review is limited to questions of procedure and not substance.

Coping with Uncertainty

Uncertainty is the bureaucrat's chief problem. Job, reputation, and agency budget are always at risk in an environment that often resists control. Antagonistic forces, actual or potential, threaten to hinder bureaucrats or to eliminate them from the policy arena altogether. Resources are always insufficient to accomplish all their objectives and they can never be sure they have chosen the "best" resource allocation. An effort to maximize individual interests and gain control over a hostile or indifferent environment normally leads, as stated in Chapter 2, to an effort to maximize their agency's budget.[43] This effort is well understood by the central staff agencies (especially OMB) and by Congress.[44] It is in fact required by the logic of the situation; the reviewing authorities would not know how to approach their tasks if other expectations were involved.

The net consequence for society of agency advocacy is not a settled matter. As noted in Chapter 2, Niskanen argues that it produces an *oversupply* of public goods and services. Since elections are blunt instruments for informing politicians about public wants, and since politicians offer obscure policies in any event, public tastes cannot be known through elections.[45] Policy advocacy by bureaucrats does not reflect public tastes accurately either. The congressional committees and subcommittees that review agency budgets are normally staffed by *supporters* of the agencies they review. Moreover, since by far the majority of Americans (excluding the poorest 10 percent and the richest 10 percent) pay about the same proportion of their incomes in taxes (28 percent), public goods and services have a higher marginal value to upper-income groups than to lower-income groups. In Niskanen's opinion, agency advocacy, a sympathetic Congress, a proportional tax rate, and the decision-rule by which Congress usually operates (simple majority rule) combine to benefit the affluent at the expense of the poor. Ironically, this result is often produced by social and political forces self-assertedly aligned with the interests of the poor.

Niskanen's view is not unchallenged. One authority argues that budgets in democracies are "too small" inasmuch as voter/taxpayers and their representatives are keenly aware of costs but not of the full range of benefits which government does or could provide.[46] Others suggest that public budgets are "too big"; voter/taxpayers are aware of the benefits supplied by government but believe (erroneously, because of hidden taxes) that someone else is paying the bill.[47]

The truth is undoubtedly more complex. Some people are more aware of the costs than they are of the benefits of government. Others are well informed on benefits but innocent of the true costs of government activity. Still others have a fairly accurate understanding of both the costs and benefits associated with government. In all cases, individual judgments are approximations at best. The "real" benefits, if any, to the individual from foreign aid or national defense expenditures cannot be closely calibrated.

COSTS AND BENEFITS OF BUREAUCRACY

Governmental agencies are established through the political process to achieve ends which powerful interests deem important. Bureaucracy has certain frequently deplored characteristics: red tape, passing the buck, inflexibility, impersonality, excessive centralization. These traits are real and annoying but do not exhaust the social costs involved in choosing a bureaucracy to achieve desired ends.

The incentives for government bureaucrats to minimize wasting their scarce resources of personnel, materials, and money are not always compelling. The situation is compounded when they have no precise understanding of the objectives they are supposed to advance or, as sometimes happens, when they are expected to advance conflicting aims. The Bureau of Prisons is supposed to provide protective custody of convicted criminals *and* to rehabilitate them; the Council of Economic Advisers is supposed to develop a plan to reduce unemployment *and* maintain price stability; the Forest Service is supposed to protect the recreational values of the national forests *and* allow logging interests access to the forests at the same time. Since many bureaucrats are involved in this confused juggling match, no wonder their means are often deployed inefficiently.

Bureaucracies entail major inequalities. Power is not shared widely but gets concentrated in the hands of those at the top. This "iron law of oligarchy" is among the most ironic political developments of the century. Many of the great bureaucratic organizations involving public education, public health, and social welfare were created at the insistence of political movements whose formal goal was equality of power, status, and income. But hierarchy as a *means* to eliminate inequality has not succeeded; rather it produces inequalities in "dignity, respect, opportunity, education, housing, recreation, leisure, security."[48] Political equality is also undermined by bureaucracy: "The plain fact is, of course, that a leader at the top of a modern hierarchy — corporations, trade unions, government agencies, political parties — tends inevitably to exert more control over government policy than does any one of his subordinates."[49]

Bureaucracies tend to resist external control. Although the president has constitutional authority over the executive agencies, it is not always possible to secure the desired responses. Members of Congress have felt the same frustration in performing their oversight functions. And so have ordinary citizens who find that public officials sometimes act arbitrarily and insensitively with respect to their legitimate interests. The inertia, complexity, size of operations, and power of bureaucracies — plus the inclination of officials to fight against threats to their status, power, and security — make external controls over bureaucracy difficult to effect.

But identifying the costs of bureaucracy is not enough. Bureaucracy bestows great benefits which, without it, would have to be foregone. For example, while bureaucracies may be powerful, they perform within a legal-rational framework that limits the discretion of officials at all levels. Narrowing the range of alternatives an official can consider or act upon exerts a measure of social control. The secretary of defense cannot divert funds from social security to defense, nor can the secretary of agriculture suspend the labor laws.

Bureaucracies also seek consciously to adapt means to ends. If this search never fully succeeds, at least it is undertaken, often with some good results. Most importantly, perhaps, gains can be secured through the division of labor. Decisions in a complex society must be made which are beyond the competence of any single person. It is said that no one entirely understands the postal system or the problems of sending people to the moon. Hence, when there is a need to coordinate large numbers of people and/or to integrate very different skills and specialties, formal organization may be the way to do it. Of course, the imperialistic impulses of bureaucrats themselves or the misplaced faith of some special interests in bureaucratic solutions may account for the growth of bureaucracy, as well as rational assessment of the costs and benefits provided by bureaucracy in any given case.

Whenever a desired social objective is involved, certain alternatives should be considered: What is the most efficient way to achieve the goal being sought? The price system, perhaps by raising or reducing incentives through the tax system? Direct subsidies to some private organization? Contracts with private interests? A joint public-private corporation? Or a government bureaucracy? The facts will determine the "best" answer while politics (which may take the facts at least partially into account) will determine the actual answer.

SUMMARY

Until well into the twentieth century, the major issues that agitated the American polity did not involve large-scale permanent expansion in the size of government. The Revolution, the debate over the Constitution, the extension of voting rights, slavery, nationalism versus regionalism, individual liberties, immigration, and business monopoly did not, however resolved, necessarily require a much larger share of the social product for government.

In our age the situation is reversed. The continuing issues of the social services and national security are in large part conflicts over the physical scope of government. In 1902 all government spending in the United States amounted to less than 8 percent of gross national product (GNP). The percentage had increased to 32 percent by 1975. National defense, space, and veterans' programs accounted for about 25 percent of all government spending (federal, state, and local) in 1975; education comprised some 16 percent, while social security, health, and welfare amounted to 30 percent. Transportation, general government, interest on the public debt, and miscellaneous activities received the rest.

The expansion in the size of government can be explained — or justified — as a response to many forces. Population increases required the deployment of more public goods and services. Rising incomes meant increased demands for more and better services and amenities. Inflation caused considerable growth in the size of government. Effectively mobilized interest groups prevailed upon government for a redistribution of resources. Efforts to cope with the negative spillover effects of private activity (as in the environmental field) and to secure social benefits which private activity does not fully provide (as in transportation or outdoor recreation) enlarged government. So did efforts to stabilize the economy through manipulation of monetary and fiscal affairs.

The institution often chosen to provide public goods and services is bureaucracy. Bureaucrats, however, may be more committed to their personal goals than to the formal-legal goals they are hired to achieve. When, as often happens, budget-maximizing bureaucrats manage to secure resources in excess of what would be provided if more democratic institutions and rules were applied, a strong argument exists for new institutional arrangements aligning the personal interests of political decision-makers with those of the voting/taxpaying public.

As an instrument for achieving social ends, bureaucracy involves the costs of red tape, buck-passing, rigidity, remoteness, and, most importantly, inequalities of control, power, status, and income. But benefits are also secured: large-scale enterprises that could not otherwise be undertaken, advantages from the division of labor, and the conscious adaptation of means to ends.

NOTES

1. Richard Hofstadter, ed., *Ten Major Issues in American Politics* (New York: Oxford University Press, 1968).

2. This point is made nicely in Robert Dahl and Charles E. Lindblom, *Politics, Economics and Welfare* (New York: Harper & Row, 1953), Chapter 1.

3. See, for example, M.A. Robinson et al., "The Scope of the Public Economy," in James Davis, *Politics, Programs, and Budgets* (Englewood Cliffs, N.J.: Prentice-Hall, 1969), p. 6.

4. The implications of individual insecurity for politics at all levels, especially the international, are developed in Harold D. Lasswell, *World Politics and Personal Insecurity,* 3rd ed. (New York: McGraw-Hill, 1970). Mature students in search of exciting reading in the social sciences are urged to consult this book.

5. This point is emphasized in Theodore Lowi, *The End of Liberalism* (New York: Norton, 1969).

6. See Richard M. Johnson, *The Dynamics of Compliance* (Evanston, Ill.: Northwestern University Press, 1967).
7. See Anthony Downs, *Inside Bureaucracy* (Boston: Little, Brown, 1967), pp. 24–31.
8. Barbara Ward, "The Gap Between Social Needs and Public Expenditures," in Terrance A. Almquist and Gary R. Blodick, eds., *Readings in Contemporary American Society* (Englewood Cliffs, N.J.: Prentice-Hall, 1968), pp. 271–272.
9. Ibid., p. 271.
10. See Norman Uphoff and L.L. Wade, "The Paradox of Affluence for Political Development," *Proceedings of the Annual Meeting of the American Political Science Association,* 1971, in which it is suggested that the effective political demand for public expansion begins to slacken in democracies at some point in economic development *before* the welfare state has been extended to all segments of society.
11. For further discussion of this point, see James M. Buchanan, *The Public Finances,* 3rd ed. (Homewood, Ill.: Irwin, 1970), pp. 50–54.
12. This presumption is central to the excellent book by James C. Davies, *Human Nature in Politics* (New York: Wiley, 1963).
13. Buchanan, *The Public Finances,* p. 49.
14. C. Wright Mills, *The Power Elite* (New York: Oxford University Press, 1956).
15. G. William Domhoff, *Who Rules America* (Englewood Cliffs, N.J.: Prentice-Hall, 1967).
16. Sidney Lens, *The Military-Industrial Complex* (London: Kahn & Averill, 1971). Lens writes that "convincing the American people that they ought to spend nine times as much on guns as on human welfare is an act of mesmerism by the military without parallel." Actually, public spending on education, social security, welfare, health, and other "human welfare" programs far exceeds expenditures on the military.
17. Ralph K. White, *Nobody Wanted War* (Garden City, N.Y.: Doubleday, 1968).
18. Robert Ardrey, *The Territorial Imperative* (New York: Atheneum, 1966).
19. W. Lee Hansen and Burton A. Weisbrod, *Benefits, Costs, and Finance of Public Higher Education* (Chicago: Markham, 1969).
20. Efforts to discover the extent of redistribution by comparing the taxes and benefits paid and received by individuals or income groups rest upon assumptions of varying degrees of plausibility. Available studies do provide insights, however; see George A. Bishop, "Income Redistribution in the Framework of the National Income Accounts," *National Tax Journal,* December 1966, pp. 378–390.
21. Unfortunately, the same laws may work to the disadvantage of those who are most exposed: unorganized workers and the unemployed. See Kenneth Boulding, *Conflict and Defense* (New York: Harper, 1962).

22. F. William Howton, *Functionaries* (Chicago: Quadrangle, 1969), p. 124.
23. Harold Seidman, *Politics, Position, and Power* (New York: Oxford University Press, 1970), pp. 102–103.
24. Ibid., pp. 104–107.
25. Ibid., p. 104.
26. Ibid., pp. 104–105. See also Dean E. Mann and Jameson W. Doig, *The Assistant Secretaries* (Washington: Brookings, 1965), and David T. Stanley, Dean E. Mann, and Jameson W. Doig, *Men Who Govern* (Washington: Brookings, 1967).
27. See the report of the National Commission on Urban Problems, *Building the American City* (Washington: Government Printing Office, 1968).
28. Herbert Kaufman, *The Forest Ranger: A Study in Administrative Behavior* (Baltimore: Johns Hopkins University Press, 1960).
29. Daniel P. Moynihan, *Maximum Feasible Misunderstanding* (New York: Free Press, 1969).
30. One heroic effort may be found in W. Lloyd Warner et al., *The American Federal Executive* (New Haven, Conn.: Yale University Press. 1963).
31. A view put most persuasively perhaps by Robert Dahl, *Preface to Democratic Theory* (Chicago: University of Chicago Press, 1956).
32. Detroit: Gale Tower Research, 1970.
33. An effort to develop a systematic understanding of these phenomena is found in Frederick C. Mosher, ed., *Governmental Reorganizations: Cases and Commentary* (Indianapolis: Bobbs-Merrill, 1967).
34. Murray J. Edelman, "Symbols and Political Quiescence," *American Political Science Review*, 54 (September 1960), 695–704; and Edelman, *The Symbolic Uses of Politics* (Urbana: University of Illinois Press, 1964).
35. A case study pointing up the impact of specialists on policy decisions is Ronald J. Terchek, *The Making of the Test Ban Treaty* (The Hague: Nijhoff, 1970).
36. James E. Webb, former administrator of NASA, comments upon the problems of the "political administrator" in his *Space-Age Management* (New York: McGraw-Hill, 1969).
37. 44 U.S.C. 1507.
38. June 19, 1974, p. 3.
39. Theodore J. Lowi, *The End of Liberalism* (New York: Norton, 1969).
40. Ibid., p. 292.
41. Ibid., p. 298. In *Schechter Poultry Corp* v. *United States*, 295 U.S. 495 (1935), the Supreme Court ruled that the Congress could not delegate "unfettered" discretion to the executive. It is the Schechter rule that Lowi suggests should be more stringently applied.
42. An interesting case study of alleged injudicious application of an agency's quasi-judicial authority by one of its employees is William H. Riker, "The National Labor Relations Board Field Examiner," in

Harold Stein, ed., *Public Administration and Policy Development* (New York: Harcourt, Brace & World, 1952).

43. William Niskanen, *Bureaucracy and Representative Government* (Chicago: Aldine, 1971).

44. Aaron Wildavsky, *The Politics of the Budgetary Process* (Boston: Little, Brown, 1964).

45. Niskanen, *Bureaucracy and Representative Government*. Anthony Downs, *An Economic Theory of Democracy* (New York: Harper & Row, 1957), asserts a more important role for elections.

46. Anthony Downs, "Why the Government Budget Is Too Small in a Democracy," *World Politics,* 12 (July 1960), 541–563.

47. James M. Buchanan, *Public Finance in Democratic Process* (Chapel Hill: University of North Carolina Press, 1967).

48. Robert A. Dahl and Charles E. Lindblom, *Politics, Economics and Welfare* (New York: Harper, 1953).

49. Ibid.

12 An Orientation to Further Study in Political Science

It is not unusual for students to choose a major course of study because their interest was piqued by their first course in the subject. Because of the intrinsic excitement and importance of politics, many readers of this volume will undoubtedly continue their inquiry into political matters. For them, and for those who will be pursuing studies in other social sciences, the following discussion may be of assistance. It is not usually necessary to proselytize on behalf of political science, but too often a book fails to alert its readers to the wider context or academic field of which its subject and approach are merely a small part.

This chapter provides, then, a brief orientation to issues in the broad and complex field of political science which will be met at other stages in political investigations. Readers who have come this far should be well prepared to confront these additional issues, if only because they have been studying a not untypical example of the kind of political theorizing and analysis that one must understand and do in the field of political science.

POLITICS, POLITICAL SCIENCE, AND THE POLITICAL SCIENTIST

Everyone awakens to the world as a part of a social group. Individuals find themselves in a world shaped by a structure of power that they did not choose and over which they have little immediate control. The things they can and cannot do are largely determined by the public choices made by others. The political structures, processes, rules, and actors that control their existence may become objects of articulated concern or remain shadowy forces beyond their comprehension. These factors, as they involve the making of public choices, are the primary stuff of politics. The public choices that are made — whether purposeful or accidental, freely chosen or imposed, good or bad, wise or foolish, efficient or wasteful — are the core of the political process. The political life of every person is concerned with learning the requirements prescribed by public choices; adapting personal values and behavior to these requirements; evaluating the goodness, appropriateness, and bindingness of these choices and the state of affairs created by them; and, perhaps, shaping future choices in a manner that is more compatible with wants, interests, and ideals.

People are intensely interested in better understanding and more effectively controlling their destiny. Since the dawn of history, they have sought knowledge about their relations with other persons and the social groups of which they are members. One aspect of the search has come to be known as political science. This branch of learning, which Aristotle called the master science, devotes itself to understanding, describing, and evaluating the substance and process of making decisions which have community-wide impact and thus affect the lives of all community members. The contemporary academic discipline of political science is only a modern variant of the historic search.

The student of politics faces an often bewildering array of factors that influence the making of public choices in any society. A large and frequently confusing vocabulary describes these factors and the relationships among them. The resulting jargon appears to have little to do with the experiences or the needs of the student, who lives in the real world of politics. There is a temptation to agree with Aristotle:

> ... The young are not fit to be students of political science, for they have no experience of life and conduct, and it is these that supply the premises and subject matter of this branch of philosophy. And moreover they are led by their feelings; so

that they will study the subject to no purpose or advantage, since the end of this science is not knowledge but action.[1]

However, the problem may not be so much with the young as with the political scientist. There is a very obvious and intense connection between the everyday experiences of the young and the political world. It is up to the political scientist to reveal that link by making the complex world of politics understandable. To argue that only through experience is it possible to learn of political things is to argue either for a polity controlled by ignorance (most people have limited political experience) or for one in which political participation and power are the prerogatives of the old, experienced, and (perhaps) "wise." These alternatives have not been found attractive in our own age, although we should not underestimate the importance of either ignorance or experience in the political process. In any case, the political scientist has an obligation to make the political events of the ages available to the young so that false turns and blind alleys can be avoided. There is no need for every generation to reinvent the wheel. Thus students can be guided to evaluate their political system in the light of their own values and interests and work toward the goals that most concern them.

Three related goals have been pursued throughout this book. First, a simple and logically coherent schema of analysis was developed to guide the interpretation of political phenomena. Second, this schema was applied to the contemporary American polity and the forces that have shaped, and are shaping, its structures, processes, and choices. Third, and by example, an effort was made to show how ways of thinking about politics enable students to understand the vast amount of political information that impinges upon them in everyday life.

It is appropriate now to place this particular study in its historical context. All contemporary scientific endeavors are dependent upon a historic tradition, and the student needs a basis for evaluating the work at hand. Although political science is one of the most ancient disciplines, it continues to deal with the same classic problems that faced it from the beginning. Its progress has not — for very good reasons — been so dramatic as that of the physical sciences, and scholars often find themselves turning to very old contributions for ways to handle present problems. While we would not think of consulting the medical literature current at the time of James Madison and Thomas Jefferson in the treatment of disease, we do look to such persons and to those who lived much earlier for advice on how we should behave politically.

The political process has been perceived by different thinkers as both a straitjacket and a necessary means for fulfilling aspirations, as the source of the greatest hope for and the greatest threat to the achievement of noble human purposes. This paradox has made politics both the most feared and the most respected of social processes, the object of naive optimism and cynical pessimism.

The Negative State

"Man is born free; however he is everywhere in chains."[2] This classic statement vividly expresses a continuing perspective on the nature of politics. People's choices are limited by the dirty, corrupting, and unjust business of politics. Free expression is impoverished by it. The state uses its vast resources — symbols, authorities, armed might, decision-rules —

"Gotcha!"
Drawing by Dedini; © *1973 The New Yorker Magazine, Inc.*

to destroy natural freedom. People are oppressed, restricted, and debased by the political decisions of the society of which they are a part.

The police officer on the beat, the draft board, the narcotics agent, the tax collector, and the judge are often cited by social critics as examples of the repressive agents of the state. The intervention — real or potential — of government has a profound effect on individual lives. Its rules may ordain that people abstain from activities considered pleasurable; risk their lives in wars they do not support; or forgo benefits that would otherwise by available because resources are allocated in a manner they regard as contrary to their own interests. If individuals should reject the dictates of the political system in the pursuit of their self-interest, certain political institutions may use extraordinary power and sometimes violence to deprive them of their property, their liberty, or their life.

This view of politics sees government as a negative force vis-à-vis the individual. Obligations, responsibilities, requirements, restrictions, deprivations, checks, threats, denials, confinements, and sometimes fear constitute the typical impact of political decisions upon the everyday life. Thus an ever present conflict exists between the desire of the individual to be free and the decrees of the state which restrict individual liberty. It is believed that an understanding of this conflict will alienate the individual from the state and reveal the state as the greatest enemy of humankind. Intense concern for this aspect of the political often leads to demands that the state be destroyed. This was the conclusion reached by many nineteenth-century anarchists and reached again by their modern counterparts.[3] The argument, put simply, is that the state is of necessity the enemy of the individual and individual freedom. The only viable political course available to the freedom-loving person is to destroy the state and dissolve the political system. When the political system is destroyed, people can achieve a life of virtue, happiness, and freedom. From this perspective, the only rational political choice is to seek the end of all political choices.

The Positive State

A strong and countervailing tradition of political thought, however, conceives of the state as a natural and necessary extension of the individual. The state is essential to the satisfaction of the needs of its people and is the indispensable source of all meaningful individual liberties. This position is clearly reflected in the Aristotelian argument that a person outside the state is either a "beast or a God." While life may be possible outside the state, the "good" life can be achieved only within the polity. The state is a positive institution which can help people secure individual freedom and achieve their true and highest nature.

The political dimension of social existence involves coming together in an organized manner so that each person, in combination with others, may establish and seek collective goals which could not be achieved alone. This joint pursuit of common goals may entail little more than individuals banding together to protect themselves against threats to their safety by the forces of nature or against abuses of their freedoms by other members of their own or another society. Advocates of this general conception differ radically on the proper role and scope of government. The ideal state may be thought to be little more than a police officer who *protects* the interests of the many from the abuses of the few. However, in a positive view of the state, complicated and vigorous efforts may be required to gain positive goals, such as a more equitable distribution of income, universal education, or better health care. The principle of division of labor as an efficient means of achieving goals is an integral aspect of the positive view of the state. The pursuit of collective goals through the political system involves the generation of power needed to gain satisfactions that are not possible without cooperation and the organization of individual talents and skills available in society. The consequent inevitable regimentation results in the loss of certain kinds of unstructured freedoms, but that loss is thought by some to be justified by the attainment of social goals which are superior to those of the individual.

Thus government, by extending the power and potentialities of persons, brings the good life within the reach of all. The central issues of politics become problems in selecting the means by which common goals are to be pursued, establishing the ways in which a society should be organized to seek these goals, and distributing costs and benefits equitably. Variations on the idea of the positive state have dominated "informed" political discourse in the United States throughout this century. The political system or the state is not generally seen by political reformers as the inevitable enemy of people but as a human institution to be used for the fulfillment of individuals' needs and ideals.

The Negative-Positive Mix

Is the state a destructive force in society, inimical to human freedom, a necessary evil based upon the weakness or evilness of people? Or is it a positive force with the capacity to make people truly free? The somewhat perplexing answer is that it is or has been both at different times, with different people, in different societies. The dictates of the most benign political state do restrain individuals from pursuing all conceivable ends; they may also promote the achievement of a broader range of goals than would be possible in the absence of the state. In all societies, even the most morally hideous, there is *some* mix of negative and positive features. In some times and in some places, the primary emphasis of government has been upon the protection of the individual and the achievement of individual interests through the collective action of the polity. In other places at other times, the balance has clearly been cast against individual freedom and toward narrowing individual choices.

A critical problem for the political scientist is to determine the factors that influence this mix of positive and negative elements of any given state. It is necessary to consider the ancient problem of distributive justice, which includes (1) analyses of the distribution of indulgences and deprivations among the population, (2) explanations for the uneven nature of that distribution, and (3) a normative evaluation of that distribution from some compelling ethical perspective. These three related issues are at the heart of virtually all political inquiry. The division of labor in political science means that not all working political scientists analyze all three problems (although some do) or even that they are interested in all three issues. But as a *social* activity, that is what political science is all about.

THE STUDY OF THE POLITY
IN HISTORICAL PERSPECTIVE

The history of political science has been marked by philosophical and metaphysical speculation about humankind and the state from a moral perspective. In every age people have also sought empirical understanding of their political conditions. While the methods chosen for gaining knowledge of the political world have varied from deductive logic to careful inductive reasoning based on vast amounts of systematic data, the discipline has been just as concerned to identify the values that should be maximized through the political system and to prescribe how the polity and the society should be organized to achieve them.

Although many great writings in the history of political thought have a timeless significance, they were generally produced in response to a specific political and social setting. Normally they contain an ideological component designed either to justify existing political institutions, processes, or allocations or to promote some desired change expected to achieve a "better" state of affairs.[4] Thus, the history of political science is composed of three interconnected streams of thought. The political scientist has attempted to determine philosophically the appropriate ends of, and interrelationships between, people and the state; to develop ideological justifications for maintaining the status quo or for changing it; and to discover empirically the factors that determine political circumstances and behavior.[5]

The political goals and values discussed in the classical writings recur as major issues in the modern world, albeit often in restructured forms. Many questions raised by political scientists today have had their basic dimensions fixed by much earlier treatments in Western political thought. We cannot present here any complete analysis of how political scientists came to be what they are. But all students of politics should become familiar with what has gone on before in their discipline. The following discussion touches on a few key points in the history of political ideas; it is merely illustrative, however, and is not even a cursory introduction to the field. The simplified analysis below does violence to the richness of the great traditions from which our political concepts are drawn, but it does express a feeling for the continuity of the issues and for the roots and variants of some of our current political ideas.

POLITICAL THOUGHT: THE CLASSICAL TRADITION

A central issue in political thought has concerned the means of organizing the collective elements of human existence so as to allow for the achievement of the "good life." Search for those elements requires a definition of the good life based, explicitly or implicitly, upon some conception of human nature and the ends toward which people should properly strive. Determining appropriate ends may involve careful observations of human activities or logical deductions from premises about human nature. Both approaches require structuring the polity so that it will aid in achieving the important goals of people, consistent with their (usually) higher nature. Thus, the study of politics is above all else the study of people as they relate to the collectivity of which they are members. No matter how technologically advanced political research may become, political science is, therefore, a homocentric or person-centered science. Some discussion of this fact is in order.

Although there is general consensus about the *objects* of political science (people and the state) at a very abstract level of discussion, political scientists disagree over the *methods* that are most suitable for political inquiry and the *aspects* of persons and the collectivity that should be central to political analysis. The units of analysis used, the problems selected, the relative importance assigned to the elements of problems, and the ways of approaching problems vary greatly among the different schools of political science. Some thinkers seek explicitly and primarily to discover the nature and proper ends of people before extrapolating prescriptions for the proper organization of the polity. Other thinkers simply *assume*, often implicitly, something about the nature and goals of people and focus their attention on the structural and organizational aspects of the polity. The major concern is to identify the values that ought to be maximized through the polity, to determine how the polity can best be ordered to achieve these values, and to develop justifications for these identifications and determinations.

Justice and Human Nature

Although many different dimensions of "human nature" have been regarded as vital by classical thinkers, the two issues most frequently discussed involve the problems of equality versus stratification and the inherent goodness or wickedness of persons. These issues are usually considered in light of the guiding principle that justice is the highest value to be sought in society. A common thread runs through most conceptions of justice: Justice requires that all persons assume responsibilities and receive rewards that are compatible with their nature, their contributions to society, or both. The idea can be stated most simply as a rule which requires that every person be given his or her due, a notion at least as old as the writings of Plato.[6] He argued that persons have different talents and desires. In accordance with the principle of the social and personal utility of the division of labor, he depicted the just state as one in which all persons performed the role for which they were most qualified and that rewarded them in a manner consistent with their basic natures and the continued performance of their proper social role. The wise (i.e., the philosopher kings) should properly rule society, and power should not be possessed by anyone else. This argument for elitist rule by the wise has been echoed and reechoed, with many variations in the composition of the elite having been suggested: The wealthy should rule, or the proletariat, or the strong, or the meek, or the ruthless, or those chosen by God. Justice will be served in each of these systems, inasmuch as each person is to receive his or her due.

Interestingly enough, writers who take the view that all people are equal do not define justice very differently. For example, Karl Marx argued that when all exploitation of individual by individual ends, as it must, the principle of justice that will prevail will be "From each according to his abilities; and to each according to his needs."[7] This is not far from Plato's definition. But, while the principle of justice remains relatively constant, the determination of what a person's due is varies considerably. Death may be the due of one who is unfortunate enough to belong to a racial, ethnic, economic, or other group which a writer or politician despises: the "bourgeoisie" under Stalin; Jews under Hitler. The argument for equality is that all should share in the governance of society and all should receive, or have a chance to receive, whatever rewards society has to offer.

Justice, then, requires that rewards, powers, and responsibilities be allotted appropriately to individuals in the polity. However, the allocations and political organizations that actually develop are determined in part by people's inherent qualities. This issue involves a judgment as to whether people are basically good, evil, or both. Human nature, it has been argued frequently, requires that the state limit natural proclivities of avarice, corruption, and exploitation. This idea of the negative state is embedded in the writings of St. Augustine[8] and Thomas Hobbes. They argue, from quite different perspectives, that the major function of the state is to preserve the peace against people's naturally evil propensities. Left to their own devices, people would soon destroy the rights of others and in the end would destroy themselves. Hobbes's characterization that, in the absence of a state to exercise control, "the life of man [is] solitary, poor, nasty, brutish, and short"[9] is a famous statement of this view.

There have also been arguments by serious political philosophers that people are basically good, and that only deranged social institutions have led to the corruption and oppression that can be observed on every hand. If institutions were corrected, people would be perfected. No state would then be needed to coerce them; only means to facilitate voluntary cooperation would be required. This theme was sounded in its most compelling form by the nineteenth-century anarchists, such as William Godwin and Pierre Proudhon.[10] The basic conception is that humans are fundamentally cooperative animals and that only the illegitimate power of the state prevents the attainment of justice and equality for all. Therefore, justice cannot be secured until the state is destroyed. This view was shared by Marx. (Some carping critics have asked how good persons could construct corrupt institutions, but that is a question we must leave to our readers.)

One begins to see why the history of political thought contains so much concern for the essence of human nature. Whether the "natural" condition is one of equality or hierarchy affects our judgments concerning the just allocation of rewards and responsibilities. Normally, a commitment to equality leads to the belief that political power should be widely shared. Commitments to stratification theories lead to opposite conclusions. Strong belief in human goodness usually goes with the idea that government should not limit people's development and freedom to any major degree. Conversely, the notion that people are basically evil often results in support for a powerful state to limit their naturally destructive impulses in order to ensure safety and security. We reiterate: All of these positions seek to have values distributed in a just pattern (all should receive their due), but the content of the distribution varies dramatically depending on the nature and inherent worth imputed to particular individuals or groups.[11]

Change and Stability

The idea that justice should be pursued through the polity is central to the critical problem of stability and change in society. The extent to which a society is just determines, for most political thinkers, whether change is regarded as a positive value (likely to achieve more justice) or a threat (likely to eliminate or reduce justice). There have been no more keenly debated issues in the history of political thought than the appropriateness of change, whether through peaceful adjustment or violent revolution. Revolution has been considered the greatest threat to justice in what is looked upon as the conservative tradition. Persons who believe that the good society has already been achieved have, for the most part, sought means to guarantee that change will be controlled or even eliminated. The doctrine of Plato that when the perfectly balanced society has been achieved any change involves retrogression and less justice is consistent with the view of all utopian writers. A rather less utopian version of this animus toward change is based on the notion that people are incapable of controlling their destiny and, although present conditions may not be perfect, any meddling with society will probably bring about a less rather than a more just situation. Rejection of revolution and skepticism toward moderate change are well stated in the writings of Edmund Burke.[12] There is, then, a powerful tradition in Western thought which distrusts change and seeks to limit it in the polity.

The means that have been espoused to restrict change show what kinds of issues enter into the critical problems of change versus stability. The Platonic idea involved a drastic system of character-building and selection of individuals into a caste system that would inhibit positive attitudes toward change. Aristotle preferred a balance of power among the social classes, with the bulk of the power being held by a middle class which would operate as a stabilizing buffer between rich and poor in the society.[13] Machiavelli issued a set of instructions for use by the ruler concerned to conserve and maintain his power containing such maxims as "It is better to be feared than to be loved."[14] The Roman lawyers looked to an equilibrium of forces in the legal powers of different segments of government as the primary means to prevent revolution or broad social change.[15] These examples illustrate the many devices and social arrangements that have been relied upon to restrict social change. They involve changing people's perceptions and values, balancing social classes, balancing interests through the legal powers of government, and using power and manipulation to maintain the status quo.

In our time a radical or liberal tradition supports social transformations as of positive value and argues that, under certain conditions, there is a right and perhaps a responsibility to launch (even violent) revolutions. Variations abound in defense of the idea that revolution or dramatic change is justified in specified circumstances. The earliest ideas were that revolution occurred naturally if imbalance developed in the political system[16] and sometimes involved discussion of the acceptability of tyrannicide, or the removal of a tyrant from power by violent means.[17] The obvious assumption was that there are limits to the power of the ruler and that, when they are exceeded, citizens have the right to remove the ruler. This concept of limited government finds its fullest expression in the natural rights tradition represented in the writings of the social contract theorists, such as John Locke[18] and J.J. Rousseau.[19] Basically they felt that every individual is entitled to certain natural rights simply by virtue of being human. The purpose of the state is to protect and guarantee these rights. When the state ceases to do so, individuals have a right to rebel and to establish a new government. It was primarily in the writings of John Locke that the American Declaration of Independence had its origin, as does the frequently expressed American version of the right of revolution. The main concern of this branch of political doctrine has been to establish appropriate limits and responsibilities for government and to institute means through which the rights of the people can be guaranteed. Change is good when it extends the fundamental rights of people. The liberal tradition is biased toward change, toward the belief that change is likely to lead to the progressive fulfillment of human rights.

The question of the right of revolution is a fundamental issue of political philosophy. It involves the obligation, if any, of the individual to accept and obey the decisions of political authority. There have been countless arguments justifying and requiring obedience to the rules of the state. A traditional aristocratic argument is that the rules should be obeyed because they were made by the superior elements of society — the rich, the wise, the well-born, or the holy; everyone else is obligated to accept their judgment.[20] To oppose their decisions would be to pursue a mistaken view, or perhaps to oppose the will of God. In most modern democratic thought obedience is required when the government rests on the consent of the governed. Ideally, each person should participate in the governance of society, making the decrees of government her or his own (in effect). There are real if imprecise limits to the obligation of the individual to obey under this doctrine. The whole idea of the right of revolution is an argument for the severing of obligations when government ceases to carry out its legitimate functions in an appropriate manner. The idea of limited constitutional government — which some would say is the greatest achievement in political history — rests on this view of the nature of political obligation.

The most difficult practical question concerning political obligation is: How does one determine when an obligation to obey government has ceased? Although a number of theorists have struggled with this problem, their answers are not fully satisfactory. If a majority is to decide, how is it to do so?[21] If the individual may decide alone, would not chaos result? Should the church decide?[22] In the final analysis the best empirical index (excluding martyrdom) of when obligation ends is when sufficient power has been mobilized to ensure a successful revolution.

The Continuing Questions

We have now identified some enduring questions raised in the history of Western political thought. Who should rule (i.e., should power be concentrated in the one, the few, or the many, the rich, the wise, the powerful)? Does human nature require that the state be used to limit corrupt proclivities or does it allow for the state to build on people's natural goodness? What are the relative values, if any, implicit in political stability and change? How can stability be achieved? What factors produce change in society? How does one judge when the maximum degree of justice in society has been achieved? Should the organization of the society reflect the basic equality or basic inequality of people? What is the nature of political obligation and what are its limits? How does one judge the extent of one's political obligation? What makes the decisions of government legitimate?

The answers that have been given to these questions make up a major part of the history of political thought. The primary emphasis in this tradition is on the normative dimensions of the questions. However, normative evaluations are frequently, even usually, based upon empirical statements which are subject to testing under modern conditions. This body of great literature is the foundation upon which modern political science rests and the source of much of its direction.

POLITICAL THOUGHT:
THE MODERN PERSPECTIVE

The philosophical tradition from Plato to Marx and beyond saw the study of politics as an aspect of the general philosophical enterprise. Although many writers in that tradition based their understanding upon observations of people, the state, and society, their empirical analyses were often subordinate to their normative concerns. In the nineteenth century there began to develop a specialized academic discipline of political science with its roots in this philosophical tradition.

All disciplines develop a dominant way of looking at their subject matter. In the most advanced scientific fields of study, theoretical models dictate the questions that will be asked, the data that will be analyzed, the methods to be used, and the interpretations that will be formulated. Research is guided by theoretical constructs and its findings are used to systematically inform the theory.[23] When critical observations do not match the theory, or are unexplainable in its terms, a new theory is required. At some point, a different way of looking at the field may produce a new paradigm to direct the activities of the field. This is the phenomenon that Kuhn has called the scientific revolution.[24] Political science has never developed the kind of general theory described in Kuhn's analysis, but there have been prevailing ways of looking at politics in different historical periods. These loosely organized theories and assumptions have largely directed the kinds of questions posed and the interests of practitioners at various times. American political science has been marked by at least three more or less general political periods. Each had assumptions that directed the questions asked and the collection, analysis, and evaluation of political data. They can be characterized, in terms of emphasis, as the descriptive, analytic, and synthetic periods.

AMERICAN POLITICAL SCIENCE

The Descriptive Period

The central concept of academic political science in America during the descriptive period was the **state**. Attention was given in this period (roughly 1870–1930) to such issues as the nature, origin, organization, and evaluation of the state in general and of American government in particular. The term **political science** was used "to describe the body of knowledge relating to the phenomenon of the state."[25] There were many attempts at defining the state, most of which contained some common elements. Garner provided a typical example:

> . . . The state, as a concept of political science and public law, is a community of persons more or less numerous, permanently occupying a definite portion of territory, independent, or nearly so, of external control, and possessing an organized government to which the great body of inhabitants render habitual obedience.[26]

The study of political science was meant to develop understanding of the state and the way it is governed.

The early professional political scientists in the United States were often trained in the German universities and they brought to their task a strong commitment to historical and legal analysis.[27] Systematic descriptions of the legal structures by which the state is governed were made. Evaluations of these structures were based on the comparative analysis of constitutions, laws, and institutions of modern states, with frequent attention given to earlier historical examples of the state. Political science tended in one sense to be a branch of public law; indeed, these two fields of knowledge were at some points virtually identical. The desirability of representative government was generally accepted, and a great deal of attention was given to the problem of preserving, refining, and extending representative institutions.

There was, then, an active reform orientation that ran through the early period of the discipline. Much writing was prescriptive in nature, with the political scientists criticizing the organization of the government or various political practices and recommending changes that would make the political process better able to achieve the goals of responsibility and accountability. The recommendations were often formalistic, with major changes to be secured through new legal structures or by shifting responsibilities within existent legal structures. A relatively high value was placed on "experts" in government, and frequent appeals were made to remove so-called administrative problems from the world of politics.[28]

Optimism and belief in progress permeated the field. The general orientation was that "good" government could be achieved if only "proper" governmental structures were created. Panaceas were developed to remedy the ills of the state. Among other things, these included: establishing the parliamentary system, installing the direct primary, creating independent regulatory commissions, spreading the instruments of direct democracy (e.g., through the initiative, referendum, and recall), and using proportional representation. The legal forms of public institutions were considered the critical factors in government; cultural, historical, and ideological variables were minimized or avoided altogether. The data ordinarily utilized were legal documents and historical records. Woodrow Wilson's performance in writing his book *Congressional Government* without ever entering the halls of Congress is typical of the period.[29]

Very little attention was given to political beliefs and activities outside of government. There was some small interest in the organization and functioning of political parties and an occasional reference to the character of the people as being relevant to the selection of the proper form of government. Judgments in these areas seldom rested upon systematic observation and were often mere speculations based on concepts as imprecise as ethnic origin, climate, and geography. Such matters were clearly subordinate to the central concern of developing institutional analyses of the legal aspects of government.

This general approach dominated the field into the 1930s and even into the 1950s. Legal and institutional analyses as aspects of civic education are still reflected in the many "civics" books used in the secondary schools. But, as with any paradigm, signs of discontent with the legal-structural approach appeared long before it lost its preeminence. It was attacked mainly on the ground that it did not adequately explain the governmental process. The criticisms remained relatively isolated and ignored by the bulk of the profession until the middle of this century.

The major attacks upon the "traditional" paradigm had overlapping substantive and methodological elements. On the one hand, the legal approach to governmental institutions was charged with being too narrow for the understanding, explanation, and evaluation of politics.[30] On the other hand, it was argued that political science should develop along the lines of other sciences by using scientific methods in the study of political phenomena. This argument insisted on the need for a "value-free" approach based upon systematic empirical analysis of political behavior. The conflict between traditional orientations and the "new science of politics" was reflected in the debates over "**behavioralism**" that took place in the 1960s. Many scholars insist that a "behavioral" pattern has dominated the field for the last two decades, but these matters are never clear-cut. It appears that the behavioral period has had two main segments, an analytic and a synthetic phase.

The Analytic Period

Substantively, the new approach broke the traditional institutional bounds of the discipline and ended the preoccupation with legal documents and formal institutions. Politics came to be defined in a way that omitted *government*. A widely accepted definition of politics was simply that it was the "pursuit of power."[31] Any place in society where power was pursued was an appropriate subject for the political scientist. Power relations in industry, in the family, or in any organized group were aspects of politics. Nonetheless, most political scientists continued to give primary attention to power relations involving the governance of the society.

Nongovernmental institutions such as political parties and interest groups were emphasized as key elements in the political process. Political scientists became interested in a broad range of social and psychological factors related (in sometimes distant ways) to political behavior. The organized group, the family, social class, the school, the church, occupations, economic resources, demographic factors were analyzed as determinants of political behavior. Similarly, political scientists began to study attitude and opinion formation, child-rearing practices and socialization patterns, and the impact of propaganda upon political behavior.

The basic orientation was that the formal institutions of government are not always or even necessarily most important in explaining how politics operates. They are mere reflections of the economic, social, and psychological factors that shape society. If one could identify the social, psychological, and economic bases of power, political behavior could be explained and predicted adequately. At best, the analysis of legal structures and documents was a waste of time. At worst, it was a conspiracy to conceal the *real* determinants of political decisions.

The dramatic shift in the substantive concerns of the political scientist during this period was accompanied by changes in the methodological orientations of the field. Emphasis upon detailed descriptions of political institutions gave way to emphasis upon scientific explanation and, in the long term, prediction. Reliance shifted from legal analysis to the use of quantitative data, often collected through the emerging technique of survey research. Broad evaluations of the government and its institutions were replaced by narrowly conceived empirical studies, and a self-conscious concern developed over questions of scientific theory-building, methods of data collection, and means of analyzing new data sources.

The behavioral paradigm — emphasizing *actual* behavior and beliefs as well as methodological rigor — attempted to emulate the approach to observation taken in the natural sciences, and new interest was sparked in the philosophy of science. Two different conceptions influenced the research of the period. One involved an inductive approach to politics through the collection of data and the discovery of relationships contained in the data. The other involved efforts to build systematic and deductive theory which could help researchers correct and refine the theory. In both cases, there was emphasis on separating questions of fact and questions of value and on limiting the impact of the values of researchers on their scientific endeavors. Of course, the problems chosen for analysis were in part determined by the values of researchers, and the interpretations they rendered were also shaped to some extent by these values, but between the selection of the problem and the completion of the analysis, the effect of personal values could be minimized. The problem for the political scientist is not necessarily greater in this regard than for other scientists.

Methodological concerns were often given precedence over substantive concerns. The analytic period tended to focus on determining appropriate units of analysis, identifying measures and indices, and analyzing narrow problems which were manageable within the rigid strictures of the scientific method. More able practitioners were not diverted by such limitations but used behavioralism when it could assist in illuminating important problems. They gave attention to the empirical basis of conflict and the distribution of power among the participants in conflict.[32] Much of the current dialogue about politics is shaped by this approach to the political process. Perhaps no term is more popular today in political discussions than *power structure* — a term created during the analytic period. The paradigm of political conflict, based upon social, psychological, and economic explanations of political behavior, has been internalized in the rhetoric and understanding of many contemporary journalists, politicians, agitators, and opinion leaders in American society.

The development of **"radical" behavioralism** was criticized from a number of perspectives. There were attacks upon its attempt to find a value-free approach to a value-laden process. Its failure to emphasize normative questions was looked upon as a threat to the highest values of the society.[33] It was also regarded as being irrelevant to the pressing issues of the time. Its interest in technique and its commitment to quantification were looked upon as useless and a means of avoiding real social problems. The problems chosen for investigation were allegedly dictated by the technique rather than the importance of the problem. Paradoxically, behavioralism itself had arisen primarily as a reaction to the inability of traditional political science to deal with the problems generated by the Great Depression, the rise of Nazism, and World War II. The narrow analytic nature of many behavioral studies restricted the ability of the discipline to study the "big issues" of politics.

The Synthetic Period

Currently, the central theme of political science is synthetic. The synthetic phase answers some if not all of the criticisms levied against the analytic phase. An example of work conducted from a synthetic perspective is the present book, which proceeds from self-conscious assumptions, erects a model of politics, uses both legal reasoning and empirical studies in describing American politics, and raises, but does not seek to resolve, normative issues.

The synthetic phase aims to integrate the findings and orientations of the significant political traditions into a more complete description, explanation, and evaluation of politics. Its primary emphasis is upon the search for interrelationships among variables with a view to determining what effect changes in one variable have upon other aspects of the polity.

The new orientation maintains the commitment to the scientific method broadly understood but stresses the importance of theory to order the findings of research into a more meaningful context. There is also a keener interest in the role of values in political behavior, as well as explicit evaluation of government's performance with well-articulated normative standards.

The definition of politics provided by David Easton has become conventional in this period. Politics entails "the authoritative allocation of values for the society as a whole."[34] No reference to the governmental institutions of the society is included. However, in the United States, the allocations made through government are central to politics. Currently, the basic understanding of politics is that it involves many factors (requiring identification) which influence decisions of government and that the decisions made affect the positions of individuals and groups in society.

Many versions of this "systems" conception have been developed and have influenced the stream of political research and interpretation in the last decade. Whether designated as "general systems analysis," "structural-functional analysis," or "the public choice approach," the essential formulations of the synthetic period are rather similar.[35] The basic view is that the polity is a social system through which authoritative, society-wide decisions are made. Innumerable structural and behavioral factors enter into the making of binding political decisions; the task of the political scientist is to discover those factors and to explain the effects of their different combinations upon governmental and individual political behavior.

Political Science Today

The emphasis in the emerging paradigm of political science is upon thinking about politics in a relational manner. The interest is not so much upon any politically important variable or set of variables as upon the evaluation and explanation of their effects on the political system as a whole. This way of looking at politics lends broader meaning to individual research findings and emphasizes that political science is a cooperative and social enterprise.

A widespread criticism of this orientation is that it is either purposely or unwittingly conservative. The argument is that efforts to know how political systems "hang together" or manage to persist focus on the sources of stability, of equilibrium, and away from the sources of stress, conflict, and change. Such focus is said to lead to pessimism about the possibility of making substantial changes through the political system. But, as we noted in Chapter 2, the argument that equilibrium concepts lead to conservatism is weak. One must understand the factors that maintain a system before knowing which factors might lead to the destruction of that system. The findings of research into political equilibriums can be used either to develop stability or to promote change. A demand not to search for understanding is really a demand to remain ignorant of the political system. It would, if accepted, destroy any legitimate function for political science. Unfortunately, there has been a good bit of academic demagogy on this subject.

The analysis of the systemic nature of political activity does have a conservative dimension of a somewhat different kind. Looking at politics as a highly complex, interactive system of behavior one sees that simple solutions and magical formulations are not likely to reorder the polity successfully. Understanding the complexity of polity and society does reduce one's faith in simple-minded radical programs and reduces the propensity of informed persons to join movements that offer primitive solutions to complex problems. However, it should be remembered that successful revolutions have involved persons who understood the system they wanted to overthrow: Neither Danton, Jefferson, nor Lenin maintained particularly simple or totemistic understandings of the political process, although two of them could be thoroughly disagreeable characters.

SUMMARY

Humankind is by nature political. Every person lives within a social group, and collective decisions that are made by the group shape the kind of life that individuals may live. Politics refers in large measure to the processes through which collective decisions are made and implemented. Political science is the study of these activities. Attempts to understand the political world are as old as recorded history, and the modern discipline of political science stands on foundations laid down by centuries of political speculation and analysis.

The classical tradition of political science is marked by attempts to determine the proper nature of people and the state. The primary interest of political thinkers has been to develop means of defining and installing justice in the political system. Subordinate interests have involved the great (and related) questions of equality, liberty, change, stability, and political obligation.

Modern political science in America is less than a century old. It has had three general phases. Scholars of the first period concentrated on the nature and organization of the state and its structural and legal problems. A strong normative element marked this legal-descriptive period, with most proposed reforms entailing structural-legal changes in the formal organization of the polity. The incapacity of this approach to comprehend major changes in domestic and international politics led to an emphasis upon the scientific study of politics, beginning during the 1950s (although important contributions were made much earlier). The first stage of this scientific or analytic period was marked frequently by rather narrow methodological concerns having little obvious or direct relation to large political questions. The present emphasis in political science is on the integration of systematic empirical political theory, the findings of well-designed research efforts, and normative principles of evaluation. This we have called the synthetic approach, the approach adopted in the present book.

NOTES

1. Aristotle, *The Nicomachean Ethics,* trans. by H. Rackham (Cambridge, Mass.: Harvard University Press, 1926), p. 9.
2. Jean Jacques Rousseau, *The Social Contract and Discourses,* trans. by G.D.H. Cole (New York: E.P. Dutton, 1950), p. 3.
3. The classic statement of the doctrine that justice demands the destruction of the state is found in Pierre J. Proudhon, *What Is Property?* trans. by Benjamin R. Tucker (New York: Humboldt, 1876).
4. The argument is best expressed in Karl Mannheim, *Ideology and Utopia* (New York: Harcourt, Brace, 1936).
5. See Andrew Hacker, *Political Theory: Philosophy, Ideology, and Science* (New York: Macmillan, 1961), pp. 1–20, for a useful treatment of these issues.
6. See *The Republic of Plato,* trans. by Francis M. Cornford (New York: Oxford University Press, 1945). An important modern argument of justice as fairness may be found in John Rawls, *A Theory of Justice* (Cambridge, Mass.: Harvard University Press, 1971).
7. Karl Marx and Friedrich Engels, *Selected Works* (Moscow: Foreign Languages Publishing House, 1951), Vol. II, p. 21.
8. St. Augustine, *The City of God,* trans. by Marcus Dods (New York: Hafner, 1948).

9. Thomas Hobbes, *Leviathan,* Library of Liberal Arts Edition (Indianapolis: Bobbs-Merrill, 1958), p. 107.
10. See William Godwin, *An Enquiry Concerning Political Justice,* F.E.L. Priestly, ed., (London: H.S. Key, 1876), and Proudhon, *What Is Property?*
11. Harold D. Lasswell and Abraham Kaplan, *Power and Society* (New Haven, Conn.: Yale University Press, 1950), p. 131.
12. See, particularly, Edmund Burke, *Reflections on the Revolution in France* (Indianapolis: Bobbs-Merrill, 1955).
13. Aristotle, *Politics,* trans. by Benjamin Jowett (New York: Modern Library, 1943), Books V and VII.
14. Niccolò Machiavelli, *The Prince and the Discourses* (New York: Modern Library, 1950), p. 61.
15. See, particularly, Cicero, *De Re Publica, De Legibus,* trans. by Clinton W. Keyes (Cambridge, Mass.: Harvard University Press, 1928).
16. For example, see Thucydides, *The Peloponnesian War,* Cawley trans. (New York: Modern Library, 1951).
17. George H. Sabine, *A History of Political Theory,* 4th ed. (New York: Holt, Rinehart & Winston, 1973), pp. 241–250.
18. John Locke, *Two Treatises on Government,* Laslett edition (Cambridge, Eng.: Cambridge University Press, 1960).
19. Rousseau, *The Social Contract and Discourses.*
20. For a useful discussion of religion as a basis for the right to rule, see John N. Figgis, *The Divine Right of Kings* (New York: Harper & Row, 1965).
21. This issue is a central concern in the writings of Locke, *Two Treatises on Government,* and Rousseau, *The Social Contract and Discourses.*
22. See Sabine, *A History of Political Theory,* pp. 287–311.
23. See Abraham Kaplan, *The Conduct of Inquiry* (San Francisco: Chandler, 1964), and Karl Popper, *The Logic of Scientific Discovery* (New York: Science Editions, 1961), for descriptions of this process and its importance in the scientific enterprise.
24. Thomas Kuhn, *The Structure of Scientific Revolutions,* 2nd ed. (Chicago: University of Chicago Press, 1970).
25. James W. Garner, *Political Science and Government* (New York: American Book, 1928), p. 3.
26. Ibid., p. 62.
27. See Bernard Crick, *The American Science of Politics* (Berkeley: University of California Press, 1959), and Albert Somit and Joseph Tanenhaus, *The Development of American Political Science: From Burgess to Behavioralism* (Boston: Allyn & Bacon, 1967), for two quite different views of the evolution of the discipline of political science in the United States.
28. See, for example, Frank Goodnow, *Politics and Administration* (New York: Russell and Russell, 1967).
29. Boston: Houghton Mifflin, 1885.

30. The most useful critique is found in David Easton, *The Political System* (New York: Knopf, 1953).
31. See Lasswell and Kaplan, *Power and Society.*
32. Ibid., and David Truman, *The Governmental Process* (New York: Knopf, 1951) were the two most influential sources of this view.
33. A vigorous critique may be found in Leo Strauss, "An Epilogue," in Herbert J. Storing et al., eds., *Essays on the Scientific Study of Politics* (New York: Holt, Rinehart, & Winston, 1962), pp. 305–328.
34. See David Easton, *A Systems Analysis of Political Life* (New York: Wiley, 1965), and Karl W. Deutsch, *The Nerves of Government* (New York: Free Press, 1963), for leading examples.
35. The first and most influential version of this approach that was directly related to political science is found in Gabriel A. Almond and James S. Coleman, eds., *The Politics of the Developing Areas* (Princeton, N.J.: Princeton University Press, 1960), pp. 3–64. For a more elaborate account of the same approach see Gabriel A. Almond and G. Bingham Powell, Jr., *Comparative Politics: A Developmental Approach* (Boston: Little, Brown, 1966).

Glossary

Administrative Law   In American law, a body of rules created by administrative agencies and the judicial interpretations of these rules.

Amicus Curiae   A friend of the Court, a term usually used in the United States to refer to persons who are not parties to a case who present legal arguments before a court in an attempt to influence a judicial decision.

Assistance in Kind   Contributions of goods or services rather than money made by government to individuals.

Behavioralism   In political science, the study of actual behavior of individuals and political structures as opposed to the study of formal rules, institutions, and legal norms.

Bill of Attainder   Punishment or deprivations imposed upon an individual or a clearly identifiable group of persons directly by legislative action without the benefit of a judicial hearing.

Categoric groups   Groups consisting of individuals with shared characteristics (e.g., sex, age, weight) rather than shared attitudes or interests.

Caucus   The bringing together of all members of a political party in a legislative body or geographic region to discuss issues and make decisions of relevance to the party.

417

Checks and Balances The practice or effort to control and limit the powers of formal institutions of government by establishing countervailing powers in other institutions of government.

Class Action A technique that is available in limited situations in which a party to a suit in a court can argue for a decision that will apply to all persons who find themselves in a similar legal situation to the litigant in the case.

Cloture A technique for limiting debate in the Senate of the United States which requires that 60 percent of the membership must agree that debate should be ended on an issue before the Senate.

Common Law A body of law that has developed through the decisions of courts in individual cases over a long period of time.

Conference Committee An *Ad Hoc* or temporary committee composed of members drawn from both Houses of Congress who are charged with resolving the differences in a bill that has been passed in different forms by the two houses of Congress.

Conservative In politics, one who is skeptical of fundamental change, concerned with social order, and committed to individual responsibility.

Consistency In social analysis, the requirement that, under the same conditions, an individual's preferences must be the same.

Constitutional Law The fundamental law of the polity which consists of the provisions of the Constitution and the major judicial interpretations of these provisions.

Decision-Rules The criteria, either formal or informal, that are folled in making choices.

Descriptive Rationality The assumption that behavior in the real world can be understood or analyzed as if individuals behave rationally.

Descriptive Theory A set of statements purporting to describe the actual state of some portion of the world.

Determinant System A collection of variables sufficient to explain all relevant aspects of a system.

Diminishing Marginal Utility The view that total utility or satisfaction afforded by something of value increases with its supply but at a decreasing rate.

Eminent Domain The power of governmental units to take private property for a public use and generally requires that just compensation be given to the property holder.

Empirical Question A question that can be answered only by an examination of factual evidence and not by logic alone.

Equal Marginal Utilities   A condition that exists when the utility or satisfaction provided by the last increment of different values is the same.

Equilibrium   A state of balance between and among opposing forces or actions.

Equity   An element of Anglo-American law which allows remedies in cases involving potentially irreparable harm when the general remedies of the common law are inadequate or inappropriate.

Externalities   Consequences, both beneficial and costly, of decisions taken by others.

Factions   Normally, a political interest group.

Free Rider   An individual who enjoys benefits from an activity the cost of which were borne by others.

Filibuster   In the U.S. Senate, a technique that makes use of the rule allowing unlimited debate to block or delay action on a bill on the floor of the Senate.

Grand Jury   A group of persons called together to determine if adequate evidence is present in a criminal case to warrant a formal trial of an individual.

Group Theory   An explanation of politics based on the view that groups are the basic units in the political process.

Habeus Corpus   A process available to any person held in custody by a governmental official which forces the official to legally justify holding the person or the person must be set free.

Hamiltonianism   The political perspective associated with that of Alexander Hamilton emphasizing a strong central government, aid to manufacturing, and economic freedom.

Hypothesis   A supposition provisionally accepted to explain certain facts and to guide further investigation.

Impeachment   A process through which any civil officer of the United States can be removed from office when convicted by a two-thirds vote in the Senate on charges brought by a majority vote of the House of Representatives.

Income Effect   The new pattern of choices that an individual will make following an increase or decrease in income.

Insatiable Wants   The contention or assumption that human wants always exceed their satisfaction.

Instrumentality   As used, the view that the most efficient known means will be chosen to secure one's objectives.

Inflation   A disporporationate increase in the quantity of money or credit relative to the goods available for purchase.

Intensity   Degree of concern of willingness to expend resources to achieve a given outcome.

Interest Group   A collection of individuals actually or potentially organized on the basis of shared concerns and outlooks.

Jacksonianism   The political tendency associated with Andrew Jackson emphasizing the desirability of popular participation in government, the diffusion of economic power, and union supremacy vis-a-vis the states.

Jeffersonianism   The political outlook associated with Thomas Jefferson emphasizing limited government, civil liberties, and the efficacy of education.

Judicial Activism   An approach to the judicial role that justifies a broad use of the power of judicial review and a substantial role for the courts in public policy-making.

Judicial Review   The power of courts to hold any executive or legislative action to be null and void on the grounds that it is in conflict with some provision of the Constitution.

Judicial Self-Restraint   An approach to the judicial role that limits the exercise of judicial review to very clear cases and limits the extent of intervention of the courts in public policy-making.

Liberalism   In politics, a set of ideas which emphasize the ability of man to control external conditions and places high value upon civil liberty and social change.

Liberal Democracies   Political systems organized on the principles of competitive popular participation, limited government, civil liberties, and majority rule.

Lobbying   Activities undertaken to influence the activities of political decision makers.

Logrolling   Agreements, either tacit or overt, among political decision-makers to exchange support on various matters, thus allowing each participant to achieve an outcome not otherwise attainable.

Natural Law   A position that there are rules that should guide human behavior that transcend mere man made rules and that all human laws should be judged by this set of rules.

Normative Theory   In Political Science, a statement describing a preferred political condition, whether it exists or not.

Organic Fallacy   As used, the false notion that collectivities of individuals give rise to groups with preferences other than those held by the individuals themselves.

Patronage   Awarding governmental jobs to supporters of a political party as an incentive for greater participation in party activities.

Pluralism   In contemporary political science, the view that American society is composed of heterogeneous groups, each possessing some measure of political influence.

Political Party   In America, a coalition of groups united in their effort to maintain or ensconce their members in elected political positions.

Political Science   The study of people using power to achieve values they desire.

Polity   Either a nation-state or that portion of a nation-state organized to make authoritative decisions.

Positive Law   An approach to law which defines law as the rules decreed by governmental agents acting in their official capacities.

Power   The ability to influence the behavior of others.

Prescriptive Rationality   Normative advice concerning the most efficient way to achieve some goal.

Pressure Group   An interest group that engages in political activity.

Public Choice Theory   An approach to the study of politics which seeks to discover how rational individuals will behave politically.

Public (collective) goods   A good or service for which it is impossible or impractical to ration to selected individuals.

Reapportionment   The redrawing of legislative district boundaries to bring them in better conformity with the distribution of the population.

Revenue Sharing   The practice of allocating federally collected taxes to state and local governments for purposes to be decided upon by those governments.

Separation of Powers   In the American case, a doctrine that holds that the powers of government are divided among the executive, legislative, and judicial branches of government by the Constitution.

Spoils System   A system of rotation of office in which virtually all public jobs are given to members of a political party that have been successful in an election.

State   A geographic area which has developed a governmental system which makes decisions that are binding upon persons who reside in the area independent of the requirements of another governmental system.

Stare Decisis   A rule of Anglo-American law which holds that similar cases should be decided in similar ways which makes each judicial decision a precedent to be used in deciding future cases.

Statutory Laws   That part of the total body of law in the legal system which consists of enactments of the legislature.

Strategic Bargaining   A plan of action by which one's position in a bargaining situation is maximized.

Swing State   Usually, a large state with a history of shifting support between Republican and Democratic presidential nominees.

Transfer Payments   Money contributions by government to individuals for which the individuals need not have made reciprocal contributions.

Transitivity   A ordering of preferences such that, if A is preferred to B, and B to C, then A is preferred to C.

White Primary   A now illegal practice, once common in the South, which excluded Blacks from participating in primary elections on the grounds that political parties were private associations.

Writ of Appeal   A means of appeal to a higher court from the decision of a lower court in which the higher court must review the legal questions decided in the lower court if certain criteria have been met.

Writ of Certiorari   An order from a higher court to a lower court that the records of a proceeding be submitted for review that is issued on the sound discretion of the higher court.

Constitution of the United States of America[1]

We the People of the United States, in Order to form a more perfect Union, establish Justice, insure domestic Tranquility, provide for the common defence, promote the general Welfare, and secure the Blessings of Liberty to ourselves and our Posterity, do ordain and establish this Constitution for the United States of America.

ARTICLE I

Section 1. All legislative Powers herein granted shall be vested in a Congress of the United States, which shall consist of a Senate and House of Representatives.

Section 2. The House of Representatives shall be composed of Members chosen every second Year by the People of the several States, and the Electors in each State shall have the Qualifications requisite for Electors of the most numerous Branch of the State Legislature.

No Person shall be a Representative who shall not have attained to the Age of twenty-five Years, and been seven Years a Citizen of the United States, and who shall not, when elected, be an Inhabitant of that State in which he shall be chosen.

[Representatives and direct Taxes[2] shall be apportioned among the several States which may be included within this Union, according to their respective Numbers, which shall be determined by adding to the whole Number of free Persons, including those bound to Service for a Term of Years, and excluding Indians not taxed, three fifths of all other Persons.][3] The actual Enumeration shall be made within three Years after the first Meeting of the Congress of the United States, and within every subsequent Term of ten Years, in such Manner as they shall by Law direct. The Number of Representatives shall not exceed one for every thirty Thousand, but each State shall have at Least one Representative; and until such enumeration shall be made, the State of New Hampshire shall be entitled to chuse three,

---

[1]This version, which follows the original Constitution in capitalization and spelling, was published by the United States Department of the Interior, Office of Education, in 1935.
[2]Altered by the Sixteenth Amendment.
[3]Negated by the Fourteenth Amendment.

Massachusetts eight, Rhode-Island and Providence Plantations one, Connecticut five, New York six, New Jersey four, Pennsylvania eight, Delaware one, Maryland six, Virginia ten, North Carolina five, South Carolina five, and Georgia three.

When vacancies happen in the Representation from any State, the Executive Authority thereof shall issue Writs of Election to fill such Vacancies.

The House of Representatives shall chuse their Speaker and other Officers; and shall have the sole Power of Impeachment.

Section 3. The Senate of the United States shall be composed of two Senators from each State, chosen by the Legislature thereof, for six Years; and each Senator shall have one Vote.

Immediately after they shall be assembled in Consequence of the first Election, they shall be divided as equally as may be into three Classes. The Seats of the Senators of the first Class shall be vacated at the Expiration of the second Year, of the second Class at the Expiration of the fourth Year, and of the third Class at the Expiration of the sixth Year, so that one-third may be chosen every second Year; and if Vacancies happen by Resignation, or otherwise, during the Recess of the Legislature of any State, the Executive thereof may make temporary Appointments until the next Meeting of the Legislature, which shall then fill such Vacancies.

No Person shall be a Senator who shall not have attained to the Age of thirty Years, and been nine Years a Citizen of the United States, and who shall not, when elected, be an Inhabitant of that State for which he shall be chosen.

The Vice President of the United States shall be President of the Senate, but shall have no vote, unless they be equally divided.

The Senate shall chuse their other Officers, and also a President pro tempore, in the absence of the Vice President, or when he shall exercise the Office of President of the United States.

The Senate shall have the sole Power to try all Impeachments. When sitting for that purpose, they shall be on Oath or Affirmation. When the President of the United States is tried, the Chief Justice shall preside: And no person shall be convicted without the Concurrence of two thirds of the Members present.

Judgment in Cases of Impeachment shall not extend further than to removal from Office, and disqualification to hold and enjoy any Office of honor, Trust, or Profit under the United States: but the Party convicted shall nevertheless be liable and subject to Indict ment, Trial, Judgment, and Punishment, according to Law.

Section 4. The Times, Places and Manner of holding Elections for Senators and Representatives, shall be prescribed in each State by the Legislature thereof; but the Congress may at any time by Law make or alter such Regulations, except as to the Places of Chusing Senators.

The Congress shall assemble at least once in every Year, and such Meeting shall be on the first Monday in December, unless they shall by Law appoint a different Day.

Section 5. Each House shall be the Judge of the Elections, Returns and Qualifications of its own Members, and a Majority of each shall constitute a Quorum to do Business; but a smaller number may adjourn from day to day, and may be authorized to compel the Attendance of absent Members, in such Manner, and under such Penalties, as each House may provide.

Each House may determine the Rules of its Proceedings, punish its Members for disorderly Behavior, and, with the Concurrence of two thirds, expel a Member.

Each House shall keep a Journal of its Proceedings, and from time to time publish the same, excepting such Parts as may in their Judgment require Secrecy; and the Yeas and Nays of the Members of either House on any question shall, at the Desire of one fifth of those Present, be entered on the Journal.

Neither House, during the Session of Congress, shall, without the Consent of the other, adjourn for more than three days, nor to any other Place than that in which the two Houses shall be sitting.

Section 6. The Senators and Representatives shall receive a Compensation for their Services, to be ascertained by Law, and paid out of the Treasury of the United States. They shall in all Cases, except Treason, Felony, and Breach of the Peace, be privileged from Arrest during their Attendance at the Session of their respective Houses, and in going to and returning from the same; and for any Speech or Debate in either House, they shall not be questioned in any other Place.

No Senator or Representative shall, during the Time for which he was elected, be appointed to any civil Office under the Authority of the United States, which shall have been created, or the Emoluments whereof shall have been increased, during such time; and no Person holding any Office under the United States shall be a Member of either House during his continuance in Office.

Section 7. All Bills for raising Revenue shall originate in the House of Representatives; but the Senate may propose or concur with Amendments as on other bills.

Every Bill which shall have passed the House of Representatives and the Senate, shall, before it becomes a Law, be presented to the President of the United States; If he approve he shall sign it, but if not he shall return it, with his Objections, to that House in which it shall have originated, who shall enter the Objections at large on their Journal, and proceed to reconsider it. If after such Reconsideration two thirds of that House shall agree to pass the bill, it shall be sent, together with the objections, to the other House, by which it shall likewise be reconsidered, and if approved by two thirds of that House, it shall become a Law. But in all such Cases the Votes of both Houses shall be determined by Yeas and Nays, and the Names of the Persons voting for and against the Bill shall be entered on the Journal of each House respectively. If any Bill shall not be returned by the President within ten Days (Sundays excepted) after it shall have been presented to him, the Same shall be a Law, in like Manner as if he had signed it, unless the Congress by their Adjournment prevent its Return, in which Case it shall not be a Law.

Every Order, Resolution, or Vote to which the Concurrence of the Senate and House of Representatives may be necessary (except on a question of Adjournment) shall be presented to the President of the United States; and befor the Same shall take Effect, shall be approved by him, or being disapproved by him, shall be repassed by two thirds of the Senate and House of Representatives, according to the Rules and Limitations prescribed in the Case of a Bill.

Section 8. The Congress shall have Power To lay and collect Taxes, Duties, Imposts and Excises, to pay the Debts and provide for the common Defence and general Welfare of the United States; but all Duties, Imposts and Excises shall be uniform throughout the United States;

To borrow money on the credit of the United States;

To regulate Commerce with foreign Nations, and among the several States, and with the Indian Tribes;

To establish an uniform Rule of Naturalization, and uniform Laws on the subject of Bankruptcies throughout the United States;

To coin Money, regulate the Value thereof, and of foreign Coin, and fix the Standard of Weights and Measures;

To provide for the Punishment of counterfeiting the Securities and current Coin of the United States;

To establish Post Offices and post Roads;

To promote the Progress of Science and useful Arts, by securing for limited Times to Authors and Inventors the exclusive Right to their respective Writings and Discoveries;

To constitute Tribunals inferior to the Supreme Court;

To define and punish Piracies and Felonies committed on the high Seas, and Offenses against the Law of Nations;

To declare War, grant Letters of Marque and Reprisal, and make Rules concerning Captures on Land and Water;

To raise and support Armies, but no Appropriation of Money to that Use shall be for a longer Term than two Years;

To provide and maintain a Navy;

To make Rules for the Government and Regulation of the land and naval forces;

To provide for calling forth the Militia to execute the Laws of the Union, suppress Insurrections and repel Invasions;

To provide for organizing, arming, and disciplining the Militia, and for governing such Part of them as may be employed in the Service of the United States, reserving to the States respectively, the Appointment of the Officers, and the Authority of training the Militia according to the discipline prescribed by Congress;

To exercise exclusive Legislation in all Cases whatsoever, over such District (not exceeding ten Miles square) as may, by Cession of particular States, and the acceptance of Congress, become the Seat of the Government of the United States, and to exercise like Authority over all Places purchased by the Consent of the Legislature of the State in which the Same shall be, for the Erection of Forts, Magazines, Arsenals, dock-Yards, and other needful Buildings; — And

To make all Laws which shall be necessary and proper for carrying into Execution the foregoing Powers, and all other Powers vested by this Constitution in the Government of the United States, or in any Department or Officer thereof.

Section 9. The Migration or Importation of such Persons as any of the States now existing shall think proper to admit, shall not be prohibited by the Congress prior to the Year one thousand eight hundred and eight, but a tax or duty may be imposed on such Importation, not exceeding ten dollars for each Person.

The privilege of the Writ of Habeas Corpus shall not be suspended, unless when in Cases of Rebellion or Invasion the public Safety may require it.

No bill of Attainder or ex post facto Law shall be passed.

No capitation, or other direct, Tax shall be laid unless in Proportion to the Census or Enumeration herein before directed to be taken.

No Tax or Duty shall be laid on Articles exported from any State.

No Preference shall be given by any Regulation of Commerce or Revenue to the Ports of one State over those of another: nor shall Vessels bound to, or from, one State, be obliged to enter, clear, or pay Duties in another.

No Money shall be drawn from the Treasury, but in Consequence of Appropriations made by Law; and a regular Statement and Account of the Receipts and Expenditures of all public Money shall be published from time to time.

No Title of Nobility shall be granted by the United States: And no Person holding any Office of Profit or Trust under them, shall, without the Consent of the Congress, accept of any present, Emolument, Office, or Title, of any kind whatever, from any King, Prince, or foreign State.

Section 10. No State shall enter into any Treaty, Alliance, or Confederation; grant Letters of Marque and Reprisal; coin Money; emit Bills of Credit; make any Thing but gold and silver Coin a Tender in Payment of Debts; pass any Bill of Attainder, ex post facto Law, or Law impairing the Obligation of Contracts, or grant any Title of Nobility.

No State shall, without the Consent of the Congress, lay any Imposts or Duties on Imports or Exports, except what may be absolutely necessary for executing its inspection Laws: and the net Produce of all Duties and Imposts, laid by any State on Imports or Exports, shall be for the Use of the Treasury of the United States; and all such Laws shall be subject to the Revision and Control of the Congress.

No state shall, without the Consent of Congress, lay any duty of Tonnage, keep Troops, or Ships of War in time of Peace, enter into any Agreement or Compact with another State, or with a foreign Power, or engage in War, unless actually invaded, or in such imminent Danger as will not admit of delay.

ARTICLE II

Section 1. The executive Power shall be vested in a President of the United States of America. He shall hold his Office during the Term of four years, and, together with the Vice-President, chosen for the same Term, be elected, as follows:

Each State shall appoint, in such Manner as the Legislature thereof may direct, a Number of Electors, equal to the whole Number of Senators and Representatives to which the State may be entitled in the Congress: but no Senator or Representative, or Person holding an Office of Trust or Profit under the United States, shall be appointed an Elector.

[The Electors shall meet in their respective States, and vote by Ballot for two persons, of whom one at least shall not be an Inhabitant of the same State with themselves. And they shall make a List of all the Persons voted for, and of the Number of Votes for each; which List they shall sign and certify, and transmit sealed to the Seat of the Government of the United States, directed to the President of the Senate. The President of the Senate shall, in the Presence of the Senate and House of Representatives, open all the Certificates, and the Votes shall then be counted. The Person having the greatest Number of Votes shall be the President, if such Number be a Majority of the whole Number of Electors appointed; and if there be more than one who have such Majority, and have an equal Number of Votes, then the House of Representatives shall immediately chuse by Ballot one of them for President; and if no Person have a Majority, then from the five highest on the List the said House shall in the Manner chuse the President. But in chusing the President, the Votes shall be taken by States, the Representation from each State having one Vote; a quorum for this Purpose shall consist of a Member or Members from two-thirds of the States, and a Majority of all the States shall be necessary to a Choice. In every Case, after the Choice of the President, the Person having the greatest Number of Votes of the Electors shall be the Vice President. But if there should remain two or more who have equal votes, the Senate shall chuse from them by Ballot the Vice-President.]⁴

---

⁴Revised by the Twelfth Amendment.

The Congress may determine the Time of chusing the Electors, and the Day on which they shall give their Votes; which Day shall be the same throughout the United States.

No person except a natural-born Citizen, or a Citizen of the United States, at the time of the Adoption of this Constitution, shall be eligible to the Office of President; neither shall any Person be eligible to that Office who shall not have attained to the Age of thirty-five years, and been fourteen Years a Resident within the United States.

In Case of the Removal of the President from Office, or of his Death, Resignation, or Inability to discharge the Powers and Duties of the said Office, the same shall devolve on the Vice President, and the Congress may by Law provide for the Case of Removal, Death, Resignation, or Inability, both of the President and Vice President, declaring what Officer shall then act as President, and such Officer shall act accordingly, until the disability be removed, or a President shall be elected.

The President shall, at stated Times, receive for his Services a Compensation, which shall neither be increased nor diminished during the Period for which he shall have been elected, and he shall not receive within that Period any other Emolument from the United States, or any of them.

Before he enter on the execution of his Office, he shall take the following Oath or Affirmation: — "I do solemnly swear (or affirm) that I will faithfully execute the Office of President of the United States, and will, to the best of my Ability, preserve, protect, and defend the Constitution of the United States."

Section 2. The President shall be Commander in Chief of the Army and Navy of the United States, and of the Militia of the several States, when called into the actual Service of the United States; he may require the Opinion, in writing, of the principal Officer in each of the executive Departments, upon any subject relating to the Duties of their respective Offices, and he shall have Power to Grant Reprieves and Pardons for Offenses against the United States, except in Cases of Impeachment.

He shall have Power, by and with the Advice and Consent of the Senate, to make Treaties, provided two thirds of the Senators present concur; and he shall nominate, and by and with the Advice and Consent of the Senate, shall appoint Ambassadors, other public Ministers and Consuls, Judges of the supreme Court, and all other Officers of the United States, whose Appointments are not herein otherwise provided for, and which shall be established by Law: but the Congress may by Law vest the Appointment of such inferior Officers, as they think proper, in the President alone, in the Courts of Law, or in the Heads of Departments.

The President shall have Power to fill up all Vacancies that may happen during the Recess of the Senate, by granting Commissions which shall expire at the End of their next Session.

Section 3. He shall from time to time give to the Congress Information of the State of the Union, and recommend to their Consideration such Measures as he shall judge necessary and expedient; he may, on extraordinary occasions, convene both Houses, or either of them, and in Case of Disagreement between them, with respect to the Time of Adjournment, he may adjourn them to such Time as he shall think proper; he shall receive Ambassadors and other public Ministers; he shall take care that the Laws be faithfully executed, and shall Commission all the Officers of the United States.

Section 4. The President, Vice President and all civil Officers of the United States, shall be removed from Office on Impeachment for, and Conviction of, Treason, Bribery, or other high Crimes and Misdemeanors.

ARTICLE III

Section 1. The judicial Power of the United States, shall be vested in one supreme Court, and in such inferior Courts as the Congress may from time to time ordain and establish. The Judges, both of the supreme and inferior Courts, shall hold their Offices during good Behaviour, and shall, at stated Times, receive for their Services, a Compensation, which shall not be diminished during their Continuance in Office.

Section 2. The judicial Power shall extend to all Cases, in Law and Equity, arising under this Constitution, the Laws of the United States, and Treaties made, or which shall be made, under their Authority; — to all Cases affecting ambassadors, other public ministers and consuls; — to all cases of admiralty and maritime Jurisdiction; — to Controversies to which the United States shall be a Party; — to Controversies between two or more States; — between a State and Citizens of another State;[5] — between Citizens of different

---

[5]Qualified by the Eleventh Amendment.

States, — between Citizens of the same State claiming Lands under Grants of different States, and between a State, or the Citizens thereof, and foreign States, Citizens or Subjects.

In all Cases affecting Ambassadors, other public Ministers and Consuls, and those in which a State shall be Party, the supreme Court shall have original Jurisdiction. In all the other Cases before mentioned, the supreme Court shall have appellate Jurisdiction, both as to Law and Fact, with such Exceptions, and under such Regulations as the Congress shall make.

The trial of all Crimes, except in Cases of Impeachment, shall be by Jury; and such Trial shall be held in the State where the said Crimes shall have been committed; but when not committed within any State, the Trial shall be at such Place or Places as the Congress may by Law have directed.

Section 3. Treason against the United States, shall consist only in levying War against them, or in adhering to their Enemies, giving them Aid and Comfort. No Person shall be convicted of Treason unless on the Testimony of two Witnesses to the same overt Act, or on Confession in open Court.

The Congress shall have power to declare the Punishment of Treason, but no Attainder of Treason shall work Corruption of Blood, or Forfeiture except during the Life of the Person attainted.

ARTICLE IV

Section 1. Full Faith and Credit shall be given in each State to the public Acts, Records, and judicial Proceedings of every other State. And the Congress may by general Laws prescribe the Manner in which such Acts, Records and Proceedings shall be proved, and the Effect thereof.

Section 2. The Citizens of each State shall be entitled to all Privileges and Immunities of Citizens in the several States.

A Person charged in any State with Treason, Felony, or other Crime, who shall flee from Justice, and be found in another State, shall on demand of the executive Authority of the State from which he fled, be delivered up, to be removed to the State having Jurisdiction of the crime.

No Person held to Service or Labour in one State, under the Laws thereof, escaping into another, shall, in Consequence of any Law or Regulation therein, be discharged from such Service or Labour, but shall be delivered up on Claim of the Party to whom such Service or Labour may be due.

Section 3. New States may be admitted by the Congress into this Union; but no new State shall be formed or erected within the Jurisdiction of any other State; nor any State be formed by the Junction of two or more States, or parts of States, without the Consent of the Legislatures of the States concerned as well as of the Congress.

The Congress shall have Power to dispose of and make all needful Rules and Regulations respecting the Territory or other Property belonging to the United States; and nothing in this Constitution shall be so construed as to Prejudice any Claims of the United States, or of any particular State.

Section 4. The United States shall guarantee to every State in this Union a Republican Form of Government, and shall protect each of them against Invasion; and on Application of the Legislature, or of the Executive (when the Legislature cannot be convened) against domestic Violence.

ARTICLE V

The Congress, whenever two thirds of both Houses shall deem it necessary, shall propose Amendments to this Constitution, or, on the Application of the Legislatures of two-thirds of the several States, shall call a Convention for proposing Amendments, which, in either Case, shall be valid to all Intents and Purposes, as part of this Constitution, when ratified by the Legislatures of three-fourths of the several States, or by Conventions in three-fourths thereof, as the one or the other Mode of Ratification may be proposed by the Congress; Provided that no Amendment which may be made prior to the Year One thousand eight hundred and eight shall in any Manner affect the first and fourth Clauses in the Ninth Section of the first Article; and that no State, without its Consent, shall be deprived of its equal Suffrage in the Senate.

ARTICLE VI

All Debts contracted and Engagements entered into, before the Adoption of this Constitution, shall be as valid against the United States under this Constitution, as under the Confederation.

This Constitution, and the Laws of the United States which shall be made in Pursuance thereof; and all Treaties made, or which shall be made, under the Authority of the United States, shall be the supreme Law of the Land; and the Judges in every State shall be bound thereby, any Thing in the Constitution or Laws of any State to the Contrary notwithstanding.

The Senators and Representatives before mentioned, and the Members of the several State Legislatures, and all executive and judicial Officers, both of the United States and of the several States, shall be bound by Oath or Affirmation to support this Constitution; but no religious Test shall ever be required as a qualification to any Office or public Trust under the United States.

ARTICLE VII

The Ratification of the Conventions of nine States shall be sufficient for the Establishment of this Constitution between the States so ratifying the same.

Done in Convention by the Unanimous Consent of the States present the Seventeenth Day of September in the Year of our Lord one thousand seven hundred and Eighty seven, and of the Independence of the United States of America the Twelfth. In Witness whereof We have hereunto subscribed our Names.

[The first ten Amendments were ratified in 1791 and form what is known as the Bill of Rights.]

Amendment I

Congress shall make no law respecting an establishment of religion, or prohibiting the free exercise thereof; or abridging the freedom of speech, or of the press; or the right of the people peaceably to assemble, and to petition the Government for a redress of grievances.

Amendment II

A well regulated Militia, being necessary to the security of a free State, the right of the people to keep and bear Arms shall not be infringed.

Amendment III

No Soldier shall, in time of peace, be quartered in any house, without the consent of the Owner, nor in time of war, but in a manner to be prescribed by law.

Amendment IV

The right of the people to be secure in their persons, houses, papers, and effects, against unreasonable searches and seizures, shall not be violated, and no Warrants shall issue, but upon probable cause, supported by Oath or affirmation, and particularly describing the place to be searched, and the persons or things to be seized.

Amendment V

No person shall be held to answer for a capital or otherwise infamous crime, unless on a presentment or indictment of a Grand Jury, except in cases arising in the land or naval forces, or in the Militia, when in actual service in time of War or public danger, nor shall any person be subject for the same offence to be twice put in jeopardy of life or limb; nor shall be compelled in any criminal case to be a witness against himself, nor be deprived of life, liberty, or property, without due process of law; nor shall private property be taken for public use, without just compensation.

Amendment VI

In all criminal prosecutions, the accused shall enjoy the right to a speedy and public trial, by an impartial jury of the State and district wherein the crime shall have been committed, which district shall have been previously ascertained by law, and to be informed of the nature and cause of the accusation; to be confronted with the witnesses against him; to have compulsory process for obtaining witnesses in his favour, and to have the Assistance of Counsel for his defence.

Amendment VII

In suits at common law, where the value in controversy shall exceed twenty dollars, the right of trial by jury shall be preserved, and no fact tried by a jury, shall be otherwise reexamined in any Court of the United States, than according to the rules of the common law.

Amendment VIII

Excessive bail shall not be required, nor excessive fines imposed, nor cruel and unusual punishments inflicted.

Amendment IX

The enumeration in the Constitution, of certain rights, shall not be construed to deny or disparage others retained by the people.

Amendment X

The powers not delegated to the United States by the Constitution, nor prohibited by it to the States, are reserved to the States respectively, or to the people.

. . . . Amendment XI [1795]

The Judicial power of the United States shall not be construed to extend to any suit in law or equity, commenced or prosecuted against one of the United States by Citizens of another State, or by Citizens or Subjects of any Foreign State.

. . . . Amendment XII [1804]

The Electors shall meet in their respective States and vote by ballot for President and Vice-President, one of whom, at least, shall not be an inhabitant of the same State with themselves; they shall name in their ballots the person voted for as President, and in distinct ballots the person voted for as Vice-President, and they shall make distinct lists of all persons voted for as President, and of all persons voted for as Vice-President, and of the number of votes for each, which lists they shall sign and certify, and transmit sealed to the seat of the government of the United States, directed to the President of the Senate; — The President of the Senate shall, in the presence of the Senate and House of Representatives, open all the certificates and the votes shall then be counted; — The person having the greatest number of votes for President, shall be the President, if such number be a majority of the whole number of Electors appointed; and if no person have such majority, then from the persons having the highest numbers not exceeding three on the list of those voted for as President, the House of Representatives shall choose immediately, by ballot, the President. But in choosing the President, the votes shall be taken by states, the representation from each state having one vote; a quorum for this purpose shall consist of a member or members from two-thirds of the states, and a majority of all the states shall be necessary to a choice. And if the House of Representatives shall not choose a President whenever the right of choice shall devolve upon them, before the fourth day of March next following, then the Vice-President shall act as President, as in the case of the death or other constitutional disability of the President. — The person having the greatest number of votes as Vice-President, shall be the Vice-President, if such number be a majority of the whole number of Electors appointed, and if no person have a majority, then from the two highest numbers on the list, the Senate shall choose the Vice-President; a quorum for the purpose shall consist of two-thirds of the whole number of Senators, and a majority of the whole number shall be necessary to a choice. But no person constitutionally ineligible to the office of President shall be eligible to that of Vice-President of the United States.

. . . . Amendment XIII [1865]

Section 1. Neither slavery nor involuntary servitude, except as a punishment for crime whereof the party shall have been duly convicted, shall exist within the United States, or any place subject to their jurisdiction.

Section 2. Congress shall have power to enforce this article by appropriate legislation.

. . . . Amendment XIV [1868]

Section 1. All persons born or naturalized in the United States, and subject to the jurisdiction thereof, are citizens of the United States and of the State wherein they reside. No State shall abridge the privileges or immunities of citizens of the United States; nor shall any State deprive any person of life, liberty, or property, without due process of law; nor deny to any person within its jurisdiction the equal protection of the laws.

Section 2. Representatives shall be apportioned among the several States according to their respective numbers, counting the whole number of persons in each State, excluding Indians not taxed. But when the right to vote at any election for the choice of electors for President and Vice-President of the United States, Representatives in Congress, the Executive and Judicial officers of a State, or the members of the Legislature thereof, is denied to any of the male inhabitants of such State, being twenty-one years of age, and citizens of the United States, or in any way abridged, except for participation in rebellion, or other crime, the basis of representation therein shall be reduced in the proportion which the number of such male citizens shall bear to the whole number of male citizens twenty-one years of age in such State.

Section 3. No person shall be a Senator or Representative in Congress, or elector of President and Vice-President, or hold any office, civil or military, under the United States, or under any State, who, having previousls aken an oath, as a member of

Congress, or as an officer of the United States, or as a member of any State legislature, or as an executive or judicial officer of any State, to support the Constitution of the United States, shall have engaged in insurrection or rebellion against the same, or given aid or comfort to the enemies thereof. But Congress may by a vote of two-thirds of each House, remove such disability.

Section 4. The validity of the public debt of the United States, authorized by law, including debts incurred for payment of pensions and bounties for services in suppressing insurrection or rebellion, shall not be questioned. But neither the United States nor any State shall assume or pay any debts or obligation incurred in aid of insurrection or rebellion against the United States, or any claim for the loss or emancipation of any slave; but all such debts, obligations, and claims shall be held illegal and void.

Section 5. The Congress shall have the power to enforce, by appropriate legislation, the provisions of this article.

. . . . Amendment XV [1870]

Section 1. The right of citizens of the United States to vote shall not be denied or abridged by the United States or by any State on account of race, color, or previous condition of servitude.

Section 2. The Congress shall have power to enforce this article by appropriate legislation.

. . . . Amendment XVI [1913]

The Congress shall have power to lay and collect taxes on incomes, from whatever source derived, without apportionment among the several States, and without regard to any census or enumeration.

. . . . Amendment XVII [1913]

The Senate of the United States shall be composed of two Senators from each State, elected by the people thereof, for six years; and each Senator shall have one vote. The electors in each State shall have the qualifications requisite for electors of the most numerous branch of the State legislatures.

When vacancies happen in the representation of any State in the Senate, the executive authority of such State shall issue writs of election to fill such vacancies: *Provided,* That the legislature of any State may empower the executive thereof to make temporary appointments until the people fill the vacancies by election as the legislature may direct.

This amendment shall not be so construed as to affect the election or term of any Senator chosen before it becomes valid as part of the Constitution.

. . . . Amendment XVIII [1919]

Section 1. After one year from the ratification of this article the manfuacture, sale, or transportation of intoxicating liquors within, the importation thereof into, or the exportation thereof from the United States and all territory subject to the jurisdiction thereof for beverage purposes is hereby prohibited.

Section 2. The Congress and the several States shall have concurrent power to enforce this article by appropriate legislation.

Section 3. This article shall be inoperative unless it shall have been ratified as an amendment to the Constitution by the legislatures of the several States, as provided in the Constitution, within seven years from the date of the submission hereof to the States by the Congress.

. . . . Amendment XIX [1920]

The right of citizens of the United States to vote shall not be denied or abridged by the United States or by any State on account of sex.

Congress shall have power to enforce this article by appropriate legislation.

Amendment XX [1933]

Section 1. The terms of the President and Vice-President shall end at noon on the 20th day of January, and the terms of Senators and Representatives at noon on the 3d day of January, of the years in which such terms would have ended if this article had not been ratified; and the terms of their successors shall then begin.

Section 2. The Congress shall assemble at least once in every year, and such meeting shall begin at noon on the 3d day of January, unless they shall by law appoint a different day.

Section 3. If, at the time fixed for the beginning of the term of the President, the President elect shall have died, the Vice-President elect shall become President. If a President shall not have been chosen before the time fixed for the beginning of his term, or if the President elect shall have failed to qualify, then the Vice-President elect shall act as President until a President shall have qualified; and the Congress may by law provide for the case wherein neither a President elect nor a Vice-President elect shall have qualified, declaring who shall then act as President, or the manner in which one who is to act shall be selected, and such person shall act accordingly until a President or Vice-President shall have qualified.

Section 4. The Congress may by law provide for the case of the death of any of the persons from whom the House of Representatives may choose a President whenever the right of choice shall have devolved upon them, and for the case of the death of any of the persons from whom the Senate may choose a Vice-President whenever the right of choice shall have devolved upon them.

Section 5. Sections 1 and 2 shall take effect on the 15th day of October following the ratification of this article.

Section 6. This article shall be inoperative unless it shall have been ratified as an amendment to the Constitution by the legislatures of three-fourths of the several States within seven years from the date of its submission.

. . . . Amendment XXI [1933]

Section 1. The eighteenth article of amendment to the Constitution of the United States is hereby repealed.

Section 2. The transportation or importation into any State, Territory, or possession of the United States for delivery or use therein of intoxicating liquors, in violation of the laws thereof, is hereby prohibited.

Section 3. This article shall be inoperative unless it shall have been ratified as an amendment to the Constitution by conventions in the several States, as provided in the Constitution, within seven years from the date of the submission hereof to the States by the Congress.

. . . . Amendment XXII [1951]

No person shall be elected to the office of the President more than twice, and no person who has held the office of President, or acted as President, for more than two years of a term to which some other person was elected President shall be elected to the office of the President more than once.

But this Article shall not apply to any person holding the office of President when this Article was proposed by the Congress, and

shall not prevent any person who may be holding the office of President, or acting as President, during the term within which this Article becomes operative from holding the office of President or acting as President during the remainder of such term.

This article shall be inoperative unless it shall have been ratified as an amendment to the Constitution by the legislatures of three-fourths of the several states within seven years from the date of its submission to the states by the Congress.

. . . . Amendment XXIII [1961]

Section 1. The District consituting the seat of Government of the United States shall appoint in such manner as the Congress may direct:

A number of electors of President and Vice-President equal to the whole number of Senators and Representatives in Congress to which the District would be entitled if it were a State, but in no event more than the least populous State; they shall be in addition to those appointed by the States, but they shall be considered, for the purposes of the election of President and Vice-President, to be electors appointed by a State; and they shall meet in the District and perform such duties as provided by the twelfth aritcle of amendment.

Section 2. The Congress shall have power to enforce this article by appropriate legislation.

. . . . Amendment XXIV [1964]

Section 1. The right of citizens of the United States to vote in any primary or other election for President or Vice-President, for electors for President or Vice-President, or for Senator or Representative in Congress, shall not be denied or abridged by the United States or any state by reason of failure to pay any poll tax or other tax.

Section 2. The Congress shall have the power to enforce this article by appropriate legislation.

. . . . Amendment XXV [1967]

Section 1. In case of the removal of the President from office or of his death or resignation, the Vice-President shall become President.

Section 2. Whenever there is a vacancy in the office of the Vice-President, the President shall nominate a Vice-President who shall take office upon confirmation by a majority vote of both Houses of Congress.

Section 3. Whenever the President transmits to the President Pro Tempore of the Senate and the Speaker of the House of Representatives his written declaration that he is unable to discharge the powers and duties of his office, and until he transmits to them a written declaration to the contrary, such powers and duties shall be discharged by the Vice-President as Acting President.

Section 4. Whenever the Vice-President and a majority of either the principal officers of the executive departments or of such other body as Congress may by law provide, transmit to the President Pro Tempore of the Senate and the Speaker of the House of Representatives their written declaration that the President is unable to discharge the powers and duties of his office, the Vice-President shall immediately assume the powers and duties of the office as Acting President.

Thereafter, when the President transmits to the President Pro Tempore of the Senate and the Speaker of the House of Representatives his written declaration that no inability exists, he shall resume the powers and duties of his office unless the Vice-President and a majority of either the principal officers of the executive departments or of such other body as Congress may by law provide, transmit within four days to the President Pro Tempore of the Senate and the Speaker of the House of Representatives their written declaration that the President is unable to discharge the powers and duties of his office. Thereupon Congress shall decide the issue, assembling within forty-eight hours for that purpose if not in session. If the Congress, within twenty-one days after receipt of the latter written declaration, or, if Congress is not in session, within twenty-one days after Congress is required to assemble, determines by two-thirds vote of both Houses that the President is unable to discharge the powers and duties of his office, the Vice-President shall continue to discharge the same as Acting President; otherwise, the President shall resume the powers and duties of his office.

. . . . Amendment XXVI [1971]

Section 1. The right of citizens of the United States, who are eighteen years of age or older, to vote shall not be denied or abridged by the United States or by any State on account of age.

Section 2. The Congress shall have the power to enforce this article by appropriate legislation.

Index

tional defense expenditures, 352, 354, 356-359, 360, 387; social services expenditures, 351-359, 360, 363-364, 367-369, 370, 372, 387; subsidies, 355

Federal Bureau of Investigation: 367

Federal Communications Commission: 370

Federalism: 45, 77, 86, 91-93, 114; central government and, 92, 93, 94, 95, 99-100; "cooperative", 91, 98, 99; "dual", 91, 93-98; Fourteenth Amendment, 108, 110, 111-113; political parties, 200; regulation of commerce and, 96-98; state's rights, 93-96, 100-101, 111-113, 177; Supreme Court and, 96; Tenth Amendment, 94, 111

Federalist: 2, 3, 159, 315

Federalist Papers: 302

Federalist Party: 316, 341

Federal judicial system: 50-51, 57, 74, 96, 108, 109, 116-154; access to, 140-141; compliance with rulings of, 147-149, 150, 151; Congress and, 81, 83, 85, 130, 280, 284; court organization in, 130-133; decision-making in, 143-150; grand jury, 106, 107; interest groups and, 141-143, 179, 186, 188-190; judicial process, 139-150; judicial review, 74-76, 81, 85, 126-128, 132; passive nature of, 123-124, 139; powers of, 80-81, 85, 86; President and, 84-85, 186, 280, 284; regulation of commerce by, 96, 97; religious freedom and, 104-105; rules governing disposition of cases in, 141; U.S. Supreme Court, 51, 70, 74, 80-81, 85-86, 113, 114, 131-133, 143-146, 147, 148-150, 151, 179-180, 246, 249, 374. *See also* Judges; State judicial system

Federal Power Commission: 370

Federal Reserve System: 47, 370, 371

Federal system: *See* Federalism

Federal Trade Commission: 47, 370

Felonies: 122, 129

Fichte, Johann Gottlieb: 157

Fifteenth Amendment: 244, 245

Fifth Amendment: 70, 73, 106-108

Filibuster: 293

Finland: 353

First Amendment: 61-62, 69-70, 73, 102-105, 147, 382, 383

Fisher, Louis: 219

Food: federal subsidy of, 354, 355

Food stamps: 354

Food and Drug Administration: 47, 384

Ford, Gerald: 84, 302, 327, 329

Foreign affairs: 75-76, 94; Congress and, 82, 84, 280, 328; interest groups and, 37; President and, 74-76, 84, 327, 328, 339, 341

Forest Service: 47, 372, 375, 386

Fortas, Abraham: 137

Founding Fathers: 61; distrust of political parties, 200; economic interests of, 314-315; fear of central government, 63-64, 65, 66, 67, 68, 313, 314, 315

Fourteenth Amendment: 71, 73, 74, 76, 108, 110, 111-113, 148, 178, 245

Fourth Amendment: 70, 73, 105-106

France: 316, 353

Free exercise clause: 104

"Free-rider": 17, 18, 35, 39, 163, 169, 192, 235, 378

"Free World": 354

Function: defined, 22

"Gag rule": 292

Gandhi, Mahatma: 12

Garfield, James Abram: 319, 327

Garner, James W.: quoted, 406

General Services Administration: 372

George III: 313

Godwin, William: 401

Goldwater, Barry: 43, 199, 255, 257, 270, 273

"Good life": 397, 399

Goods: *See* Public Goods and Services

Government: employees in, 351, 353; expenditures for national defense, 352, 354, 356-359, 360, 366-367, 387, 388; expenditures in public sector, 351-359, 360, 363-364, 367-369, 370, 372, 373, 387; growth of, 354-355, 361,